THE FRENCH-CANADIAN HERITAGE IN NEW ENGLAND

FREE PUBLIC LIBRARY
DALTON, MASSACHUSETTS

First opened, May 1861   Accepted by Town, March 1885

THE FRENCH-CANADIAN HERITAGE IN NEW ENGLAND

Gerard J. Brault

Published by
University Press of New England
Hanover and London
and
McGill-Queen's University Press
Kingston and Montreal

Published simultaneously by
University Press of New England
Hanover, NH 03755
and
McGill-Queen's University Press
Kingston and Montreal, Canada

University Press of New England
Brandeis University
Brown University
Clark University
University of Connecticut
Dartmouth College
University of New Hampshire
University of Rhode Island
Tufts University
University of Vermont

© 1986 by University Press of New England   Second printing 1986

Legal deposit second quarter 1986
Bibliothèque nationale du Québec

Printed in the United States of America
5   4   3

Library of Congress Cataloging-in-Publication Data
Brault, Gerard J.
  The French-Canadian heritage in New England.

  Bibliography: p.
  Includes index.
  1. French-Canadians—New England—History.
2. New England—History.   I. Title.
F15.F85B73   1986   974'.004114   85–22512
ISBN 0–87451–358–8
ISBN 0–87451–359–6 (pbk.)

Canadian Cataloguing in Publication Data
Brault, Gerard J.
  The French-Canadian heritage in New England

  Bibliography: p.
  Includes index.
  ISBN 0–7735–0536–9 (bound.)
  ISBN 0–7735–0537–7 (pbk.)

  1. Canadians, French-speaking—New England—History.*
  2. New England—History.

  I. Title.

F15.F85B73   1986   974'.004114   C86–093508–6

C O N T E N T S

Illustrations follow page 82

PREFACE

This book aims to provide an introduction to Franco-American studies for specialists and nonspecialists alike. Franco-Americans have called for something similar since the 1950s,[1] as have a growing number of scholars since the surge of interest in ethnic studies of the 1960s.

What I present in this work is mostly descriptive, and, whenever I have passed judgment, I have endeavored to be even handed. Some may feel that I have let slip an opportunity to plead the cause of, say, the Acadians, biculturalism, or bilingualism. I prefer to let the facts speak for themselves.

Much has been written about the French Canadians of New England, but a lot of the information is scattered or difficult of access. Nearly all the relevant material is written in French which is an added obstacle for many persons. The works by Benoît, Ducharme, Rumilly, and Perreault give a good idea of the subject but are either outdated or offer insufficient coverage and documentation.[2]

Parish histories contain much valuable information, especially about priests, physicians, lawyers, and other notables, but usually furnish few particulars concerning the living and working conditions of ordinary Franco-Americans. The present work views Franco-Americans not only as parishioners but as individuals earning a living and relating to other members of society.

World War I and World War II were watersheds in Franco-American history, but other periods are not as well defined. Also, the field of Franco-American studies encompasses subjects that do not lend themselves readily to chronological presentation. For these reasons I use a topical approach within a loose time frame.

Some Franco-Americans have not welcomed scholarly investigations of their culture or history by outsiders;[3] also, the group has tended to favor clerical, elitist, and self-congratulatory interpretations. However, since the 1960s the trend has moved away from such views, and a new openness characterizes discussions at conferences and meetings. In no way does this change indicate a diminution of pride. Quite the contrary, it shows that Franco-Americans now have a more realistic opinion of themselves and have gained greater self-confidence.

Although by no means definitive, this study will acquaint readers with the present state of knowledge about the Franco-Americans and should stimulate further research.

However, culture is not always something one can measure, compare, or otherwise quantify the way one analyzes minority-group voting patterns or rates of upward mobility.[4] Culture is also a matter of the heart. The amount of ethnic culture one is fortunate enough to experience, in addition to the valuable heritage of being an American, is directly proportional to the knowledge one has of its folkways, its customs, its speech patterns, its wisdom. It is the capacity to recognize these things when one sees, hears, or remembers them. It is the enrichment one feels.

Thus, discovering one's ethnic heritage is a different experience for each person. At times, it can be an epiphany. One afternoon in 1952, in the city of Reims, I noticed an unusual sculpture over a sixteenth-century school doorway. Chiseled in stone, I could see two boys' heads, one smiling, the other sad. I consulted my guidebook, wondering why the masks of Comedy and Tragedy had been carved there of all places. To my great surprise, I read that the faces represented *Jean qui pleure et Jean qui rit*.

I had always assumed that that expression, which was used in my family when one of the children was crying but could easily be teased into laughing, was a private one. It suddenly dawned on me that the locution was not even exclusively a Canadianism but a time-honored French expression. The experience was Proustian, only the association was centuries old, and I felt indissolubly joined with my French past.

Chapter 4 ("Pages from a Family History"), while presented as a straight narrative, was actually pieced together from bits of information gathered during more than a quarter of a century of searching. This investigation made me realize that one cannot truly speak of the French-Canadian heritage in New England and, more particularly, of the personal cultural legacy one has received without considering family history. Consequently, while I trust that this book provides some of the information readers are seeking, I hope, too, that chapter 4 helps them arrive at a better understanding of what it means to be Franco-American.

In 1976 Claire Bolduc, a young Franco-American, best expressed what I have tried to accomplish in this book: "It won't do to present a romanticized history of Franco-American exploits. What we need is the truth . . . and the truth is that we are a small unappreciated people, endowed with tremendous energy; we are only human beings like everyone else. . . . But we are not less than that."[5]

I take pleasure in acknowledging the help I have received on this project over the years. I started to collect material, to teach, and to write about the Franco-Americans in the late 1950s, but due to other teaching and research commitments I worked on this book only in fits and starts until my sabbatical in 1980. Meanwhile I had received an American Philosophical Society grant in 1972 and continued support from the Pennsylvania State University's Faculty Research Fund and Institute for the Arts and Humanistic Studies. Finally, I was able to spend six months in Quebec City in the spring of 1984 thanks to a Senior Fellowship in Canadian Studies from the government of Canada and a grant-in-aid from the Ministère des Affaires Intergouvernementales of the government of Quebec.

For all this encouragement and financial assistance I wish to thank in particular the following persons: Stanley F. Paulson, former dean of the College of the Liberal Arts; Richard L. Frautschi, head of the Department of French; Thomas F. Magner, former associate dean for Research and Graduate Studies; Stanley Weintraub, director of the Institute for the Arts and Humanistic Studies at the Pennsylvania State University; Norman T. London, academic relations officer, Embassy of Canada, Washington, D.C.; and Jean-Marc Nicole, conseiller, Direction Etats-Unis, Ministère des Affaires Intergouvernementales, government of Quebec, Quebec City, Canada.

I am also grateful to Jacques Mathieu, director of the Centre d'Etudes sur la langue, les arts et les traditions populaires des francophones en Amérique du Nord (CELAT) at Laval University, and his colleagues, especially Jean-Claude Dupont, Carole Saulnier, and Yves Roby, for their many courtesies during my stay in Quebec City.

Armand B. Chartier, a professor at the University of Rhode Island, and Claire Quintal, director of the French Institute at Assumption College, kindly read my typescript critically and offered many useful comments. I am happy to acknowledge their assistance here. They in no way accept responsibility for the flaws in this work, nor do they necessarily share the views expressed.

My wife Jeanne was, more than ever, my helpmate in this undertaking. Sharing the same background as I, she was my sounding board and also an excellent source of information. More important, she made it possible for me to say: This is my best effort. For this I shall always be in her debt.

State College, Pennsylvania   G.J.B.
December 1985

THE
FRENCH-CANADIAN
HERITAGE IN
NEW ENGLAND

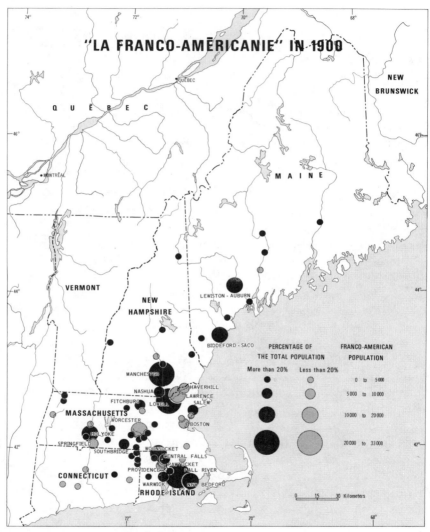

"LA FRANCO-AMĒRICANIE" IN 1900

QUÉBEC

NEW BRUNSWICK

MONTRÉAL

MAINE

VERMONT

NEW HAMPSHIRE

LEWISTON - AUBURN

BIDDEFORD - SACO

MANCHESTER

NASHUA HAVERHILL
LAWRENCE
FITCHBURG LOWELL SALEM

MASSACHUSETTS
WORCESTER
BOSTON

HOLYOKE
SPRINGFIELD
SOUTHBRIDGE WOONSOCKET
CENTRAL FALLS
PAWTUCKET
PROVIDENCE FALL RIVER
CONNECTICUT WARWICK NEW BEDFORD
RHODE ISLAND

PERCENTAGE OF
THE TOTAL POPULATION

More than 20%   Less than 20%

FRANCO-AMERICAN
POPULATION

0   to   5000

5000   to   10000

10000   to   20000

20000   to   33000

0   15   30 Kilometers

Map 1. The concentration of Franco-Americans in certain areas of New England today is
largely the result of a settlement pattern begun after the Civil War. It was clearly fixed by
the turn of the century. (Source: Vicero, *Immigration*, p. 4, fig. 1, as adapted by Louder and
Waddell, *Continent perdu*, p. 29, fig. 1. Courtesy Laboratoire de cartographie, Département
de géographie, Université Laval, Ste-Foy, Québec.)

INTRODUCTION

The French Canadians are a small people whose historic heartland is in southern Quebec but who also settled elsewhere, often in distinct patterns, on the North American continent, for example in the Midwest.

This book is about the French Canadians who moved to New England beginning a little over a century ago. The migration was massive but of relatively short duration, lasting only about sixty years. Perhaps as many as half who came to the region during this period returned home. Most who stayed in the Northeast remained strongly attached to their roots, and today many of their descendants share their beliefs and values.

The story of the French Canadians in New England resembles that of other American ethnic groups—early hardship and discrimination followed by gradual acculturation and rise to a higher social and economic position. But it differs markedly from this experience, too, and even from that of French Canadians who settled in other parts of the United States. Imbued with a strict brand of Catholicism and convinced that preserving their cultural heritage involved a fight against long odds, a considerable number became absorbed in the group's inner life and stood on the defensive in their relations with others throughout most of their history. The citadels they constructed were both marvelous and gratifying, but the price may have been a lag in upward mobility and a loss of influence. This much is certain: Over the years, French Canadians in New England developed the great cultural, moral, and spiritual legacy they received from their ancestors. Today, many still cherish these ideals and are dedicated to passing them on to generations yet to come.

According to the 1980 census, persons of French origin constitute the fifth largest ancestry group in the United States:[1]

1

English	50 million
German	49 million
Irish	40 million
Afro-American	21 million
French	13 million
Italian	12 million
Scottish	10 million
Polish	8 million
Mexican	8 million
American Indian	7 million
Dutch	6 million

From an ethnic point of view, the Cajuns of Louisiana and the Franco-Americans of New England and upper New York State stand out from the population of French origin because of the density and cohesiveness of their groups. Both have a common national origin but each also has a distinctive culture, history, and identity. Cajuns are predominantly descendants of Acadians who came to Louisiana in the mid-1760s; however, other Cajuns spring from immigrants who arrived from France, Santo Domingo, or elsewhere about this time.[2]

Many Franco-Americans—the term caught on with the elite toward the end of the 1890s and gained wider acceptance in the 1920s[3]—also have Acadian ancestors, but an overwhelming majority are descended from Quebecois. Emigration to the United States occurred mainly from 1870 to 1930, peaking in the 1880s.[4] (Incidentally, although persons of Acadian origin were included in the French figure mentioned earlier, Americans who claimed French-Canadian ancestry were listed separately.)

Once bolstered by a formidable network of churches, media, schools, and societies dedicated to the ideal of *survivance,* or loyalty to the French-Canadian heritage, the Franco-American group today is not what it used to be. The period of its greatest vigor may have been at the turn of the century or, at the latest, in the decade following World War I. But Franco-Americans still have a great reserve of strength, and in recent years a resurgence of their ethnic awareness and pride appears to be gaining momentum and scope after a period of steady decline.[5]

Population centers

According to official and unofficial censuses, the vast majority of persons of French-Canadian descent residing in the Northeast are concentrated in three distinct regions sometimes referred to as *Franco-Américanie.*[6]

1. Northern Maine, in particular the upper St. John Valley (Aroostook County). This section, made up of small towns and rural areas along the

Canadian border, became American territory by virtue of the Webster-Ashburton Treaty between Great Britain and the United States in 1842. Many of its inhabitants are of Acadian extraction, their ancestors having settled here as early as the latter part of the eighteenth century; others are descended from Quebecois who began arriving not long afterward.[7]

2. Western Vermont and upper New York State.[8] Franco-Americans in this region are located mainly in cities and towns just south of Quebec and in a string of rural communities along the boundary between these two northeastern states. Many early French-Canadian immigrants settled in Vermont temporarily before moving on to larger population centers elsewhere in New England. Burlington and Winooski, Vermont, and Cohoes, New York, are mill towns that belong in the third category.

3. Central and southeastern New England including southern Maine. By far the greatest number of Franco-Americans reside in former textile centers in this area. More often than not, these centers are small- or medium-sized cities and towns situated along rivers that once were an important source of power for local industries. Some, like Lowell, Massachusetts, and Manchester, New Hampshire, were planned communities created in the first part of the nineteenth century for the express purpose of manufacturing. Others, like Brunswick, Maine, or Chicopee, Massachusetts, date back to colonial times but were transformed in the early 1800s into factory towns.

Communities with a high Franco-American population—where this group constitutes 20 percent or more of the total inhabitants—have tended to remain more "French" than others. However, other factors of a geographical and historical nature—for example, relative proximity to the Canadian border or to other Franco-American centers, and number of recent arrivals—must also be considered.[9] In any event, Franco-American cities and towns in the third region have, since the turn of the century, fallen into the four categories identified in Appendix A, "Size and Percentage of Franco-American Population."[10]

French mother tongue statistics

It is not easy to determine the size of any American ethnic group. Figures vary a good deal according to the reliability of the source, the basis of the information (for example, the specific question that was asked), and the passage of time. One estimate that may offer the most satisfactory statistics is provided by the answers given to a question asked of heads of households in the 1970 census (15 percent sample), that is, "What language other than English was spoken in this person's home when he was a child?" (see Appendix B, table 1). These figures do not necessarily imply fluency or use of French on the part of the respondents. On the other hand, they are more dependable than, say, census figures relating to country of birth, which do not distinguish regions of Canada and only take immediate parentage into account, not later generations.

Not all New Englanders having a French mother tongue are of French-Canadian origin, the most obvious exception being individuals either born in France or of French parentage, virtually all of whom consider themselves ethnically distinct from the Franco-American group. French emigration to the United States has always been relatively small compared to that of many other European nations. According to the U.S. Immigration and Naturalization Service, only 730,150 French natives settled in this country from 1820 to 1970 as opposed to 6,917,097 Germans, 5,176,488 Italians, and 4,713,868 Irish.[11] In 1970 the Bureau of the Census reported that persons of French stock constituted less than 0.03 percent of the New England population. If one subtracts this segment of the French mother tongue population, one arrives at the adjusted figures given in Appendix B, table 2.

Other estimates of the Franco-American population

Of course, that a person heard French spoken at home as a child is far from a perfect test of membership in the Franco-American group. However, other statistics are also open to question. The long form used in the 1980 census asked: "What is this person's ancestry?" The Bureau of the Census listed separate totals for French and French-Canadian, and for persons of single and multiple ancestry (that is, say, French and no more than one other descent) (Appendix B, tables 3 and 4). Acadian was included in the French category. Comparison with the mother tongue figures provided in Appendix 2 suggests that many Franco-Americans reported their ancestry as French rather than French-Canadian.

Parishes

Though lacking the objectivity and precision of census statistics, other data concerning the Franco-American population merit consideration. A high percentage of persons of French-Canadian extraction residing in New England belong to Catholic parishes. In this region a distinction is sometimes drawn between national and territorial parishes; in the latter group a distinction is also made—though the concept has become increasingly shaky—between churches where traditionally priests have been Franco-

American and those where they have not. Thus, in 1949 one authoritative source referred to 427 Franco-American parishes, broken down as follows: 178 Franco-American national parishes, 107 "mixed" Franco-American parishes with Franco-American clergy, and 142 others. In this survey, the total Franco-American population of New England was given as nearly 1.5 million, that is, 925,000 parishioners constituting the *population catholique franco-américaine organisée,* or Franco-Americans concentrated in identifiable Catholic parishes, plus an additional 500,000 Franco-Americans scattered throughout the area.[12]

Since 1949, urban renewal projects, the arrival of new immigrant groups, and other sociocultural factors have occasioned major demographic changes in Franco-Américanie. Nevertheless, the bulk of those who take an interest in their French-Canadian heritage or are at least conscious of it can still be found in these parishes.

Though by no means official, the list in Appendix A, "Selected Franco-American parishes," includes all the congregations usually regarded as Franco-American national parishes as well as most of the others associated with the group. Acadians from the Maritime Provinces but also from northern Maine have tended to gather in Massachusetts parishes, chiefly in Amesbury, Cambridge, Chelsea, Fitchburg, Gardner, Lynn, New Bedford, Salem, Waltham, and Worcester.[13]

This book endeavors to provide a reasonably complete picture of the Franco-American achievement in New England. After outlining the chief features of traditional French-Canadian culture, the first two phases in Franco-American history—1865–1920 and 1920–60—are discussed. This account is illustrated by one family's story, the author's own, in a separate chapter that also touches on the distant origins of the Franco-Americans. This second look, as it were, is followed by a survey of the present situation.

1

THE ROOTS OF
FRANCO-AMERICAN
CULTURE

Quebec City, founded in 1608, was the first permanent French settlement in North America. More than two-and-a-half centuries of history, high in color and drama, separate the establishment of the earliest French trading posts along the St. Lawrence River and, to the east, in Acadia, and the first great wave of the French-Canadian emigration to New England.

In 1759 a battle lasting a mere twenty minutes on the Plains of Abraham, before the walls of Quebec City, sealed the fate of New France. Although the British would henceforth predominate in Canada, the French inhabitants of Quebec and certain other areas of that country would succeed in maintaining their language, traditions, and separate nationality. This historic struggle is indelibly engraved on the French-Canadian mind and explains, in a large measure, the extraordinary persistence of certain cultural traits among Franco-Americans even after several generations.

Another factor that contributed to this remarkable survival was the French-Canadian immigrants' sentimental conception of their ancestral way of life—for many it was a deep attachment—and their frequent return trips to their native villages to keep in close touch with relatives and revive old memories. Their descendants, too, kept such feelings alive with repeated visits.

Lately, many French Canadians and Franco-Americans have taken an interest in their French ancestors and, thanks to vastly enhanced travel opportunities, have been able to visit France and experience French life and culture. They have also begun to learn more about their forebears who lived during the early years of the colony. Their ancestors are no longer remote and vague participants in a kind of costume drama; with the help of genealogists and family historians, and of living museums in historic areas of French Canada, their forebears have become real people, their own flesh and blood, relatives with everyday concerns. One such voyage of discovery, the author's own, is discussed later in chapter 4.

Until recently, however, most French Canadians and Franco-Americans conceived of their roots in terms of their immediate past—the kind of people their parents and grandparents were, and how they lived not so long ago in rural French Canada.

Ideology

In the nineteenth century, nationalistic ideologues in Quebec developed the concept that French Canadians were duty bound to preserve their cultural identity. For many, this notion became indistinguishable from the view that French Canadians were called upon to fulfill a sacred mission, namely to preserve Catholicism in America, and that this mission could best be accomplished by maintaining their mother tongue and customs, and by staying on the land.[1] *La survivance,* as this view came to be called, animated contemporary patriotic speeches and tracts, and inspired literary works such as Antoine Gérin-Lajoie's novel *Jean Rivard* (1862, 1864, 2 vols.).[2]

This messianic and agrarian ideology was associated with the myth of a Golden Age, a time when habitants were devout, hardworking farmers, toiling in peace and harmony, benevolently watched over by wise old parish priests.[3] A series of sketches by Edmond J. Massicotte transposed this long-ago period of great happiness and prosperity to the recent past. For example, *La bénédiction du Jour de l'An* (1912) is a dramatic rendering of the traditional New Year's Day blessing, and *Le Saint Viatique à la campagne* (1916) shows farmers kneeling with heads bowed respectfully as the pastor brings the last sacrament to a dying parishioner.[4] Massicotte's drawings depict real-life people in authentic settings, but like Norman Rockwell's illustrations of the American scene, they are suffused with sentimentality and nostalgia.

At first, Anglo-Saxons in Canada (*les Anglais*) posed the main threat. But, beginning about the middle of the nineteenth century, emigration to New England loomed as an equally disturbing menace.[5]

Better than anyone else perhaps, Louis Hémon (1880–1913) summed up turn-of-the-century French-Canadian survivance ideology in his novel *Maria Chapdelaine,* first published in 1914.[6] (A Frenchman, Hémon only lived two-and-a-half years in Quebec before being accidentally killed by a train at the age of thirty-three.) On the surface, the story of a young woman's gradual resignation to frontier life in Quebec's Lake St. John country, portrayed in realistic terms as filled with endless toil and danger, the novel is also a paean to deep-seated loyalties.

At the end of the book Maria rejects a Franco-American suitor who offers to deliver her from this harsh and desolate land and accepts the proposal of a good-hearted but plain French-Canadian farmer. She reaches this decision after much soul-searching, culminating in a nocturnal revelation that provides an affirmative answer to the question: Is life on the frontier worthwhile? The three voices that convince Maria are the joys of each passing season, the sweet sounds of French, and, especially, the mystical "voix du pays de Québec." Subsequently regarded as supplying the correct reply to a more general query about the value of persisting in Quebec, this celebrated passage, notably the proud affirmation "Nous sommes venus il y a trois cents ans, et nous sommes restés" (We came three hundred years ago, and we stayed), strikes a responsive chord in most French Canadians to this day.

French-Canadian traditional culture at the turn of the century

Social historians and students of traditional culture have described in more objective fashion the lifeways of the inhabitants of rural Quebec at the turn of the century—olden times many French Canadians and their descendants still remember vividly.[7] The grandparents and great-grandparents of most Franco-Americans came from all the settled regions of eastern Canada, including cities and towns, but the vast majority emigrated from small communities (with populations of under a thousand) along the St. Lawrence and Richelieu rivers. At the time, many Quebec villages were scarcely more than a crossroads where the parish priest and a few craftsmen and merchants serviced an essentially rural area. Retired persons of modest means (*rentiers*) without families, and day laborers (*journaliers*), also tended to live in town.

Social organization

French-Canadian society was gradually undergoing a transformation from a subsistence to a market economy,[8] but in the countryside life went on as usual and in fact would remain largely unchanged until World War II. Villages were isolated from one another and people traveled very little. Houses were generally aligned along the road that traversed each *rang* (range, i.e., a subdivision of a tract of land), and often were no more than two or three hundred feet apart from one another, but a neighborhood concept was practically nonexistent.[9] Villagers in the first rang considered their situation to be superior to that of farmers in the second rang, those in the second more advantageous than habitants in the third, and so on. A few tasks required cooperative effort—for example, cornhusking, pig slaughtering, repair work on local roads or the parish church, and some harvesting—but as a rule individuals had few dealings with the people next door. Everyone loved to gossip and talk politics on the church steps before and after mass on Sunday mornings and on infrequent visits to village craftsmen, but the rest of the time they socialized almost exclusively with relatives.

Then as now, laws in Quebec were made by a bicameral parliament with elected deputies and appointed senators. The two leading provincial parties of the day were the Conservatives (*les Bleus*) and the Liberals (*les Rouges*).[10] Each village elected a mayor and a council for a two-year term (women did not have the right to vote in federal elections until 1918, in provincial or local contests until 1940), but these officials mostly concerned themselves with road maintenance and other small projects. The local school board met occasionally, for example to discuss the hiring of a new teacher, but important policy matters relating to curriculum and textbooks were decided at the provincial level by the church-controlled *Comité catholique* which sent an *inspecteur* to each village once a year.[11]

The *curé,* or pastor, was the most powerful figure at the local level. His influence extended far beyond the sacred sphere as he was routinely consulted by parishioners concerning all manner of secular decisions.

Each Quebec parish is owned and managed by a corporation known as the *fabrique.*[12] *Marguilliers,* or board members—usually three or six depending on the size of the community, elected for a three-year term on a rotating basis—function as a council supervising all parish activities and financial matters: hence they enjoy special status. However, in dealing with this group as well as with other parishioners, the turn-of-the-century curé usually managed to get his way.

The lines between French-Canadian village and parish life were blurred. The social structure of the parish can be shown schematically as a circle representing the entire community, the greater prestige being at the top (see figure 1).[13] In the middle section marked B, one finds the majority of the parishioners, owners of small farms, organized into a hierarchy based not so much on wealth as on family and rang lines. The crescent C includes all the nonfarmers living in the village—bankers, day laborers, small tradesmen, and such—with prestige according to wealth, which rarely exceeded that of the average farmer and often ranked below it. Day laborers and others in the lower reaches of the crescent often abandoned traditional values and mores, and were looked down upon by all other members of the

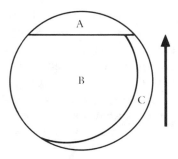

Figure 1. Social organization of a traditional French-Canadian rural community before World War II. (Source: Miner, *St. Denis,* p. 250.)

parish. At the top, the section marked A is made up of a distinct class that rarely associated with the remainder of the community. It included the curé, his relatives, and any deputy or senator who happened to live in town, and his family and relatives.

The most striking aspect of this culture was its orderliness and the relative security resulting from a shared understanding of life's goals and everyone's place in society. The curé played a particularly important role in defining this view. The existence of a world beyond the village was only dimly perceived and regarded as culturally disorienting and a danger to the soul.

Housing

A few fieldstone houses with steep roofs, which dated back to the French regime, could still be found in some areas,[14] and log cabins were plentiful in the backcountry. (The rugged life in pioneer settlements around Lake St. John is described in Hémon's *Maria Chapdelaine*.)[15] Some habitations were indistinguishable from contemporary farmhouses in other parts of Canada or in the United States, and in many cases their construction and appearance had been influenced by them. However, a large number of French-Canadian homesteads were unlike any of these.

A popular type of dwelling in the area surrounding Quebec City consisted of a rectangular frame structure resting on a foundation several feet high with an open porch and steps front and rear (*galerie*) protected by an overhang.[16] The siding was clapboard and the double-sloping roof, in which three or more dormer windows (*lucarnes*) were set, was generally covered with tar paper, asbestos shingles, or tin. A chimney usually protruded from each gable. (Mansard roofs were also fashionable about this time, but the vogue was relatively short-lived in Quebec.)[17] The raised porch facilitated access in the winter when snow accumulated on the ground, and the eaves offered protection from sun and rain the rest of the year. Narrow wooden pillars and a railing were sometimes added to suggest the form of a veranda. Windows and doors were often outlined in color.

Even houses located in the village usually had a number of attached or detached annexes associated with rural living: a barn, a privy, a shed, and a stable. Farmhouses had more such structures spread over a larger area: a henhouse, a pigpen, storage buildings, a summer kitchen, and so on. A bed of flowers often decorated the frontage. Vegetable and herb gardens could be found in sunny spots on the side of the house or at the rear. A swing was another fixture here.[18]

Inside, the two-storied building contained, on the first floor, a kitchen, dining room, parlor, and one or two bedrooms; the second level, reached by a staircase, was divided into bedrooms and a storage area.[19] All rooms except the kitchen were wallpapered or painted white. Most houses also included a cellar and attic.

Furniture

Quebec houses contained a good deal of furniture, most of it home-made: beds, benches, bureaus, chairs, chests, cupboards, rocking chairs, tables, and so forth. Peddlers sold small articles, for example, rush-bottom chairs. Finer pieces, especially those in the parlor, were usually purchased from the local cabinetmaker. Clocks, knick-knacks, and sets of upholstered furniture manufactured in the city also found their way into parlors. A large kitchen stove was one of the first items purchased by any family along with pots, pans, earthenware dishes, jugs, pottery, and utensils. Tallow candles were no longer widely used: kerosene lamps provided light at the close of day. Looms, skein-winding reels, spinning wheels, and other essential appliances needed to produce cloth, thread, or yarn were also bought objects and stored in the attic when not in use.

Kitchen walls were decorated with holy pictures and a religious calendar listing saints' feast days, holy days of obligation, and reminders of periods of fast and abstinence. Family photographs were displayed in the parlor. Crucifixes—often traversed by a palm or spruce branch renewed once a year on Palm Sunday—and holy pictures could be found everywhere. Large matching portraits of the Blessed Virgin and the Sacred Heart were fixtures in the parents' bedroom. An image of the Guardian Angel adorned the children's room.[20]

Clothing

Women still produced knitted goods and various kinds of homespun (*drayet* or *droguet*—drugget, a coarse, durable wool fabric—flannel, fulled cloth, and ticking) for bedclothes and garments. But they also purchased small quantities of inexpensive manufactured material, notably gingham, poplin, and prints (*indienne*).[21]

The costumes worn by troupes that perform French-Canadian folk dances today are adaptations of apparel once considered suitable for either work or formal occasions, either summer or winter.[22] However, all clothing tended to be much more somber and uniform.

To go about his daily tasks in the warm months, the farmer usually put on loose-fitting gray or brown trousers made of drugget (*culotte bavaloise*), fastened with a broad leather belt or held up by suspenders; he also wore a checkered flannel shirt, woolen stockings, mocassin boots (*bottes sauvages*), and, on sunny days, a handmade straw hat.[23] In cold weather, he would add a sweater or vest and, outdoors, a fur or heavy wool hooded overcoat (*capot*) tied about the waist with a sash (*ceinture fléchée*).[24] A fur cap (*casque*) or woolen *tuque,* and flannel-lined calfskin mittens were added as well.[25]

The ceinture fléchée deserves special note. Bright-colored sashes are known to have been worn by French-Canadian *coureurs de bois* and *voyageurs* as early as the eighteenth century. The modern handwoven, worsted sash seems to have been first produced in quantity about 1810 for the North West Company, a firm that joined the Hudson's Bay Company in 1821. About this time, female finger-weavers at L'Assomption, near Montreal, obtained a monopoly on their manufacture and developed a distinctive lightning-bolt pattern. Various styles of sashes were popular items of male wearing apparel in the nineteenth century. They appear frequently in paintings by Cornelius Krieghoff, and in the mid-1830s they were worn as a kind of emblem by the Patriotes. The arrowhead sash that once belonged to Dr. Jean-Olivier Chénier, who was slain at St. Eustache in 1837, is preserved in the National Museum at Ottawa. The sash industry declined at the turn of the century but was revived in the 1930s.

In the summer, a woman wore a plain flannel skirt (over a heavy *jupon,* or slip), a long-sleeved gingham bodice (*polka*) buttoned down the front and closely fitted around the neck, woolen stockings, mocassins, and a sturdy apron. To work in the fields, she covered her head with a cotton bonnet (*capine*) tied under the chin or a straw hat.[26] A baggy, heavy cotton cap with bows front and back but exposing the chignon was a popular headpiece for girls.[27] Indoors during the winter, a woman wore a skirt and blouse of a heavier material, and she often wrapped a gray flannel shawl with fringe around her shoulders and put on a capine or *capuche* made of cotton or wool bordered with lace and fastened with a bow under the chin.[28]

On formal occasions, a man wore the same Sunday suit summer or winter (the jacket was fastened with four buttons and had narrow lapels), a white shirt, and dark tie. In the summertime, a woman had a number of simple, homemade dresses, but to go to church she covered her shoulders with a short cape (*collerette*) and always donned a store-bought hat. In the winter, she wore an outfit of matching material with a fitted jacket and puffed sleeves, and a wool overcoat and hat. Older ladies covered their heads with a crocheted capine.[29]

Family

Quebec society was family oriented. Anthropologists note that French Canadians developed kinship recognition to a high degree; in other words, they were able to identify many relatives, often up to third cousins.[30] Weddings, christenings, funerals, holidays, and anniversaries were occasions for family gatherings, frequently lasting well into the night, but outings and more extended trips away from home also normally involved dropping in or staying with relatives. During these visits, much time was spent catching up on the latest offspring and family doings.

For the habitant, there was a practical side to family solidarity. To this day—the same thing holds in the United States—one cannot generally make a go of a small farm unless members of a household pitch in, contributing their labor and their earnings to this common endeavor. A large family was therefore a decided advantage.

The lines of authority were clearly drawn: the father made all the important decisions relative to the farm, and the mother ran the house.[31] At times, however, the two spheres of activity overlapped, as, for example, when the entire family dropped everything to go berrying (the mother was usually in charge),[32] or to gather in the crops (the father's area of responsibility).

Each person's situation was usually determined early on. One of the sons would inherit the farm, another would become a priest, the others would eventually acquire land to settle on and establish new homesteads, be apprenticed to local craftsmen, or become day laborers. The family did what it could to give each child a good start in life, but vocational choices were limited by custom and meager resources. Youngsters were expected to be self-sufficient at a relatively early age. However, they were also morally bound to help out on the farm until their late teens. During the winter, many young men worked in lumber camps (*chantiers*) or, after the thaw, in rafting the timber downstream to the sawmills and shipyards (*la drave*). The greater part of their wages was usually turned over to their parents.[33]

Elder children usually married first and moved out of the house. Logically, then, the family farm was handed down from the father to one of the younger sons.[34] After the latter married, three generations often dwelled under the same roof. Young women were brought up to be wives and mothers. But if they did not marry or enter religious life they often became the backbone of the home, caring for the young children or elderly parents and making enormous contributions to everyone's welfare on the farm.

The economic and demographic factors that produced the exodus of French Canadians to New England altered these traditional patterns. Emigration drained the Quebec countryside of its young men and women, leaving behind a population that tended to be either under fourteen or about forty and over.

Daily living

The cycle of life in rural Quebec was tied to the need to produce essential goods on the farm and in the home. The daily routine varied according to the season but the long hours and backbreaking labor never ceased. The typical habitant owned a minuscule piece of land—under fifty acres—about ten cows, a dozen hens, a sow, a pair of oxen, a horse, a dog, and a cat. Some farmers also kept ducks, goats, rabbits, or sheep.[35] Farm animals at that time were generally of an inferior quality.[36]

Rural families rose early, generally before 5:00 A.M. in the summer, a bit later in the winter, and performed a number of chores before breakfast. Hearty, countrystyle meals were consumed at about 7:00 A.M., noon, and 5:00 P.M.[37] Typical households included ten or more persons.

"Women's work"—preparing meals from scratch; washing, drying, and storing dishes and kitchen utensils; cleaning the house; keeping everything in order; mending clothes; caring for small children—took much time and required considerable organizational skills.[38] Additional tasks—washing and ironing clothes once a week; baking bread (*pain de ménage*) twice a month; heavy wash twice a year, in the spring and fall; cleaning the entire house from top to bottom (*le grand ménage*) and making soap from rendered beef fat (*savon du pays*) in the spring; planting, weeding, and harvesting garden vegetables and herbs in the warm months; canning in the fall; spinning wool thread, weaving cloth, fashioning clothes; knitting wool mittens, scarves, stockings, and tuques; hooking rugs and making quilts—all had to be accomplished on schedule, too.

The men returned to the house for all meals but could scarcely delay getting back to work. In the spring, the farmer repaired fences, and split and corded firewood. Calves and offspring of other farm animals were also born at this time and had to be looked after. However, he was mostly occupied with plowing (at times, this was accomplished in the autumn), harrowing, fertilizing the soil, and sowing the grain. Summer was the time for repairing equipment and farm buildings, cutting and storing hay, and gathering berries; autumn for harvesting and threshing grain and flax, and picking fruit; winter for sawing firewood and cutting fenceposts, feeding and watering livestock, cleaning out stalls in stables, and slaughtering pigs.[39]

By the turn of the century, manufactured implements and tools were beginning to appear on Quebec farms—axes, hatchets, harrows, mauls, pitchforks, plows, saws, seed spreaders, sickles, spades, wedges—but many habitants were still fashioning these items by hand with metal parts produced by the local blacksmith. The farmer generally built most of his furniture and all wooden structures, beginning with his own house and barns. For his own use, he constructed carts, flails, rakes, snowshoes, sledges (*traîneaux*), sleighs (*berlines, carrioles*), two-wheeled wagons (*banneaux, cabarouets*), and wheelbarrows, and, for the women, looms (*métiers*), skein-winding reels (*dévidoirs*), and all sorts of kitchen utensils. He also fashioned leather objects such as harnesses and mittens.[40]

Few Quebec farmers owned automobiles, tractors, or trucks before the late 1930s.[41] The most elegant mode of transportation was the buggy or surrey, always referred to by their English designations.[42]

Food

French-Canadian farm families ate hearty but, except for holidays, unvarying meals:[43] for breakfast, pancakes, salt pork spread on bread and toast, coffee or tea, and, at times, fried eggs; for lunch and dinner, soup, pork, potatoes, bread and butter with maple syrup (and cream) or molasses, and fresh berries, fruit, and vegetables in season (at other times, whatever was available from home canning). Soups were made of vegetables (cabbage, peas) or barley. Beef, chicken, and veal were rarely served; blood sausage (*boudin*) was considered a delicacy. The beverage was milk or water. Everyone abstained from meat on Fridays and, during Lent, on Wednesdays as well; adults also fasted during the forty weekdays before Easter, which meant consuming only two ounces of food in the morning, eight ounces in the evening.[44] At Christmastime special platters were prepared: pork terrine (*cretons*), beef, chicken, or veal ragout (*ragoût aux boulettes* or *boules*), roast beef, pork-and-spice pies (*tourtières*), fritters (*croccignoles* or *croquignoles*), and raisin and sugar pies. Easter often called for many of the same treats as well as for salt pork and deep-fried eggs.[45]

As their names imply traditional dishes were prepared in characteristic fashion but, being handed down orally from generation to generation, varied a good deal from one family to another. There is, therefore, no set way of making or serving this food. Regional delicacies also could be found.

Religion

Few Franco-Americans today yearn to return to the rigors and ordinary fare of such an existence, but many are inspired by the courage and religious convictions of their ancestors. In French Canada, an abiding and orthodox faith in a just and merciful God gave meaning to daily tasks and to the yearly round, and enabled people to surmount many adversities.[46]

The Patriote movement of the 1830s, an attempt by leaders in Quebec to secure political reforms, ended with an ill-fated uprising; the movement itself had pronounced anticlerical tendencies. After the Rebellion of 1837–38, the Catholic hierarchy in Quebec acted swiftly and effectively to counter this trend and to consolidate its position.[47] Bishop Ignace Bourget of Montreal (1840–76) worked with set purpose to this end. His initial efforts coincided with a visit by Bishop Charles de Forbin-Janson of Nancy in 1840–41, which caused a sensation. The French prelate's preaching and organizational zeal, exhibited in a series of appearances throughout the province, contributed enormously to a Catholic revival whose effects were still being felt a century later. Vigorous proselytizing resulted in a great increase in religious vocations and rapid growth of parish organizations. Aided by the arrival of numerous congregations from France and the foundation of specialized religious communities in Quebec, the Catholic church assumed control of education and social service at all levels. It also constituted a formidable lobby that persuaded public officials to enact rigorous laws designed to regulate conduct and morals in accordance with a conservative brand of Roman Catholicism. Relations between the curé and his flock—and between upright parishioners, on the one hand, and their more libertine neighbors, on the other—were sometimes strained; conflicts arose, for example, over proper conduct or tithing.[48]

Also, many French Canadians did not feel bound by the prevailing political philosophy and succeeded, for example, in getting Liberal party candidates elected to office. Many, too, scoffed at puritanism, and the vast majority, no doubt, were convivial at family gatherings, notably at Christmastime.

In the post–Vatican II era it is sometimes difficult to appreciate the formalism that characterized public and private worship in the Catholic church at the turn of the century. Prayers were always recited in exactly the same way, the liturgy of the mass and other devotions remained unchanged year after year, and rites relating to the seven sacraments were invariable.

Yet spiritual life was no less intense or rich because of adherence to prescribed forms. French-Canadian habitants felt close to God and believed He intervened not infrequently in their affairs. Everyone knew of miraculous occurrences: disasters averted, sicknesses cured. Certain saints were the object of intense devotion. At the same time, a strong undercurrent of folk beliefs was also present among the people and gave rise to many superstitious practices.[49]

Holy days and other seasonal events

Scholars have found it useful to analyze traditional life on the basis of the liturgical year and the stages of life. Here are some illustrations of French-Canadian customs and mores, using these categories for the sake of convenience.

Advent. A time of prayer and fasting in anticipation of Christmas—as the great feast approached, the faithful sang "Venez, Divin Messie" in church—this season also called for extensive preparations for the holiday.[50] Beef and hog butchering was an elaborate, exciting, and noisy activity that required the cooperation of the entire family and often involved neighbors. When pigs were slaughtered, the blood was kept for sausage (*boudin*) made by combining the fluid with milk, mixing it with salt pork, onions, and seasoning, stuffing it in casings of the swine's intestines, and cooking (not boiling) it in hot water for fifteen minutes. It was customary to give choice morsels to relatives and friends, especially those who helped on this occasion. Chickens and turkeys were also prepared for cooking at this busy time of the year.

Christmastide (Le temps des fêtes). In Catholic countries and in other areas where Christianity has been implanted, the feast of the Savior's birth is marked by joyous celebrations.[51]

For French Canadians at the turn of the century, the annual commemoration centered on the religious service and the singing of carols in church. The image of sleighs bearing happy parishioners returning home after midnight mass in the snow-covered village is fixed in the collective consciousness. The popular belief that a special favor, implored by reciting one thousand Hail Mary's on Christmas Eve, will surely be granted is immortalized in *Maria Chapdelaine.* (Some believed that one could achieve the same end by saying sixty-six rosaries during Advent, the sixty-seventh on Christmas Eve.)[52] At midnight, farm animals were said to kneel in the stable in adoration of the Christ Child.[53]

A manger (*la crèche*) framed with spruce trees decorated with bright-colored ribbons was erected near the main altar, and a simple pageant with children playing the roles of angels, shepherds, Mary, and Joseph preceded the high mass. At precisely midnight, the lights in church were extinguished, a statue of the Baby Jesus was placed in the manger, and the lead male voice in the choir sang the solemn "O! Holy Night" ("Minuit chrétien").

During mass, the pastor usually rose to the occasion and delivered a fine sermon, and practically everyone received communion. The choir always intoned "O Come All Ye Faithful" in Latin ("Adeste Fideles"), but such popular songs of religious joy as "Les Anges dans nos campagnes" ("Angels We Have Heard on High") were sung in French. A low mass (*la messe de l'aurore*) followed and was attended by all.

When the family returned from church at about two o'clock in the morning, an elaborate meal was served (*le réveillon*). Traditional dishes included croquignoles, ragoût, tourtières, fruit, and pies. Small gifts were then exchanged. (This custom dates back only to the second half of the nineteenth century: earlier, the presents were exchanged on New Year's Day.)[54] Rural children of the time were accustomed to very little in the way of playthings or treats. Christmas was no exception. In their stockings, or by the manger in the parlor, children might find a bit of candy, an orange—rarely seen in Quebec at any other time of the year—or a simple toy. Sometimes they were told that these presents came from Father Christmas (*le Père Noël*), imagined, as in England, as a tall, thin version of Santa Claus who wore a long red robe rather than breeches and boots.[55] More often, the gifts were said to have been left by *l'Enfant Jésus*.[56]

The feasting generally lasted until dawn, so everyone slept late on Christmas Day and no special meals were prepared. However, a *bûche de Nöel,* or cake shaped and decorated to resemble a Yule log, was often served on that day.

There was much visiting of relatives and friends on the days after Christmas, and there were also many nightlong parties in the home (*veillées*). On the last Sunday of the year, unrented church pews were auctioned off in the parish hall by the *crieur* and the election of the marguilliers was held.[57] A special door-to-door collection of goods for the poor (*la guignolée*) was sometimes made on Christmas or on New Year's Day.[58]

January 1 was one of the most important feasts of the year. The family gathered early at the grandparents' or parents' home, and the eldest son asked for the blessing. For French Canadians, it was a solemn and emotional moment. (The practice was not common among Acadians who, incidentally, believed it was bad luck if the first visitor were a woman.)[59] Everyone knelt before the grandfather who gave a benediction similar to that of the priest at the end of mass. As he made the sign of the cross over everyone, or each individual, he said: "Que Dieu vous bénisse au nom du Père et du Fils et du Saint Esprit. Amen." Traditionally, this blessing was immediately followed by a wish along the following lines: "Je vous souhaite une bonne et heureuse année, une bonne santé, et le paradis à la fin de vos jours!" (I wish you a prosperous and happy New Year, good health, and eternal bliss when you pass on.)[60] Though always associated with this custom, the phrase alluding to paradise is now generally recognized as the classic French-Canadian New Year's wish. After the blessing, everyone rose, kissed or shook hands, and exchanged expressions of good fortune.

In many families, boys kissed both parents on this occasion and when greeting. (French Canadians usually kiss twice in succession.) In former times, Acadians rarely kissed one another in public.[61] The small gifts for children were sometimes given, according to French custom, only on New Year's Day.[62]

Before and after mass—January 1 is a Holy Day of Obligation for Catholics—further greetings and good wishes were exchanged with relatives and friends on the church steps. At the conclusion of his sermon, the pastor expressed his wishes for his parishioners and gave his formal blessing, as usual, in Latin. After the sermon, the newly elected marguillier was installed in a simple ceremony: the outgoing officer, accompanied by an altar boy or the sexton holding a lighted taper, led his successor to the pew reserved for the wardens.

At home, after a round or two of drinks during which informal toasts were exchanged with everyone, a hearty and joyous meal was served. This generally consisted of roast beef or turkey; mashed potatoes, peas, pickles, beets, and onions; tourtières; croquignoles and other desserts. A New Year's Day visit to relatives in the area was customary during the afternoon or evening.

The holiday season ended with Epiphany (*la Fête des Rois*) on January 6, commemorating the coming of the Magi. On this day, statues of the Wise Men made their appearance in church. At the evening meal or during the veillée, the Twelfth Night Cake (*le gâteau des Rois*) was served.[63] A pea and a bean were baked inside the cake. Whoever got the slice with the pea was proclaimed king; the bean, queen; and each was crowned with a colored paper diadem. The king was expected to kiss the queen. In France, only a bean is involved—today usually an imitation seed in the form of a crown or other ornament—and the cake is called *la galette des Rois*.

February 2. Candlemas (La Chandeleur). Forty days after the birth of Our Lord, Mary went to the temple at Jerusalem to be purified and to present her son to God as required by the Law of Moses. At a special mass on this day (or the following Sunday), candles were lighted and held by the faithful during parts of the service, and then brought home. When lighted, the candles were believed to protect the home during storms, to ward off evil, and to comfort individuals who were seriously ill or in death throes.[64]

On Candlemas night, French Canadians often had pancake parties (*veillées de crêpes*), for eating flapjacks on this occasion was said to bring good luck. In the United States, February 2 is Groundhog Day. According to tradition, the woodchuck comes out on this day; but if the sun is shining, the animal is frightened by his own shadow and goes back into hibernation, thus portending six more weeks of winter. The legend is widespread in

European (and French-Canadian) folklore, but it is often associated with a bear or other hibernating animal. Various French sayings and rhymes allude to this popular myth and offer explanations of why the days are growing longer at this time of year. For example:

A la Chandeleur,
Les jours rallongent d'une heure.

(At Candlemas,
The days grow an hour longer.)

Or: Les jours croissent de plus d'une heure (The days grow more than an hour longer); Les plus grandes douleurs (The greatest woes, i.e., the worst part of the winter); La neige est à sa hauteur (The snow will not get any deeper); and so on. In certain parts of Quebec, a similar tradition is associated with the feasts of Saint Mathias (February 24) or Saint Joseph (March 19).[65]

An old custom associated with Candlemas, *courir la Chandeleur* (to make the Candlemas rounds), is only attested among the Acadians.[66] Groups of young men went from door to door on the afternoon of February 2 (but never on a Sunday) taking up a collection—food, clothing, money—for the needy or, simply, for an evening party. Many such collections were taken in Europe and Quebec (cf. *la guignolée* on Christmas or New Year's Day) but, it would appear, never in connection with Candlemas.

The Acadian alms collectors (*quêteux*), sometimes as many as thirty bachelors or young married men, would smudge on mustaches or beards, don outlandish costumes, and ride in horse-drawn sledges. At the head of the cortege would be the leader, dressed in fancy clothes and holding a baton surmounted by a replica of a rooster. After knocking at a door and inquiring politely if the occupants wished to *recevoir la Chandeleur* (invite Candlemas collectors in), the group would enter in single file, sing and dance for a few minutes, gather whatever items were offered in boxes, sacks, or other containers, and, after having a drink, perhaps, and singing a little ditty to thank their hosts, proceed to the next house. The music was traditional but some of the words were adapted to the circumstances. It was considered bad luck to refuse to contribute, and the leader could even put a hex on the house. The collected goods were distributed to indigent families, but enough was generally kept for a veillée to which everyone was invited that evening.

With the advent of social security in the 1930s and, above all, with the departure of virtually all young men from the Maritime Provinces during World War II for military service or for work in city factories, the custom died out. In its day, it improved the welfare of the poor and provided a welcome diversion in the dead of winter.

February 14. Saint Valentine's Day. Widely celebrated as a secular event in Europe since the Middle Ages, Saint Valentine's Day in France seems to have been reserved for the nobility until modern times.[67] No commemorations are recorded in Quebec during the French regime. Influenced by contemporary English fashion, valentines in turn-of-the-century French Canada were either romantic or satiric. The latter could be quite cruel, for example, pointing out alleged bad habits, moral flaws, or physical deformities. Sent anonymously for the most part, malicious messages of this sort eventually went out of vogue.

February 29. Leap year. Every fourth year an extra day is added to the calendar.[68] According to an old custom, unmarried women are allowed to take the initiative in proposing marriage in the course of that year or, on February 29, in asking for a date. In Quebec, an old saying reflecting folk misgivings about anything out of the ordinary—but suggested in part, no doubt, by the rhyme—claims that Leap Year children are feebleminded: *l'année bissextile, l'année des imbéciles* (Leap Year, year of the imbeciles).

March 17. Saint Patrick's Day. The Irish in French Canada have long made their presence known in a variety of ways, including public celebrations of their patron saint's feast day.[69] Crows—at Percé, seagulls (*goélands*)—are said to return to Quebec on Saint Patrick's Day, an occasion often marked by winter's last snowstorm. This explains the Quebecois proverb *Il va faire mauvais, c'est la fête des Irlandais* (It's going to be stormy, it's the Irish holiday); but it is also a wry commentary on Irish pugnaciousness.

March 19. Saint Joseph's Day. Very popular in French Canada from the early days of the colony when fireworks were set off in his honor on his feast day, Saint Joseph was named the patron saint of Canada in 1834. The Oratory that bears his name in Montreal was begun in 1924 by Brother Alfred Bessette (Frère André), a renowned faith healer.[70]

In Quebec, many farmers waited until after *la tempête de saint Joseph* to tap maple trees. The saint's feast day was also said to be a propitious time to sow tomatoes (indoors). According to a French-Canadian proverb, Saint Joseph's Day was a forecaster of spring: *La Saint-Joseph belle, le printemps vilain* (when Saint Joseph's Day is fair, spring is foul).

Shrovetide and Carnival (Les Jours gras et le temps du Carnaval). In Catholic countries, the weeks before Lent, and especially, the days immediately preceding Ash Wednesday, have, since the Middle Ages, been a season of feasting and merrymaking.[71] Lent was a somber time of fasting and penitence, hence the popular saying:

Mardi Gras
Va t'en donc pas.

(Shrove Tuesday
Don't go away.)

At the turn of the century, French Canadians celebrated with veillées at which card playing, dancing, singing, storytelling, and partaking of elaborate meals played an important part. No special food was reserved for this period of the year, although crêpes were popular and, of course, meat dishes. Commonly served drinks included moonshine (*bagosse*) and a mixture of whiskey and wine (*caribou*).

At Shrovetide, groups of children and sometimes grown-ups went about in disguises consisting mainly of bizarre clothes and homemade masks constructed out of cardboard or sacks.[72] After making the rounds of neighborhood homes, where they provided brief indoor entertainment—dancing, singing, and playing pranks—and were rewarded with fruit, taffy, or some other form of candy, the revelers would end up at a veillée, where they removed their masks.

Priests frowned on excessive partying and scolded parishioners for carousing, as opposed to moderate social drinking (taking *un p'tit coup*), and indecent dancing. It was considered morally objectionable for a woman to allow herself to be held by the waist (*se laisser prendre par la taille*). In many areas, the curé imposed a year-round ban on all kinds of mixed dances and even refused absolution to any person who confessed having engaged in this activity. However, people often adopted the commonsense view that, except during Lent, chaperoned dancing, especially in the home, was no sin. In any event, all partying stopped promptly at midnight on Mardi Gras. The prohibition against dancing on Ash Wednesday (*sur le Mercredi des Cendres*) is immortalized in the legend of Rose Latulipe, whose mysterious partner after midnight on one such occasion turned out to be Satan.

In the latter part of the nineteenth century, Montreal and Quebec City began organizing huge public celebrations, largely to attract tourists during the off-season. These events lasting several days included costume balls, fireworks, ice palaces, illuminations, parades with floats (*chars allégoriques*), and snow sculpture competitions. The tradition gradually died out but was successfully revived in Quebec City in 1955. The festivities there today have little connection with the pre-Lenten season and have been transformed into a winter carnival. In 1984 the ten-day event, presided over by Bonhomme Carnaval and featuring a queen and her court (referred to as *duchesses*), culminated on February 12, more than three weeks before Mardi Gras.

Lent. The forty days from Ash Wednesday to Easter were marked, in French Canada, by several religious observances and secular customs that are no longer witnessed today.[73] In the early days of the colony, everyone twenty-one years of age or older was required to fast and to abstain from meat (also butter, eggs, and lard) from the beginning to the end of Lent. By the middle of the nineteenth century, the Catholic church had eased lenten rules slightly, limiting fasting to weekdays and total abstinence to Wednesdays, Fridays, and certain other days (meat could be consumed at one meal on the other weekdays).

In turn-of-the-century Quebec, the regulations concerning fasting were interpreted strictly; the two ounces of food allowed in the morning and eight ounces at night were often carefully weighed. Typically, such meals would consist of black coffee and bread mixed in a bit of water sweetened with molasses (*la tambane*). On days of abstinence, crêpes, fish (cod, eel, herring), and pea soup were standard fare. Technically, the rules concerning abstinence applied only to persons fourteen years of age and over, but the entire household generally partook of the same food.

Everyone was expected to perform private acts of mortification, for example to give up card playing, drinking, smoking, or social engagements, and to recite the rosary or attend mass every day. Children were strongly urged to make sacrifices and practice self-denial.

Like their ancestors in France, many French Canadians broke Lent about midway, usually on Thursday of the third week but sometimes for as long as three days. A popular custom involving masquerading and feasting as at Shrovetide, *la Mi-Carême,* was roundly condemned by the church and by stern individuals who scorned those who were unwilling to tough out the entire forty days of Lent (*toffer tout leur Carême*).[74] The tradition was allegorized as *la Bonne femme Mi-Carême,* an old woman in rags riding a nag, who left candy for children.

On Passion Sunday many people took cuttings from fruit trees indoors, putting them in buckets or jars of water to force them for use as a decoration in the home on Easter Sunday.

In rural French Canada about 1900, palms were not generally available so parishioners brought spruce branches, often decorated with paper flowers or ribbons, to be blessed at mass and to be held during the traditional procession commemorating Christ's triumphal entry into Jerusalem. These branches were treated with reverence and preserved in the home throughout the entire year. Like Candlemas tapers and holy water, they were believed to give protection against natural disasters and to bring blessings. The weather on Palm Sunday was said to indicate the atmospheric conditions ahead.

On Maundy Thursday the organ and the bells rung by the altarboy during mass as well as those in the belfry tolled by the sexton were stilled after the Gloria, until Holy Saturday. A clapper or a wooden instrument with a crank (*crécelle*) was used instead to signal certain parts of the service. Grown-ups pretended that the church bells had flown off to Rome—to see the pope, to get salt pork, or something of the sort—and teased small children into watching them leave or return on Easter morn. When toddlers did not see the bells go by, parents explained that they were probably too high in the sky.[75]

Toward the end of the service, a consecrated host was removed from the tabernacle, put in a chalice, and placed in a repository on a side altar. Throughout the rest of the day and part of the night, parishioners made visits to the Blessed Sacrament, often spending an hour or more in pious adoration.

The solemn liturgy of Holy Week climaxed on Good Friday. Many French Canadians observed the day by abstaining from all food except bread and water (*le grand jeûne*). Even farm animals were sometimes made to fast all day. Most families accomplished only essential tasks and kept silence from noon until three o'clock in the afternoon, the hours Christ spent upon the cross. *Le Vendredi saint* was such a special day that it gave rise to the belief that, if one asked for three favors during the three hours of prayerful silence, or while standing ramrod straight as an act of mortification throughout the entire reading of the Passion of Our Lord, God would surely grant one request. Finally, it was widely held that it always grew dark about three o'clock on Good Friday, the hour when Christ yielded up His spirit.

The long liturgy on Holy Saturday morning included the blessing of new fire, the paschal candle, and water. At the Gloria, the organ burst into music and all the bells suddenly rang out in unison, bringing expressions of joy to everyone's face. After mass, parishioners filled small containers, brought along for this purpose, with holy water that had been placed in large tubs at the entrance of the church. Lent was now over, and few could avoid immediately having the candy, drink, or smoke they had denied themselves for so long, especially the many stalwarts who had not indulged themselves on Sundays. A slightly irreverent ditty, sung to the tune of "O filii et filiae," conveyed the joy and relief felt on this occasion:

Alleluia, le Carême s'en va,
On mangera plus de la soupe aux pois,
On va manger du bouillon gras.[76]

(Alleluia, Lent will soon be over,
Say good-bye to pea soup,
Say hello to meat broth.)

Easter. The most important day in the liturgical year, Easter was celebrated with great pomp at church and was associated with many beliefs
and customs.[77] A large number of French-Canadian families would rise before dawn to fetch water from a stream.[78] Opinions differed as to whether
l'eau de Pâques should be collected with or against the flow, but people felt
that it had miraculous properties. They washed their faces and hands in it,
drank it, and preserved it in bottles and other containers. It was believed
that this water stayed pure indefinitely and never went flat. Many persons
also claimed having seen the sun on the horizon at the crack of dawn dance
with joy at Christ's resurrection.

At mass on Easter morning, French Canadians wore their best clothes
and tried to include at least one new article of personal attire, thus adher-
ing to an ancient custom said to reflect Saint Paul's appeal to "put on the
new self" (Ephesians 4:24). On the menu that day, one found many favorite foods that had been prohibited during Lent, for example, salt pork
cooked on a griddle and smoked ham. Easter ham was said to have important medicinal value.

At the end of the nineteenth century, Catholics had until Low Sunday,
or Quasimodo, that is, the Sunday following Easter, to fulfill their Easter
duty (*faire ses pâques, son devoir pascal*). The angelus bell at six o'clock in the
evening on that day was said to toll for those who had violated this obligation. Those who waited until the last minute to confess themselves did so,
in the popular view, to outfox the priest who would surely not deny a sin-
ner absolution at this late date, whence the expression *faire des pâques de
renard* (*renard* is French for *fox*). In French-Canadian folklore, a werewolf,
or person who, possessed by the devil, turned into a wolf or other animal
(*virer loup-garou*) at midnight, was often an individual being punished for
not having gone to confession in seven years. The only way to set the victim free was to make it bleed with a knife or other sharp object.[79]

Maple-Sugaring Time (Le temps des sucres). Early in the spring, many
French-Canadian farmers devoted a month or so to maple sugaring on
their own land or, more commonly, in nearby wooded areas where maple
trees were plentiful (*sucreries*).[80] Sucreries were often exploited by the same
family for several generations. The process involved tapping the trees for
their sap (*l'eau d'érable*) and reducing the fluid to syrup and, eventually, to
sugar by boiling it in a cast-iron cauldron. The best time for drawing off
the sap was on sunny days following cold nights. Animal behavior and
other phenomena in nature were believed to announce the beginning and
end of the season. For example, it was time to start when the titmouse
(*oiseau de sucre*) made its appearance, time to finish when woodpeckers
(*pique-bois*) struck the buckets with their bills.

Maple sugar products were intended mainly for home use, an average family requiring about 100 pounds of sugar and 150 pounds of syrup each year. A small amount was also produced for barter with local craftsmen and for sale to itinerant middlemen who distributed the products in the cities.

At the turn of the century, the process was inefficient and time consuming. The sap dripped along crude boards into birchbark or wooden receptacles; much fluid was also lost in transferring it from one container to another (when the sap was flowing, each bucket had to be emptied into a keg that was hauled by hand on a sledge); the distilling apparatus, heated over outdoor fires, was primitive and wasteful. But it was customary for family and relations—often numbering thirty to fifty persons, including the obligatory fiancés—to gather once or twice at the *cabane à sucre* to help out and to have a good time. The sugaring off (*partie de sucre*) was well on the way to becoming a Quebec institution.

The outing was generally held in the afternoon, on a Sunday or at Mi-Carême. Visitors would reach the cabin on snowshoes and begin drinking, singing, and telling jokes. When the syrup was ready, it could be tasted by dipping a flat stick shaped like a spoon (*palette*) into the boiling fluid. Some was also ladled out onto the snow to make clumps of *tire*, which were picked up with the palette and consumed. Later, a meal was served, usually consisting of baked beans, bread, eggs fried in maple syrup, grilled salt pork, and smoked ham. Almost always, the frolicking involved teasing, hide-and-seek, a snowball fight, and smearing others' hands and faces with *tire* and soot. The party ended with everyone carrying home containers of syrup and a supply of sugar molded into one- or two-pound blocks (*pains de sucre*).

Today, Quebec produces 70 percent (30 million pounds) of the world's maple sugar, and it exports 80 percent of its yield to the United States.[81] Most of the industry uses modern distilling and packaging processes. Parties de sucre are still enormously popular in French Canada but are often held in a cabane adjoining a large public facility, charging admission and featuring a bar, restaurant, and live music. The traditional menu has been expanded to include crêpes, pancake batter cooked in boiling syrup (*pépères*), and slices of bread soaked with heavy cream and covered with shredded maple sugar (*tartines*). But many people enjoy reminiscing about and, whenever possible, actually going to a *vraie* cabane à sucre, that is, a small, family-owned enterprise in a rustic setting.

April 1. April Fool's Day (Poisson d'avril). In many places today, practical jokers have a field day on the first of April.[82] For obscure reasons, the custom in Francophone countries is associated with fish. One shouts "Poisson d'avril!" or makes an allusion to fishing—for instance: "Est-ce que ça mord?" (Are they biting?)—when the prank is revealed. Schoolchildren love to pin a paper fish on someone's back, and the possibilities for such mischievous acts, ranging from making someone look up "at the bird" to elaborate hoaxes, are endless. Popular tricks include sending an unsuspecting individual for a fanciful or ridiculous object: a single-ended rod (*un bâton à un bout*), a pail of smoke (*une chaudière à boucane*), checkered paint (*de la peinture carreautée*), or a brand-new skyhook (*un petit rien tout neuf*).

April 25. Saint Mark's Day. At a special mass each year on this day, farmers in French Canada ask God to protect their crops. An indoor or outdoor procession precedes the Rogation Day mass.[83] A handful of the seeds to be planted are brought to church and are blessed by the priest. In former times, habitants viewed anything to do with fertility or reproduction with awe and set great store by blessed seeds. Farming families often recited additional prayers in the field and signed themselves before sowing the first seeds which always included some of the sacred grains. The youngest child, regarded as more innocent than adults, was frequently asked to put the first seeds in the ground.

In Quebec, as in other regions having the same general climactic conditions, April showers are proverbial. One saying in this connection is worth noting:

En avril
Ne te découvre pas d'un fil.[84]

(In April,
Don't remove a stitch.)

May 1. May Day. During the French regime and for many years afterward, it was customary on May Day for villagers to set a tall spruce or pole into the ground before the manor house to pay homage to the local lord.[85] Rounds were fired into the trunk throughout the day, and the ceremony was the occasion of revelry. Sometimes the ceremony honored the community's captain of the militia. At the turn of the century, townspeople along the St. Lawrence River had a similar practice of planting the trunk of a tree into the ice at midstream if it had not broken up by that day. Rain or water derived from melted snow on the first day of May was considered by many persons to have curative powers, especially for eye ailments. In the spring, animals were often put to pasture on the first rainy day of May for the same reason. May Day was also considered to be a good time to plant potatoes and trees.[86]

For Catholics, May is the month of Mary. In rural French Canada, parishioners would gather for devotions every evening at church, at a cross by the side of the road, or at the *école de rang*.[87] The faithful would recite the rosary and sing hymns in honor of the Blessed Virgin. The most popular song of praise is familiar to most Franco-Americans:

C'est le mois de Marie
C'est le mois le plus beau
A la Vierge chérie
Chantons un chant nouveau.

Ornons le sanctuaire
De nos plus belles fleurs
Offrons à notre Mère
Et nos chants et nos coeurs.

('Tis the month of Mary,
'Tis the most beautiful month of all,
Join in singing a new song
To our beloved Virgin.

Deck the shrine
With the most beautiful flowers of all,
Offering our Mother
Our voices and our hearts.)

Often, the outdoor religious exercises were organized by the local schoolmarm who led the group in prayer and song. Statues or portraits of Mary, in church or in the home, were generally adorned with fresh flowers throughout the month.

Corpus Christi (La Fête-Dieu). On the Thursday after the feast of the Trinity, or the following Sunday, the church holds a special celebration honoring the Eucharist.[88] In Catholic countries the day is marked by public religious ceremonies, highlighted by a procession through the streets.

The feast was very popular in rural French Canada. The entire parish would take part, either as members of one of the men's, women's, or children's organizations moving solemnly through the village streets and nearby countryside, banners displayed, or as spectators joining in the singing of hymns and repeating prayers as the procession went by. Houses and streets were embellished with bunting and other ornaments. The spectacle of the priest in dazzling cope and velum bearing the monstrance under a canopy carried by the marguilliers inspired everyone with awe and fervor.

At one or two points along the way—different places each year—a temporary altar was set up in front of someone's home, and the honor of decorating the site with flowers, greens, and tree boughs was conferred upon the occupants. A benediction was held here before the procession returned to the church. The event, which generally occurred in front of one's own house only once in a lifetime, was considered to be one of the great moments in a family's history.

June 24. Saint John the Baptist Day. Declared the patron saint of the French Canadians by Pope Pius X in 1908, John the Baptist had been honored during the French regime with religious ceremonies and also with bonfires associated with the summer solstice.[89] In 1834 the Société Saint-Jean-Baptiste was founded and began to place emphasis on patriotic celebrations—banquets, parades, speeches—especially in the cities. In certain rural communities the day was commemorated with similar events, but these were usually scaled down to modest proportions. The modern holiday throughout Quebec is a post–World War II phenomenon.

August 15. Assumption of the Virgin Mary. Since 1881 Acadians, whose patron saint is Our Lady of the Assumption, have celebrated this day with patriotic as well as religious fervor.[90]

November 1. All Saints' Day (La Toussaint). Long associated throughout Europe with All Souls' Day (November 2, *Le Jour des Morts*)—whence Halloween observed on October 31—All Saints' Day often reminded Quebecois of the souls in purgatory.[91] Because of this connection, country people in former times believed that spirits roamed about at this time of the year; prudent individuals remained indoors whenever possible, especially at night. Halloween activities such as those that have become traditional in the United States were unknown in French Canada.

November 25. Saint Catherine's Day. It was a French-Canadian custom to make taffy (*tire*) on *la Sainte-Catherine,* which was also a day when one was supposed to accord special attention to women twenty-five years old and over who were unmarried.[92]

The stages of life

Birth and Baptism. Rural French Canadians had large families—ten surviving children were not uncommon—which meant that young wives generally had babies every year.[93] Women viewed frequent childbearing as a burden but as their lot. Little prenatal or postnatal care was available for mother and child, with the result that the incidence of miscarriages, infant mortality, and childbed fever was high. When a doctor was unavailable, a midwife (*sage-femme*) usually delivered the baby and helped out for a few days. A handcrafted wooden cradle (*ber*) could be found in every home. Spindles at each corner facilitated rocking which was also sometimes accomplished by a string attached to the parents' bed.

Many folk beliefs surrounded childbirth, for example, ways to predict the sex of the child or the number of children one would have. Discussing procreation with children was taboo: they were told that the Indian (*le sauvage*) or the Gypsy (*le Bolomien* or *Bohémien*) brought babies. Youngsters usually managed to acquire essential biological information from peers or from observation of farm animals.

Baptism was immediate if the child was sickly; otherwise, the ceremony was usually performed within a day or two of birth. The name Joseph for a boy or Marie for a girl was routinely given to each child and was entered first in the baptismal register, but it was rarely used afterward. Many children were named after relatives, and middle names usually recalled a godparent. Then as now, certain designations were in fashion for a time. At the turn of the century, many girls were given names like Adélina, Délima, and Sophie; many boys were called Amédée, Cléophas, and Herménégilde. Popular nicknames included Da-Bé, Ti-Bé; Gros-Bi, Ti-Bi; Jos (the *s* was silent and the *j* pronounced as in English), and Pit, for Pierre.

Close relatives served as godparents (grandparents often sponsored the first child) and considered it a serious responsibility. As the mother was still confined, the christening was normally attended only by the father, godparents, and a few close relatives. The midwife was often asked to be the *porteuse,* that is, to hold the child. The baby was dressed in an elaborate chrisom which was often used for every child in the family and at times handed down as one of the few heirlooms. It was customary for the sponsors to bestow small gifts on their godchild (for example, a silver cup), as well as on the mother (a bottle of wine), the porteuse (a pair of gloves), and the sexton. The latter's enthusiasm in ringing the church bell following the ceremony could be expected to vary according to the size of the tip. A modest meal for the christening party followed at the parents' home.

Childhood. Infants and toddlers were mostly cared for and watched over by the mother, but older brothers and sisters were expected to assist whenever possible. Nursery rhymes and finger games, comparable to those found in most cultures, amused and instructed little children about parts of the body and familiar animals and objects. For example, one might pat or tickle the baby from tummy to forehead while reciting: "Ventre de son,—Stomac de plomb,—Fale de pigeon,—Menton fourchu,—Bouche d'argent,—Nez cancan,—Joue bouillie,—Joue rôtie,—Petit oeil,—Gros oeil,—Cillon, cillette,—Casse-baguette!"[94] Or the child might learn that a horse moves forward at different gaits—walk, trot, canter, and gallop—by being playfully bounced on daddy's knee or foot:

Le pas, le pas,
Le trot, le trot,
Le galop, le galop,
GROS GALOP! GROS GALOP![95]

Elementary religious concepts were inculcated early on, for example, by pointing to pictures of Jesus, the Blessed Virgin, or angels and affirming that certain behavior pleased or displeased these personages. Simple prayers were learned as soon as the child could talk. Kindness, politeness, and sharing were also emphasized.

Boys as well as girls normally wore dresses until the age of four or five, but sex roles were defined from the outset by associating them with approved activities and behavior. Little children played outdoors for the most part, usually with a brother or sister, but always under the mother's watchful eye and within sound of her voice. They amused themselves with simple toys—a doll, a sled, a wagon—or pretend games like giddap.

At the age of six, the child went off to the local *école de rang* usually accompanied by an older brother or sister. For most youngsters, this was the first encounter with children other than members of the extended family.

Until World War II, and in many areas for more than two decades afterward, the one-room frame schoolhouse was a fixture in rural Quebec.[96] Whitewashed and surmounted by a belfry crowned with a cross, the turn-of-the-century école de rang, attended by thirty to fifty pupils in grades one through seven taught by a lone teacher, was sparingly furnished and notoriously cold, dark, and drafty during the winter. The building was usually isolated so as to minimize distractions and fenced in to keep strays out. A large wooden cross, planted not too far from the front door, a woodshed, herb and vegetable garden, and outhouse completed the picture.

Inside, a woodburning stove, tended by one of the schoolboys, was the only source of heat for the entire building, which also had a small room in the rear or attic for the teacher (many, however, found lodgings elsewhere). Kerosene lamps provided light—as late as 1949, only 38 percent of rural schoolhouses had electricity. Desks were bolted to the floor, and framed pictures of the Blessed Virgin and the Sacred Heart, a crucifix, and a few visual aids—for example, alphabet cards and a map of Canada—were the only decoration.

Male instructors were in preponderance when public schools were first established in the province in 1846, but by the end of the century 95 percent of the instruction was provided by females. In 1900 the average annual salary for males was $220; for *maîtresses d'école* engaged in exactly the same work, $105. Schoolmarms were often the butt of gossip and shabbily treated. Many stalwart and exemplary teachers managed nevertheless to overcome these obstacles and exerted a positive influence on generations of students.

La petite école was regarded as a church annex, where religion and morality were taught along with the three Rs.[97] Instruction reflected the philosophy that there was only one proper way to look at things. Consequently, there was little classroom discussion and most lessons were learned by rote.

Loud recitations punctuated the daily routine. Boys sat on one side of the room, girls on the other.[98]

Toward the end of the first grade, after having mastered, at home and at school, certain tenets of Catholic doctrine, the class received first communion (*la petite communion*) in a body at an informal ceremony in the sacristy.[99] Parents often witnessed this ritual. Also about this time a number of boys learned to assist the priest at mass and at other religious ceremonies.

During recreation, children learned different games—boys and girls separately, as a rule—by observing older schoolmates, then by gradually joining in.[100] Sports requiring equipment or special clothing were not played. Most games were age-old forms of play found in many lands but for the most part were inherited from France and, naturally, were conducted in French: blindman's buff (*colin-maillard*), giant steps (*le pas de puce*), hide-and-seek (*la cachette*), hopscotch (*le paradis*), jump rope (*sauter à la corde*), leapfrog (*le saut-mouton*), and so on. In the 1940s one researcher in Beauce recorded no fewer than two hundred such games.[101] Counting-out rhymes (*comptines*) were also popular. For example, to choose a player, one might use the following verse:

Un, deux, trois. Nous allons aux bois.
Quatre, cinq, six. Pour cueillir des cerises.
Sept, huit, neuf. Dans mon panier plein d'oeufs.
Dix, onze, douze. Elles seront toutes ROUGES.[102]

(One, two, three. Into the woods we go.
Four, five, six. To gather cherries.
Seven, eight, nine. A basketful of eggs.
Ten, eleven, twelve. They'll all be RED.)

More than three hundred French-Canadian variations are attested.[103]

Round dances, some of them dating back to the Middle Ages, were among the most interesting traditional pastimes engaged in by schoolgirls: "La Boulangère," "C'était une bergère," "Où vas-tu, Germaine?," "Ramenez vos moutons," and "Savez-vous planter des choux?," to name but a few.[104] In the latter selection, children danced around in a circle, miming the different ways to plant cabbage indicated in the song by touching the ground with an index finger, a palm, a foot, or a knee:

Savez-vous planter des choux?
A la mode, à la mode,
Savez-vous planter des choux,
A la mode de chez-nous?

On les plante avec nos doigts . . .
A la mode des Chinois.

On les plante avec nos mains . . .
A la mode des Romains.

On les plante avec nos pieds . . .
A la mode des pompiers.

On les plante avec nos g'noux . . .
A la mode de chez-nous.

(Can you plant cabbages?
The way, the way,
Can you plant cabbages,
The way we do?

We plant them with our fingers . . .
The way the Chinese do.

We plant them with our hands . . .
The way the Romans do.

We plant them with our feet . . .
The way the firemen do.

We plant them with our knees . . .
That's the way we do.)

At the turn of the century, similar round dances were also performed by grown-ups during veillées. By the 1940s, only old-timers still knew the words and figures of a few rounds such as "La Bastringue," "La Danse du rosier," "La Ronde des cocus," and "La Ronde des oignons."[105] In the case of children and adults, these dances were both sung and performed by the same players without instrumental accompaniment.

Education was not popular with rural French Canadians. Many farmers considered it a luxury and insisted that their children were needed at home. Absenteeism at school was high during planting and harvesting seasons. A large number of pupils were allowed and even encouraged by their parents to drop out after four or five years.

At about this point, the formal "first" communion ceremony (*la communion solennelle*) was held, preceded by about a month of daily instruction provided by the pastor. Children walked to and from the village for these lessons, often two or three miles, and the experience was referred to as *marcher au catéchisme*.[106] First communion was an impressive ritual. Girls wore white dresses, gloves, shoes, stockings, and veils; boys dark blue suits with a white armband. At mass, the communicant was given a cloth scapular to wear and a certificate that was often framed and proudly displayed in the parlor. A festive meal in the young person's honor followed in the home. It was customary for parents and godparents to present their child with gifts on this occasion: a missal, rosary, holy pictures. Later the two first communion ceremonies were combined. (Today in Quebec, it generally occurs at the end of the third grade.)

Children returned home after school each day and, as they grew older, assumed added household and farm responsibilities. Those who finished grammar school were presented with diplomas and small awards by the pastor in a graduation ceremony. Many girls attended nearby boarding schools for two or three years. Instruction in these establishments, conducted by nuns, was superior to that provided in the école de rang and conferred status on the graduate and her family.[107] A few boys continued their education in one of the province's many *collèges classiques* operated by male religious. About half generally became priests, the remainder businessmen or professionals. Such an education required a substantial investment on the part of the family.[108]

Adolescence. Regarded as golden years, the teenage years in rural French-Canadian society were generally not full of the conflicts and traumas associated with this time of life in modern industrialized nations.[109] The transition from childhood to maturity was relatively short, vocational choices limited, and youthful activities prescribed by custom. Girls participated fully in housework; boys farmed, began serving an apprenticeship, or found some form of gainful employment. In the winter, many youths went off to lumbering camps. Card playing, moderate drinking (and, for males, smoking), like a wholesome interest in the opposite sex, were considered appropriate behavior for persons in their midteens.

The socially approved way for young people to meet was at veillées, one of the few occasions when neighbors might be invited. Married persons would customarily withdraw to the parlor and allow the younger set to take over the kitchen. Card playing (especially *quatre septs*), singing popular and traditional songs, and storytelling alternated with dancing and party games.

In addition to rounds, traditional dances included jigs (*gigues*) and quadrilles.[110] Jigs seem to have been introduced by Irish and Scottish settlers, but by 1900 the dance had become distinctively French-Canadian. The quadrille called for musical accompaniment, a reel played by a fiddle, harmonica, Jew's harp, spoons, or simply the human voice imitating an instrument. Originally a graceful contredanse necessitating a full hour and a half to execute all five parts, the dance represented a maiden fleeing a suitor's advances and eventually relenting. Girls were held by the arm, not the waist. Square dances imported from the United States were gaining in popularity. These differed from quadrilles in that they required calls and did not always follow the same routine. (After World War II, square dances in public halls, with accordion and guitar accompaniment but many calls in French, practically eliminated all other forms of folk dancing in the province.[111] Today, traditional dances in Quebec are for watching and are maintained almost exclusively by costumed folklore groups.)

Courtship and Marriage. In many cultures, much folklore, taken more or less seriously, discusses ways to determine whether or not a young woman will eventually marry and, if so, how to divine the appearance or initials of her future husband.[112] For example, French-Canadian girls might pull petals from a daisy, saying: "Religieuse,—vieille fille,—mariée," study the letter an apple peel cut in one piece forms when tossed behind her back, or look for a reflection in a moonlit pond.[113]

Having become interested in a marriageable young woman—sometimes a girl no older than sixteen—a youth would come calling on a Sunday evening. Traditionally, he visited the entire family at first and tried to be as casual as possible. (Sisters would sometimes wonder which one of them was being courted.)

During group conversations or card games, glances would be exchanged, hints given, and, ideally, encouragement received from the young woman in the form of a smile or a friendly look. Thus emboldened, the young man intensified his visits and began making small gifts. Unless there was more than one suitor, acceptance of presents generally signaled that the courtship was progressing well; the girl became the boy's *blonde,* the young man her *cavalier.*

At this point, it was customary for the couple to spend Sunday afternoons together in proper Victorian pursuits: looking at autograph and photograph albums or singing popular sentimental songs in the parlor, sitting in a swing or playing croquet—a recent English importation[114]—outdoors, or, grandest experience of all, taking a buggy ride to the village and back.

Eventually—at times, rather abruptly—the young man would ask the father for his daughter's hand in marriage (*la grande demande*). A frank discussion of the young man's prospects ensued. From time to time, the youth's father would accompany him on this occasion. If not, he would make an appearance when the time came to negotiate the marriage contract, a matter arranged between the parents. This verbal agreement spelling out what each fiancé brought in marriage (dowry, farm animals, property) was sometimes itemized with the aid of a notary. At times, the engagement was formalized with a small ceremony in the woman's home during which the pastor blessed the ring. A family celebration followed.[115]

Parents expected the young man to be twenty-one years of age or nearly so and to show promise. The contract was designed to give the couple a modest start, nothing more. An engagement lasting more than six months was discouraged. Considerable social pressure was applied on single persons in their twenties to get married.

Two practices, one canonical, the other profane, preceded the wedding day. On three successive Sundays, the banns were read in the parishes of both fiancés. In the Catholic church, this was (and is) intended to forestall any impediment to a lawful marriage. In rural Quebec, the young couple considered this public announcement to be embarrassing. Consequently, the pastor generally agreed to limit the reading of the banns to one occasion, and the fiancés arranged to attend mass elsewhere on this morning.

A few days before the wedding, the young man's bachelor relatives and friends often organized a stag party in his honor. The ritual was known as the *enterrement de la vie de garçon,* for it was highlighted by a mock funeral. The bridegroom was forced to lie down on bed boards or a cot made to resemble a coffin while a solemn or bawdy eulogy was read over him. A purse was usually presented at the conclusion of the ensuing revelry. The bride was also occasionally feted by her girl friends and relatives. Many showers climaxed in the reading of a flowery address emphasizing the joys and spiritual rewards of married life.[116]

In rural Quebec, fashions were influenced to some extent by city and, ultimately, upper-class English styles. At the turn of the century, these modes, followed in clothing catalogs and newspaper advertisements, had an effect on traditional wedding attire. For example, brides began to carry a bouquet and bridegrooms to wear a gray hat and gloves.[117] The class of wedding differed with individuals, that is, the ceremony and the decorations in church could be elaborate or simple, and the ringing of the bell perfunctory or enthusiastic. However, there was usually little public display.[118] Invitations to the wedding were made orally, the nuptial mass was always in the morning, and the bride and groom each had only one attendant (a *fille d'honneur* and a *garçon d'honneur*). The reception started at the home of the bride but often continued in other family residences and lasted for days. There was much kissing, singing, and dancing, and many expressions of good wishes. After a few rounds of drinks, there was sometimes a bit of boisterousness and ribald songs, too. At night, unpopular newlyweds—for example, an older man who married a young woman, or a person taking a husband or wife too soon after the first spouse had passed away—could expect a shivaree (*charivari*). To accommodate relatives and friends, the honeymoon, if such a trip were made at all, came after the festivities had spent themselves.[119] It frequently consisted of a few days' stay with relatives living at a distance. Many French Canadians also visited the shrine of Saint Anne de Beaupré near Quebec City on this occasion.[120]

French Canadians generally dressed more conservatively after marriage. Women were expected to wear darker dresses with long sleeves and skirts. Men often wore a gold watch and chain, and grew a mustache.

Old Age. The son who expected to inherit the family farm would often continue to reside with his parents.[121] After he married, he would generally occupy a separate section of the house, or an addition, with his wife and children. As parents began to need care, the younger family took over more and more of the house. The happiest retired persons, of course, were those who were loved and respected by their children and who continued to feel useful.

At about age seventy, the elderly couple at times consigned themselves to a married or unmarried son or daughter dwelling with them by means of a contract drawn up by a notary (*la donation*). This agreement amounted to a last will and testament, and was intended to make it possible for the parents to live their remaining years in relative security and tranquility. However, many elderly strove to remain independent to the end. Then as now, there were no easy solutions to the problems of aging and of people of different generations living at close quarters.

Death and Mourning. In French Canada, sudden death (*la mort subite*) was greatly feared. Throughout their lives people prayed there would be suitable opportunity to prepare to meet their Maker and, in particular, to receive extreme unction. (Saint Joseph is the patron saint of *la bonne mort*.) One of the most solemn family duties was to make sure the priest arrived on time. If an individual in the parish were known to be dying, special prayers were offered during Sunday mass. In popular belief, many signs foretold death, for instance, a bird flying indoors, a howling dog, or a hearse stopping in front of one's house. Dreaming of flowers or of anything else associated with funerals was another ominous indication.[122]

When a person passed away, the sexton was immediately notified and he began to sound the death knell (*les glas*: the word is singular in standard French). The bell invited parishioners to pray for the soul of the departed one, but it also signaled key information, for example, three strokes in succession for a man, two for a woman, and one for a child. (The prescribed number varied but always preceded the tolling.)

Until the day of the funeral, all arrangements were handled by the family. Embalming was rare. A room was made ready, and the deceased was laid out in it on boards (*sur les planches*) set on benches.[123] To give the appearance of a chapel, this frame and, at times, the room's ceiling, floor, and walls were covered with white sheets; a cross was set between lighted tapers at the head of the bed. A handkerchief or white cloth was usually placed over the dead person's face. No flowers were displayed.

During the three-day wake, visitors entered this mortuary where members of the family were always keeping watch. They knelt, prayed for the deceased, and often touched the body as a sign of respect. Once every hour, all mourners present gathered before the bier to recite the rosary to-

gether. Then they withdrew to the parlor or kitchen where, after express-
ing sympathy to the bereaved, they chatted quietly with others attending
the wake. Late in the evening, refreshments were often served. As a rule,
drinking and hilarity were frowned upon.

On the day of the funeral, always held in the morning, an undertaker
placed the body in a black wooden coffin and conveyed it to church in a
horse-drawn hearse. In smaller communities, family members attended to
this themselves. It was customary for relatives and friends to walk to the
church in a group behind this vehicle. Pallbearers were usually close relatives of the deceased.

Three categories of funerals were offered by the church. A family could
arrange to have a first-class ceremony in which the altar and church walls
were hung with black crepe, lighted candles in tall candelabra were placed
behind the casket, and low masses were celebrated on the two side altars at
the same time as a high mass was being sung. Second- and third-class funerals omitted these ornaments, and the requiem mass was scaled down
accordingly. At the time, the pall draped over the coffin was always black,
except for a child who had not yet received first communion, in which case
the cloth was white. No eulogy or homily was ever given nor was communion distributed. During high mass, the awe-inspiring "Dies irae" and the
affecting hymn "J'irai la voir un jour" (I'll visit her some day), with its rising phrase "Au ciel, au ciel, au ciel" representing the soul's ascent heaven-
ward, were sung by the choir. The Libera responsary signaled the ap-
proaching end of the service. At the cemetery, which was normally located
next to the church, brief prayers were recited by the priest before the casket
was lowered into the ground. Afterward, a simple meal was served at home
before relatives departed.

Holy pictures bearing, on the back, a prayer and the name, dates, and a
small photograph of the deceased were distributed to members of the family attending the funeral and mailed to those who lived too far away to be
present. On the Sunday preceding or following the ceremony, prayers were
offered in church for the repose of the parishioner's soul. During the year,
several commemorative masses were celebrated. The first anniversary mass,
sometimes replicating the funeral with a catafalque representing the pall-
covered coffin, was usually attended by members of the family who resided
in the area.

In French Canada, protocol dictated which relatives wore mourning
and for how long. For example, two years' *grand deuil* was expected for a
spouse and one year for a parent. A woman in mourning wore a black
dress, coat, hat, long veil, and accessories; a man, a black suit (or armband)
and tie. (For women, a third year of *demi-deuil,* that is, a combination of

black and white, was also customary.) Children were dressed in black for shorter periods. Social activities were sharply reduced in periods of mourning. Many rural French-Canadian families adhered strictly to these practices until after World War II.

Folklore

Folktales. Storytelling played an important role in French-Canadian life.[124] Recited by parents as bedtime stories, or by *mémère* or *pépère* to amuse their grandchildren, these wonderful tales were also appreciated by adults. For example, storytelling was a favorite pastime at veillées and in lumber camps. One person generally had the reputation of being the best *conteur* in the village, and when this individual could be cajoled into performing, the narration was the highlight of the evening. A few peddlers (e.g., Boily le Remancheur and Louis l'Aveugle [Simard]) were renowned for their ability to hold audiences spellbound as they spun out their stories.[125] However, though conteurs cadged many a drink as a reward for their prowess, none earned their livelihood in this fashion.

The advent of radio and modern forms of entertainment undermined storytelling to such an extent that the tradition has practically disappeared in French Canada today. Fortunately, a large number of French-Canadian folktales have been recorded. On the basis of this archival material, scholars have been able to determine to a remarkable degree the nature and extent of this rich heritage. For example, using an elaborate classification system of types and motifs, that is, major constituent elements, they have been able to categorize practically all known French-Canadian stories.

The bulk of the narratives in the French-Canadian repertory originated in France and are attested throughout Europe.[126] For instance, Cinderella (Cendrillon, and, in certain Acadian versions, Cendrillouse), the best known of all fairy tales, in all French-Canadian accounts wears glass slippers to the ball, a trait found only in the French tradition immortalized by Charles Perrault in 1697.[127] (It is often said, but it is by no means certain, that this feature is based on the homonymic confusion of *verre,* or glass, and *vair,* a kind of fur.) Specialists who have studied the tales preserved in the Archives de Folklore at Laval University (see *CELAT,* Appendix C) report that the most popular types concern devils, followed in popularity by werewolves, elves (*lutins*), and ghosts. Legends about haunted places and buried treasure are also quite common. Other widely disseminated stories include Hansel and Gretel—known in French as *Le Petit Poucet*— Little Red Riding Hood (*Le Petit Chaperon Rouge*), the Maiden without Hands (*La Fille aux Mains Coupées*), and the Master Thief (*Le Fin Voleur*). Another tale, the Dragon Slayer, is associated in French-Canadian tradition with Ti-Jean, the young hero of numerous adventures, including those re-ferred to as The Boy Steals the Giant's Treasure and The Clever Horse.

The following stories, my mother's entire repertory, were recorded by me on July 13, 1962. Not long afterward, a copy was deposited in the Ar-chives de Folklore at Laval University where it is now part of that perma-nent collection. The grandmother my mother refers to was Victorine Dozois, who married Pierre Gustave Thibodeau at Napierville, Quebec, on February 8, 1864. After the recording session, my mother volunteered that she had tried hard to visualize and to imitate her grandmother reciting the stories.

All three narratives are well known to specialists, the third to every American child. As I indicated earlier, Le Petit Poucet, or Tom Thumb, is a name that is also associated in French tradition with the Hansel and Gretel story. Persons familiar with colloquial Canadian French should have no dif-ficulty reading the original, rendered here in a modified phonetic transcrip-tion, except perhaps for the word *paparmanes,* today more often associated with peppermint candy. I shall limit my remarks to the second of these stories which has special significance for me.

Le Petit Poucet

Je vais vous raconter un conte de ma grand-mère.

Alors cette femme avait un petit garçon qui se nommait P'tit Poucet.

A dit: "Mon p'tit garçon, va donc dans le jardin me chercher un chou. Mais," a dit, "ferme ta barrière, par exemple."

Le petit garçon s'en va en sautillant, rentre dans le jardin; i oublie de fermer sa barrière.

Le gros boeu caille, i rentre, pi il l'a aperçu. I avait peur, i dit: "Qu'est-ce que j'va faire? J'va me cacher en d'sous du chou." C'te gros boeu caille, i rentre, mange des choux, mange des choux . . . mange P'tit Poucet avec! Ah!

Sa mère trouvait qu'i prenait du temps à venir. A l'appelle: "P'tit Poucet! P'tit Poucet!"

"J'dans le ventre du gros boeu caille, maman!"

"P'tit Poucet!"

"J'dans le ventre du gros boeu caille, maman!"

Ça fait que son père, i vient, il tue le gros boeu caille. P'tit Poucet a sorti. Pi là il s'est promis qu'il l'obéirait, sa maman, après.

(Tom Thumb

I'm going to tell you one of my grandmother's stories.

A woman had a little boy called Tom Thumb.

She says: "My son, please go into the garden and fetch me a cabbage. But," she says, "be sure to close the gate, though."

The little boy goes skipping into the garden but forgets to close the gate.

A big piebald ox enters the garden and notices him. Frightened, the little boy says: "What am I going to do? I know, I'll hide under a cabbage." The ox gobbles up cabbages one after another, and . . . gobbles up Tom Thumb, too! Oh!

His mother thought he was taking a long time. She calls him: "Tom Thumb! Tom Thumb!"

"Mama, I'm in the big ox's belly!"

"Tom Thumb!"

"Mama, I'm in the big ox's belly!"

So his father comes and kills the big ox. Tom Thumb came out. Right then and there, he resolved to mind his mother from that point on.)

LES P'TITES PAPARMANES

Encore un conte de ma grand-mère.

La mère, a dit à son p'tit garçon pi sa p'tite fille: "Allez donc me chercher des p'tites paparmanes pi j'va vous faire un beau gâteau."

Ça fait que les p'tits enfants s'en vont du long de la p'tite rivière. Marche, marche.

Pi le p'tit garçon s'amusait, lui, pi la p'tite fille, a ramassait, pi al emplissait, al emplissait sa p'tite chaudière. Ça fait que quand sa p'tite chaudière a été pleine, le p'tit garçon, i dit: "Donne-moi-z-en donc!" I dit: "J'en ai pas, moi."

A dit: "T'avais en bel d'en ramasser."

Ça fait que, "Ben," a dit, "i est assez tard. On va s'en aller à maison."

Ça fait que le p'tit garçon l' . . . l' . . . i l'a frappée pi l'a jetée dans rivière. Pi prend la p'tite chaudière pi s'en va chez eux.

Pi sa mère, a dit: "Où c'est que ta p'tite soeur?"

"Oh, je sais pas. Al avait pas ramassé encore. Pi a va venir plus tard. A s'en vient, là."

Sa mère a laissé faire une escousse. Attend, attend. La p'tite fille ne venait pas. A dit: "Tu vas venir avec moi." Pi a dit: "On va aller la chercher."

I voulait pas. I aimait pas ça.

Ça fait qu'i s'en vont du long de la rivière. Marche, marche. Tout d'un coup, i entendait . . . un p'tit queuqu' chose qui était sous la rivière qui disait:

"C'est mon p'tit frère
Qui m'a tuée
Pour cinq ou six p'tites paparmanes
Que j'avais trouvées,
Que j'avais trouvées."

(THE PEPPERMINT LEAVES

Another one of my grandmother's stories.

A mother says to her little boy and girl: "Please go fetch me some peppermint leaves and I'll make you a nice cake."

So the children set out along a river. They walk and walk.

While the little girl was busy gathering leaves and filling her pail, the little boy was playing. When her pail was full, the little boy said: "Come on, give me some: I don't have any."

She says: "You should have gathered some yourself."

Then she says: "Well, it's late now: we're going home."

So the little boy . . . struck her and threw her into the river. He takes the pail and returns home.

His mother says: "Where's your little sister?"

"Oh, I don't know. She hadn't gathered any yet. She'll be back later. She's coming."

The mother waited awhile but, when the little girl didn't show up, she said: "You're coming with me. We're going to look for her."

He didn't want to go. He was worried.

They walk along the river. They walk and walk. Suddenly, they heard a mysterious voice in the water singing:

"It was my little brother
Who killed me
For five or six peppermint leaves
That I had found.")

Le P'tit Chaperon Rouge

Je me souviens d'un autre conte de ma grand-mère: "Le P'tit Chaperon Rouge."

La grand-mère était malade, était au lit. Ça fait qu'al attendait sa p'tite fille qui devait venir la voir.

Pi al entend frapper à la porte. A dit: "Entrez!"

C'était le gros loup qui entre! Saute sur la grand-mère, dévore la grand-mère. Pi i s'habille, i met la jaquette et le bonnet de la grand-mère, pi i se met au lit à place de la grand-mère. I attend.

Tout d'un coup, i entend frapper: "Entrez!"

Pi la p'tite fille i rentre avec son p'tit panier en sautant: "Bonjour, grand-mère! . . . Mais vous avez ben des grandes oreilles, grand-mère!"

"Mais c'est pour mieux t'entendre, ma p'tite fille."

"Mais vous avez ben des grands yeux, grand-mère!"

"Mais c'est pour mieux te voir."

"Vous avez ben des GRANDES dents!"

"C'est pour mieux te manger!"

Pi i saute sur la p'tite fille pi i la dévore.

On demandait à grand-mère qu'i était arrivé de la p'tite fille. Ça fait qu'a nous a dit que le père était venu pi i avait tué le gros loup. Pi la p'tite fille avait sorti.

(Little Red Riding Hood

I remember another one of my grandmother's stories: "Little Red Riding Hood."

A grandmother was sick in bed waiting for her granddaughter who was supposed to come by to visit her.

She hears someone knock at the door. "Come in," she says.

The Big Wolf comes in, leaps on the grandmother, and eats her up. Then he puts on the grandmother's nightgown and cap, and lays down in her place in the bed. He waits.

Suddenly, he hears someone knock at the door: "Come in!"

The little girl comes skipping in with her little basket: "Good day, grandmother! . . . My, but you have big ears, grandmother!"

"Why, the better to hear you with, granddaughter."

"My, but you have big eyes, grandmother!"

"Why, the better to see you with."

"My, but you have BIG teeth!"

"The better to eat you with!"

Then he leaps on the little girl and eats her up.

We would ask grandmother what became of the little girl. She told us that the father came and killed the Big Wolf. Then the little girl had come out.)

Much of my mother's narrative style and dramatic flair is lost in the transition from oral to written form, and in the loose English translation I have provided. For example, a number of conjunctions (*pi, ça fait que*) and diminutives (*p'tites paparmanes, p'tite chaudière*) have been eliminated. Also, my mother put great emotion into certain phrases: "le p'tit garçon l'. . . l'. . . i l'a frappée"; "Vous avez ben des GRANDES dents!" She made effective use of traditional narrative devices and techniques, for example, direct discourse (conversations are quoted) and repetition to indicate the passage of time (*Marche, marche; al emplissait, al emplissait; Attend, attend*). She rarely interrupted the story to make personal observations (*I avait peur; I voulait pas*).

It is difficult to convey the horror "Les P'tites Paparmanes" inspired in me as a child. It was years later that I learned of an equally shocking conclusion. My mother did not know or perhaps spared me from hearing this ending. (At times, the narrator may inadvertently abridge the story. This may explain why the customary preliminary encounter between Little Red Riding Hood and the wolf in the woods is omitted above.) Folktales do not often have a moral, although "Le P'tit Poucet" here certainly does. So far as "Les P'tites Paparmanes" is concerned, I have always felt that the point was: do not be mean to your sister!

Like the two other stories my mother told, the latter tale is well attested in European folklore (one study analyzed nearly two hundred versions).[128] It is known to scholars as The Singing Bone (type 780; Stith Thompson's *Motif-Index* lists it as E 632) because in most versions the crime is revealed by a whistle or a flute made from one of the murdered person's bones, for instance a finger, or from a branch of a tree growing from the grave.[129]

As usual, the frame and details vary with each storyteller, who may even blend in an entirely separate tale (this is the case in certain variants recorded in New Brunswick). There may be two parents and they may be royalty; the children may be named and they may be brothers or sisters, as in the English and Scottish ballad "The Two Sisters." What is sought may be a bird, a flower, or a plant (in certain French-Canadian versions, it is a *tourte*, interpreted either as a cake, a red-breasted bird, or a turtle). Often, this object has magical properties capable of healing the parent, who is ailing, and the finder is promised a rich reward, thus providing a less frivolous motive for the crime. Instead of being drowned, the victim is sometimes buried after being slain. The telltale object may be found by a passerby. My interpretation of the phrase *un p'tit queuqu' chose* (a mysterious voice) is based, in part, on my mother's inflection as she uttered these words and, in part, on the eerie song that followed.

More often than not, the parents punish the child by killing him. At times, to serve the ends of poetic justice, they dispose of the body at the scene of the crime.

The haunting song is not always the same, and it usually emanates from a wind instrument. Often, in French, it begins with the thrice-repeated word *siffle(z)* or *souffle(z)*. In different French versions, the names of the flowers the children seek bear a certain homonymic resemblance to one another, for example, *bouquet d'éternelles, jufernelle, rose de sainte Ernelle, rose paternelle, rose de pimprenelle, rose de Pimperlé*. Canadian-French *paparmanes* may thus be akin to pimpernel, a medicinal herb of the primrose family.

Folk songs. Thousands of traditional French songs have been preserved in French Canada, where they are associated with canoeists and voyageurs of times long past and with veillées of not so long ago. Three of the best known songs are "A la claire fontaine," "A Saint-Malo," and "V'là l'bon vent."

"A la claire fontaine" is the lament of a lover who waits in vain for his mistress who left him because he failed to give her a bunch of flowers. Sung to various melodies, it appears to date back to the late Middle Ages.[130]

"A Saint-Malo" seems to owe its popularity to the Patriotes of the 1830s, who evidently felt it evoked Quebec's maritime past and historic ties with France.[131] Jacques Cartier hailed from St. Malo and set forth from that port in 1534 on a voyage that led to the discovery of Canada. However, a French-Canadian variant provides the name Nantes instead of St. Malo, and the French prototype appears to have been Bordeaux. The abridged version widely known in French Canada recounts the ostensibly innocent banter between ladies and sailors over the price of barley and wheat, the women managing to talk the mariners into giving them grain for nothing. The complete song adds a bawdy ending to the tale. Accepting an invitation to come aboard, the youngest woman protests when the ship sails away: "I am a councillor's wife," she says. The sailor replies: "If you were the king's wife I would still sleep with you." "But I've never had a child," she objects. To which the seaman responds: "You'll have one now!"

"V'là l'bon vent" (also known as "En roulant ma boule") was one of the songs in the French-Canadian repertory that underwent the most changes.[132] It relates that after a king's son has shot a white duck with his silver gun, three maidens pick up the feathers to make a marriage bed and raise a family. A sad and senseless killing is thus repaired through love and procreation. Mention of the gun permits dating after the fifteenth century. The words were originally sung to many different tunes, but both have now become fairly uniform. The refrain "En roulant ma boule" and others are of French origin; "V'là l'bon vent" is merely a variation of one of these phrases (e.g., "C'est le vent qui va frivolant"). On the other hand, "C'est l'aviron qui nous monte, qui nous mène" and other choruses alluding to canoeing or logging are specifically French-Canadian.

Like "A Saint-Malo," the first verse of another much-appreciated song known by the last of these refrains ("C'est l'aviron qui nous monte, qui nous mène") contains the name of a French port associated with Canadian history: "M'en revenant de la joli' Rochelle." It tells how a fair maiden, taken for a horseback ride, asks her naïve companion to stop for a drink. When he fails to grasp her meaning (it is obviously a pass), she refuses to take the proffered water, and later, having returned home, she mocks the young man by drinking deeply. A lesser-known song—"Ah! Qui me passera le bois?"—recounts a similar adventure.[133]

Many other once-popular songs are now practically forgotten. "Dans les prisons de Nantes" is the story of a prisoner set free by the jailer's compassionate daughter. In French-Canadian versions, the scene is often London, not Nantes. "La complainte de Cadieux" is based on the legend of Jean Cayeux, a French-Canadian voyageur who, about 1709, lost his life to Iroquois marauders along the upper Ottawa River after sending his wife and children downstream to safety in a canoe. The song is filled with devotion to the Blessed Virgin.[134]

One of the world's most famous ditties—"Alouette!"—is of French origin, but it first caught on in Quebec at the end of the nineteenth century.[135] In French folk songs the lark is said to be prized for its feathers. "Alouette!" is well liked today because it lends itself to boisterous singing and is a good icebreaker, even with people who do not understand French.

A recent catalog of traditional French songs has no fewer than seventy thousand entries identified as belonging to about six thousand types.[136]

Traditional trades

French-Canadian farmers were largely self-sufficient and tended to purchase relatively few items from the general store or itinerant peddlers. However, they routinely turned to local craftsmen for certain products and services.

At times, artisans handed down their skills from father to son; for example, several instances of five generations of blacksmiths are recorded in Quebec. However, most craftsmen learned their trade by serving an apprenticeship of two years or more.[137] In the nineteenth century, boys age ten or younger were at times apprenticed for ten or twelve years. Such arrangements could involve formal contracts negotiated with the aid of a notary, but equally binding verbal understandings were also commonplace. Apprentices received little or no pay but were clothed, fed, and housed by the master. Guilds never existed in Quebec before or after the English

Conquest in 1760.[138] Masters kept close watch over their charges and often required them to work from five o'clock in the morning until eight o'clock in the evening in the summer, and until nine o'clock in the evening in the winter.

Best known perhaps as a farrier, that is, one who shoes horses, the blacksmith performed many other essential tasks for the community. He forged hinges, latches, and locks for doors as well as hooks, nails, farm tools, and kitchen utensils. He formed iron bands and installed them on carriage and wagon wheels. Though not accustomed to producing elaborate or elegant pieces such as ornamental grills and roadside or steeple crosses, he could and did at times fashion carefully wrought objects.[139]

The blacksmith shop was a single-story structure averaging twenty-five feet square.[140] It usually had a few windows, doors wide enough to let in horses, and a dirt floor. Inside, one would find the forge, that is, a brick or cement fireplace or a wooden stand with tray filled with sand; hood to draw off fumes and smoke; and bellows that were operated by hand or a pedal. There would also be a work table, a tub containing water to which salt had been added, an anvil securely fastened to a block of wood, and a great variety of tools—pincers, scrapers, vises, and so on.

The smithy was a fascinating place for children, and for grown-ups too, who could always pick up the latest news and gossip from idlers there. Usually a powerfully built man, the blacksmith, wearing his long leather apron, worked in a world of hammering, hissing, and ringing noises, pungent odors, and glowing metal.

In folk song and folktales, the blacksmith is generally a strong and fearless figure, and his workplace is associated with hell.[141] According to a popular French-Canadian story, one day the devil enters a blacksmith's shop and inquires where a certain person lives. Recognizing the fiend, the smith lifts a plow with one hand and, using one of the handles as a pointer, shows him the way. Frightened, the devil departs in haste. In one version, it is the legendary strongman Jos Monferrand who is awed by the blacksmith's feat.

With changes in modes of transportation and travel, and with the influx of manufactured goods replacing products once made by hand, the blacksmith's trade gradually declined in America after the turn of the century. By 1960 it had virtually disappeared from the Quebec scene.[142]

Throughout the French regime and until the 1940s, the village cobbler in Quebec produced shoes and boots in his home or shop.[143] He customarily sat on a bench fitted with a tray or toolbox and worked at a wooden or cast-iron last with an awl, hammer, knife, measuring instruments, pincers, pliers, and other tools. He wore a leather apron and, on his left hand, a half glove.

The shoemaker generally did not enjoy high standing. Though he normally served an apprenticeship of three years, his trade was said to require more endurance than skill or strength. French-Canadian folk songs made him out to be a dishonest person and a carouser. However, he also had a reputation for being philosophic.[144]

Roadside crosses

Croix de chemin are one of the most picturesque features of the Quebec landscape.[145] Few are more than a century old (in fact most came into existence a good deal more recently), but many replace similar sacred objects that stood in the same place years earlier. Some are crucifixes, but the most popular form consists of a cross bearing, at the center, a Sacred Heart emblem, often surmounted by rays, and instruments of the Passion of Our Lord (crown of thorns, nails, lance, etc.), or both. Time was when local organizations raised and maintained crosses to mark the foundation of a parish, a memorable mission or retreat, or the limits of a rang, but many pious individuals also erected them as votive offerings, to implore God's help—for example, in combating alcoholism—or in recognition of divine intervention on a particular occasion.

Parishioners showed great reverence for their crosses and gathered before them to pray, with or without their priests, during the month of May, on feast days, when a drought threatened crops, or in other times of calamity.

These customs have all but disappeared since the 1960s. But for many French Canadians today, roadside crosses are still enveloped with a mystique and symbolize the faith and traditions of their forefathers.

Language

Quebec's isolation from France, especially after the British Conquest in 1760, is a well-known fact. This remoteness and the dialect leveling that characterizes colonial languages in America, together with other factors of a historical and sociological nature, gradually differentiated Canadian French from its parent language.[146]

From the outset, education in Canada always involved a certain amount of language training. And, with the rise of the school system, formal instruction in grammar, pronunciation, and vocabulary played an increasingly important role in the development of cultivated Canadian French. In nearly all cultures, "correct" speech is a sign of high status. In the case of Canadian French, correctness is, naturally, associated with standard French, but there is a threshold in pronunciation and, to a lesser extent, in vocabulary that even elite speakers of Canadian French generally do not cross.[147]

Emigration from France to Canada crested toward the middle of the seventeenth century, before stopping altogether after the Conquest. However, contact with the motherland was never completely lost; French religious and, of course, written material continued to arrive in the province. French-born priests, brothers, and nuns were actively recruited by the Quebec hierarchy, especially after the Patriote Rebellion of 1837–38, and they had a considerable effect on the development of cultivated Canadian French.[148] Initially, this was simply an accommodation of nineteenth-century standard French, made in the collèges classiques and boarding schools maintained by the French religious for young ladies.

The continuous influence of standard French on Canadian French did not prevent the latter from going its own way. By the beginning of the present century, the lexical, syntactical, and phonological differences between the two—noted by French visitors on earlier occasions—were still extensive and varied.

There is no lack of dictionaries and glossaries listing anglicisms, archaisms, neologisms, and other features of Canadian French,[149] but one recent publication deserves special note because it provides a wealth of information about the language spoken by the parents and grandparents of present-day Franco-Americans.[150] From 1973 to 1978 a team of dialectologists from Laval University interviewed seven hundred persons, all sixty years old or over, living in 169 different rural areas of Quebec, Ontario, and the Maritime Provinces. Using a list of twenty-five hundred questions, the researchers gathered data enabling specialists to plot a linguistic atlas of French Canada at the turn of the century. This ten-volume work makes it possible to situate with great precision the range of terms used to refer to every aspect of daily living in a rural milieu.

However, the most exhaustive documentation of Canadian French, from the settlement of New France to the present, is contained in *Trésor de la langue française au Québec*. This computerized dictionary based on historical principles is being compiled at CELAT (Laval University).[151]

Disregarding for the moment historical and other considerations, it may be useful to list a few of the most striking phonetic traits that distinguish the French spoken today in France from that heard in Canada and New England.[152]

Opening of accented vowels having a reduced aperture before certain final consonants

In Canadian French, a variant occurs in the second of the following paired items:

[i] / [I]	[u] / [U]	[y] / [Y]
dimanche/dime	bouchon/bouche	jupon/jupe
filer/fil	bouleau/boule	lunette/lune
guider/guide	bouquin/bouc	pruneau/prune
mitaine/mite	coucher/couche	reculer/recule
siffler/siffle	ouvrir/ouvre	sucer/suce

However, when the final consonant is [r], [v], [z], or [ʒ], the two vowels are identical, as in standard French.

[i]	[u]	[y]
friser/frise	douzaine/douze	amuser/amuse
livrer/livre	rougir/rouge	juger/juge
tirer/tire	trouver/trouve	purée/pure

Lengthening and diphthongization of accented, open midvowels before certain consonants

Many variants are found here, the same vowel being arbitrarily pronounced several different ways:

	Standard French	Canadian French
chêne	[ʃɛn]	[ʃɛjn, ʃejn, ʃaɛn]
dehors	[dəɔr]	[dəhɔwr, dəhɔ:r]
dimanche	[dimãʃ]	[dzimãw̃ʃ]
linge	[lɛ̃ʒ]	[lɛ̃ʒ, lɛ̃jʒ]
longue	[lɔ̃g]	[lɔ̃w̃g, lɔ̃w̃ŋ]

The variant [ɒ]

This sound resembles standard French [ɔ], as in *porte,* but it requires more lip rounding and lip protrusion. It appears where standard French has an anterior [a] or a posterior [ɑ], even though the latter two are also represented. Diphthongization is to be expected when the vowel is accented before certain final consonants: *lâche* [lɒwʃ], *vase* [vɒwz].

The variant [ã]

This phenomenon, or the diphthong [ãw̃], [ãw̃], appears wherever standard French has [ã].

	Standard French	Canadian French
ange	[ãʒ]	[ãw̃ʒ]
cent	[sã]	[sã]
chanter	[ʃãte]	[ʃãte]
tremper	[trãpe]	[trãw̃pe]

Assibilation of voiced and unvoiced dentals
[t, d] *before* [i], [y], [j], *and* [ɥ]

Whenever [t] or [d] is followed by [u] or a mid or open vowel in Canadian French, it is pronounced as in standard French. Otherwise, these consonants become [tˢ] and [dᶻ] respectively.

Trilling of r

Canadian French has several different *r* sounds, the most common being the single-flap apical *r* produced by placing the tip of the tongue against the teethridge.

Other characteristics of Canadian French include implosion of final plosives; sounding of final *t* in such terms as *bout, fouet,* and *lit* as well as in proper names like Talbot; reduction of certain consonantal clusters; and the appearance of [ɛ], [ɒ], or [æ] after [w] where standard French has [a] as in *droit, soir,* and *voile.*

Speakers of cultivated Canadian French endeavor to pronounce words "correctly" and often substitute standard French sounds for many of those listed above, especially where assibilation and diphthongization have been noted. However, like all speech habits, Canadian phonological features are difficult to eradicate.

Joual, that is the speech of French Canadians who either lack education or care little for correct pronunciation—the term is derived from a way to produce the word for horse (*cheval*) and is usually used disparagingly—varies a good deal from standard French. A few examples are as follows: substitution of the sound [ɛ̃] for [œ̃] and even [ɑ̃] in such words as *chacun* and *champ;* frequent use of [a] and [a] for [ɛ] in such expressions as *français* and *lait;* palatalization of [k] and [g]; articulation of *h;* consonantal glides and metatheses of the *donnez-moi-z-en* and *ercule-toi* type.

Speakers of cultivated Canadian French consider *grasseyement* and the pronunciation [mwe] for *moi* and [twe] for *toi* to be particularly offensive and low class.

2

THE IMMIGRATION
PHASE, 1865–1920

French Canadians came to New England individually or in small family groups. Except for the relatively small number who, in the troubled 1830s, fled Quebec because of the Patriote Rebellion—nearly all the insurrectionists were eventually repatriated—the immigrants came on their own initiative seeking to improve their lot.

More often than not, the French Canadians fully intended to return home after earning enough money to achieve a modest objective, typically the purchase of a small farm or the paying off of a mortgage. At times, fed up with rural life, feeling that they were a burden on their family or simply wanting to become independent, young men and women struck out for themselves with no goal other than to be on their own.

Most headed for cities and towns where relatives or friends had preceded them and where they had reason to believe they could find work. By the last quarter of the nineteenth century, the names, if not the precise location, of many Franco-American population centers and the tales of high wages available there were known throughout French Canada, even in some of the remotest areas.

Devout Catholics, the French-Canadian immigrants generally attended Sunday mass. They soon discovered that Franco-American parishes offered not only religious services in their native language but also a broad range of social activities and contacts not unlike those they had enjoyed at home. These parishes often constituted havens that enabled recent immigrants to adapt to or at least survive the harsh living and working conditions of the time. Eventually, about half the new arrivals from French Canada settled permanently in New England, not infrequently after one or more false starts.

Background

The St. Lawrence Lowland lies within a triangle with the Laurentians to the north and the Appalachians to the south of what is referred to as Logan's Line. Climate is obviously a very important consideration in an agricultural economy. While Quebec has ample precipitation, only in the St. Lawrence Lowland is it warm enough for successful farming—a degree-day measurement of 3,000 to 3,500 is regarded as the absolute minimum for the hardier grains such as barley and for hay. Only in the St. Lawrence Lowland upstream from Quebec City is this condition met within the province.[1]

What strikes us today as an elementary fact, namely that Quebec is simply not suited for most types of farming and certainly not for growing wheat, was not clearly understood until the twentieth century with the advent of more scientific methods of agriculture.[2] The nineteenth-century Quebec farmer, like his New England counterpart, tilled the soil, planted, and harvested according to age-old custom and stubbornly resisted any change. He did not use manure or any other kind of fertilizer, kept turning over the same old top soil with a shallow plow, sowed unclean and unimproved seed, allowed weeds to grow everywhere, and knew nothing about crop rotation. As if this were not enough, Quebec farms were also infested by insect pests and suffered the injurious effects of blight.

All these factors contributed to a 70 percent drop in the province's production of wheat, the chief cash crop, between 1827 and 1844. In some counties, the decrease was as much as 95 percent. When efforts were made to introduce potatoes, a similar disaster was caused by the potato blight.[3]

The only harvest that did not fail was the human one. The population of Quebec was about 60,000 at the time of the Conquest. Less than a century later, in 1851, the French-Canadian population had increased to nearly 670,000.

With farms no longer able to support the burgeoning population and with little capital to purchase tillable land in the eastern townships or anywhere else, an acute crisis developed in the province. The solution arrived at is a familiar one to historians. When the population is expanding rapidly and the land is declining in productivity, people emigrate. For this reason an estimated 800,000 New Englanders left their farm lands for the West in the thirty years between 1790 and 1820. Also for this reason 10 million people, mostly Scandinavians, Irish, and Germans, emigrated to the United States between 1840 and 1880. And for this reason more than 23 million people, chiefly from eastern and southern Europe, came to America between 1880 and 1920.

Thousands of Canadians left Quebec in the years following the British Conquest, settling in no particular pattern in other Canadian provinces and throughout the United States except for important concentrations in Ontario and along the northern tier of American states.[4] In 1850 the permanent French-Canadian immigration to New England probably totaled less than 20,000 persons, 62 percent of whom settled in Vermont, particularly in the northern and western sections of that state. An estimated 3,700 French Canadians had settled in Maine by that date, but only 800 or 900 of that number, clustered in Waterville, Orono, and Old Town, may be termed true immigrants. The balance became Americans when the Webster-Ashburton Treaty between Great Britain and the United States in 1842 declared that seven thousand square miles of disputed territory in the St. John Valley belonged to Maine.

By 1860, 12,000 new French-Canadian immigrants had reached New England; together with the natural increase, these new immigrants doubled the Franco-American population. Most continued to live in the same areas, but important concentrations now became apparent in about two dozen central Massachusetts towns in the area around Worcester, south along the Blackstone Valley into Rhode Island, and along the Merrimack Valley including Manchester, New Hampshire. Franco-Americans continued to be engaged in a variety of occupations, but prophetically, in southern New England towns a large number were recruited as contract laborers for the textile mills.

Many French Canadians served in the Union Army during the Civil War—a much smaller number joined the Confederate forces—but it has not been possible to determine the total of enlistments or the number of veterans who settled in New England after the conflict.[5] The figures 40,000 and even 50,000 have been bandied about but are no doubt greatly exaggerated. Two well-documented cases deserve special mention. Cited for gallantry in action and wounded while charging enemy trenches at the Battle of Cold Harbor (1864), Edmond Mallet (1842–1907) was promoted to the rank of major and later distinguished himself as a career civil servant in the United States Department of the Interior.[6] Calixa Lavallée (1842–91) also served in the Union Army and was wounded at the Battle of Antietam. A brilliant musician, he is best remembered for having composed in 1880 "O Canada," the national anthem of Canada.[7]

Two Franco-American novels depict the Civil War in a harsh light. Rémi Tremblay's *Un Revenant* (1884) is in part the autobiographical account of a young soldier who, after having been captured at the Battle of Petersburg and incarcerated in the Confederates' notorious Libby Prison, is later paroled and then deserts.[8] Adélard Lambert's *L'Innocente Victime* (1936) tells the tragic story of a young French Canadian who is tricked into enlisting in the Union Army in 1864. (There were apparently a number of incidents of the sort; however, most French Canadians doubtless volunteered.) Wounded in battle and stricken with amnesia, he fails to locate his wife who set out to find him but was murdered in a case of mistaken identity.[9]

What caused the explosion in French-Canadian immigration in the thirty years that followed the Civil War can be traced back to twelve Boston merchants who in 1813 started the famous Boston Manufacturing Company.[10] This group, which included members of the Appleton, Cabot, Lawrence, Lowell, and other Brahmin families, hit upon the idea of starting a large integrated cotton mill for the mass production of cloth. The first mill of its kind opened its doors at Waltham, Massachusetts, in 1815. The period between 1830 and 1850 witnessed an extraordinary development of industry in New England, largely resting on the integrated mill concept, particularly in the manufacture of cotton and woolen textiles, boots, and shoes.

Cheap water power was of primary importance in this development. A map showing the major rivers of southern New England or this area's chief cotton textile mills is at the same time a chart of Franco-American demography to this day.[11]

Before the Civil War, the textile industry had employed mostly unmarried girls, recruited locally but also from northern New England farm communities. By the mid-1840s, as greater demands were made on mill operatives, American-born employees began to abandon this kind of work. Their places were filled for a short period by the newly arrived Irish immigrants. As the Irish in turn began to desert the mills, and with the post–Civil War boom in textiles, factory managers began increasingly to draw on the abundant human resources of Quebec. Appendix B, tables 5 and 6 tell the rest of the story. They show dramatic increases in the Franco-American population, particularly in southern New England, in 1870, 1880, and 1900—the latter year closely reflecting present-day concentrations.

The relative proximity of New England and the availability of cheap, rapid transportation by rail were major factors contributing to this growth. The French Canadians have the distinction of being the only major ethnic group to have immigrated to the United States in any significant number by train.

In 1900 Massachusetts included nearly half the entire Franco-American population, southern Maine and New Hampshire sharing another quarter about equally. The impact of the Franco-American element as a percentage of the total local population in 1900 was particularly noteworthy in cities like Biddeford, Maine (62 percent), Southbridge, Massachusetts (60 percent), Woonsocket, Rhode Island (60 percent), Lewiston, Maine (46 percent), Waterville, Maine (45 percent), Manchester (40 percent) and Nashua, New Hampshire (35 percent), but also in towns like Daniel-son, Connecticut (64 percent), Suncook, New Hampshire (60 percent), Plainfield, Connecticut (58 percent), Brunswick, Maine (54 percent), Old Town, Maine (52 percent), and Spencer, Massachusetts (52 percent). The Franco-American distribution of 1900 has remained fairly constant up to the present day with some notable exceptions. The St. John Valley still retains its more than 95 percent Franco-American percentage although Aroostock County experienced a major out-migration during World War II.[12] There have also been significant Franco-American increases in some of the former mill towns. For example, Lewiston's Franco-American popula-tion is estimated to have grown by about 15 percent since 1900, currently making that city about 61 percent French. A kind of corona effect appears to be working here since most people claim that Lewiston is 75 percent or even 80 percent Franco-American today. However, the French population in other centers has not kept pace with the area's growth as a whole.

Some industries actively recruited labor from Canada, especially in the years immediately before and after the Civil War. For example, in 1859–60 I. M. Boynton hired several French Canadians who lived in the vicinity of St. Hyacinthe for work in textile mills in Chicopee and Lowell, Mass-achusetts, and Salmon Falls, New Hampshire.[13] Many agents appear to have been Franco-Americans; among them were Joseph Proulx, a resi-dent of Holyoke, Massachusetts, who operated near St. Hyacinthe on be-half of the Lyman Mills at this time,[14] and Samuel P. Marin of Lowell, Massachusetts.[15]

Immigrants wrote enthusiastic letters home or, when visiting, forcefully pointed out the advantages of living and working in New England mill towns. Lorenzo Surprenant incarnates this role in Hémon's *Maria Chap-delaine*. Seeking—in vain, as it turns out—to persuade the heroine to for-sake her hard life on a small farm near Lake St. John to become his wife in Lowell, Massachusetts, where he has moved, he draws a dazzling picture of the city with its bright lights and broad asphalt sidewalks for strolling in the evening; its crowds, electric trolleys, and stores; its amusements (cir-cuses, illustrated newspapers, motion pictures, theaters); its well-dressed people living in comfortable, brick apartment houses complete with gas and hot water. She would not have to work in a mill because he earned enough for the both of them. And last but not least, the local parish had a French-Canadian priest from St. Hyacinthe looking after their many com-patriots who had settled in that city.

This word-of-mouth recruitment resulted in the implantation of many immigrants from one area, and even from one village, into a given New England community. For example, a family from St. Ours in the Richelieu Valley reached Woonsocket, Rhode Island, about 1814 or 1815 and was joined there by several more families from the same area before 1840. Other persons from St. Ours settled in nearby Southbridge and Worcester, Massachusetts, about this time.[16] Most French Canadians in Brunswick, Maine, came from the south bank of the St. Lawrence River from Montreal to Rivière du Loup, more than half from contiguous counties.[17] Numerous inhabitants of Salem, Massachusetts, are said to have emigrated from Rimouski.[18] Similar claims have been made for Berlin, New Hampshire (Coaticook); Fall River, Massachusetts (Richelieu and Yamaska River valleys, and also counties downstream from Quebec City); Manchester, New Hampshire (Nicolet, Yamaska, Lotbinière, and St. Maurice counties); Warren, Rhode Island (Berthier, Joliette, Maskinongé, and St. Maurice counties); and Westbrook, Maine (vicinity of Quebec City).[19] One scholar found clusterings from several Beauce villages in Augusta and Waterville, Maine, and theorized that a significant number of the latter came down the Kennebec Road on foot or in horse-drawn wagons, while the Grand Trunk and Maine Central railroads carried the majority of Maine's other Franco-Americans from a much broader area of Quebec to such cities as Biddeford, Brunswick, Lewiston, Rumford, Sanford, and Westbrook. He also traced the routes followed by Acadian immigrants from New Brunswick and Prince Edward Island, and Acadian-Canadian French from the upper St. John to several areas, notably the paper mill towns.[20]

Social and economic conditions

In 1878 Honoré Beaugrand, who had been a resident of Fall River, Massachusetts, in the early years of that decade, published *Jeanne la fileuse,* the first Franco-American novel.[21] Though far from painting a complete or objective picture, the author's account of the immigrant's voyage to a New England mill town and the settling-in there in October 1873 has exceptional documentary value.

In Beaugrand's novel, the sixteen-year-old orphaned heroine and her foster family, the Dupuises, leave Montreal at 4:00 P.M. and arrive at Fall River at 2:00 P.M. the next day on the Passumpsic Railroad. They manage the transfer at Lowell and the change of stations at Boston without any difficulty thanks to helpful bilingual attendants. Tickets cost $10 each and include shipping and delivery of all baggage. Michel, the Dupuis's seventeen-year-old son, who had gone on ahead a year earlier, had reserved a tenement in a company house and secured work for the entire family. The family's remaining resources amount to $30, with which they purchase furniture and kitchen utensils.

French Canadians have only been in Fall River since 1868 but already number 6,000 (12 percent of the local population). Their group includes a few professionals and a number of small businessmen, notably food retailers who enjoy a monopoly of the French-Canadian trade. The Dupuises open up charge accounts with the baker, butcher, and grocer, who send employees around each day to take orders and to deliver. Bills come due in thirty days. Most French Canadians continue to purchase on credit. The tenements in company houses are said to be very comfortable, and the modest rent is deducted from the family's pay.

Having rested for a few days after their journey, the father and older children begin work at the Granite Mill. Massachusetts law requires the three youngest Dupuis children, ages twelve, ten, and eight, to attend school twenty weeks a year. After fulfilling this obligation, the children find employment at the mill.

Everyone rises early and arrives at the factory promptly at 6:30 A.M. A sixty-hour week is the rule. Beaugrand mentions the rigors of mill work and the subjugation of the workers, which he acknowledges to be a kind of slavery—domination by foreigners, regimentation, strict supervision by exacting foremen—but he glosses over these negative aspects and claims they mainly affect newcomers: "One is very unhappy the first weeks but when payday arrives, this unhappiness generally changes into satisfaction at the prospect of receiving regular wages, which is only natural." [22]

A first-time employee must initially serve an apprenticeship at a reduced hourly wage rate. Consequently, the family's combined first-month income is low. However, the Dupuises pay off most of their debts the second month, and on the third payday they are able to start putting some of their earnings into a savings account. Adjustment to life and work in Fall River is said to take about three months. Mill workers are paid an average of $1.22 an hour. Children receive 28 cents to $1.00 an hour. According to the author, salaries were higher when the Dupuises arrived in Fall River in 1873; however, a depression already in its fifth year was forcing wages down. (A 10 percent reduction in 1875 was followed by another in 1877.)

Beaugrand provides a certain amount of information about mill operatives' leisure-time activities. Franco-Americans socialize among themselves evenings and Sundays, and the Dupuises attend Saint Anne's Catholic Church. The father reads the local French-language newspaper (*L'Echo du Canada*) and is a member of the Société Saint-Jean-Baptiste. Michel belongs to the Cercle Montcalm, a local Franco-American cultural organization. One Sunday afternoon the boy shows Jeanne and his sisters around town. He also attends, on June 24, 1874, an important gathering in Montreal of French Canadians and Franco-Americans organized by the Société Saint-Jean-Baptiste. Jeanne sews and studies English in the evening and somehow also finds time to give French lessons to a group of French-Canadian children attending public school. In December 1874 she returns to Canada to marry her fiancé, who has the responsibility of managing the family farm. Her brother Jules, who has been working in a lumber camp, comes to Fall River and goes into business for himself as a grocer. The elder Dupuis, having saved enough in three years to pay off the mortgage, also returns home.

The apparent ease with which the habitant made the transition to a better life in New England affected another contemporary observer. In 1890 Father Edmond Hamon, a Jesuit missionary who served ten years in French-speaking parishes in New England, wrote:

> A habitant, poor in earthly possessions but rich in progeny, decides to emi-
> grate to the United States. The family arrives now in a manufacturing center,
> Lowell, Holyoke, Worcester, for example; together with the father and mother,
> there are eight or ten children of different ages. All these people are dressed in
> homespun, that is to say clothing woven by the mistress of the house. This *butin,*
> or gear, is tied in bundles which the father has distributed among the eldest
> boys, while he himself holds on to the gunny sack containing what he regards as
> his most valuable property. The train pulls in at the station. The mother scoops
> up her offspring, who, scattered all over the railroad car, noses pressed to the
> window, are gazing in wide-eyed astonishment at this new country. She hastily
> stows away the many objects forgotten on the seat, and finally gets out of the
> train in the land of liberty, pushing her brood before her. . . .
> Friends and relatives of the newcomers await to welcome them at the station.
> They exchange hearty handshakes, they kiss each other warmly, then they lead
> the emigrants to their lodgings prepared in advance for them. Visit these fami-
> lies a year later. You'd be surprised to see the changes in their faces. The boys,
> wearing clean and well cared for clothes, now look like little gentlemen. The
> girls are elegantly dressed and, to be sure, there are plenty of ribbons. Even the
> grandparents have been won over; the oldtimer and his wife are very nearly con-
> verted to American fashions. And all these folks seem pleased with their lot:
> "We live well here," they tell you. "We are well housed, heated, clothed; we have
> fresh meat every day and more money at the end of the month than we had in
> Canada at the end of an entire year."[23]

On the whole, Hamon was favorably impressed by the Franco-Americans' standard of living. The following is his account of a typical worker's home in Marlboro, Massachusetts:

> The head of the household greets you with open-hearted civility and shows
> you into a very clean, very elegant little parlor with rug, sofa, piano or harmo-
> nium. Pictures they brought with them from Canada are hanging on the walls,
> the Sacred Hearts of Jesus and Mary, and Saint Anne, the great patron saint of

the Canadians. Next to these, one finds needlepoint executed by the girls who are attending convent school, a crown and a cross and the superimposed motto *Pas de croix, pas de couronne* [No crown without the cross], or the English greeting *Welcome!* Soon, behind the mother you'll see blond-haired children peeking through the parlor door that is ajar. Beckon ever so slightly. Immediately a half dozen little boys and girls surround you, looking at you and playing with you like an old friend. The eldest daughter will play a tune on the piano to welcome you, the youngest will recite a fable learned at school, and, if you have the time, her mother will detail the qualities and faults of each member of the family.[24]

The author describes a summer evening in the French-Canadian section of Holyoke near Precious Blood Church in similarly idyllic terms.[25] The streets, which are lined with blocks four and five stories high, are filled with playing children and young girls strolling about in groups of three or four, chatting excitedly. On stoops and in entryways men are seated quietly smoking their pipes or engaged in animated conversation. There is laughter and singing everywhere; flowers decorate each windowsill.

Like Beaugrand, Hamon was well aware of the dark side of factory work.[26] It was, he conceded, boring and debilitating labor. Operatives were on their feet from six in the morning until six at night, except for the lunch hour, watching three and even four looms. The noise was deafening, heat prostration was common. Cotton dust choked the lungs. A high percentage of workers, especially females, developed eye problems. (The grinding drudgery of mill work is described by two Franco-American authors who experienced it in Emma Dumas's *Mirbah* and Camille Lessard's *Canuck*.)[27] Few French Canadians, Hamon conceded, could stand it for more than about ten years. However, he pointed out that for many, work in textile mills or shoe factories was but a means to an end: they later became small businessmen or learned less physically demanding trades. Meanwhile, wages earned in the mill also made it possible for them to buy private homes.[28]

Scholars who have studied Franco-Americans of the day in more objective fashion have confirmed the settling-in process described by Beaugrand and Hamon but have painted a far more somber picture of living conditions in the Little Canadas of New England.

Taking in relatives or friends for more than a few days was a gesture of solidarity, but since compensation was usually involved it was also an important way for the family to earn extra income. For example, in Lowell in 1870, nearly one-third of French-Canadian households included at least one person who was not a member of the nuclear family (father, mother, children). At least one enterprising Franco-American, Félix Albert, went into business for himself, meeting new arrivals at the railroad station, renting them tenements, and helping them find work.[29]

Also, Lessard's realistic novel, *Canuck,* set in Lowell in 1900, presents the French-Canadian immigrant's initial contact with a factory city as a grim and disheartening experience. At the train station, babies are crying and everyone is filthy from the journey. The buildings near the depot are dingy and ramshackle. Climbing to the top of a nearby hill, the young heroine is overwhelmed by the sight of sooty factories and row upon row of tediously uniform tenement houses. In the run-down flat the family finds along a muddy canal, windowpanes are missing, plaster is falling from the ceiling, and the floor is splintering. Cupboards and sink are crawling with cockroaches, and the faucet is a moldy green.

In Lowell, French Canadians initially settled especially in the Old Depot and New Depot districts. By 1880 they were beginning to move into an extension of the Old Depot area destined to become the city's Little Canada. In that year, this quarter was still only 46 percent French-Canadian. Ten years later the entire zone, one square mile, was a French-Canadian enclave.[30]

Lowell's Little Canada consisted largely of flimsy multiple-family dwellings, averaging between twenty-four and thirty-six units, built after the Civil War. Conditions were extremely crowded and unsanitary. There were no regular garbage collections. Health officials deplored the squalor but for years did little to improve the situation. In 1880 the mortality rate in this district was 29.6 per thousand and rising, the highest in the city; in one part of Little Canada (Ward 5) it was 47 per thousand. Children under five were the chief victims, accounting for 50 percent of all French-Canadian deaths. Lacking proper nutrition and medical care—few parents had their offspring inoculated—children were prey to common diseases that often proved fatal.[31] In the 1870s and 1880s, housing and health conditions in many other cities where there was a large influx of French-Canadian immigrants, for example Fall River and Holyoke, were equally appalling.[32] The situation began to improve in the 1890s, but in 1900 the mortality rate among Lowell's Franco-Americans was still 24 per thousand. A survey published in 1912 revealed that in one block (the Harris), 300 persons were living in forty-eight tenements of four rooms each, an average of 6.25 per room; forty rooms had no windows. The same study notes the existence of a playground in Lowell's Little Canada in 1909 but charges that it is unsupervised and the scene of many fights.[33]

In the last quarter of the nineteenth century, Franco-Americans residing in smaller mill towns often managed no better. In Brunswick, Maine, the Cabot Company constructed wooden tenements on and near Mill Street near the river, as did a number of private enterpreneurs. Virtually the entire Franco-American population until 1900 could be found in this crowded quarter. Many of the buildings were originally purchased for between $75 and $125 and paid for themselves every three or four years.[34] Contacts between the French and the rest of Brunswick's population, except for the foremen at the mill, were nonexistent. The town's other inhabitants simply looked the other way, pretending that a quarter and later more than half of the population did not exist.[35] For many years the local newspaper did not even record Franco-American births, marriages, and deaths.

In the spring of 1886, diphtheria broke out in the French quarter.[36] A. G. Tenney, the remarkable man who edited the *Brunswick Telegraph,* started a campaign to alert the local citizenry about the threat posed by certain revolting conditions near the company houses. Tenney's analysis of the cause of the epidemic was incorrect, but his increasingly strident weekly editorials, castigating the owners of the Cabot mill for their greed and negligence, drew attention to the plight of the Franco-Americans. Between May 1 and September 10 of that year (1886), seventy-four persons died in the French district of Brunswick, mostly from diphtheria; nearly all were children.[37]

One concrete result of the 1886 epidemic in Brunswick was Tenney's befriending of the young doctor, Onésime Paré, who worked heroically through the summer to stem the tide of the disease, only to die of pneumonia himself the following January.[38] Dr. Paré was born in Canada but attended the University of Michigan, where he earned his M.D. degree in 1884. He died at the age of thirty-two.

In 1875, 41 percent of Lowell's Franco-Americans lived below the poverty line; an additional 11 percent were barely over it.[39] In 1880 two-thirds of the cotton mill workers in Cohoes, New York, a one-company town with a large Franco-American population, could be classified as poor.[40] Families with working children and with fathers who were or eventually became skilled laborers fared best.[41] Typically, Franco-American fathers worked as laborers, mothers kept house, and unmarried children, especially females, found jobs in the mill. (In 1900 the percentage of the French-Canadian labor force employed in the textile industry in some representative cities was as follows: Fall River, males 52.8, females 83.9; Lawrence, males 32.4, females 81.7; Lowell, males 40.6, females 80.5; Manchester, males 36.3, females 71.1; New Bedford, males 61.0, females 87.9.)[42] Mothers rarely worked outside the home but contributed enormously to the household economy by caring for children, cooking, cleaning, sewing, and washing. Boarders meant extra labor for them. Wives also kept families on a schedule and maintained order, a function humorously referred to in Franco-American slang of the day as that of a policeman.[43]

Many families succeeded in laying aside respectable sums but most never managed to do so. When debts were paid off, workers often spent the balance of their earnings on the luxuries deplored by the Franco-American clergy: amusements, fine clothes, picnics, trips to Canada, and so on. Single persons and those whose stay was brief—that is, the greatest number—generally did not prosper.[44]

Nevertheless, Hamon's positive view of the economic advantages of factory work finds an echo in the recollections of many Franco-Americans who got their start in this way. Most seem to have been successful in coping with the harsh realities of existence in an industrial setting. Interviews with former Franco-American employees of the Amoskeag Manufacturing Company of Manchester, New Hampshire, revealed that they exercised a good deal more control over their own lives than was earlier believed.[45] Workers left their jobs very casually, virtually certain that they would be rehired by the company. Discriminated against in the 1870s and 1880s, Franco-Americans were able, early in the twentieth century, to develop their own informal network of contacts along kinship and ethnic lines to obtain better jobs and treatment in the mill, and even to move from one mill town to another in New England. Though overseers, that is, individuals in charge of a department, were rarely Franco-Americans, many relied upon foremen or other key persons who were members of the group to implement decisions and handle day-to-day problems. Such individuals were often useful in reconciling differences between employers and workers.[46]

Labor problems

Nineteenth-century French-Canadian immigrants were sometimes stigmatized as antilabor.[47] It is true that most were preoccupied with concerns of an ideological and practical nature that were far removed from those of union organizers. However, except for isolated instances of strikebreaking, notably in Fall River in 1879,[48] French Canadians behaved no differently from other recent immigrants in this respect. In fact, after initially being subjected to considerable abuse by labor leaders, they ceased being the scapegoats when, in the latter part of the century, other nationalities began arriving in large numbers and soon bore the brunt of such attacks.

In Fall River, discriminatory practices by English and Irish mill operatives undermined working-class solidarity.[49] Until well into the present century, the latter controlled higher-paying jobs and forced French-Canadian males to seek employment in other occupations. Local religious disputes between Irish and French-Canadian Catholics also poisoned the atmosphere.[50] In Cohoes, New York, French-Canadian cotton mill operatives, ably organized by Samuel Sault, joined forces with Irish fellow workers and, in 1880, participated in a successful nine-day walkout.[51] Two years later they were defeated in a bitter four-month strike.

In New England, French Canadians joined some labor organizations, notably the carpenters' union; in Springfield, Massachusetts, they formed a French-speaking local in 1885, and in nearby Holyoke, in 1889.[52] However, unskilled textile workers—the bulk of Franco-American laborers—were not successfully unionized before World War I.[53] Most were shocked by labor violence and were instructed by their pastors not to participate in work stoppages. This happened, for example, in Fall River during the turbulent 1870s and in Lawrence during the famous eight-week strike in 1912 led by the Industrial Workers of the World, or Wobblies, and the American Federation of Labor. In Biddeford, Maine, in 1886, three hundred Franco-Americans formed their own local of the Knights of Labor but soon disbanded.[54]

Like many other immigrant groups, French Canadians did not hesitate to send their children to work in the mills. In many cases, this was the only way the family could escape grinding poverty. In addition to being exposed to conditions that were hazardous to their health, children who worked in factories were also denied an education, which all too often sentenced them to more years of manual labor.

Though many states adopted child labor legislation in the nineteenth and early twentieth centuries, these laws were not strictly enforced. It has been estimated that at the turn of the century nearly one-fifth of all American children between the ages of ten and sixteen were employed in various commercial enterprises.[55]

The Prints and Photographs Division of the Library of Congress preserves nearly fifty-three hundred numbered photographs taken by Lewis W. Hine (1874–1940) for the National Child Labor Committee of New York from 1908 to 1931. The pictures were part of a campaign waged by the committee and other organizations to put an end to the employment of children.

Lot 7,479 consists of seven albums of prints—about nineteen hundred in all—of boys and girls fourteen years old or younger entering or leaving factories, or at work. Hine's captions and negatives are also on file.[56] Many of the photographs were taken surreptitiously to avoid alerting mill agents or having children run away in fear of being discovered underage. However, most children were happy to oblige, and captions frequently provide the names and addresses of subjects. A few children are shown outside their homes or in family groups. Only rarely are they seen inside their homes.

Hine was much affected by the deplorable living and working conditions he recorded, but he also harbored prejudices. He poked fun at the French Canadians' English and was shocked by some of the girls' shameless flirting or vulgarity. In the following caption (2,741), for example, he reveals himself to be full of compassion mixed with disgust:

> Slovenly kitchen living-room of family of Alfred Benoit, 191 N. Front St. [New Bedford, Massachusetts], a sweeper in Bennett Mill; has been there for two months. Mother works in the same mill; father is a canvasser (and shiftless). Said, "I'm de father of 11 children." The baby in the girl's arms is one they are keeping for another woman. The mother would not get in the photo. Alfred had bad eyes this morning (influenza apparently) and moping [*sic*] them with a filthy rag. One of the little ones had the same trouble. Another had a boil on his face.

Hine performed his task conscientiously, and his striking photographs testify that many and perhaps most French-Canadian children led a hard life in New England mill towns at the turn of the century. But Hine also had an eye for a pretty face: he took no fewer than ten photographs—several of them close-up portraits—of Mamie Laberge, a spinner in the Spring Village Mill, Winchendon, Massachusetts, whom he described as "A modest young French girl of 13 years."

The plight of older adolescents who were also compelled to spend years in factory work and to contribute their salaries to a family fund instead of preparing their own futures has been given less publicity. This problem was dealt with in Lessard's *Canuck*, the story of a fifteen-year-old girl forced to work in a mill in Lowell for three years by a tyrannical father. The author drew on her experiences in Lewiston, Maine, where she was employed in a textile mill for four years at the turn of the century.

Social classes

In Lowell in 1870, 95 percent of employed males were working class. In Holyoke, the percentage was even higher: an 1871 city directory listing 258 French Canadians included only 2 professionals and 5 merchants, 3 of them grocers.[57] In the years that followed, the number of middle-class Franco-Americans, especially retail businessmen, rose steadily, but the percentage remained low. Joseph Chalifoux (1850-1911), who emigrated to Lowell in 1868, was one of the first Franco-Americans to achieve high status in business circles. He amassed a fortune by opening large department stores in Lowell, Massachusetts; Manchester, New Hampshire; and Birmingham, Alabama.[58]

It was only natural that French-Canadian immigrants should turn to store owners and professionals of their own nationality for services and for leadership. This group generally prospered in good times but, like the working class, was also faced with ruin during economic downturns. To cite but one example, nearly three hundred small businesses were started by Franco-Americans in Augusta, Maine, from 1880 to 1920, but not a single one survived.[59]

Most of the individuals who founded and guided parish and regional organizations, and engaged in local politics, were members of the middle class. These persons collaborated with clerics in developing a distinctive ideology whose contours can be found in Franco-American newspapers and in the proceedings of Franco-American conventions of the day.

Ideology

In the second half of the nineteenth century, as French Canadians began to emigrate at an alarming rate, many politicians and priests in Quebec condemned this phenomenon as a serious threat to survivance, or the continued vitality of the French-Canadian people. Georges Etienne Cartier, prime minister of Canada, is alleged to have said: "Laissez-les partir: c'est la canaille qui s'en va" (Let them depart: it's the rabble who are leaving).[60]

A smaller but no less influential number of leaders saw emigration in a more positive light. In 1869 Louis Joseph de Goësbriand, first bishop of the Diocese of Burlington (Vermont), described the exodus toward the south as providential, that is, the way God intended to bring about the conversion of New England.[61] A few even suggested that the region might someday become part of Quebec, especially if the latter became independent.[62] New England could at least become as French-Canadian as, say, parts of Ontario bordering on Quebec. By World War I it was clear that this notion was a pipe dream.

The French-Canadian immigrants who settled permanently in New England realized that they now owed allegiance to their adoptive country and that, living for the most part in cities rather than rural villages, they needed to adapt to this milieu. Many rapidly became integrated into American society; however, a greater number reacted warily to their new environment.

A majority of those who resisted assimilation were influenced by leaders who developed a theory, derived from nineteenth-century Quebec survivance ideology, about the group's life and culture.[63] According to this view, Franco-Americans may have ignored the call of the land—that is, the agrarian life for which they were supposedly destined—and left their native country, but they would continue to exist and prosper as a people if they cherished and safeguarded the other elements of their French-Canadian heritage, namely their mother tongue, Catholic faith, and customs. To do this, it was important to remain attached to traditional ways, and it was absolutely essential to combat the godlessness, materialism, and promiscuity they believed existed all around them.

This austere attitude and cautious approach to American life, sometimes ascribed to the strain of Jansenism in French-Canadian Catholicism of the day, gradually attenuated.[64] However, until World War II many Franco-American leaders maintained a siege mentality and spoke proudly of certain parishes as *citadelles*.[65]

Franco-American merchants and professionals benefited greatly from the loyalty of members of their ethnic group and never hesitated to encourage this kind of solidarity by advertising and other means. Because throughout this period (and well into the next) Franco-American merchants and professionals virtually monopolized their compatriots' patronage, one scholar has suggested that they consciously promoted survivance ideology in order to perpetuate this control.[66] Self-interest no doubt played a role; but in the main, Franco-American ideology appears to have developed spontaneously as a continuation of the struggle against the assimilation that began in Quebec in the aftermath of the British Conquest.

Politics

Stimulated by naturalization campaigns, French-Canadian immigrants became United States citizens in growing numbers beginning in the 1870s. However, initially they were slower to claim citizenship than many other ethnic groups—partly because of language problems but, above all, because of uncertainty about returning home. Younger immigrants were the first to make the decision. In 1885, 75 percent of the French Canadians admitted to citizenship in Holyoke, Massachusetts, were thirty years old or younger.[67]

Franco-American voting in national elections followed broad national trends from 1896 to 1924. Analysis of returns from a sampling of thirty communities with a high percentage of Franco-Americans reveals that, except in 1908 (when they favored William Jennings Bryan) and in 1916 (Woodrow Wilson), they tended to vote Republican.[68] However, they rarely voted as a bloc, and local factors influenced state and, especially, municipal elections. In southern New England, Irish control of Democratic politics drove many Franco-Americans into the Republic party; but this was apparently not the case in smaller towns in central Massachusetts where French Canadians settled early and were the predominant ethnic group.[69] Also, in Fall River, the French Canadians and Irish joined forces in the second decade of the present century, a unity that resulted in the election of the city's first Franco-American mayor, Democrat Edmond P. Talbot, in 1922.[70]

In many cities and towns Franco-American votes were regarded as pivotal, and members of the group succeeded in gaining a number of seats in municipal councils and in state houses; where in a majority, they usually chose one of their own as mayor. However, Franco-Americans were never able to control party politics at the state level, although Aram J. Pothier was elected governor of Rhode Island on the Republican ticket in 1908 and remained in power until 1915, and then was reelected in 1924 and served until his death in 1928.[71] In the interim, Pothier's friend Emery J. San Souci served as governor for one term beginning in 1920.

Perception of Franco-Americans by others

When French Canadians began arriving in large numbers in New England, they were often regarded as amiable, good-natured, and hard working people, but negative stereotypes—for example, they were thought to lack ambition and to be priest ridden or turned inward—also surfaced from time to time.[72] Like all generalizations about ethnic groups, such views usually betrayed a patronizing or prejudiced attitude.

Often associated with the foreign-born in the nineteenth century, alcoholism was not regarded by most outside observers as a major vice among French-Canadian immigrants.[73] Hamon, who was active in promoting temperance among Franco-Americans in the latter part of the century, supports this view.[74] However, one scholar has noted many incidents of public drunkenness and numerous arrests for illegal liquor sales by Maine's Franco-Americans. (Maine was a dry state from 1851 to 1933.)[75]

Two groups were instrumental in disseminating negative stereotypes about the recent arrivals from Quebec. In cultivated circles the Boston Brahmins, who regarded American democracy and culture as fixed, monolithic, and essentially Anglo-Saxon, viewed most immigrants with suspicion, especially those who did not quickly embrace their beliefs and way of life. They tended to confuse the French Canadians in their midst with French peasants, felt threatened by their attachment to their own language and religion, and resented that many had no intention of settling permanently in New England.

Many members of the working class were antagonistic to the French Canadians for a different reason. They believed their own wages were being driven down because the new arrivals seemingly agreed to work for very little.

Matters reached the boiling point in 1881 with the publication of the

Twelfth Annual Report of the Massachusetts Bureau of Statistics of Labor.[76] Reflecting the biased opinion of unionized textile workers interviewed by his agents, Commissioner Carroll D. Wright issued a stinging indictment of French Canadians as a group:

> With some exceptions the Canadian French are the Chinese of the Eastern States. They care nothing for our institutions, civil, political, or educational. They do not come to make a home among us, to dwell with us as citizens, and so become a part of us; but their purpose is merely to sojourn a few years as aliens, touching us only at a single point, that of work, and, when they have gathered out of us what will satisfy their ends, to get them away to whence they came, and bestow it there. They are a horde of industrial invaders, not a stream of stable settlers. Voting with all that it implies, they care nothing about. Rarely does one of them become naturalized. They will not send their children to school if they can help it, but endeavor to crowd them into the mills at the earliest possible age.[77]

At a hearing held before Wright on October 25, 1881, Franco-Americans from Cohoes, Fall River, Lewiston, Manchester, Nashua, Woonsocket, and Worcester, and their friends rebutted these sweeping and unfair charges and presented ample evidence of the group's achievements and contribution to American society. Wright conceded as much and, in the *Report* that appeared the following year, presented a more balanced view. However, the 1881 account was widely distributed and caused great harm.[78]

About this time several Protestant groups—Baptists, Congregationalists, and Methodists—began proselytizing among French-Canadian immigrants in New England. Often equating Americanism with the Protestant faith, these missionaries founded several French-language newspapers beginning in 1880, including *Le Franco-Américain* at Fall River in 1888, incidentally one of the earliest attestations of the term.[79]

The most aggressive of these missionaries was the Rev. Calvin E. Amaron who was active in Lowell, then in Springfield, Massachusetts. Of Swiss extraction, Amaron founded the Collège Franco-Américain, ancestor of American International College, at Springfield in 1885 and published the alarmist tract *Your Heritage, or New England Threatened* (1891; the first edition in 1885 was entitled *The Evangelization of the French Canadians*). None of these efforts at conversion gained much success.

Religion

Like Catholic immigrants from other lands, French Canadians continued to attend church in New England. Local clergymen and parishioners, who were predominantly Irish, sometimes welcomed them; often, however, the reception was cool and even unfriendly. Cultural differences, the language barrier, and rivalry among workers created these tensions. Many of the new arrivals began to stay away from church; nearly all felt uncomfortable in these surroundings. They longed to participate in devotions conducted in French and according to their customs. Their prayers were soon answered.

A number of communities boast early Franco-American parishes, notably Van Buren (Saint Bruno, 1838) and Upper Frenchville (Saint Luce, 1843) in rural northern Maine, but the foundation by immigrants of Saint Joseph's Church in Burlington, Vermont, in 1850 signaled the dawn of a new urban era in the group's history (see next section, "National Parishes"). By 1900 there were no fewer than eighty-two Franco-American parishes.[80] (For a historical listing, see Appendix A, "Some Early Franco-American Parishes.")

This growth was not gradual but came in fits and starts. One scholar, noting a hiatus in the mid-1860s and again in the 1870s, has made the plausible suggestion that the foundation dates reflect the cyclical character of the French-Canadian immigration, which responded quickly to economic conditions in New England—that is, more immigration during boom years, 1867–73 and 1886–93, less during the Civil War and the depression of 1873–79.[81]

The procedure for founding a new parish was repeated over and over again throughout New England. Often convened by a local merchant or professional, and following a visit by a missionary priest, French-Canadian immigrants assembled and, after taking a census and making inquiries about renting a building or hall, or securing land to build a church, petitioned the bishop to form a parish with a French-speaking pastor.

"The curé, guardian and head of parish life, saved our people from annihilation at crucial junctures in their history; he prevented our ancestors from going under."[82] Historians today may demur at such exaltation of parish priests, but few would deny the key role many played in maintaining the group's identity and shaping its outlook on life.

Among the most active secular priests of the day, Father Louis Gagnier founded no fewer than eleven parishes in six years, from 1869 to 1874, in Vermont and Massachusetts. Other prominent founding fathers include the Rev. J. B. Bédard of Fall River, Joseph A. Chevalier of Manchester, Charles Dauray of Woonsocket, and Pierre Hévey of Lewiston and Manchester. Three religious orders, the Dominicans, Marists, and Oblates, also provided many early pastors. Several French and Belgian priests figured among these pioneers. For example, in 1855 Bishop de Goësbriand, himself a Breton, recruited seven fellow countrymen for parish work in Vermont (another Breton, Father Hervé Cardinal, arrived in Vermont independently two years later). And ten Belgian missionaries are known to have served in Connecticut beginning in 1862.[83] However, the vast majority were French Canadians.

Services were initially held in public halls, storefronts, or abandoned Protestant churches rented or purchased for this purpose. One of the pastor's first duties was to perform baptisms and weddings, many of which had been postponed until his arrival. All were duly entered in the brand-new parish register. Marriages performed by justices of the peace or Protestant ministers were usually rehabilitated in a special ceremony.[84] Many names of French-Canadian immigrants are garbled in contemporary records kept by non-French-speaking city clerks and pastors. Early on, too, like other recent arrivals, some Franco-Americans began seeking an accommodation with their non-Francophone neighbors and employers by anglicizing their names. However, the practice of giving popular American first names to children did not become widespread until the third generation.

One of the first priorities of the new parish was to collect funds to build a suitable church, rectory, convent, and school. Money came from a variety of sources: door-to-door solicitations, pew rentals, and, above all, bazaars, raffles, picnics, and suppers.[85] In addition to bringing in income, these social gatherings developed parish solidarity.

National parishes

In the second half of the nineteenth century, the Catholic hierarchy in the United States, which was largely Irish, opposed efforts by various ethnic groups to establish parishes based on nationality.[86] Most prelates were convinced that immigrants (and fellow Catholics) would suffer less discrimination and persecution if the recent arrivals became assimilated rapidly. Opponents charged that the Irish were forcing assimilation needlessly in order to control the church at the parish level as well. The argument that Catholics were leaving the church in droves usually persuaded bishops to authorize national parishes. However, the large number of requests, the obstinacy—and, at times, the obstreperousness—of the parishioners, and the duration of the phenomenon perplexed high-ranking ecclesiastics.

Even when in a majority, Franco-Americans in so-called mixed parishes often found it acceptable to have a French-speaking pastor or curate, whether the latter was French-Canadian or not. At any rate, most put up with this situation throughout their history. Others found these circumstances intolerable and agitated to change conditions more to their liking or to form a separate national parish. At times, only French-Canadian or Franco-American priests, not French or Belgian, would do. Activists usually managed to obtain a guarantee that the parish would remain permanently national, but the understanding reached about the nationality of priests for mixed parishes was generally less clear.

From the outset, Franco-Americans had run-ins with Irish coreligionists. In 1850 Irish members of Saint Mary's Church in Burlington, Vermont, resisted efforts by French-Canadian fellow parishioners to form a separate congregation—eventually historic Saint Joseph's parish—by preventing them from building on land owned by Saint Mary's. The tactic proved unavailing when the French Canadians purchased a lot some distance away. In Ware, Massachusetts, in the mid-1880s, Franco-Americans rebelled against their Irish pastor for forcing acceptance of a drive to pay off the parish debt; they even protested to Rome before the commotion subsided.[87] Many more skirmishes pitted Franco-Americans against the Irish hierarchy before the end of the century, but three major confrontations deserve special note.

The Flint Affair

When young Father Bédard died suddenly in 1884 after a meteoric career, the pastorate of Notre Dame de Lourdes parish which he had founded in Fall River became vacant. Archetype of the activist and dedicated Franco-American pastor, Bédard was revered by most of his parishioners but had antagonized Bishop Thomas F. Hendricken on a number of occasions. He had, for example, pioneered in the development of the *syndique* concept in New England whereby a parish corporation, as in Quebec, not the bishop, controlled the congregation's financial affairs.

Determined to nip this challenge in the bud and smarting from other slights, Hendricken pointedly named an Irish pastor to succeed Bédard, in spite of the fact that Irish members of the congregation had separated to form another parish. What happened next is known as the Flint Affair from the name of the mill and village where Notre Dame is located. For two years, Franco-Americans resisted their bishop in a highly publicized clash of wills, hounding three Irish pastors in succession from this post and appealing to Rome. Prodded by the Vatican and fellow bishops, Hendricken finally acceded to their wishes, thus consecrating the principle of national parishes. Beginning in 1886, the next bishop worked successfully at effecting a reconciliation.[88]

Danielson and North Brookfield

In two other causes célèbres during the next decade, determined efforts to wrest concessions from bishops in the Hartford, Connecticut, and Springfield, Massachusetts, dioceses proved futile.[89]

Saint James Church in Danielson, Connecticut, was 87 percent Franco-American but without a French-speaking priest. Prolonged negotiations, culminating in a lengthy strike and a refusal to pay pew rent, were unavailing. Having come this far, many protesters, led by Charles J. Leclaire, declined to accept a French pastor and attempted to establish an autonomous national parish to be headed by a French-Canadian curé. In 1897 a petition to Rome was turned down; increasingly isolated, the dissidents eventually yielded.

At the turn of the century, Bishop Thomas D. Beaven rejected a petition by Franco-Americans to establish a national parish in North Brookfield, Massachusetts. Defying him by building a chapel and welcoming an independent-minded French priest, many dissidents incurred excommunication.

Once vested in bishops, authority to establish national parishes was transferred to Rome in 1918.[90] By then, French-Canadian emigration to New England had declined sharply and the pressure to found new parishes was lessening. Henceforth, Franco-American leaders increasingly focused their attention on the quality of their ethnic life as opposed to the quantity of their national parishes.

The Corporation Sole Controversy

The related struggle over control of parish financial matters, which had been simmering for a quarter of a century in New England, reached the boiling point in 1909. At a convention held in Brunswick, Maine, in that year, Franco-Americans, vexed by what they perceived to be highhanded steps taken by Bishop Louis Walsh, decided to push for revision of the state's corporation sole law, which stipulated that the bishop owned all church property in his diocese.

In a hearing before the Maine legislature's Judicial Affairs Committee, Attorney Godfroy Dupré, speaking in favor of new legislation, invoked the hallowed principle of no taxation without representation. More impressed by the argument submitted by an array of bankers that to alter the law would be fiscally unwise, the committee recommended that no change be made.

A few months later, six Franco-American leaders, five of them residents of Biddeford, hotbed of opposition to the bishop, having persisted in their challenge, were interdicted by Walsh. An example was also made of a seventh leader who, having died suddenly, was accorded obsequies consisting of a Libera but no mass. Bishop Walsh's harsh handling of this entire matter offended the moral sense of many observers.

Responding to an appeal by several Franco-Americans, Rome, that same year, pronounced itself in favor of New York State's parish corporation sys-

tem. Initially viewed by some as a compromise, this arrangement autho-
rized a five-member body—the bishop, his vicar, the pastor, and two
parishioners—to act as a single person in this respect. However, because
the parishioners were to be designated by majority vote of the other three
members, the bishop would retain absolute control. In 1913 the Maine
legislature approved this measure.[91]

The first Franco-American bishop

In the latter part of the nineteenth century, Franco-American leaders
complained increasingly that no member of their group had ever been elevated to the rank of bishop, in spite of the fact that Franco-Americans constituted nearly one-third of the Catholic population of New England (in
1890). Bishop Louis de Goësbriand of Burlington (1853–92), a Frenchman, was succeeded by John Stephen Michaud who was French-Canadian
only on his father's side and did not readily identify with Franco-Americans.
Finally, in 1907 George Albert Guertin, pastor of Saint Anthony of Padua
parish in Manchester, New Hampshire, and a bona fide Franco-American
(he was born in Nashua), was named bishop of his diocese. A quiet but
efficient administrator, he served with distinction until his death in 1931
and was a disappointment only to certain militants.[92]

Schools

In the earliest days, some mills instituted schools, essentially to teach
Franco-American children a bit of English and the three Rs. As the number
of Franco-Americans grew in New England and parishes were established,
pastors felt the need to found their own schools in order to provide proper
training in a milieu regarded as a grave danger to faith and morals. The
cornerstone on which the Franco-American school was built was the profound conviction that abandoning the French language was tantamount to
abandoning the Catholic faith.

The first teachers were recruited from among the Franco-Americans
themselves, usually young women who had attended convent schools in
Canada. Among the earliest were a Mrs. Salvail at Fall River about 1869;
Alphonse Paré at Biddeford shortly after 1870; a Miss Lacourse at Lewis-
ton in 1870–71, and Vidal Bourbeau in the same city in 1873; Hélène
Paquet at Biddeford in 1875; and two laywomen at Holyoke in 1876.[93] In
Biddeford, the wife (i.e., Hélène Paquet) and the daughter of Dr. Narcisse
Thivierge, a local pharmacist, started a school together with Misses Dion
and Rhéaume in the early 1880s which enrolled about a hundred chil-
dren.[94] About this time, Gaspard Drainville, assisted by Wilfrid Rouleau,

operated a similar program for children in Woonsocket.[95] In 1881 J. H. Guillet, a lawyer, opened a free night school for youngsters in Lowell.[96] A Miss Daignault and several assistants were providing instruction to about two hundred children in Brunswick in 1887.[97] Many of the early classes were held in private homes, church basements, or vestries. The first French school in Sanford, Maine, opened by Vidal Bourbeau of Lewiston in 1895, was in a room above a store.[98]

Very little is known about what lay persons taught in these early Franco-American schools. They no doubt improvised as well as used the écoles de rang or convent schools they had attended as models. Most of the instruction was probably in French. This phase ended with the arrival of the religious teaching orders, bringing with them a different concept of what a parochial school ought to be.

The first full-fledged Franco-American parochial school was founded by the Soeurs des Saints Noms de Jésus et de Marie of Hochelaga (Montreal) in Immaculate Heart of Mary parish, Rutland, Vermont, in 1870. (The establishment was closed in 1882.)[99] The second and third schools were in Notre Dame de Lourdes parish, Fall River, Massachusetts (Religieuses [or Soeurs] de Jésus-Marie of Sillery) in 1877, and in Saint Peter's parish, Lewiston, Maine (Grey Nuns) in 1878. In 1881 the Dominican Fathers in the latter city constructed an imposing edifice, which began to be used as an elementary school in 1883. In those days, parents paid fifty cents a month for each child's tuition. The Dominican Block and most other buildings of the sort, were more than mere schools: they also served as vital community centers for the local Franco-American population. When the school sponsored dramatic and musical performances by pupils (séances) like the Christmas pageant in Lewiston in 1885, the entire parish turned out.[100]

The religious orders introduced a new dimension into Franco-American education. They did not just teach subjects; rather, they strove to implant an ideology of how to live according to well-defined rules.[101] Early Franco-American society, like most ethnic cultures, was a prefigurative community—the parents often learning from their children, not the other way around, as is usually the case. Enrollment in the parish schools grew steadily, at times mushrooming as parents found the instruction authoritative and thoroughgoing, especially after the system of grades was introduced.

It is easy to criticize these early parochial schools with their iron discipline and simplistic view of life, but late-nineteenth-century and early-twentieth-century public schools had a comparable atmosphere. The difference, of course, was that the Catholic faith, the French language, and French-Canadian culture were at the heart of parochial school programs. Nativists worried about all efforts to maintain ethnic culture in America but concentrated their attacks on the use of foreign languages as a medium of instruction in elementary schools.

In test cases involving Franco-Americans, authorities in Haverhill and Fitchburg, Massachusetts, in 1888 and 1893, respectively, refused to recognize parochial schools because instruction was not in English.[102] In the end, the right of these private establishments to teach in French was sustained, but it was also acknowledged by Franco-Americans that some instruction in English was desirable and necessary.

Under increasing pressure from local school commissions and the Catholic hierarchy, Franco-American parochial schools eventually settled into the routine they maintained until the 1950s: half a day was taught in French, with subjects such as French grammar, catechism, Canadian history, art, and music; half a day was taught in English, with subjects such as American history, arithmetic, geography, and so on. This system was in effect by 1912, for example, in the schools maintained in New England by the Sisters of the Assumption (Nicolet).[103]

Except for such communities as the Dominicans, many of whom were French, the first religious were Canadian born. Over the years, the French-language subjects gradually became the province of the Canadian religious, English-language subjects the specialty of the Americans; the former, in a sense, transmitting the old traditions, the latter the new.

In the early days, relatively few Franco-Americans went on to high school or college. Many who did attended institutions in Canada. Two of the earliest Franco-American boarding schools for girls were under the supervision of the Sisters of Saint Anne at Marlboro, Massachusetts (1887), and the Ursulines at Waterville, Maine (1900). (The first school at Rutland, Vermont, in 1870 took in female boarders.)

In October 1904 a group of Assumptionist Fathers, recently arrived from France, established a small school for boys in Greendale, a suburb of Worcester, Massachusetts.[104] Almost immediately the school undertook the mission of becoming a Franco-American institution of higher learning. Inspired by French and French-Canadian educational ideals, the Collège de l'Assomption soon offered an eight-year high school and college program. (Its charter authorizing the school to award bachelor's degrees was granted in 1917.) Over the next half century this bilingual institution exerted a great influence on the Franco-American community.

Organizations

Until World War II, the parish, that is its church and school, was the focus of Franco-American life. Much leisure time was taken up by parish activities which often involved the whole family: morning mass on Sundays, holy days, and daily during Advent and Lent; Benediction, Stations of the Cross, Vespers; bazaars, jubilees, and week-long retreats; baptisms, first communions, confirmations, weddings, funerals, and so forth.

Early on, Franco-Americans established religious and social organizations in virtually every community where they settled. These associations resembled one another, tending to give uniformity to parish life throughout New England and to produce institutionalized values.

Parish societies

Shortly after his arrival, the founding pastor would organize an altar boy group and a usually all-male choir for the proper celebration of mass. He also established sodalities for men (Sacred Heart League), married women (under the patronage of Saint Anne), and girls (Children of Mary), all on the French-Canadian model.[105] Though essentially devotional in nature—for example, sodality members were required to attend mass and receive communion as a group on certain occasions—these organizations also fostered a standard of behavior based on moral principles. Members of the Sacred Heart League generally pledged not to curse or to frequent saloons.

Other associations

The line between Franco-American parish and community organizations was blurred. Many of the latter excluded persons who were not regular churchgoers; also, the organizations attended mass in a body at least once a year (often in full regalia in spite of a ban on such displays promulgated by the Council of Baltimore in 1889), supported parish endeavors, and had a chaplain who was normally the local pastor or curate.

In 1834 the first Société Saint-Jean-Baptiste was established in Montreal by the Patriote Ludger Duvernay to promote solidarity among French Canadians and to provide a welfare fund that included sickness and death benefits. The idea of an annual celebration of the saint's feast day, June 24, also dates from that year. Independent sister societies sprang up throughout Canada and, as early as 1848, in New England (La Société Jacques-Cartier, St. Albans, Vermont).[106]

Many associations founded by French-Canadian immigrants in the second half of the nineteenth century were small, autonomous, and often short-lived organizations whose chief purpose was to provide insurance.[107] Their designations reflect a French-Canadian prototype or the nationality of its members, for example:

Association Canadienne-Française—Concord, New Hampshire (1868)
Institut Canadien-Français—Biddeford, Maine (1868); Lowell, Massachusetts (1868); Woonsocket, Rhode Island (1876)

Institut Jacques Cartier—Lewiston, Maine (1872)
Société (or Union) St-Joseph—Burlington, Vermont (1859); Lowell, Massa-
chusetts (1870); Lewiston, Maine (1879); Holyoke, Massachusetts(1880);
Biddeford, Maine (1886)
Union Canadienne—Holyoke, Massachusetts (1881)

Their designations also reflect the name of their policyholders' parish—
Société St-Augustin, Manchester, New Hampshire (1878); Union St-
Georges, Manchester, New Hampshire (1891)—or a patron saint—Union
St-Pierre, Manchester, New Hampshire (1894), in honor of Monsignor
Pierre Hévey, pastor of Saint Mary's.

However, the most popular name by far was the Société Saint-
Jean-Baptiste. Groups were formed in Pittsfield-Springfield, Massachusetts
(1864); Meriden, Connecticut (1865); St. Albans, Vermont (1866);
Biddeford, Maine (1867); Holyoke, Massachusetts, and Woonsocket,
Rhode Island (1868); Fitchburg and Worcester, Massachusetts (1869);
Haverhill, Northampton, and Southbridge, Massachusetts, and Nashua,
New Hampshire (1870); Fall River and Webster, Massachusetts, and Man-
chester, New Hampshire (1871), to list but a few. (Societies bearing this
name were also started in Malone [1848], New York City [1850], Plattsburgh [1863], Albany and Cohoes [1868], and Troy, New York [1870].)

Efforts to federate Franco-American mutuals were to no avail until two
such groups formed the Association Canado-Américaine at Manchester,
New Hampshire, in 1896, and eighteen organizations merged into the
Union Saint-Jean-Baptiste d'Amérique at Woonsocket, Rhode Island, in
1900. These two fraternal societies were to play a major role in Franco-
American history.

Other mutuals with branches in Canada as well as New England about
this time included the Catholic Order of Foresters (Chicago, 1883; a
splinter group, the Ordre des Forestiers Franco-Américains, formed at
Springfield, Massachusetts, in 1906, merged with the Association Canado-
Américaine in 1938); the Société des Artisans Canadiens-Français (Montreal, 1876); and the Société L'Assomption, which recruited many Franco-
Americans of Acadian heritage. (Founded at Waltham, Massachusetts, in
1903, the group's headquarters was moved to Moncton, New Brunswick,
in 1913.) Franco-American mutuals began holding congresses every year
or so beginning in 1865.[108]

Many local branches stressed fraternalism and engaged in cultural, educational, and social activities such as banquets, excursions to Canada,
musicales, and naturalization programs (including evening courses in
English).

Similar Franco-American organizations without insurance benefits also
sprang up, for example:

Cercle Canadien—Fall River and Southbridge, Massachusetts (1876); Bidde-
ford, Maine (1902)
Cercle Montcalm—Fall River, Massachusetts (1868)
Cercle National—Manchester, New Hampshire (1895)
Cercle Rochambeau—Holyoke, Massachusetts (1900)
Club Calumet—Fall River, Massachusetts (1909)
Club Jolliet—Manchester, New Hampshire (1884)
Club Littéraire Musical—Lewiston, Maine (1888)
Corporation des Membres de l'Association Catholique—Lowell, Massachusetts
(1878)
Ligue des Patriotes—Fall River (1886) and New Bedford, Massachusetts (1902)

It is believed that by 1900, over four hundred such organizations had
been founded in New England.[109] Many initially held their meetings in
parish or public halls but later acquired their own building, for example,
the five-storied Saint John the Baptist Hall in Biddeford (1896) and the
wooden Corporation des Membres de l'Association Catholique (CMAC)
in Lowell (1900).[110]

Women's groups began to appear at the turn of the century. There were
female Société Saint-Jean-Baptiste and Union St-Joseph mutuals in Springfield, Massachusetts, in 1901 and 1902, respectively.[111] The Cercle Jeanne
Mance of Worcester was founded in 1913.[112]

One of the major events every year was the Saint John the Baptist Day
celebration organized by Franco-American clubs and societies. In large cities there was usually a mass followed by a parade, a picnic, and speeches.
On one memorable occasion in Lowell in 1881, the procession included
two thousand marchers, 150 carriages, and many bands and floats.[113]

Musical ensembles were very popular, and parishes often had their own
organizations. Among the earliest were Pierre Painchaud's band at Biddeford, Maine, in 1872, and J. R. Lafricain's Bande Canadienne at Manchester, New Hampshire, in 1874.[114] In Lewiston, Maine, the Fanfare St-
Dominique was formed in 1894, the Fanfare Ste-Cécile in 1896, and the
Orphéon in 1912.[115]

Many amateur theatrical groups were also formed, the earliest on record
being the Club Dramatique at Marlboro, Massachusetts, in 1868.[116] Another group of Franco-American thespians performed the following year
in a church basement at Worcester. The first French play at Lowell was
produced in 1870, at Southbridge in 1876.[117] According to one tally, some
150 Franco-American dramatic groups performed no fewer than nine hundred plays from 1868 to 1930. Usually comedies and melodramas, these
compositions were mostly works by French or French-Canadian authors,
or translations. More than fifty Franco-American plays are known but
most have never been published.[118]

French, French-Canadian, and Franco-American troupes also toured

New England about this time.[119] In *Mirbah,* Emma Dumas described the emotions of fictitious working-class Franco-Americans from Holyoke who attended a play called *Repentir,* said to have been presented on tour at Gilmore's Court Square Theatre in nearby Springfield in 1889. Many claimed the performances by local theatrical groups at the Opera in Holyoke were just as good.[120]

Operettas were popular. For example, Robert Blanquette's *Les cloches de Corneville* was performed at Lewiston in 1904, 1912, and 1940, and at Holyoke in 1908 and 1926. (It was revived at Lewiston on April 29–30, 1983.)[121]

Mention should also be made of the hundreds of séances, or pageants—many of them including skits or playlets in French performed by schoolchildren—that were a fixture in every Franco-American parish until World War II.

Founded in 1899, the Société Historique Franco-Américaine was an early effort to highlight French, French-Canadian, and Franco-American contributions to the development of the United States.[122] Its meetings also afforded useful interaction with local French natives and visitors from France. In many Franco-American centers, the area's Alliance Française served the same purpose.[123] A chapter of this association was active in Lowell as early as 1902.

The Franco-American brigade

In the latter part of the nineteenth century, paramilitary units were formed throughout the United States to foster patriotism and preparedness. Many were affiliated with state militias which lent them equipment. Franco-Americans constituted many such groups, which drilled regularly, marched in parades, and served as honor guards on ceremonial occasions. Each of these organizations, called a *garde,* was named for a French or French-Canadian hero (e.g., the Garde Napoléon at Fall River, Massachusetts, and the Garde Montcalm at Manchester, New Hampshire) or the parish to which its members belonged (the Garde St-Joseph at Fitchburg, Massachusetts). One of the earliest units was the Garde Lafayette founded at Manchester in 1887. In 1916 it was called up by President Woodrow Wilson during the Mexican Border Campaign.[124]

A separate organization, the Papal or Pontifical Zouaves, noted for its colorful uniforms, also attracted a number of Franco-Americans. One unit was established at Manchester in 1887 but only lasted a few years.[125] (The international force by the same name, which defended Pope Pius IX, was organized in 1860 and disbanded in 1871.)

In 1906 twenty-three groups of guards united to form the Brigade des Volontaires Franco-Américains. It had three regiments complete with band

and drum and bugle corps. Annual three-day encampments were held around Labor Day. In 1911 it boasted eleven hundred members.[126] Shortly before the United States declared war in 1917, the brigade sent a telegram to Wilson offering to serve as a unit.[127] However, before anything came of this, so many members volunteered on an individual basis that the brigade was disbanded. After World War I efforts were made to reestablish the brigade and to form new units. For example, in 1920 the Garde Foch was founded at Manchester. In 1930 one regiment still had three hundred members, but the vogue for such organizations was clearly past.

Credit unions

The Banque Coopérative Lafayette, founded in Fall River, Massachusetts, in 1894, is believed to have been the first financial institution in New England controlled by Franco-Americans.[128] Taking a different tack, Alphonse Desjardins, a disciple of Friedrich Wilhelm Raiffeisen, who created the first credit union in Germany in 1864, established the earliest such association (*caisse populaire*) in North America at Lévis, Quebec, in 1900.

Invited to Manchester, New Hampshire, in 1908, Desjardins helped Franco-Americans in Saint Mary's parish found the first credit union in the United States.[129] This historic bank was incorporated on April 6, 1909, as Saint Mary's Cooperative Association. More than forty credit unions were later created by Franco-Americans throughout New England.

Newspapers

According to a recent survey, no fewer than 330 Franco-American newspapers were founded from 1869 to the present day, more than half of them between 1880 and 1900, their golden age.[130]

French-language newspapers have existed in the United States since the time of the American Revolution, and several were launched in Vermont in the aftermath of the Patriote Rebellion of 1837–38. The earliest, *Le Patriote Canadien,* a weekly published in Burlington by Ludger Duvernay, lasted six months (1839–40).[131] But the first newspaper aimed at the French-Canadian immigrants in New England was *Le Protecteur Canadien*, which was published in St. Albans from 1868 to 1871.

Most Franco-American newspapers were short-lived, had a tiny circulation, and produced little or no effect. A number were printed with one occasion in mind or transformed to serve a particular purpose. For example, in 1892 Benjamin Lenthier purchased or founded nineteen Franco-American newspapers with the financial banking of Josiah Quincy, wealthy secretary of the National Democratic party, in the campaign to elect Grover Cleveland president of the United States. After the election, the newspapers, which had all been published at Lowell for distribution throughout New England, folded.[132] Others, however, were high-minded undertakings that exerted a lasting influence on Franco-American history.

Ferdinand Gagnon (1849–86), who founded several newspapers beginning with *La Voix du Peuple* at Manchester in 1869, is regarded as the father of Franco-American journalism.[133] His years at the helm of *Le Travailleur* in Worcester from 1874 to 1886 climaxed a brilliant career that was cut short by his untimely death at the age of thirty-six. Initially ambivalent on the question of naturalization—he was employed by the Quebec government to promote repatriation[134]—Gagnon became a United States citizen in 1882. Impulsive and contentious (he was a bitter adversary of fellow publisher Honoré Beaugrand who once challenged him to a duel), this big hulk of a man threw himself heart and soul into a host of Franco-American endeavors and left a durable legacy of fine editorials.

In addition to *Le Travailleur,* which, unlike much of the other French-language press, was widely read throughout New England, the chief newspapers of the day were:

Le Jean-Baptiste, Northampton, Massachusetts (1875)
Le Messager, Lewiston, Maine (1880)
Le National, Plattsburgh, New York (1883); Lowell, Massachusetts (1890)
L'Indépendant, Fall River, Massachusetts (1885)
L'Etoile, Lowell, Massachusetts (1886)
L'Opinion Publique, Worcester, Massachusetts (1893)
L'Avenir National, Manchester, New Hampshire (1894)
La Tribune, Woonsocket, Rhode Island (1895)
La Justice, Biddeford, Maine (1896)
L'Impartial, Nashua, New Hampshire (1898)
Le Courrier, Lawrence, Massachusetts (1899)
Le Courrier, Salem, Massachusetts (1902)
La Justice, Holyoke, Massachusetts (1902)
Le Citoyen, Haverhill, Massachusetts (1906)
La Liberté, Fitchburg, Massachusetts (1908)
Le Lynnois, Lynn, Massachusetts (1910)

Le Messager typifies this early journalism.[135] Founded in 1880 by Louis J. Martel, an energetic and politically ambitious young doctor, the weekly presented a Franco-American world view, that is, a potpourri of articles chronicling the group's many activities locally and throughout New England as organized by a small but influential middle class, and reviewing Canadian news of the day. Occurrences outside this sphere were mentioned in passing, but what really mattered was Franco-American life and the furtherance of its ideology. In politics, *Le Messager* was a staunch supporter of the Democratic party. The newspaper was placed on a solid business footing by Jean-Baptiste Couture, who became its editor-proprietor in 1892, increased its circulation and frequency of publication to biweekly, and expanded its coverage of sports, and national and world events. One of the most successful Franco-American journalistic efforts, the venerable *Messager* published its last issue in 1968.

The repatriation movement

After years of indecision, Quebec finally acted in 1875 to encourage French-Canadian immigrants to return home.[136] The preceding year, repatriation had been one of the hot topics at a mammoth Saint John the Baptist Day meeting in Montreal attended by thousands of Franco-Americans. Over the next half century, repatriation efforts by the governments of Quebec and Canada assumed various forms but consisted mainly of offers of free or inexpensive farmland in the Saguenay–Lake St. John area, the eastern townships, the Gaspé region, western Canada, or the Maritime Provinces. Colonization societies were organized in Montreal (1879) and Quebec City (1880).[137] Sometimes special railroad cars or fare rebates were provided. Many agents were hired to visit Franco-American population centers, give lectures, and offer assistance. A number of journalists, notably Ferdinand Gagnon, respected editor of *Le Travailleur,* played a key role in this movement. The economic benefits of repatriation were stressed, but these were usually accompanied by appeals to patriotism.

One of the target cities was Biddeford, Maine, site of several huge textile mills with a history of layoffs and low wages.[138] In 1898, 60 percent of the mill city's population was Franco-American. The campaign here featured visits by noted French-Canadian clergymen, including the legendary Curé Antoine Labelle, the hiring of a Biddeford native as a resident agent for sixteen years beginning in 1899, and the publication of weekly or monthly advertisements from 1907 to 1914, and then from 1918 to 1922, in *La Justice,* the city's popular French-language newspaper. The editor, Alfred Bonneau, was an agent of the Colonization Society of Montreal and an earnest advocate of repatriation.

It has been estimated that fully half of the French Canadians who emigrated to New England before 1900 subsequently returned to Quebec.[139] While difficult to gauge the effect the repatriation campaign may have had on this vast population shift, the ideas that furthered this cause fueled anti-French-Canadian sentiment among nativists who asserted that the possibility of returning home delayed assimilation for many of those who elected to settle permanently in New England.

The Amoskeag Manu-
facturing Company and,
in the distance, Saint
Mary's Church, Man-
chester, New Hamp-
shire, in 1927. When
photographer Ulric
Bourgeois (1874–
1963) recorded this
scene, parish and mill
dominated Franco-
American life. Today
many Franco-American
values and ideals can be
traced back to this en-
vironment and to rural
French Canada at the
turn of the century.
(Courtesy Department
of Media Services, Di-
mond Library, Univer-
sity of New Hamp-
shire.)

Massicotte's depictions
of French-Canadian cus-
toms not only convey a
sense of time and place—
turn-of-the-century
Quebec—but also ideal-
ize traditional ways.
This portrayal of the solemn New Year's Day
blessing underlines fam-
ily solidarity and respect
for elders.

In this sketch showing
the curé bringing the
eucharist to a parishio-
ner in danger of death,
Massicotte places em-
phasis on rural French-
Canadian reverence for
priests, glossing over relations that were not in-
frequently tense.

At the turn of the century, most Franco-Americans returned home at least once a year to visit relatives. On one such trip about 1908, Bourgeois photographed the farmhouse and connecting barn where his wife's family lived at Valcourt d'Ely, a few miles northwest of Sherbrooke, Quebec. (Courtesy Department of Media Services, Dimond Library, University of New Hampshire.)

Interior of the Laverdure summer kitchen at Valcourt d'Ely showing a woman drawing out and twisting wool fiber into thread with the aid of a foot-driven spinning wheel. (Courtesy Department of Media Services, Dimond Library, University of New Hampshire.)

Illustrations by Marc-Aurèle Suzor-Côté (1869–1937) of the 1916 edition of Louis Hémon's *Maria Chapdelaine*, a tale of pioneer life in the Lake Saint John country. Here farmers are depicted in homespun work clothes.

Massicotte's 1919 drawing of rural folk returning home by moonlight after midnight mass captures the mood of the traditional French-Canadian Christmas celebration.

As Lent approached, French Canadians fortified themselves with celebrations. Massicotte's sketch, drawn in 1911, depicts country people making the rounds of neighboring homes on Ash Wednesday eve.

Family gatherings in the evening were often enlivened with singing and dancing. The veilleux in Massicotte's 1915 drawing are dressed in their Sunday best and the two couples are said to be dancing a gigue carrée. The musical accompaniment is provided by a violoneux.

Massicotte portrays a wedding party arriving at the bride's home for the traditional reception following the marriage ceremony. The bride dismounting from the buggy, which has a calash or folding top, is decked out in a muslin dress trimmed with *falbalas* (flounces).

Calixa Lavallée, talented musician and composer, was born at Sainte-Théodosie near Verchères, Quebec, in 1842. He ran away from home at the age of 15, joined a traveling minstrel show at New Orleans, and, in 1861, enlisted as a trumpeter in the Fourth Rhode Island Regiment. Wounded in the leg at Antietam (1862), he settled at Montreal but, in 1882, returned to New England. He died in Boston at the age of 49, having composed, among other marches and songs, "O Canada," which would later become the national anthem of Canada. (Courtesy Archives Nationales du Québec.)

Born in Lanoraie, Quebec, Honoré Beaugrand (1848–1906) was an inveterate traveler from the age of seventeen when he joined the French forces who had occupied Mexico City. He worked as a journalist in France and in the United States where, while a resident of Fall River, Massachusetts, he wrote *Jeanne la fileuse*, the first Franco-American novel (1878). Twice mayor of Montreal (1886 and 1887), Beaugrand published numerous travel accounts and folktales. (From Beaugrand, *Jeanne La Fileuse*, ed. Roger Le Moine.)

This interior view of the Bourgeois home in Manchester, New Hampshire, about 1905— evidently at Christmastime—suggests that the young photographer and his family led a reasonably comfortable existence. (Courtesy Department of Media Services, Dimond Library, University of New Hampshire.)

The Harris, corner of Hall and Aiken Streets, an example of an overcrowded tenement house in Lowell's Little Canada in 1912. (From Kenngott, *Record of a City*.)

One of the rare photographs of the interior of a mill worker's tenement, this picture of Alfred Benoît's home in New Bedford was taken by Lewis W. Hine in January 1912 for the National Child Labor Committee of New York. (Courtesy Library of Congress.)

Mamie Laberge at her machine, Winchendon, Massachusetts, September 1911. Hine noted that Mamie belonged to a family of thirteen, nine of whom worked in the Spring Village Mill. (Courtesy Library of Congress.)

Joseph Rouillard (the proprietor of Rouillard's Grocery) and his family in front of their home on Cochran Street, Chicopee Falls, Massachusetts, about 1918. (Courtesy Rouillard family.)

Assumption College began in this small building in Greendale, a suburb of Worcester, Massachusetts, in 1904. Founded by the Augustinians of the Assumption, a French religious order, it eventually became the most important Franco-American educational institution. (From Marcelin A. Parent, *An Album of Assumption Life 1904–1954* [n.p., 1954].)

Seal of the Association Canado-Américaine. (The arm and hammer and fasces in the middle of the shield represent the City of Manchester and the State of New Hampshire, respectively.) The first successful attempt at forming a federation of Franco-American mutual benefit societies, the ACA, like other similar organizations, provides insurance but also fosters group consciousness and pride and affords many opportunities for socializing. (Courtesy Association Canado-Américaine.)

Photograph taken at the foundation of the Union Saint-Jean-Baptiste d'Amérique, Woonsocket, Rhode Island, in 1900. From its inception, the Union has been one of the bulwarks of survivance in New England. (Courtesy Union Saint-Jean-Baptiste d'Amérique.)

Bronze medal of the Société Historique Franco-Américaine. Designed by Franco-American sculptor Lucien H. Gosselin in 1934, it represents the allegorical figures of Marianne (France) and Columbia (United States). The reverse side shows an open book (Science), a torch (Truth), and a laurel wreath, and bears the Latin words Lux (Light) and Veritas (Truth). (From *BSHFA* [1936].)

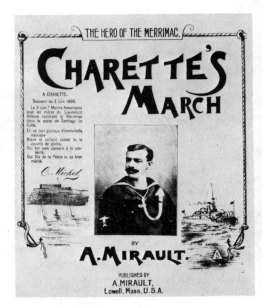

George Charette of Lowell, Massachusetts, Spanish-American War hero. (From Santerre, *Franco-Americans of Lowell*.)

Dame Emma Lajeunesse, whose stage name was Albani, was one of the leading prima donnas of her time. She was an intimate friend of Queen Victoria and other royalty, and her concerts throughout Europe and North America were notable successes. (Livernois Studio, Quebec City, courtesy of Archives Nationales du Québec, Quebec City.)

Famous French-Canadian strongman Louis Cyr had close ties with Lowell, Massachusetts. (From Santerre, *Franco-Americans of Lowell*.)

Saint Anne's Church, Fall River, Massachusetts, one of the strongholds of French-Canadian survivance in New England. (Courtesy St. Anne's Church, Fall River, Mass.)

A tablet in the National Baseball Hall of Fame and Museum in Cooperstown, New York, describes Napoleon Lajoie as a "great hitter and most graceful and effective second-baseman of his era." (Courtesy National Baseball Library, Cooperstown, N.Y.)

Elphège-J. Daignault, crusading editor of *La Sentinelle* and President of the Association Canado-Américaine from 1922 to 1936, was the acknowledged leader of a group of militants who contended with the Bishop of Providence, Rhode Island, in the most controversial episode in Franco-American history. (Courtesy Association Canado-Américaine.)

For nearly a half century, Wilfrid Beaulieu, editor of *Le Travailleur*, advocated a hard-line policy toward assimilationism. Unyielding in his opinions, he campaigned tirelessly against those he perceived as undermining the group's solidarity, irritating many but leaving a legacy of dedication to the Franco-American cause. (Courtesy Boston Public Library.)

First Aubuchon Hardware Store, Fitchburg, Massachusetts, in 1908. (Courtesy Aubuchon family.)

moi ne   la voi le   a voi ne

La peti te poi re, la toi tu re de la ca-
ba ne, la voi le du na vi re, le voi le de la
veu ve, la ro be de toi le de l'A ra be, la
joie de l'â me pu re. Soi gne ma bê te. La
pou le *est* à moi. La boî te est à toi.
A mé dée fe ra boi re l'â ne. Le roi rè gne.

goûte la joie de l'âme pure.

(1) La grande sœur dit : Pouah ! que c'est vilain **de fumer la cigarette** !

Above left: *La Lecture par la
méthode phonique*, a widely-
used primer in Franco-
American schools, had an
unequivocally religious
theme. *Above*: The vileness
of smoking was drummed
into the heads of Franco-
American children along
with the ABCs.

The church at L'Acadie, Quebec,
today. Built by Acadian refugees in
1800, this remarkable edifice has been
designated a historical landmark.
(Jacques Paul [courtesy of Pierre
Brault], L'Acadie, Québec.)

General view of the
Greendale campus
of Assumption High
School and College
in the 1930s. (From
Parent, *An Album of
Assumption Life*.)

Family and friends at the celebration following the wedding of Frédéric and Eugénie (Boivin) Brault at La-colle, Quebec, in 1908. The photograph was taken on the front porch of the bridegroom's parents' home. The newly-weds—who were married at nearby Ile-aux-Noix—are seated in the back row framed by two columns. Philias (Frédéric's brother) and, on his right, his future wife Bernadette Cor-bière are immediately in front of the couple. (Courtesy A. L. Bi-saillon, Lacolle, Quebec.)

Philias and Aline (Ré-millard) Brault, the au-thor's parents, about 1960. (Courtesy Hausa-mann, Steiger's Studio, Springfield, Mass.)

Brault-Pepin family gathering at the shore in Rhode Island, 1984.

Quilt designed and sewn by the author's wife in 1984, showing memorable events in the history of the Brault family. (Courtesy Graphic and Photographic Services, Pennsylvania State University.)

UNION SAINT-JEAN-BAPTISTE

The evolution of the emblem of the Union Saint-Jean-Baptiste d'Amérique from the early device, which is still the society's official seal, to its modern logo reflects changes in public taste over the years. (Courtesy Union Saint-Jean-Baptiste d'Amérique.)

Paul M. Paré, energetic secretary of ActFANE, keeps people informed about developments on the Franco-American scene and strives to coordinate as many of these activities as possible. (Courtesy ActFANE.)

Edgar J. Martel, president of the Union Saint-Jean-Baptiste d'Amérique, has been largely instrumental in rejuvenating this powerful fraternal organization and placing it on sounder financial ground. (Courtesy The Greniers, Holyoke-Springfield, Mass.)

Eugène A. Lemieux, president of the Association Canado-Américaine, has injected new life into this fraternal benefit society, which exercises great influence on the Franco-American group today. (Courtesy Association Canado-Américaine.)

One of the key persons in the current revival in Franco-Américanie, Claire Quintal is professor of French at Assumption College and director of its French Institute. A native of Central Falls, Rhode Island, she has lectured and written extensively on French, French-Canadian, and Franco-American culture. (Courtesy Patrick O'Connor, Central Massachusetts Media, Inc.)

Yvon Labbé, editor-in-chief of *Le FAROG Forum*, deserves praise for having developed a small bilingual sheet at the University of Maine at Orono into a major newspaper addressing issues that concern all Franco-Americans. (Courtesy Al Pelletier, University of Maine Public Information.)

Some early disasters

Before laws were passed in the present century protecting laborers against injury, factories were dangerous places to work. In Lawrence, Massachusetts, for example, one textile mill is reported to have had one thousand accidents in less than five years.[140]

One of the earliest tragedies involving French-Canadian immigrants occurred during the Civil War in the gunpowder works owned by Col. Augustus G. Hazard in Enfield, Connecticut. On July 23, 1862, nine persons were killed in an explosion, including at least two French Canadians, Edward Grandmont, twenty-two, and Leonard Manseau, twenty-six.[141] The Granite Mill fire in Fall River, Massachusetts, on September 19, 1874, that claimed twenty-three lives, several of them French Canadians, is described in Beaugrand's *Jeanne la fileuse* (1878), the first Franco-American novel.[142]

Probably the greatest disaster of the time involving French Canadians occurred at Holyoke, Massachusetts. At 5:00 P.M. on May 27, 1875, fire broke out during Corpus Christi devotions in a crowded temporary chapel of Precious Blood parish. Fifty-one persons died immediately, of which only three could be positively identified. Later deaths raised the total to ninety-six fatalities. Forty-eight of the victims were buried in a common grave in Precious Blood cemetery.[143] A fifty-five-page account of the incident, illustrated with woodcuts from a contemporary newspaper story, is found in Emma Dumas's *Mirbah* (1910–12).[144]

On the afternoon and evening of June 25, 1914, flames fanned by shifting winds ravaged more than three square miles of Salem, Massachusetts, causing four deaths and leaving an estimated eighteen thousand persons homeless. The congested area of South Salem near the Naumkeag Cotton Mills, inhabited by an overwhelming majority of the city's Franco-Americans, was most directly affected. Newly constructed Saint Joseph's Church and nearby school and convent buildings were completely destroyed.[145]

Celebrities

Many clergymen, newspaper editors, organization leaders, and individuals engaged in business, politics, and the professions became well known in Franco-American circles.[146] A few who acquired a reputation beyond the group have been mentioned earlier. Five others also achieved renown.

Emma Lajeunesse (1847–1930), born in Chambly, Quebec, was a popular concert artist and opera singer whose stage name (Albani) may have been suggested by Albany, New York, where she lived for several years during her adolescence with her immigrant family. (She herself, however, claimed the name honored her voice teacher, the Italian Del Lorenzo Albani.) She performed outstandingly at the Covent Garden in London from 1874 to 1896 and, in the early 1890s, was also given prominent billing at the Metropolitan Opera House in New York.[147]

George Charette (1867–1938) of Lowell, Massachusetts, was a seaman aboard the U.S.S. *New York* when the Spanish-American War broke out in 1898. After volunteering for combat duty, he was transferred to the U.S.S. *San Francisco* which participated in the mining of the harbor of Santiago de Cuba in an effort to blockade the Spanish fleet. Early on the morning of June 3, he was one of eight volunteers, led by Lt. Richard P. Hobson, who, in spite of withering fire from the enemy, succeeded in positioning the U.S.S. *Merrimac* and sinking it so as to further bottle up the Spanish force. Charette, who was awarded the Congressional Medal of Honor for this daring deed, continued to serve with distinction in the United States Navy and rose to the rank of lieutenant.[148] In 1942 a Liberty ship was named in his honor.[149]

Louis Cyr (1863–1912), born in Napierville, Quebec, was fifteen years old when his family moved to Lowell in 1878. He worked a year in a textile mill in that city and then on a nearby farm. Endowed with a powerful physique and a knack for showmanship, he embarked upon a career as a professional weight lifter. Billed as the Strongest Man in the World and accompanied by a troupe of acrobats and other performers, including his wife Mélina Comtois, the three-hundred-pound colossus toured Quebec and New England in the 1880s and 1890s giving demonstrations of prodigious strength. In 1892 he took his act to London; in 1896 his feat of lifting on his back a platform holding thirty persons seated on chairs was featured in P. T. Barnum's circus. Plagued with asthma and nephritis, Cyr retired in 1897 to a farm near Montreal and lived on an exclusively milk diet the last twelve years of his life.[150]

Napoleon "Larry" Lajoie (1875–1959) of Woonsocket, Rhode Island, was one of the best second basemen in the history of baseball. Known for his graceful movements and his batting consistency (lifetime average .339), Lajoie—sportswriters and fans pronounced his name Lah-joe-way—had a twenty-one-year career in the majors in Philadelphia and Cleveland from 1896 to 1916, led the American League in batting in 1901, 1903, and 1904, and was elected to the Baseball Hall of Fame in 1937.[151]

Eva Tanguay (1878–1947), outstanding vaudeville and musical comedy headliner in the early part of the century, was born in Marbleton, Quebec, but raised in grinding poverty in Holyoke, Massachusetts. As a child she won first prize in a local amateur night and soon embarked upon a highly successful career in show business. She was the star of Florenz

Ziegfeld's *Follies of 1909,* but she is best remembered as the "I Don't Care Girl," from a number she sang in the Broadway play *The Chaperones* in 1904. She made a fortune, earning as much as $3,500 a week with song and dance routines considered daring in her day, such as "I Want Someone to Go Wild with Me" and "It's All Been Done Before But Not the Way I Do It." However, she went through her money rapidly and experienced spectacular losses in the stock market crash of 1929. Although bedridden by severe ailments for the last ten years of her life, she maintained to the end an appearance of gaiety and insouciance.[152]

Music

For approximately forty years beginning in the 1890s, Eusèbe and Philias Champagne of Lowell, Massachusetts, composed and performed popular music for all occasions.[153] A third brother, Octave, contributed lyrics for many of their songs, including such ditties as "L'amour c'est comme la salade" (1916).

The catalog of the Orion Publishing Company, founded by the Champagne brothers in 1922—their music began appearing in print about 1912—listed nearly sixty titles together with numerous phonograph recordings and player-piano rolls, and included works by another Lowell composer, Louis Napoléon Guilbault, author of the "Lowell March" (1936) and popular French songs such as "Bravo" and "Si belle."[154] Philias, the last surviving Champagne brother, died at Lowell in 1957.

The Champagne brothers' music was revived at a public concert given at the University of Lowell in 1978. In 1982 a collection of their sheet music was acquired by the Lowell Public Library.

Architecture

Scores of churches, a number of them of cathedral-like majesty, were built by Franco-Americans during this period and the next. Many were adorned with beautiful altarpieces, wood carvings, and paintings. The grandest edifices include Notre Dame of Southbridge, Massachusetts; Saint Anne of Fall River, Massachusetts; and Saints Peter and Paul of Lewiston, Maine. Magnificent Notre Dame de Lourdes of Fall River, Massachusetts, constructed from 1890 to 1906 and housing important paintings and wood carvings, was destroyed by fire on May 11, 1982.[155] The splendid wooden altarpiece in Saint Joseph's of Cohoes, New York—the church was begun in 1874—also deserves special mention.[156]

3

THE MIDDLE
PHASE, 1920 – 1960

Most Franco-Americans who grew up between the two world wars were raised by parents who clung to traditional ways; but sooner or later, like the children of other ethnics, they came into contact with mores and values that were different from those learned in the home. The process of acculturation was stressful and often left psychological scars. Many, for example, would never get over being ridiculed for their accent in English or for cultural faux pas. Even so, a large number of Franco-Americans managed the transition, convinced that biculturalism was a good thing.

Franco-American institutions were solid and well entrenched during the 1920s and 1930s. Vigorous parish life, schools, organizations of all sorts, and newspapers attested to the group's vitality. However, the élan that animated these undertakings gradually spent itself. Crises of various sorts explain in part this decline, but the inability of the group's leaders to clearly define modern Franco-American culture and to provide programs capable of forcefully engaging the attention of the younger generation were also responsible.

Unsettling as this decline was, it did not, as many predicted, presage the end. When, in the 1960s, new leaders began to emerge and to give fresh impetus to the Franco-American movement, they discovered that many of the old structures were in need of repair but still intact, testifying to the remarkable achievements of the earlier effort.

Ideology

The economic and social changes brought about by World War I and the stepped-up campaigns, during and after the conflict, of such groups as the American Legion, the Daughters of the American Revolution, and the League of Women Voters to Americanize immigrants affected life in the Little Canadas of New England.[1]

Among Franco-American leaders, whether to make an all-out effort to counter these influences or to take a more moderate stance was a central question. How much survivance was possible? New England was not Quebec where French Canadians were the dominant group and enjoyed special rights guaranteed them by law and custom. Most Franco-Americans recognized that resisting all forms of assimilation was neither practical nor possible. But to safeguard the essential part of their cultural heritage, they continued to build their many institutions, especially those at the parish level. Large families were encouraged, and greater attention was focused on fostering ethnic pride in the home. Traditional family life was increasingly viewed as a cornerstone of survivance.[2]

On a number of occasions, Franco-Americans united against efforts by federal and state governments to curtail the use of foreign languages as a medium of instruction in private schools. For example, in 1921 they strongly opposed passage of a law in Rhode Island, introduced by Republican state representative Frederick Peck, stipulating that private schools could not be certified unless there was "thorough and efficient" teaching in English of all subjects offered in the public schools.[3] In 1923 the United States Supreme Court, in *Meyer v. Nebraska* (262 U.S. 390), invalidated all such acts as infringing upon the Fourteenth Amendment ("No State shall . . . deprive any person of life, liberty, or property, without due process of law").[4]

About this time, Franco-American leaders seized upon the notion of cultural pluralism—the theory had been advanced as early as 1900 by Edmond de Nevers,[5] and was now also being promoted by other ethnic groups—and succeeded in co-opting the Americanization issue.[6] But the heady optimism of the early 1920s was greatly dampened by the Sentinelle Affair and the Wall Street stock market crash as the decade drew to a close. Cracks now appeared in the Franco-American edifice.

The Sentinelle Affair

A bitter five-year public quarrel, named after a French-language newspaper in Woonsocket, Rhode Island, that figured in the controversy, pitted moderate against militant Franco-Americans in the mid-1920s. The disagreement centered around survivance strategy and, above all, around the proper response to growing pressure from the Irish-dominated Catholic hierarchy to support diocesan fund drives.[7]

These campaigns, perceived by militants led by lawyer-editor Elphège-J. Daignault (1879–1937) as a plot to anglicize and ultimately to assimilate national parishes, culminated in a pew-rental strike, the removal of W. A. Prince, embattled pastor of Saint Louis parish in Woonsocket, and, finally, in 1928, in the shocking excommunication of sixty-two Sentinellistes who had initiated or supported a civil suit against Bishop William Hickey. All signed repentance forms the following year, ringing the death knell of the movement.

The struggle was centered in Woonsocket—Sentinellistes were particularly in evidence in Saint Louis and Saint Anne parishes there—but attracted partisans from other parts of Rhode Island, notably Central Falls and Pawtucket; New England, especially Manchester, New Hampshire, and Worcester, Massachusetts; and even Quebec.

Elie Vézina, secretary-general of the Union Saint-Jean-Baptiste d'Amérique, took a firm stand against the Sentinellistes; many officers of the Association Canado-Américaine were in the opposite camp. However, few parish priests became involved, at least openly, in the dispute. As each event transpired, extensive coverage in the local, regional, and even national press occasioned discomfiture or jubilation for many Franco-Americans, depending on their point of view.[8]

The Sentinellistes struck a responsive chord in many ordinary Franco-Americans: at the height of the crisis, in 1927, approximately ten thousand turned out for a protest rally in Woonsocket. The controversy is far from forgotten today, especially by certain stalwarts.[9] And muted echoes of the affair reverberated in Worcester's *Le Travailleur,* founded in 1931 by the legendary Wilfrid Beaulieu (1900–79), until it ceased publication in 1978.[10]

Mount Saint Charles Academy

In the years immediately following World War I, Mount Saint Charles Academy in Woonsocket, Rhode Island, was conceived of as a Franco-American diocesan school specializing in business and technology.[11] Funds were raised for the institution—the Union Saint-Jean-Baptiste d'Amérique contributed over $500,000—as part of a drive designed to settle debts incurred by more than a score of Franco-American parishes in the Diocese of Providence. Founded in 1924 by the Brothers of the Sacred Heart as a day and boarding secondary school for boys, Mount Saint Charles became the target of much Sentinelliste invective as militants claimed its program and atmosphere were not sufficiently French.[12] The school soon severed its ties with the diocese but for years continued to emphasize French.

Known throughout the area today for its strong academic program and nationally for its championship hockey teams, "The Mount" dropped its boarding program in 1972 and became coeducational in 1973. Originally a small school—enrollment in the 1920s was about 300—with a bilingual curriculum designed for students drawn almost exclusively from the Franco-American milieu, it evolved with the times and now accepts all nationalities and denominations. The school population in 1984 was 920 young men and women.[13]

Social and economic conditions

In a study of Nashua, New Hampshire, one scholar suggested that a wide difference in attitude between French-Canadian immigrants and their children developed in that city in the years 1910 to 1930 and that thereafter the generation gap widened rapidly as a result of exogamy, military service, television, and travel. According to this source, neither the clergy nor the people themselves opposed this evolution. Between 1930 and 1950 Nashua grew in size, but the Franco-American community "at best held its own during these years."[14]

In 1930, Newburyport, Massachusetts, had seventeen hundred inhabitants. Although by no means a major Franco-American center—only 8.5 percent of the population was of French-Canadian extraction—the city deserves special note as the object of a landmark study by a team of Harvard University sociologists. The authors of the six-volume Yankee City series situated 40.1 percent of Newburyport's Franco-Americans on the lowest rung of a six-step social ladder, 23.8 percent one level higher, and 15.3 percent on the third tier from the bottom (lower middle class).[15] According to this source, Franco-Americans fared poorly because many planned to return to Quebec—hence showed little interest in upward mobility—and were kept down by a patriarchal family structure and the teachings of their priests.[16] On the matter of education, the local pastor was quoted as saying about the early years of the community: "The French Canadians couldn't send their children to school because they were very poor and had large families. But they're sending all their children to school now and have done so ever since they've become established." However, influenced by narrow ideas prevalent in the rural French Canada of the day, that at times were reinforced by the Franco-American clergy, relatively few sent their children on to college.[17]

In 1933 Franco-Americans made up 75 percent of the work force in the cotton and woolen mills of Burlington, Vermont. According to one survey, 59 percent of the total Franco-American population lived in the northern part of town and 28 percent in the extreme southern district near the factories, both areas being the poorest residential sections. A number of small businessmen, for example, 27 percent of the city's grocers and 61 percent of its barbers, were Franco-Americans. Considerable occupational strides had been made by Burlington's Irish and Jewish populations, but slower progress had been realized by the Franco-Americans: 70 percent of the first generation and 50 percent of the second were laborers or mill operatives. One informed observer was quoted as saying: "It has taken the French Canadian three generations to get out and achieve what the Irishman did in one; namely, build himself a nice home, plan a good education for his children, and strive to better himself in his work."[18]

An analysis of Woonsocket, Rhode Island, public school children and their parents in 1926 revealed that intermarriage was not as frequent among Franco-Americans as among other nationalities. However, the percentage increased significantly in the third generation (first generation: 7.8 percent—as compared with British, 32.4; Irish, 21.8; Slavs, 7.2; Italians, 7.1; Jews, 1.8—second generation: 8.8 percent; third generation: 35 percent). Franco-Americans had the largest number of children per family (4.8) and stood out among other ethnic groups for their loyalty to their mother tongue. For example, first-generation Jews were twice as likely as French Canadians to use English routinely in the home. However, Franco-American men were ranked highest in their ability to speak English in addition to their mother tongue (78.4 percent were bilingual).[19]

The long and bitter strike of 1922 at the Amoskeag Manufacturing Company in Manchester, New Hampshire, was the beginning of the end of a way of life for many of the area's Franco-Americans. The work stoppage was precipitated by a sudden increase in working hours and a 20 percent cut in wages. Faced with a host of problems, including competition from southern mills, high labor costs, and shrinking markets, most New England textile companies experienced similar difficulties and responded in similar ways.[20] The industry's steady decline in the years that followed, coupled with the inception of the Great Depression, led to a series of plant shutdowns. In Massachusetts's Connecticut Valley alone, seventeen textile mills, employing 57.5 percent of the region's industrial workers, closed between 1929 and 1933. In the latter year, 25.1 percent of Chicopee's population was on relief.[21]

It is believed that 10,580 persons (13.5 percent of the city's inhabitants) left Manchester in the 1920s, in large measure due to the strike of 1922. When the Amoskeag shut down operations in 1935, more than eleven thousand persons, about half of them Franco-Americans, were left without work. A study based upon interviews with a thousand former Amoskeag employees, questioned a year or more after the shutdown, revealed that only 24.6 percent of those who left Manchester in the 1920s—of this number a mere 18 percent were Franco-Americans—moved outside of New England. Even fewer (16.8 percent) did so after the depression began.[22]

Out-of-work families subsisted by using up their savings, borrowing money from relatives and friends, cashing in insurance policies (in one survey, 33 percent were forced to surrender all their policies), taking in boarders or roomers, moving to cheaper lodgings, and cutting down on expenditures. Before federal relief programs went into effect in 1933, public assistance varied from community to community. Some communities provided money for basic necessities, others dispensed supplies at central commissaries.[23] Wages in New England textile mills were never very high after World War I; but after the depression began, earnings fell. For example, in 1923, the median annual wage for all Amoskeag operatives was only $805; by 1934 it had declined to $577. In both cases, unskilled workers received much less.[24]

Franco-American businessmen and professionals began to see a need to form networks. Founded in 1922, the Calumet Club of Augusta, Maine, eventually became a leading civic and social organization. Until World War II, membership was strictly limited; no one engaged in an *occupation salissante,* that is, work likely to soil hands or clothes, was permitted to join. The organization sponsored many social events and entertained prominent political and sports personalities.[25]

In 1934, in the depths of the depression, the Aubuchon Hardware Company was incorporated and began the spectacular rise that made it one of the best-known Franco-American success stories.[26] William E. Aubuchon (1885–1971) emigrated to Fitchburg, Massachusetts, in 1898 at the age of thirteen. The eldest of four children—his mother had been widowed when she was twenty-four—he found a job in the Orswell Cotton Mill. After working there and in another mill in nearby Leominster for eight years, he used a $500 inheritance to purchase a small hardware store in the Cleghorn section of Fitchburg in 1908. He opened a second store in Fitchburg in 1917, then a branch store in Worcester in 1920. With 124 outlets in New England and New York State today, the Aubuchon Hardware Company is the largest merchant hardware chain in the United States. William E. Aubuchon, Jr., of Fitchburg, president of the family-owned company since 1950, has a long and distinguished record of involvement in Franco-American affairs. A cousin, Jacques Aubuchon, starred in ten Broadway plays, over twenty feature films, and more than three hundred television shows.

Education

Franco-American culture today is largely the product of an extensive school system that flourished in the period between World War I and World War II. More than any other institution, the elementary schools, founded and maintained by separate parishes, influenced and shaped individuals and gave them a sense of belonging to the Franco-American group.[27] Although far from uniform, they provided a common experience, fostered similar attitudes, and, above all, promoted identical values. Drastic changes would later occur in these schools, but traces and, at times, strong evidence of the pedagogy and philosophy of education that characterized them persist to this day in their successors.

The local pastor was generally very much involved with his parochial school. He visited classes, gave out report cards, presided at ceremonial occasions, and controlled the budget. But the school was administered and staffed by a religious community, usually a teaching order of nuns, which made a long-term commitment to serve the parish. There were minor skirmishes, of course, but as a rule parish priests and sisters saw eye to eye on school policy, and parents strongly supported their school and all its activities.

Franco-Americans considered their schools to be flatly superior to public institutions because their curricula included religious education, moral training, and French-language instruction. From the pulpit the pastor hammered home this message, making it clear that parents were morally obligated to send their children to parochial schools. A cold war isolated public and parochial schools. Public school teachers tended to regard their French-Canadian or Franco-American counterparts as poorly trained, doctrinaire, and insufficiently civic minded. They believed Franco-American establishments graduated children who had been given a narrow education and could not speak proper English. In many public schools, notably in strongly Francophone areas such as the St. John Valley in northern Maine, children were forbidden to speak French and reprimanded by teachers if overheard using that language.

On the other hand, religious considered public schools to be institutions where de facto Protestantism reigned and where discipline was entirely lacking. On both sides, anecdotes and, at times, evidence of a sort circulated, buttressing these views. It would be years before relations between the two systems were marked by mutual respect and good will. Franco-American children rarely associated with public school students. And although they sometimes longed for more freedom, Franco-American children were usually convinced that their programs were as superior as represented to them.

The method of teaching employed in Franco-American parochial schools owed much to the *Ratio Studiorum,* or plan of studies worked out by the Jesuits in the sixteenth century. This relationship is clear, for instance, in the case of the Ursulines, where the following practices were common: the review at the start of each period of what had been covered in the preceding class, the emphasis on memorization, and the principle of emulation and rewards (contests, honor rolls, prizes, rankings) to stimulate effort. One of the hallmarks of Franco-American education, firm discipline, was also a cherished Jesuit tenet. As God's representative, the teacher was expected to exercise authority resolutely and with great vigilance, and never to give in to children, parents, or outside influences. Rules and punishments abounded. The ideal student was a docile student.[28]

A dress code and rules of conduct stressing propriety, orderliness and cleanliness—equated with civilized behavior (*agir comme du monde*)—were strictly enforced.[29] Boys dressed neatly and wore a tie. Girls were required to wear uniforms, usually dark blue dresses reaching well below the knee, often with stiff white collars and cuffs that could be removed for cleaning, and long, heavy stockings. The only acceptable ornaments were small religious medals, except girls wore a long, narrow ribbon as a tie. Its color might vary according to the liturgical calendar, for example, purple for Lent, light blue for May, the month of Mary. Culottes or slacks were forbidden, and in the winter girls were made to remove snowpants in the hallway before entering the classroom.

From the first grade on, children were expected to sit, stand, or kneel straight and still, without looking about idly, at desks bolted to the floor in precise rows, boys on one side, girls on the other.[30] They were taught to answer "Oui, ma Soeur" or "Non, ma Soeur," to say "S'il vous plaît" when asking for anything, and to rise immediately and greet guests politely: "Bonjour, ma Soeur Supérieure," "Au revoir, Monsieur le Curé." Choral salutations were in order in the latter circumstances, but the children were not to shout, drag out words, or make unnecessary noise standing or sitting down. Boys normally kept arms folded, girls hands joined as in prayer, on desktops. Absolute silence was maintained everywhere in school except when answering teachers' questions. In corridors, in the schoolyard, and on the street, boys gave priests and nuns a hand salute, girls bowed their heads respectfully.

In the morning and afternoon, children arrived promptly in the school-yard and, when the bell rang, formed ranks in silence by classes facing their teachers. A similar procedure followed recesses. At a signal from Sister Superior, each group proceeded in orderly fashion to its respective classroom and filed in row by row. In ranks, hands were held together behind the back. Upon entering the building, each boy removed his hat, held it before him over his left fist, and kept his right hand behind him.

After storing coats, hats, rubbers or overshoes, and schoolbags in designated areas, row by row, children stood by their desks. Each session began and concluded in French with standard prayers and a few short devotions depending on the season, feast day, or other circumstances. Additional prayers—always in French—were said every hour on the hour.

The rosary was prayed at least once every day; however, at times decades were spaced over several hours. The routine was varied by saying the beads standing, kneeling, or sitting. Group movements inside and outside the classroom (as well as at the children's mass on Sundays) were controlled by a sharp click from Sister's clapper, two hinged pieces of wood about one inch by three inches.

Morning prayers were immediately followed by the Pledge of Allegiance in English, facing the American flag, then by a similar oath to the Sacred Heart flag (the prototype of the flag of Quebec bearing a red Sacred Heart emblem at the center of the cross) along the following lines:

> Honneur à Toi, Noble Drapeau Carillon-Sacré-Coeur; redis-nous la foi et la vaillance de nos ancêtres; et, sur ce sol d'adoption, sois toujours le ralliement de la race canadienne-française.[31]
>
> (All honor to Thee, Noble Carillon-Sacred Heart Flag; remind us of the faith and valor of our ancestors; and, in our adoptive land, always rally the French-Canadian people.)

Children were never allowed outside the classroom except at appointed times, under the teacher's supervision, and always in ranks—once each in the morning and afternoon, to go to the bathroom and again for recess. Schoolyard play was closely monitored—boys on one side, girls on the other. At the end of the day, children were dismissed class by class and maintained ranks until they reached the edge of the school property.

The school year corresponded more or less to the public school schedule, the main difference being the spring vacation which always included the latter part of Holy Week and at least a few days after Easter. There was also no school on All Saints' Day (November 1), and the Feasts of the Immaculate Conception (December 8) and of the Ascension (forty days after Easter). Other holidays varied from school to school: a feast day of particular significance to the sisters—for example, the Presentation of Mary (November 21)—or the Monday after the annual séance, an entertainment put on by the children for their parents.

Several other days were celebrated with a special mass—school might start a half hour later than usual so that the children could attend, for example, on All Souls' Day (November 2), Saint Blaise (February 3), and Ash Wednesday—or would call for commemoration on a more modest scale in the classroom. For example, a decoration (flowers or ribbons) might be placed before a picture or a hymn might be sung on the feasts of the Guardian Angels (October 2), the Magi (January 6), Saint Joseph (March 19), and the Annunciation (March 25). Three French saints enjoyed similar favor: Saint Teresa of the Child Jesus (October 3), Saint Bernadette Soubirous (February 18), and Saint Joan of Arc (May 30). Saint Cecilia, patroness of musicians, was sometimes remembered, especially if the school had a music teacher.

American holidays were observed in the traditional way: Columbus Day, Lincoln's Birthday, Washington's Birthday, and, in Massachusetts, Patriot's Day. Often the religious aspect of Thanksgiving, Saint Valentine's Day, or Mother's Day was emphasized. Naturally, Christmas and Easter received special attention as the two most important holy days of the year; Franco-Americans prepared for them weeks in advance with Advent and Lenten devotions.

Franco-American schools were bilingual, and the instructional program was a combination and an adaptation of the curricula followed in Quebec and American schools. The morning session was conducted in French, the afternoon in English, or vice versa, often in different classrooms with different teachers. French was the medium of instruction for catechism, Bible study, French language, Canadian history, art, and music, more or less in that order of importance; the remaining subjects—reading, writing, arithmetic, American history, geography, civics, hygiene—were taught in English.

This division of time is misleading because French was also used throughout the day for all prayers and public announcements, for informal conversation with teachers outside the classroom, and for all schoolwide activities. Naturally, the sisters communicated with the parents in French. Although the situation varied according to the degree of ethnicity in the area, by the 1930s Franco-American children generally spoke English among themselves at recess. However, periodic campaigns were undertaken with more or less success to encourage the use of French in the schoolyard.

Textbooks written for Quebec children were generally used to teach French-language subjects in Franco-American parochial schools. Among the most popular were the manuals of the Frères des Ecoles Chrétiennes, or Christian Brothers. Like the McGuffey readers, the two-part primer, *La Lecture par la méthode phonique*, first published in 1918, inculcated piety and moral values.[32] The frontispiece shows Jesus and the children (Mark

10 : 13 – 16). The next page depicts a middle-aged gentleman holding up an infant who beckons to a Madonna; a little girl hugs her father's knees. The close relationship between reading and religion is made more explicit in the full-page illustration, in part 2, of Saint Anne instructing the child Mary with a book.[33]

Many sentences for copying were moralistic or religious: *élève poli; vénère ta mère; la fidelité à sa parole; le riche fait la charité; goûte la joie de l'âme pure; Ami, déteste la langue bavarde; supporte tes souffrances pour l'amour de Dieu* (polite child; honor thy mother; keep your word; the rich man gives alms; delight in being pure in heart; Friend, eschew gossip; endure your suffering for God's sake). Children were urged to avoid the evils of tobacco and alcohol: *Chers amis, ne fumez pas: la cigarette est un poison; L'alcool apporte la misère dans ce ménage* (Dear friends, don't smoke: cigarettes are poison; Drinking reduces this household to want). The drawing for the diphthong *oi* shows a young woman turning her head away from a boy who tries unsuccessfully to hide a lighted cigarette behind his back. A note explains: "La grande soeur dit: 'Pouah! que c'est vilain de fumer la cigarette!'" (Big sister says: "Ugh! smoking cigarettes is nasty!").[34]

Part 2 contains sixteen poems and ten prose passages which were often memorized. The verse encourages children to listen well and speak little, to not appear to be more than one is, and to avoid bad companions ("Les oranges," by J. M. Villefranche).[35] The prose is designed to foster piety, love of family, obedience, and politeness.

Bible study at this level consisted of elementary instruction about the Creation, Annunciation, Incarnation, Baptism of Christ, Redemption, and the Prodigal Son. These fundamental notions were imparted by telling the children simple stories and showing them pictures in class, often on a series of brightly colored posterboard charts, and having them learn their catechism.[36] At home, parents helped their offspring memorize short answers to related questions; then, at school, Sister would ask each pupil to recite. Other stories dealt with Saint Joseph, Saint Anne, Saint John the Baptist. Sister also stressed the importance of keeping the Sabbath and Holy Days. The Ten Commandments were learned in rhymed form.

Lectures courantes, Deuxième Livre (1916), used in the fourth and fifth grades, included short narratives intended to develop filial devotion, honesty, industriousness, patriotism (illustrated by the heroic deeds of Dollard des Ormeaux, the French-Canadian Custer), politeness, respect for teachers, self-sacrifice, and temperance.[37] Other stories pointed out the advantages of reading and cautioned against excessive curiosity, playing with matches, and poor ventilation.

Much of this material was drawn from collections of children's stories by European writers (e.g., Louis Ratisbonne and Canon Schmid) or from seventeenth- and eighteenth-century French authors (Fénelon, Florian, La Fontaine), but French-Canadian poets were also represented, for example Octave Crémazie and Pamphile Lemay. One of the most interesting pieces was a French-Canadian variant of a tale better known as the medieval fabliau *La Housse partie.* (A man is about to turn his aged father out of doors with only an old horse blanket for protection against the cold; however he changes his mind when his little boy innocently cuts the blanket in two—whence the title—wishing to save part of it for his own father later on.) In the French-Canadian version, the old man is forced to eat from a wooden bowl, away from the family table; the four-year-old boy is then discovered fashioning a similar vessel.[38]

Canadian history was taught with an eye to showing how God had watched over his chosen people.[39] Much emphasis was given to describing the religious devotion and extraordinary heroism of the early colonists. In the third grade the teacher paid particular attention to the life and role of the missionaries in New France, the idea being to instill comparable steadfastness and zeal.[40] In most French-Canadian history textbooks published before the late 1960s, American Indians are not portrayed very favorably.[41]

It is difficult to determine the exact number of schoolchildren enrolled in Franco-American educational establishments of the day. A survey of Woonsocket, Rhode Island, in 1926 showed that three-fourths (4,890) of all children of French-Canadian extraction were attending Franco-American parochial schools.[42] But for reasons cited above, this city may not have been representative. Some statistics, subject to caution, are provided by the *Guide officiel des Franco-Américains* for 1938. They are found in Appendix B, table 7.

Assumption College

Until 1947, when they began admitting students irrespective of nationality, Assumption High School and College in Worcester, Massachusetts, were the flagship institutions of the Franco-American educational establishment. The two schools occupied separate wings of a large building on a hill in suburban Greendale, but the eight-year program was regarded as a continuum designed to promote the development of an elite consisting of priests and professional men.

Like the French-Canadian collège classique, Assumption strove to inculcate Catholic doctrine and traditional values while teaching liberal arts subjects. Throughout four years of high school (*éléments, syntaxe, méthode,* and *versification*), the core curriculum included courses such as ancient history, French, Greek, Latin, and religion, all taught in French; at the college level (*belles-lettres, rhétorique,* and two years of *philosophie*), the entire cycle of required courses in philosophy and French literature was also conducted in that language.

Assumption differed from its sister schools in Quebec in that it became increasingly bilingual. The school was founded by the Assumptionist Fathers who were French (and Belgian), and the French as opposed to the French-Canadian or Franco-American presence was real. But by the late 1930s, French-born faculty members were dwindling and their influence was on the wane. By that date, roughly half the courses (e.g., American history, biology, English, mathematics, and physics) were taught in English. Also by that time, students generally spoke English among themselves when not attending class or engaged in a Francophone activity.[43]

Assumption was a small institution whose size was seriously affected by economic conditions: 180 students (high school and college combined) in 1921, 300 in 1926, but only 197 in 1934. During World War II, the number of students attending the high school swelled (400 in 1945), but enrollment in the college dropped off sharply until only a handful remained.[44]

Recruited from all over New England but especially from nearby Franco-American population centers, the student body came from middle-class families for the most part. But aided by low-interest loans from Franco-American fraternal organizations, students also came from the working class. A great majority were first-generation college and even high school students. A scattering of native French and children of French and Belgian mill owners and administrators from Rhode Island, and a few stray non-Francophones, rounded out the otherwise homogeneous group. The Assumptionist Fathers, who did parish work on weekends, were always on the lookout for likely candidates, and Franco-American parochial schools encouraged eighth-graders to participate in an annual scholarship competition held on campus.

Progressive in certain respects, notably in its bilingual curricular offerings and extracurricular activities, unwavering in its commitment to Catholic and liberal arts educational ideals, Assumption was hindered in its quest for academic excellence by its insularity. Nevertheless, it did succeed in fostering among its students a balanced and positive view of the group's French and French-Canadian heritage. A high percentage of its graduates entered the priesthood or became professional men. Many later played an active role in Franco-American affairs.[45]

The school was already edging away from its ethnic orientation when a tornado struck the Greendale campus a few days after commencement in

June 1953. (In March 1923 a fire had gutted the central part of the edifice but classes had resumed a few weeks later.)[46] The preparatory school remained in the rebuilt building but was forced to close in May 1970, due to declining enrollment. Meanwhile, after being temporarily housed elsewhere in Worcester, the college was transferred to its present location on Salisbury Street in 1956. Assumption College became coeducational in 1969. Its current undergraduate enrollment is about fifteen hundred. Graduate courses are also offered in several departments.

Organizations

Many early Franco-American organizations at the parish, city, state, and regional levels continued to flourish; others died out. The rise and fall of these societies can sometimes be ascribed to the charisma of certain individuals whose leadership resulted in a period of great activity that successors were unable to sustain. Personal rivalries, the Sentinelle Affair, the depression, and local economic and social conditions are other reasons why many once thriving organizations became moribund or extinct.

The astonishing number of associations in certain areas attests to the local group's vitality but also indicates that many Franco-Americans preferred smaller, more intimate societies tailored to special needs or purposes. For instance, Southbridge, Massachusetts, whose Franco-American community numbered a mere six thousand in 1919, had a Saint John the Baptist society and local councils of two other mutuals; a Cercle Canadien that sponsored lectures on various topics, an astounding number of French plays, and many other events; another similar club; two temperance societies; a naturalization club; three bands, an orchestra, and several music societies; a thrift club and a cooperative bank; many other parish and school organizations; and a French newspaper.[47] In 1920, Woonsocket, Rhode Island—where more than thirty thousand Franco-Americans or 70 percent of the city's total population resided—was the headquarters of the Union Saint-Jean-Baptiste d'Amérique, which locally comprised seven councils. Woonsocket also had three locals of the Ordre des Forestiers Franco-Américains; two each of the Association Canado-Américaine, the Société des Artisans Canadiens-Français, and the Alliance Nationale; and one of the Société Jacques Cartier. It also had a daily French newspaper, *La Tribune,* and, of course, numerous parish societies.[48]

The Fédération Catholique Franco-Américaine, founded in 1916, was an umbrella organization largely political in nature. It was formed to counterbalance such associations as the School Defense Leagues seeking to

Americanize minority groups, on the one hand, and the Irish-dominated Catholic societies, in particular the National Catholic War (later Welfare) Council, on the other.[49] The federation disbanded in 1933.

In 1920 a Franco-American secret society, the Crusaders (Croisés) was established at Woonsocket, Rhode Island, along the lines of the Knights of Columbus. The organization soon came into conflict with Bishop Hickey in skirmishes foreshadowing the Sentinelle Affair. Rent by dissension, the Croisés were a casualty of this controversy.[50]

Until World War II the Cercle des Etudiants Franco-Américains, founded in 1922, was a support network for Franco-American college and graduate students who lived principally in the Boston area. In the following decade, similar organizations were created by professionals: the Association des Professeurs Franco-Américains (1933), the Association Médicale Franco-Américaine (1936)—a smaller medical society was founded in Worcester, Massachusetts, in 1915—and the Association Franco-Américaine d'Education (1938).[51] None of these groups survives today. (An Association des Professeurs Franco-Américains for elementary and secondary school teachers of French was founded in 1963 and remained active for several years in the wake of the National Defense Education Act summer institutes at Bowdoin and Assumption colleges.)[52]

A veterans organization, the Légion Franco-Américaine des Etats-Unis, was founded in 1933; its first post was at Lawrence, Massachusetts.[53] A group called the Vétérans Franco-Américains still holds annual meetings.[54]

In Maine, Lewiston's Ligue des Sociétés de Langue Française (1923) seemed to have lost its vitality but was suddenly reborn in 1976 as L'Unité Franco-Américaine. Today it concerns itself mainly with the city's annual Festival. Another Lewiston association, the Vigilants, was founded in 1936.

Among the smaller local organizations, formed in the period between World War I and World War II, that have withstood over time are the Société des Concours de Français, Fall River, Massachusetts (1926); the Marchandes de Bonheur, Lewiston, Maine (1929); the Cercle Jeanne Mance, Lowell, Massachusetts (1931); and the Dames Françaises, Springfield, Massachusetts (1931). The Survivance Française of Lewiston, Maine, dates from 1942.

Franco-American snowshoe clubs have always maintained close ties with French-Canadian counterparts in the Union Canadienne des Raquetteurs (1907). Congresses, which feature dances, coronation of a queen and princesses, races, parade with floats, and a banquet, are held annually and generate much local enthusiasm.

The Union Américaine Fraternelle des Raquetteurs (American Snowshoe Union) was founded by Louis-Philippe Gagné of Lewiston in 1924.[55]

Early Franco-American clubs still in existence include the Montagnard (1925), Jacques Cartier (1925), and Cercle Canadien (1925) of Lewiston; the Voltigeur (1926) and Rochambeau (1934) of Biddeford, Maine; the Paresseux (1929) of Rumford, Maine; the Joliette (1934) of Berlin, New Hampshire; the Alpin (1927) of Manchester, New Hampshire; the Chanteclerc (1939) of Dracut, Massachusetts; and the Coureur des Bois (1940) of Lowell, Massachusetts.[56] Most have a ladies auxiliary.

Finally, the Comité d'Orientation Franco-Américaine (1947)—known since 1957 as the Comité de Vie Franco-Américaine—and the Fédération Féminine Franco-Américaine (1951) play a major role in the life of group members today and are discussed in the next chapter.

Literature

In the opinion of one specialist who, in 1946, examined the literary output of no fewer than 217 Franco-Americans who wrote in French, the bulk of their work was mediocre. Her brief discussion of Franco-American novels consisted mainly of unfavorable criticism of their complicated or implausible plots, faults she ascribed to amateurishness. She did, however, single out for praise the poetry of Louis Dantin (*Le Coffret de Crusoé*, 1932) and Rosaire Dion-Lévesque (*Les Oasis*, 1930). She also admired Dr. Georges Boucher's "Ode à Québec," begun in 1902 and completed in 1933 (final version, 1952).[57]

A more specialized study of three Franco-American novels of the 1930s found they were not devoid of interest, particularly as they shed light on contemporary attitudes and values.[58] Alberte Gastonguay-Sasseville (1906–78), the daughter of a prosperous insurance agent in Lewiston, Maine, published *La Jeune Franco-Américaine* in 1933.[59] The novel tells of a young woman's struggle to remain faithful to her Catholic and Franco-American upbringing despite the lures of modern life (e.g., the blandishments of a divorced man, the amorous advances of her employer, the bad example of a girlfriend who leads a life of debauchery). Camille Lessard-Bissonnette (1883–1970), the author of *Canuck*, emigrated from Quebec to Lewiston with her family in 1904 at the age of twenty. Although she left that city a few years later and subsequently resided in various parts of Canada and the United States—she died at Long Beach, California—she never forgot her experiences working in a textile mill in Lewiston for four years before finding employment as a feature writer for *Le Messager*, the local French-language newspaper. Her novel, which appeared in 1936, is set in Lowell, Massachusetts, in 1900, but she drew heavily upon her experiences in Lewiston.[60] A gloomy but well-structured story that grips the reader, *Canuck* is probably the most important novel in French by a Franco-American writer. The year 1936 also witnessed the publication by Adélard Lambert (1867–1946) of *L'Innocente Victime,* a rambling narrative inspired by the American Civil War.[61] The author, who lived most of his life in Manchester, New Hampshire, but returned to Quebec in 1921 at the age of fifty-four, viewed the process of assimilation with a jaundiced eye and wished to contrast the hazards of life in the United States with the relative peace and security of rural existence in Canada. (For Lambert's contributions to the study of Franco-American folklore, see "Folklore.")

Two other French-language novels by Franco-Americans are worthy of note. *Sanatorium* by Dr. Paul Dufault (1894–1969), published in 1938, is the story of life in an establishment for the treatment of tuberculosis.[62] Dufault, who spent his entire professional career working in such an institution maintained by the commonwealth of Massachusetts at Rutland, attracted two other Quebecois physicians to the place—Drs. Armand Laroche and Gabriel Nadeau. Keenly interested in Franco-American affairs, the group nevertheless led a kind of monastic existence until the sanatorium closed in 1966. The novel has existential overtones and may also allude to the estrangement many French-Canadian immigrants of the day experienced in America.

Alienation is the theme of another contemporary novel, *Les Enfances de Fanny* by Louis Dantin, pen name of Eugène Seers (1865–1945).[63] Written from 1936 to 1943 but published posthumously in 1951, this affecting account relates the love of Donat Sylvain, a French artist residing in Roxbury near Boston, Massachusetts, for his black housekeeper. After a common-law marriage, the couple experience many hardships because of others' prejudice. In the end, Fanny's former lover, blinded by jealousy and racial hatred, slays her. The story is partly autobiographical. A brilliant French-Canadian priest who rose rapidly to become superior of his religious order, Dantin embarked early on a literary career, became associated with the Montreal School (1895–1930), and had a great influence on the young Quebecois poet Emile Nelligan whose works he edited.[64] In 1903 he suddenly left religious life and sought refuge in Boston where he found work as a typographer. In 1922 he hired a black housekeeper who became the inspiration for Fanny. Dantin, who considered himself to be a social outcast, identified with blacks, immersed himself in their culture, and eventually moved to their neighborhood in Roxbury. His poetry, and especially his literary criticism, place him in the first rank of North American French-language authors of the day.[65]

In the early days of the immigration to New England, a few transplanted French Canadians—notably Anna-Marie Duval-Thibault and Drs.

Joseph-Hormidas Roy and Joseph-Amédée Girouard, wrote melancholy and nostalgic poetry characteristic of individuals who do not feel in harmony with their surroundings.[66] Even after World War I, a number of poets, for example, Charles-Roger Daoust, Philippe Sainte-Marie, and Fathers Aristide D. M. Magnan and Louis-Alphonse Nolin, continued to publish verse on related themes or centered on contemporary French-Canadian ideology.[67]

The transition to a more distinctly Franco-American voice appears in the poetry of Louis Dantin,[68] Henri D'Arles (pseudonym of Father Henri Beaudé; 1870–1930), and Rosaire Dion-Lévesque (1900–1974). Henri D'Arles (*Laudes*, 1925), whose work has been categorized as "poetic realism," is especially noted for his sensitive descriptions of nature.[69] Rosaire Dion-Lévesque (*Vita*, 1939; *Quête*, 1963; also a translation of Walt Whitman's *Leaves of Grass*, 1933) was the first of these poets to be born in New England (Nashua, New Hampshire). A journalist by profession, he entertained friendly relations with many literary figures, in particular with Louis Dantin who became his mentor. In his poetry, Dion-Lévesque bares his soul and reveals that the spirit is indeed willing but the flesh is weak. Deeply attached to his French-Canadian heritage, he nevertheless felt more American than French and is perhaps best remembered for four sonnets in which he sang the praises of his native land (in "Amor patriae," the last section of *Quête*).[70]

In 1955 one scholar listed 109 Franco-American authors who wrote in English.[71] However, the tally included many writers not usually associated with the group—for example, Vivian (Lajeunesse) Parsons whose novel *Not without Honor* (1941) deals with the French-Canadians of her native Michigan—and numerous publications of a technical nature.

Four of these books warrant special attention. *The Delusson Family* (1939) by Jacques Ducharme and *Mill Village* (1943) by Albéric A. Archambault are fictionalized accounts of real-life French-Canadian families that emigrated to New England.[72] *Laurentian Heritage* (1948) by Corinne Rocheleau-Rouleau is a series of charming reminiscences of rural life in Quebec in the 1870s.[73] The latter work was widely used to acquaint English-speaking Canadians with the roots of Quebecois culture. In 1945 Robert Fontaine published *The Happy Time,* the story of an adolescent boy's coming-of-age in a wacky French-Canadian family living in Ottawa in the 1920s.[74] Enormously popular, the novel was adapted for the stage by Samuel A. Taylor in 1950 and ran for 614 performances on Broadway. In 1952 Columbia Pictures produced a film version featuring Charles Boyer and Louis Jourdan. A musical in 1968 starred Robert Goulet and David Wayne.

Newspapers

Important dailies and weeklies continued to serve major Franco-American centers. In addition to providing an outlet for budding as well as established authors—many of the French-language writers mentioned above first published their works here—these journals also served as a forum for discussion of the main issues concerning the group.

The Great Depression signaled the beginning of the end. In 1935 one study could still claim that twenty-eight Franco-American newspapers were in existence;[75] but vast social changes, in particular a growing preference for English-language dailies, were already undermining even the most financially sound ethnic journals. By the 1950s the Franco-American press was a mere shadow of its former self. With two or three exceptions, these newspapers were now purveying information, most of it local and of little consequence, rather than ideas. Saddest of all, they were growing increasingly out of touch with their readers.[76]

The chief Franco-American newspapers of the 1920s, 1930s, and 1940s, with the dates they ceased publishing, are as follows:[77]

L'Opinion Publique, Worcester, Massachusetts (1931)
La Tribune, Woonsocket, Rhode Island (1934)
Le Lynnois, Lynn, Massachusetts (1935)
Le Citoyen, Haverhill, Massachusetts (1939)
L'Avenir National, Manchester, New Hampshire (1949)
La Justice, Biddeford, Maine (1950)
Le Courrier, Salem, Massachusetts (1950)
L'Etoile, Lowell, Massachusetts (1957)
L'Indépendant, Fall River, Massachusetts (1962)
La Justice, Holyoke, Massachusetts (1964)
L'Impartial, Nashua, New Hampshire (1964)
La Liberté, Fitchburg, Massachusetts (1965)
Le Messager, Lewiston, Maine (1968)
Le Travailleur, Worcester, Massachusetts (1978)

Artists

The most accomplished Franco-American artists of the day were Lucien Gosselin (1883–1940) and Lorenzo de Nevers (1877–1967). Born in Whitefield, New Hampshire, Gosselin, who was the nephew of the famous French-Canadian sculptor Philippe Hébert, moved to Manchester with his family as a child. After studying in Paris under Henri Bouchard, Paul Landowski, and Antonin Mercier from 1911 to 1916, Gosselin returned to Manchester where he produced an impressive number of statues and monuments that now stand in cemeteries, churches, and squares throughout the Northeast. He also designed and engraved numerous commemorative medals.[78] De Nevers was born at St. Elphège, Quebec, but emigrated to Central Falls, Rhode Island, in 1898. The brother of the Franco-American historian Edmond de Nevers (1863–1906), he studied fine arts for fifteen years in Paris beginning in 1902. Throughout his long career, during which he resided in Montreal and New York City as well as in Central Falls, he specialized in portraits and religious paintings.[79]

Celebrities

Many Franco-Americans achieved fame during this period. The following are perhaps best remembered.

Will Durant (1885–1981), the son of a French-Canadian immigrant mill operative in North Adams, Massachusetts, was seven years old when his family moved to Kearney, New Jersey. After obtaining his Ph.D. from Columbia University in 1917, he began writing history and philosophy books. In 1935 he published the first installment of his monumental *Story of Civilization. Rousseau and Revolution,* volume 10 in the series, written in collaboration with his wife Ariel, won the Pulitzer Prize for general nonfiction in 1968. Volume 11, *The Age of Napoleon,* also coauthored with his spouse, appeared in 1975. The couple's final work, *A Dual Biography,* was issued in 1977.[80]

Leo Durocher (1905–), born in Springfield, Massachusetts, was a major league baseball player for seventeen years and a manager for twenty-four years. Under his direction, the Brooklyn Dodgers and the New York Giants won a total of three National League pennants in 1941, 1951, and 1954; in the latter year the Giants were also victorious in the World Series. Celebrated for his run-ins with players and officials—in 1947 he was suspended for the entire season by Commissioner Happy Chandler for "conduct detrimental to baseball"—and for his flamboyant life-style, "Leo the Lip" retired in 1973.[81]

Frank Fontaine (1920–78), a native of Cambridge, Massachusetts, was the son of entertainers (his grandfather was a circus strongman with the Ringling Brothers). In his youth he traveled the vaudeville circuit with his parents and got his first big break when he won first prize on "Major Bowes' Original Amateur Hour," a radio talent contest, in 1936. A comic and singer, he performed in many supper clubs and made frequent appearances on radio comedy shows in the 1940s and 1950s. Fontaine achieved stardom when he became a regular on the Columbia Broadcasting System's television program "Jackie Gleason and His American Scene Magazine" (1962–66) portraying Crazy Guggenheim, a cheerful drunk, in a skit with the host in the role of Joe the Bartender. (Fontaine also sang in a pleasant baritone.) Devoted to his wife and eleven children, he always managed to spend two weeks of every month at his home in Winchester, Massachusetts.[82]

René A. Gagnon (1924–79) was a nineteen-year-old private from Manchester, New Hampshire, when the marines landed on Iwo Jima, 750 miles from Tokyo, on February 19, 1945. Ordered to capture Mount Suribachi, a 550-foot extinct volcano at the southern tip of the island, his company encountered stubborn Japanese resistance; but on the morning of February 23 they reached the summit. As the men were raising the American flag, Associated Press photographer Joe Rosenthal captured the scene in what has been called "the most famous battle photograph ever taken." Gagnon, who is the second figure from the right (helmet barely visible), survived the battle—three other flag raisers did not—and eventually settled at Hookset, New Hampshire.[83]

John C. Garand (1888–1974) emigrated as a child from St. Rémi, Quebec, to Jewett City, Connecticut, where, at the age of fourteen, he found work as a floor sweeper and bobbin boy in Slater's Mill. He became enamored with repairing and designing machine parts and, in 1919, accepted a position at the Springfield (Massachusetts) Armory. Now an ordnance design engineer, he began work in 1923 on the .30 caliber Springfield rifle used by United States troops in World War I. The M1 rifle he invented was a greatly improved weapon that eliminated manual operation of the bolt mechanism. Adopted in 1936 as standard equipment by the United States Army, and later by the Navy and Marine Corps, it was widely used in World War II and in Korea. The Garand rifle was replaced by the M14 in 1960.[84]

Rudy Vallée (1901–) was born in Island Pond, Vermont, but raised in Westbrook, Maine. Christened Hubert Prior Vallée, the singer and orchestra leader earned the nickname Rudy while at the University of Maine—which he attended before transferring to Yale—because of his admiration for a popular saxophone player of the day, Rudy Wiedoeft. Vallée broke into the big time in 1928 while performing with his orchestra at the Heigh-Ho Club in New York City. For ten years beginning in 1929, he was host of the "Rudy Vallée Show," a radio variety hour of the National Broadcasting Corporation. He also starred in many motion pictures, including *The Vagabond Lover* (1929). He later came out of semiretirement to play a major role in the Broadway musical *How to Succeed in Business without Really Trying* (1961–64).[85]

Folklore

French-Canadian folk traditions were very much alive in New England between the two world wars.[86] The Franco-American bibliophile and amateur folklorist Adélard Lambert settled in Manchester, New Hampshire, where he lived for forty years, after residing with his parents in other northeastern cities as a child. Many of the stories, songs, and children's dances and games he collected, and which are now part of the library of the Association Canado-Américaine, were learned from informants in Albion and Warren, Rhode Island, and from close relatives.[87]

Related data are associated with Roméo Berthiaume (1907–80), who spent the greater part of his life in Woonsocket, Rhode Island, wrote six volumes of memoirs for his family, and supplied information in tape-recorded interviews for Rhode Island's Folklife Project (1979), now preserved in the Library of Congress in Washington, D.C. Yvonne Lagassé of Lowell, Massachusetts, born in 1906, also furnished an oral history of that city's Little Canada as well as other valuable material, including many songs that have been published in a recent study.[88]

This authentic material handed down orally from generation to generation is not to be confused with, say, the traditional songs transmitted via publications such as Eusèbe Viau and J.-Ernest Philie's *Chants populaires des Franco-Américains,*[89] which first appeared in 1929, and Father Charles-Emile Gadbois's *La Bonne Chanson* (1937).[90] Although admirable in many other ways, the latter create the false impression that the words and music of each song are fixed. Also, the corpus of French-Canadian folk songs is vastly more extensive and diverse than suggested by these limited and bowdlerized collections.

Veillées were held in tenement buildings wherever Little Canadas existed throughout New England, and evidence shows that the merrymaking on Saturday evenings, anniversaries, and holidays even included folk dancing. By the 1930s such gatherings generally took place in public halls and social clubs. Informants insist that the quadrilles sometimes danced on these occasions were distinct from square dances, but outside influence was evidently involved because calls were used—a distinguishing trait of the American dance.[91]

The traditional veillée, complete with dancing, drinking, singing, and storytelling, lived on until the 1940s in many homes in the Quebec countryside and in Franco-American centers. But it was already a dying social phenomenon in Quebec cities as early as 1919 when an attempt was made to revive the custom with a show staged at Montreal.[92] A sign of the times, similar entertainments were also produced in New England, for example in Lowell, Massachusetts, in 1934 and 1936. These were prototypes of the performances that have been given regularly there since 1968 by the Equipe du Bon Vieux Temps.[93]

4

PAGES FROM A
FAMILY HISTORY

In the following account I seek to individualize and give imme-
diacy to some of the preceding narrative as well as to consider
briefly the more distant origins of Franco-American culture. As I trace my
ancestors, from father to son, for nine generations, I endeavor to look at
their place in history.[1] The line of direct descent is as follows:

1. Vincent and Marie (Bourg) Brault
2. Pierre and Anne (LeBlanc) Brault
3. Joseph and Elisabeth (Thibodeau) Brault
4. Amand and Madeleine (Dupuis) Brault
5. Amand-Damien and Elisabeth (Jacques) Brault
6. Amand and Josephte (Granger) Brault
7. Julien and Domitille (Cyr) Brault
8. Julien and Agnès (Laroche) Brault
9. Philias and Aline (Rémillard) Brault

My ancestors were ordinary people, not movers and shakers of the
world. Carried along by currents they probably scarcely understood, let
alone could control, they managed nevertheless to raise families and lead
full lives. In this and other respects they were not unlike most French colonists, French-Canadian country people, and early Franco-Americans.

The colonization of Canada

For over a century after Christopher Columbus discovered America,
European explorers roamed the Atlantic coast in their ships.[2] They sailed
into its bays and harbors, and up its rivers. Leaving the protection of their
vessels, they made bold forays overland, built small forts, and encountered

and traded with the people they called Indians or savages. However, no group of colonists established a single permanent settlement in North America.

These navigators were looking chiefly for a shorter way to the Orient, source of silk, spices, and precious stones. Meanwhile, in the West Indies and in Central America, the conquistadores were shipping back vast amounts of gold, silver, and other valuables to Spain. Explorers to the north found no such treasure but quickly recognized that great profits could be made from two other abundant commodities, fish and fur.

Early in the sixteenth century, European fishermen began making regular trips to the shallow waters off Newfoundland and Acadia, or Nova Scotia. The population of Europe was increasing rapidly, and fish, particularly cod, was a cheap and popular substitute for meat.

Gradually the fur trade also began to assume importance. The St. Lawrence River loomed increasingly as a great highway, giving easy access to areas where natives would transport large quantities of fur and cured pelts for trading. The Indians were happy to exchange these items for goods they found useful and appealing: initially iron axes, knives, and pots; brandy, cloth, fishhooks, and trinkets; then hats, shirts, and other clothing; tools and weapons of various kinds; and food and tobacco. In Europe, skins, especially beaver, could be sold for gain. Fur for hats, coats, and muffs was much in demand among the gentry.

The European powers knew that the only way to hold claim to a region of the New World was to colonize it. Preoccupied with other matters that drained their energies and wealth, the French kings turned to groups of seaport merchants to accomplish this task. The plan was always the same: in return for a promise to establish a permanent colony, the merchants would be granted a monopoly of the fish and fur trade. Rival merchants promptly undermined the operation at home and abroad. More interested in making a quick profit than in any long-term investment, the French monopolists provided the colonists with scanty supplies and soon left them to their own devices.

In 1627 only about a hundred colonists were living in scattered settlements in the vast area of North America claimed by France. The French were particularly interested in two main regions—the peninsula and surrounding territory known as Acadia, and the St. Lawrence Valley referred to as Canada.

New France experienced its period of greatest growth during the administration of Intendant Jean Talon (1660–80) and during the last twenty years before the British Conquest in 1760. Before 1660 the average number of immigrants per year never exceeded twenty. The number of colonists who settled in New France before the Conquest totaled about ten thousand.

In France, the provinces situated north of the Loire and the central-western provinces played a preponderant role in the immigration to Canada, as Appendix B, table 8 shows. The provinces north of the Loire furnished far fewer emigrants to Acadia; the central and western provinces (Poitou, Aunis, Saintonge, Angoumois), far more. Cut off from France in 1713, Acadia was the destination of few French settlers after that time.[3]

Why did so few French emigrate to Canada in the seventeenth and eighteenth centuries? According to one scholar: "The essential reason must be looked for in the colony's economy itself. In order to attract immigrants, a country must offer excellent prospects for agriculture as well as industry and commerce, but New France offered nothing of this kind."[4]

The recruitment of colonists

In the early days of the colony and for a long time afterward, few French came to New France on their own initiative. They were recruited individually and in small groups by merchants for the most part, few of whom had made the voyage themselves, and by a handful of ambitious entrepreneurs willing to risk their lives and fortunes in the wilderness.

The intendants strove to recruit qualified workers, but nine-tenths of the colonists who claimed to be tradesmen when they embarked for Canada seem to have been mere apprentices or peasants who engaged in handicraft during the winter to earn a bit of money. After fulfilling the conditions of their contract, most of these so-called artisans became habitants or traders.

Military recruits comprised 35 percent of the ten thousand immigrants who settled New France. From the outset the colony was defended by soldiers, at first a small band of individuals. However, in 1665 King Louis XIV sent the Carignan-Salières regiment totaling about twelve hundred men. Recalled to France three years later, the regiment left some four hundred members in Canada. These officers and men settled on farms or traded with the Indians.

Like the military, the majority of marriageable young women who immigrated settled in Canada in the 1660s. Nine hundred are believed to have arrived from 1665 to 1673.[5] These were the famous "king's daughters" (filles du roi)—orphan girls who were given a dowery plus certain expenses: passage, clothing, "a coffer, a cap, a taffeta handkerchief, a shoe ribbon, a hundred needles, a comb, white thread, a pair of stockings, a pair of gloves, a pair of scissors, two knives, a thousand pins, a bonnet, and four laces." More than a third of the *filles du roi* were Parisian, more than a tenth Norman. They were supposed to be "in vigorous health and accustomed to farm work." Most promptly found a husband.[6]

In the seventeenth century, the French peasant led a precarious life. Weighed down by all sorts of taxes—for example, every year he paid a tithe (*la dîme*) to the church and was obliged to purchase a certain amount of salt on which a heavy charge (*la gabelle*) was imposed—he lacked money and struggled to farm a few scattered acres. Thousands died of starvation when crops failed between 1630 and 1632, 1636 and 1638, 1660 and 1664, and 1693 and 1694.[7] In such crises, many peasants begged in neighboring cities for their bread but usually returned empty-handed.

The Thirty Years' War (1618–48), especially the final phase that began in 1635, visited further calamity upon the French peasants. There were invasions of French territory, and marauders ravaged the countryside. To finance the war, Cardinal Richelieu levied a series of new taxes (*la taille*) whose burden once again fell chiefly on the peasants. Harsh measures were adopted by tax collectors, who had purchased their office and were often corrupt.

This period in French history witnessed a series of peasant revolts derisively termed *jacqueries* by the upper classes. (The insurgents themselves were called *croquants* or, in Normandy, *nu-pieds*.)[8] Typically, a mob would gather suddenly, raise a hue and cry against tax collectors—the alarm bell was often rung as a signal—and then give a good thrashing to any that could be found. Armed with sticks and farm implements, the crowd sometimes went on a rampage, administering a drubbing to officials and burning or destroying their property.

When unable to quell such revolts, local authorities requested troops, who generally subdued the rebels quickly. Hauled before a magistrate, insurgent leaders were sentenced either to be flogged, to serve years or even life on convict ships (*galères*), or to be executed. Rural tax revolts—similar disturbances also occurred in cities and towns throughout France—were common before the civil war known as the Fronde (1648–53) produced its own havoc.

Many seventeenth-century French colonists, particularly those who came from Normandy and the southwest, may have experienced such conditions and may have decided in desperation to embark upon a new life. Others may simply have been seeking adventure or short-term financial gain. Overpopulation in certain areas of France, which impelled many persons to move to Spain about this time, provides another explanation.[9]

In any event, most individuals and families probably got the idea of settling in New France—for a time, at any rate—from persons who were involved in the colonization effort. For example, from 1634 to 1663 Robert Giffard recruited some fifty heads of families who lived in his native Mortagne-au-Perche. In 1636 forty-six colonists from Normandy, mainly members of the Le Gardeur and Le Neuf families, constituted another important nucleus.[10]

At times the contact lived a great distance away. Since the Middle Ages, well-to-do noblemen and merchants routinely invested part of their wealth in farms.[11] An individual might own property in the vicinity of the city or town in which he resided, but he might also own property in another province, say, through inheritance. Peasants farmed the land, and owners paid frequent visits to oversee work and collect revenues.

Vincent Brault, ancestor of the Brault family, emigrated to Acadia as a consequence of such a relationship.

La Chaussée

Vincent Brault was born in 1631, almost certainly in La Chaussée (Vienne) or in the immediate area.[12] Located in central France in the northern part of Poitou, La Chaussée is today a quiet rural village with a population of about three hundred. It is just off Route Nationale 147, and by car it is a short ten miles northwest to Loudun and twenty-six miles southeast to Poitiers.[13] However, in the seventeenth century the village was relatively isolated from these cities; its economic and social life was closely bound up with the Seigneur d'Aulnay.[14]

Young Vincent, his sister Renée, his brother-in-law Vincent Brun (Renée's husband), and a number of other peasants from this area were recruited about 1650 by Charles de Menou d'Aulnay, governor of Acadia, on lands he owned in and around La Chaussée. Until his death at Port Royal, Acadia, in that year, d'Aulnay was the principal developer of that colony.

Notre Dame Church, a small, stocky Gothic structure in La Chaussée, no longer has a resident priest. However, it figures in the official registry of historical buildings and is well maintained. Here, no doubt, the small group bound for Acadia heard mass, received their pastor's final blessing, and bade farewell to relatives and friends before setting out on the great adventure. (A modest museum, La Maison de l'Acadie, attached to the church, houses a typical farm interior of the day, a few items of traditional clothing of the region, and the rudiments of a research library specializing in the origins of the Acadian people.)

Brault, a word derived from Gallo-Germanic Beroaldus, is a very old name borne by many French families in this and other areas.[15] It is also a

common place-name in France (these localities were designated for pro-
prietors named Beroaldus) and takes such forms as Braud (Gironde), Brault
(Cher, Vienne), and Braux (Ardennes, Aube, Basses-Alpes, and Côte
d'Or), or appears in combinations like Braucourt (Haute-Marne), Braux-
le-Châtel (Haute-Marne), Braux-le-Petit (Aube), Braumont (Meurthe-et-
Moselle), Braux-Sainte-Cohière (Marne), Braux-Saint-Rémi (Marne),
Brauvilliers (Meuse), Labraux (Aube), Le Braud (Corrèze), and Pont
du Brault (Charente-Maritime).[16] Many French Canadians and Franco-
Americans spell their name Breault; Acadians, Breaux, whence the place-
name Breaux Bridge in Louisiana.

It is possible, but by no means certain, that the Braults of La Chaussée
derive their name from a tiny locality called Brault, a few miles to the east
near the village of Dercé, in the canton of Monts-sur-Guesne (Vienne).[17] A
handsome and well-preserved stone country house, the Château de Brault,
dating back to the sixteenth century and now privately owned, marks the
place.

The voyage to Acadia

In the mid-1600s the journey from La Chaussée to La Rochelle by way
of Poitiers and Niort, a distance of 112 miles, probably took a week or
more on foot. Travel was always arduous, but the road from Poitiers to La
Rochelle was much frequented and presented no special obstacles. The
area around La Chaussée and Poitiers is a fertile plain that becomes marshy
west of Niort.

Vincent Brault must have embarked at La Rochelle since about this time
all shipping for Acadia was monopolized by this port; also, d'Aulnay's
business agent, Emmanuel Le Borgne, resided there.[18] In the 1640s several
ships were fitted out on d'Aulnay's behalf by his supplier; unfortunately, no
passenger list survives for any of these voyages.

Chances are that Vincent became an *engagé,* that is, he went before a
notary—probably Teuleron, the public officer Le Borgne dealt with in La
Rochelle—and signed an indenture.[19] This formal document would have
bound him to a specific individual for whom he worked exclusively for a
given number of years. Many of these contracts have survived, and although none mention Vincent or any known relative, they give us a clear
idea of the terms under which they probably agreed to voyage to Acadia.

Contracts never involved anyone under sixteen unaccompanied by a
relative (Vincent turned sixteen in 1647) or any youth alone under eighteen. Wages were specified and were always paid in cash, never in goods. In
New France, engagés were fed at the expense of the persons who hired

them. Craftsmen earned the highest salaries; then, in descending order, came sailors, soldiers, and plowmen. Part of the wages, ordinarily about half, were received in advance and were used to purchase clothing, tools, and the like before departure. In the early days of the colony, there were few cobblers, tailors, or weavers, and replacements for worn-out clothing and shoes were shipped from France.

La Rochelle was an exciting port in the seventeenth century, and it remains a delightful place to visit today, especially in the summertime. When Vincent Brault called there, its narrow streets were crowded with noisy wagons and carts laden with provisions destined for the rows of ships moored alongside the quay at Chef de Baie in the outer harbor—the Vieux Port, or inner harbor was too silted up to accommodate ocean-going vessels—and huge bundles of fur and piles of lumber, products of Canada, were to be seen on the wharves.[20] The briny sea air mixed with the pungent odor of codfish, rope, and tar, and shouts of harried laborers and enterprising street vendors could be heard everywhere.

Once the proud bastion of Protestantism in France, La Rochelle had successfully withstood a six-and-a-half-month siege by royal troops in 1573. However, in 1628 the Rochelais had met their match in Cardinal Richelieu. To prevent the English fleet from coming to the aid of their Huguenot allies, Richelieu constructed a stone dike sealing off the port; to block all sorties, he had a vast moat dug around the city's walls. After resisting for a year, La Rochelle capitulated and its storied fortifications were reduced to rubble. The picturesque twin towers guarding the entrance to the Vieux Port, the Tour de la Chaîne and the Tour Saint Nicolas, were spared and are popular symbols of La Rochelle today.

Not far from the dock stand the magnificent city hall and numerous splendid frame houses. These buildings and the lovely arcades along Rue Chaudrier, Rue des Merciers, and Rue du Minage, affording shoppers protection from the sun and rain, are just as they were when Vincent Brault and hundreds of other colonists passed through the city on their way to Acadia and Canada more than three centuries ago. The Musée du Nouveau Monde, inaugurated in 1981, on Rue Fleuriau, contains many exhibits recalling La Rochelle's involvement with Canada in the seventeenth century.[21] However, perhaps the most enduring memorials of this age are the thousands of pebbles, once carried as ballast in the holds of French vessels returning from Canada, with which Rue de l'Escale is now paved.

Ships usually set sail for New France at Eastertime so that they might have time for the return voyage before winter, a season that presented grave navigational difficulties.[22] Departure for New France was often delayed: time was needed to assemble a crew, to prepare the ship, and to load it, and

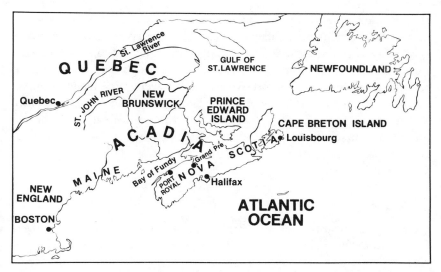

Map 2. Map of Acadia in the seventeenth century. The area known today as the Maritimes includes the Canadian provinces of New Brunswick, Nova Scotia, and Prince Edward Island. (Source: Clark, *Acadia*, p. 332, figs. 5.1 and 8.1.)

weather conditions were not always favorable. Passengers sometimes had to wait in port for weeks on end.

For Vincent Brault and his fellow colonists, most of whom had probably never ventured far from their native villages located miles inland, the two-month sea voyage represented an incredible adventure. Vincent no doubt crossed the Atlantic on a square-rigged galleon or pinnace not unlike those depicted in a sketchbook that is dated 1679 and preserved in the Service Historique de la Marine at the Château de Vincennes on the outskirts of Paris.[23]

Passenger ships did not exist in the seventeenth century although vessels were at times adapted to transport a large number of individuals. Noblemen and religious were accommodated in the officers' quarters. However, the rest of the colonists had to shift for themselves on deck amidships—braving the elements with the penned-up animals and fowl being carried to the New World or finding a cramped place to rest among the cannons, hammocks, and seamen's lockers on the fetid battery deck. On a voyage of such long duration, storms and a heavy sea were to be expected. Illness such as dysentery, scurvy, yellow fever, and, of course, mal de mer was common. One of the greatest risks was to be overtaken by pirates or, in time of war, by an enemy vessel.

Ships leaving La Rochelle routinely steered northwest along the coast of France, at times as far as the Isle of Sein or Ushant off the tip of Brittany, then headed west for Newfoundland's Grand Bank. Certain areas of this vast shallow-depth underwater plateau, well marked on navigational charts of the day, could be located by soundings, which helped captains get their bearings. Here ships going to Canada passed through the Cabot Strait to the mouth of the St. Lawrence River; those traveling to Acadia rounded Cape Sable, sailed up the Bay of Fundy, and entered the Annapolis Basin. By the mid-seventeenth century the route was well known to fishermen and merchant seamen. For instance, Samuel de Champlain made twenty-three passages along this route from France to Canada before he died at Quebec in 1635.[24]

Port Royal

Annapolis Royal—formerly Port Royal—is a pretty little town overlooking the Annapolis Basin, an inlet of the Bay of Fundy. A summer resort, today it is as thoroughly British as its name, which was changed in 1710 to honor Queen Anne.

Toward the middle of the seventeenth century, perhaps as many as three hundred people lived in and around Port Royal; approximately half lived in families.[25] Although the seigneurial system does not appear to have been maintained very strictly, colonists recognized that they held their land as a concession from d'Aulnay (or, later, from his heirs) and that they owed him dues and duties. However, the fees were nominal—each year, one sou per acre and a few chickens. The traditional services (corvées) were probably performed, if ever, in haphazard fashion, especially during the crises that continually beset the colony during d'Aulnay's administration.

Vincent Brault may initially have been one of d'Aulnay's engagés, working one of his farms, or he may have been employed by one of the many habitants developing lands held from the governor in the immediate area. Some of these farms already could be found a mile or two upstream and on both sides of the Rivière Dauphin (Annapolis River), but most were clustered on the elevated portion of a small peninsula jutting out from the south bank. The head of the Annapolis Basin was ringed by tidal marshes filled with rich grass; the marshes were flooded by the sea at high tide. D'Aulnay had some of the marshes drained and encouraged the growing of wheat there. The governor lived in a large manor house constructed of great squared beams set one on another, the colonists in smaller log cabins. Twelve Capuchin monks maintained a small school for French children and Indian youths.

After years of skirmishing with his chief rival, Charles de Saint-Etienne de La Tour, d'Aulnay was finally able to eliminate him from competition in

1645. D'Aulnay died in a canoeing accident five years later. D'Aulnay's business agent, Le Borgne, to whom the governor owed a huge sum of money, promptly sent men to take over Port Royal, raid other outposts, and commandeer anything of value that could be found by way of compensation. In 1654 a large English force sent by Oliver Cromwell seized control of Acadia, and the British remained the dominant power in the area until 1670. Left to their own devices, the French at Port Royal abandoned their homes, pushed five or ten miles up the river, and hung on until fortune favored them once again.[26]

In 1667 the Treaty of Breda restored Acadia to France, and by 1670 the French were again in effective control of the colony. Hector d'Andigné de Grandfontaine, the first of a series of new governors, arrived the following year and set up headquarters across the Bay of Fundy at Pentagouet. Grandfontaine immediately ordered a nominal census of the population which was carried out and completed by the Franciscan priest Laurent Molin.[27]

On the basis of the 1671 census—a bit difficult to interpret because of duplications and omissions—it has been estimated that the total permanent Acadian population in that year was about five hundred. The entry for Vincent Brault reads as follows:

> Laboureur—Vincent Brot aagé de quarante ans, sa femme Marie Bour [Bourg], aagée de 25 ans, leurs enfans, quatre: Marie, aagée de neuf ans; Anthoine, aagé de 5 ans; Margueritte, aagée de trois ans; Pierre, aagé d'un an; leurs bestiaus à cornes, neuf, et sept brebis; leurs terres en labour, quattre arpans.[28]

> (Plowman—Vincent Brot age forty, his wife Marie Bour [Bourg], age 25, their four children: Marie, age nine; Anthoine, age five; Margueritte, age three; Pierre, age one; nine head of cattle and seven sheep; four arpents of plowed land.)

Along the Annapolis River, groups of farming families eventually gathered into tiny villages. Besides farming, to add variety to their ordinary fare habitants engaged in berry-gathering and hunting in the nearby fields and woods, and fishing for alewives, bass, and shad in local streams. A supply of meat and fish was salted or smoked for the winter. The most popular form of travel was by bark canoe, which every member of the family learned to handle skillfully. Small skiffs were also used. The population of Port Royal, especially on the farms upstream, grew steadily over the following years.

Vincent Brault died before 1686 when he would have been fifty-five years old.[29] His widow, Marie Brault, stayed on in Port Royal where no doubt she was looked after by her son Jean Brault; born in 1675, at the time of the 1714 census he still lived in the vicinity with his wife and five children. The parish register records that Marie Brault passed away there on September 19, 1730, at the age of eighty-six.[30]

At Port Royal, D'Aulnay had built a fort, a part of whose earthworks together with a storehouse and powder magazine can still be seen. In the seventeenth and eighteenth centuries, the fort was the scene of many sieges; it changed hands several times and underwent numerous modifications. Today, however, the site of this fort—Fort Anne National Historic Park—is dominated by the old British officers' quarters, erected in 1797 (reconstructed in 1935), which houses a small museum.

Grand Pré

Shortly after the French regained control of Acadia about 1670, several young Port Royal settlers, desiring to make a fresh start in an area where there would be less interference from the French or the English, migrated up the Bay of Fundy to the Chignecto and Minas Bay areas.[31] By 1707 more than 580 persons were living here. The settlers planted oats, wheat, peas, and other vegetables in the tidal marshlands, and apple orchards soon dotted the neighboring countryside. The inhabitants traded regularly with New England merchants who sent small vessels up the Bay of Fundy to barter tools, textiles, sugar, and spices for the Acadians' fish, furs, and surplus grain and livestock. This traffic was illegal, but in view of their isolation and their neglect by the French, the trade was absolutely essential for the Acadians' well-being.

Vincent Brault's sons soon joined the earliest emigrants from Port Royal to the Minas Basin. In 1701 Pierre was living at St. Croix River with his first wife, Marie Bourgeois, and their four children. After Marie died, Pierre remarried in 1705—his second wife was Anne LeBlanc—and settled a few miles to the west at Rivière aux Canards.[32]

Rivière aux Canards is one of four roughly parallel tidal streams— Canard, Habitant, Pereau, and St. Antoine (present-day Cornwallis)— which flow east into the Minas Basin. The main settlement was a short distance to the east at Grand Pré, an ill-fated village that took its name from a thousand-acre marsh used for farming. By midcentury the population of Grand Pré and the settlements to the west along nearby streams, especially the Canard, was an estimated twenty-five hundred. Grand Pré proper, comprised of some two hundred houses situated on a slight rise at the edge of the marsh, stretched between present-day Hortonville and Wolfville.[33]

It was customary to refer to clusters of farms as "villages" because of their proximity to one another and the close family ties of their inhabitants. The name of each village was derived from the surname of the principal family residing there (for example, Village des Comeau, Village des LaPierre, Village des Trahan) or, to avoid confusion, from the Christian name of the principal head of family (Village de Claude [Boudreau] at Rivière des Habitants as opposed to Village de Michel [Boudreau] at Rivière aux Canards). In one case, an abridged form of the family name was used: Village des Coin (for Aucoin).[34]

In 1755 the Village des Brault at Rivière aux Canards included twenty different families. Pierre Brault, eighty-five years old in that year, lived in proximity to his four sons, Joseph (born 1706), Pierre (1713), Paul (1717), and Amand (1721), and his grandson Joseph (1739), Joseph's son.[35] In fact, by then Pierre senior was doubtless living with his son Joseph. Such an arrangement was normal; many Acadian households had three and even four generations living under one roof.

A few stone houses had been built at Grand Pré, but everywhere else the homes, barns, and stables were framed of timber. Churches and presbyteries were located at Grand Pré (Saint Charles parish), Canard (Saint Joseph), and Pisiquid (Assumption of the Blessed Virgin and Holy Family). Nothing remains today of any of these buildings.

Acadian marshland farming—the only kind of agriculture practiced to any great extent on the peninsula before 1755—was very distinctive. Each habitant family sealed off four or five acres of marshland that normally was covered with seawater at high tide. This task was accomplished by constructing a dike at low tide. Deep clumps of turf were cut along a line and turned over to build a compact bank about five feet high and ten feet wide at the base, tapering to about one or two feet wide at the top. Grass soon formed a thick mat over the low causeway. Sluices were cut into the wall and fitted with clapper-valve gates (*aboiteaux*), permitting fresh water from streams and rainfall to flow out at low tide but preventing sea water from seeping back in at high tide. Two or three years were needed for rain to wash out the salt from the reclaimed land.[36]

The year 1710 marked the beginning of the end of French power in North America.[37] In that year Port Royal fell, and shortly afterward the Treaty of Utrecht (1713) recognized British sovereignty over most of the area designated ever since as Nova Scotia. However, the French retained control of Cape Breton Island and the territory later known as New Brunswick and Maine.

On the surface, life continued as before for the Acadians in various parts of the peninsula. They tended their farms and remained grouped in steadily expanding communities at Annapolis Royal, the Minas Basin, and elsewhere. But much had changed. The French urged the Acadians to move to

Cape Breton, but few responded to this appeal. Having come this far largely on their own, they were reluctant to exchange a relatively secure way of life for an uncertain existence elsewhere.

For their part, the English recognized the deputies elected annually by the Acadians to represent various districts and also allowed the local notaries to continue serving as public officers. The deputies played a key role in representing Acadian interests before the governor and his council at Annapolis Royal. For forty years the Acadians presented arguments and petitions through their deputies and resisted repeated English efforts to require them to take an unqualified oath of allegiance. However, the vast majority did not aid the French in their raids on British settlements and shipping in the area. For the most part, the clergy encouraged the Acadians to remain steadfastly neutral.[38]

Louisbourg

The decision of French authorities in 1718 to build a huge fortress city near the western tip of Cape Breton complicated matters.[39] Begun in 1720, and of enormous strategic importance because it guarded the entrance to the Cabot Strait, hence the St. Lawrence, Louisbourg became a symbol of French power in North America. For twenty years the French poured vast sums into the fortress which incorporated the most advanced military engineering concepts of the day. The fort was completed on the eve of King George's War (1744–48).

In 1745 a land and naval force consisting of over five thousand New England volunteers captured Louisbourg. In New England the colonists' jubilation over the surrender of the much-vaunted citadel—Louisbourg Square in Boston commemorates this event (although most of its Greek Revival houses were built in the 1830s or 1840s)—turned to bitterness when, by the terms of the Treaty of Aix-la-Chapelle in 1748, Louisbourg was returned to French control. The following year Halifax was founded on the eastern coast of Nova Scotia for the express purpose of neutralizing the threat posed by this fortress.

When, in 1758, a year before the fall of Quebec, an English army led by Jeffrey Amherst and James Wolfe recaptured Louisbourg, the great French citadel's defenses were systematically demolished. Little but rubble remained in 1928 when the Canadian government decided to designate the area a national historic site. In 1962 a vast federal project was undertaken to restore approximately one-fifth of the original town as it existed just prior to the first siege in 1745.

Visitors to Fortress of Louisbourg National Historic Park may stroll along its impressive battlements and take guided tours through the Château Saint Louis, where the governor's sumptuous apartments and other authentically furnished rooms are located. Barracks, private residences, shops, and other facilities—fifty buildings in all—have been carefully reconstructed. Costumed guides and other personnel in period civilian and military garb add to the restoration. A small museum contains artifacts recovered in the ruins and provides an instructive account of the painstaking research that preceded the restoration.

The deportation of the Acadians

After the Treaty of Aix-la-Chapelle, few expected peace between the French and English colonists to last very long.[40] When hostilities began again in 1754, in what historians would later call the French and Indian War,[41] Gov. William Shirley of Massachusetts and Lt. Gov. Charles Lawrence of Nova Scotia sent a joint expedition under the command of Lt. Col. Robert Monckton, British commandant at Annapolis Royal, seconded by Lt. Col. John Winslow of Massachusetts, against Fort Beauséjour and Fort Gaspereau, two newly constructed French outposts on the Chignecto Isthmus, which they regarded as British territory.[42] The move was designed to break a vital link in the chain of French forts encircling the British colonies and to isolate Louisbourg from Quebec. The campaign, which was entirely successful, was also intended to stem the exodus of Acadian refugees, many of them able to bear arms, toward French-held territory.

The Acadians were willing to swear allegiance to the king of England—and had done so in 1730—but only on condition that they would never be obliged to take up arms against France. If forced to take an unqualified oath, the Acadians indicated that they would leave their homeland of their own accord. Since they depended upon the Acadians to produce food, the English hesitated for a long time to act decisively in this matter. Meanwhile, fear of Acadian support of a French counteroffensive from Louisbourg and Quebec mounted. News of Maj. Gen. Edward Braddock's stunning defeat at Fort Duquesne (Pittsburgh) on July 9, 1755, intensified British frustration.

At a meeting held in Halifax on July 28, Lawrence and the Nova Scotia council voted unanimously to deport all the French Acadians to various British colonies. Massachusetts volunteers under Winslow's command executed Lawrence's orders.

It is difficult to estimate the number of Acadians who resided in various settlements in 1755. Many emigrated from the region in the early part of the decade. Probably between 8,000 and 9,500 remained by midcentury.[43] The largest number—6,000 to 7,000 men, women, and children—were forcibly removed in the massive deportations of 1755. But hundreds more were sent out in each of the following years, perhaps an additional 2,000 in all before 1763.[44] Since the nineteenth century, historians have referred to the Acadian diaspora as Le Grand Dérangement (The Great Uprooting).

The first roundup of Acadians took place at Fort Beauséjour (now called Fort Cumberland), and other assemblies were held at Annapolis Royal and Pisiquid (Fort Edward). However, the most celebrated gathering occurred on September 5 at Saint Charles Church in Grand Pré, where 418 Acadian men and boys responded to Winslow's summons and were made prisoners. They were detained until late October in a fenced-in camp near the church or on board ships anchored offshore a short distance away. Today nothing remains of the original church. In 1922 the edifice was reconstructed, using period buildings as models. It houses a small museum with a few Acadian artifacts. The most interesting relics are perhaps two cruets and a double cup discovered in a neighboring field. The cruets may have been used to hold water and wine, the cup to serve communion under both species at mass.

Shortly after the men and boys were incarcerated, a list of the French households in the Grand Pré area was drawn up by Father François Landry, the only Catholic priest allowed to remain with his people. On September 15 Winslow entered a copy—the original has not survived—in his journal, now preserved in the library of the Massachusetts Historical Society at Boston. Many of the names were garbled by Winslow but can be interpreted with the help of other sources. The tally included 446 males listed by name and village. In each case, the number of sons (527 in all), daughters (576), and farm animals was also listed. Married women were not identified but a total of 387 was indicated. Additionally, 820 persons not already accounted for were said to be aged and infirm, for a grand total of 2,743 individuals.

According to this census, the Village des Brault consisted of households headed by the following persons: Amand Brault, Joseph Brault, Joseph Brault fils, Paul Brault, Pierre Brault fils, Olivier Daigle, Olivier Daigle fils, Etienne Deroy, Joseph Hébert, Manuel Hébert, Pierre Hébert, Simon Pitre, and Germain Richard.[45] Amand, Joseph, Paul, and Pierre fils were the sons of Pierre Brault, age eighty-five, whose name was not provided; Joseph Brault fils was his grandson. The family name appears as Brune and the village is called Burne.

The slow and confusing process of embarkation began on October 8. In his journal, Winslow described the boarding as "a Sceen of woe & Distres."[46] He was much affected by the anguished women carrying children in their arms and by the aged and infirm. He tried to make room for entire families and even villages in the same vessel; but in the haste and confusion, children became separated from their parents, wives from their husbands. To the very end, the Acadians could not believe that the deportation orders would actually be carried out. On October 27, Winslow wrote that the fleet was under sail.

This tragic episode inspired one of America's greatest writers. Henry Wadsworth Longfellow's celebrated poem, *Evangeline: A Tale of Acadie* (1847), is the story of a maiden's constancy and faithfulness throughout thirty years of wandering in search of her fiancé. Separated from her lover in the Deportation of 1755, she eventually finds him on his deathbed. Longfellow got the idea for his poem from the Rev. Horace Lorenzo Conolly, rector of Saint Matthew's Episcopal Church in South Boston, who later said he heard it from one of his parishioners, Mrs. George Mordaunt Haliburton, a French Canadian.[47]

Was there a historical prototype to Evangeline? The best-known candidate is Emmeline Labiche whose biography bears a certain resemblance to that of the heroine.[48] Whether based on a true adventure or not, the poem was greatly admired and, by 1947, had appeared in 270 different editions and at least 130 translations.[49] The poem also was evoked through many illustrations, motion pictures, musical compositions, and plays. Too sentimental for most tastes today, *Evangeline* remains, for persons of Acadian heritage, a powerful symbol of their people's unbreakable will to survive.

The fourteen transports from Grand Pré and surrounding areas rendezvoused in the Bay of Fundy with ten other ships carrying Acadians rounded up at Fort Cumberland. The twenty-four vessels held about four thousand Acadians. Three English warships, the *Halifax*, the *Nightingale*, and the *Warren*, served as a convoy. A day or two after setting out, the ships were scattered by a violent storm, and individual vessels put in wherever they could. None of the colonies for which the transports were bound had been officially apprised ahead of time.

The Acadians deported to the American colonies on this and later occasions were dispersed as follows:[50]

Massachusetts	2,000
Virginia	1,140
Maryland	1,000
Connecticut	700
Pennsylvania	500
Carolinas	500
Georgia	400
New York	300
Total	6,540

Few Acadians settled permanently in these colonies. After the Treaty of Paris was signed in 1763, nearly all moved to Quebec, the Maritime Provinces, or the French West Indies.

Acadians began arriving in Louisiana in small numbers soon after 1755. Hundreds of families, who had been transported initially to the American colonies or who had sought refuge in the French West Indies about this time, emigrated to Louisiana after the Treaty of Paris. They were joined, especially in the 1780s, by large numbers of Acadians who had been sent to France two decades earlier.[51]

Exile in Massachusetts

On November 3, 1755, the *Boston Evening Post* reported that several transports that were heading elsewhere carrying Acadians had arrived in the harbor the day before.[52] A committee of the Massachusetts House of Representatives was named to investigate rumors of deplorable conditions aboard. The inquiry revealed overcrowding, a shortage of water and provisions, and much sickness. Many passengers were lying on the decks exposed to the elements. Some of the men had been imprisoned on the ships for two months, and the ravages wrought by the storm were also evident. After deliberation, the Massachusetts General Court ordered that 134 of the 1,077 Acadians be allowed to disembark in family groups before the vessels could proceed to their original destinations. Thus, on November 7, 1755, the first Acadians—including some aged and infirm persons—were placed in private homes in Boston and surrounding towns, or in the workhouse at Charlestown.

Other groups of Acadians began arriving in Boston shortly afterward, and the influx continued until the following August. A few men were allowed to rejoin their families after that date, but larger groups were barred from entering by Massachusetts officials. On December 24, 1755, special statutes were hastily enacted by the general court directing a joint committee of both houses to distribute the Acadians in family groups to various town in Massachusetts. The families were eventually assigned to 110 communities. Sheriffs were ordered to transport them with their baggage to their respective destinations, and the selectmen and overseers of the poor were instructed to attend to their needs. It was assumed that the Acadians would be able to support themselves in due time. In spite of Massachusetts experiencing severe economic difficulties and work being scarce for the next few years, most Acadians, after an initial adjustment period, did not become burdens on the colony.

On March 6, 1756, a law was passed directing local authorities to provide a house, farming implements, and handicraft tools for all deportees who could support themselves, and suitable relief for those who could not. Each community kept a list of such expenses and was reimbursed annually by the general court. The bills submitted by the towns and the various petitions received by the committee in charge of affairs concerning the "French Neutrals" are preserved in the Massachusetts Archives and provide an extraordinarily detailed account of hardship cases and grievances.[53]

The towns were displeased by the responsibility thrust upon them, and some treated their wards shabbily. Families were often obliged to move several times before they finally found decent accommodations. On the whole, however, towns provided reasonable aid. The Acadians either managed to find work on their own or were bound out by the selectmen. The men and boys did farm work, cut firewood, fashioned wooden farm implements and kitchen utensils, and, in the 1760s in Boston, worked as fishermen and laborers. The women and girls were employed as spinners and weavers as well as servants, but they also helped the men in the fields.

Some friendships were formed between the Acadians and English, but for the most part the two groups kept to themselves. Generations of bitter conflict in North America between the French and English and religious intolerance, bred this hostility. The memory of bloody raids by the French and Indians at York in 1692, Deerfield in 1704, and many other localities had burnt itself into the minds of Massachusetts residents. A real threat of renewed attacks was present in the 1750s.[54]

Protestant ministers constantly fanned anti-Catholic passions. In February 1756 a letter addressed to Governor Shirley by both houses of the legislature alluded to the Acadians as "persons whose gross bigotry to the Roman Catholic religion is notorious."[55] The persecution of the Protestants in France was another sore point. Often both concerns were fused.[56]

The dramatic fall of Quebec City in September 1759 and the collapse of all French resistance in Canada a year later at Montreal removed the threat of a French attack upon Massachusetts. But it was not until seven years later that the Acadians were free to leave the colony.

Many members of the Brault family managed to stay together during the journey and after arriving in the Bay Colony. Until 1760 octogenarian Pierre Brault and his spouse, two of his sons, Amand and Joseph, and Joseph's son, and their families were all residing at Braintree or nearby Hingham about ten miles southeast of Boston. A third son, Paul, and his family lived across the bay at Ipswich, twenty-five miles north of Boston.

The first mention of Pierre Brault in records preserved in the Massachusetts Archives appears in an application dated February 4, 1757, from the selectmen of Braintree for reimbursement of expenses incurred in providing for three Acadian families from June 10 to November 10, 1756. The document concerns the households of François LeBlanc (Fransway Liblong), Pierre Brault (Pere Brew), and Amand Brault (Amon Brew):[57]

> 1756, June the 10th, Fransway Liblong and family, 7 in all, were put out to Board at Eighteen Shillings and Eight pence p[r] weak. . . . . £20—10—
>
> Pere Brew and family of seven were put out for thirteen and four pence p[r] weak Each of what Labour they Did. . . . . £14—13—
>
> ~~Young~~ Amon Brew and family of Seven were put out on the same terms. . . . . £14—13—
>
> Error Excep[d]   £49—17—

Since the application did not provide enough particulars, clarification was requested by the joint committee on Acadian affairs. On April 25, 1757, the selectmen complied as follows:[58]

> To the Honourable Gentleman Committy appointed to Exammin the accompts of the Charge of the Late inhabatents of Nova Scotia
>
> In Obedience to the Order of the General Court dated Jan the 21, 1757. The following is a List of the Names and Circumstances of the French Inhabitants of Nova Scotia now residing in the Town of Braintree taken by the Selectmen this 25th Day of April 1757.

Names	Age	Circumstances of Health	Capacity for Labour
1st Family			
Perre Braux	87 Years	Invalid	Incapable
Ana Braux	77	d° [ditto]	d°
Joseph Braux	51	Invalid	d°
Joseph Braux j[n]	18	. . . .	Capable
Amon Braux j[n]	17	. . . .	d°
John Sam[l] Braux	15	Invalid	Incapable
Margaret Braux	19	d°: subject to Fitts	d°
2d Family			
Ammon Braux	40	. . . .	Capable
Magdalen Braux	36	near her Time	Incapable
Mary Braux	11 or 12	weakly	d°
John Braux	9	. . . .	d°
Joseph Braux	7	. . . .	d°
Magdalen Braux	5	. . . .	d°
Margaret Braux	3	. . . .	d°

3ᵈ Family

Francis Leblond	75	Invalid	Incapable
Joan Leblond	72	dº	dº
James Leblond	51	Weakly	Capable in Part
Catharine Leblond	49	dº	Capable in Part
Mary Magdalen Leblond	14	. . . .	Capable
John Baptist Leblond	12	. . . .	Capable of his Age
Beloni Leblond	7	. . . .	Incapable

Josᵃˢ Quincy
Richard Brackett
Jonᵃ Allen
Ebenʳ Thayer Jun
} Select Men

On the back of the sheet, the selectmen added the following information:

1ˢᵗ Family but 2 beds and the Cover of both wore out. All of them destitutte of Linnen or Shirting and the old persons, very poorly cloathd, have been supplyd with what they have by Capt. Thayer with whom they livd as pʳ his accoᵗ to be rendered.

2ⁿᵈ dº but one Bed in the same Condition and the whole Family but poorly Cloathid tho in some measure provided with Cloath of their own making by Mʳ Rawson's help with whom they Live as pʳ his Accoᵗ to be rendered.

3ʳᵈ dº but one Bed middling good and the Family pretty well cloathd by their own Labour.

The document shows that Pierre and his second wife, Anne (LeBlanc), were residing with their son Joseph, a widower, and his children. Jacques LeBlanc and his spouse had their aged parents, François and Jeanne (Hébert) LeBlanc, in their care in a similar arrangement. François also came from Grand Pré and was related by marriage to Pierre Brault.[59]

The list and accompanying comments reveal the appalling state of the family's health in their first year in Massachusetts: the four grandparents, Pierre's son Joseph, and the latter's son Jean Anselme (John Samuel) and daughter Marguerite were all invalids; Amand's wife was about to have a baby, and three other persons—two adults (Jacques LeBlanc and his wife) and one eleven-year-old child, Marie Brault—were weakened by illness. Only four of the fourteen persons of working age were fully capable of being employed, three more only being able to perform tasks not requiring sustained effort. The note on the back of the document completes this picture of human misery: three beds for twenty-one people, worn-out blankets, tattered clothes.

The seven adult members of Pierre Brault's family lived in a single room in the home of a certain Captain Thayer, a wheelwright by trade. Amand

and his family resided with a man named Rawson. Thayer's accompanying statement offers valuable insight into the character of one individual charged with looking after a helpless Acadian family:[60]

Gentlemen,

As there is Dificulty in Respect of the accompt of the Charge of the French people Exhibited by the Selectmen of the Town of Braintree by Reason of its not being so perticoler as your Honners Require, I have ben at the trouble to Spend two Days in waiting upon your Hon[rs] that I might have an an opportunity when you was together to Give you my Reasons why it was a hard thing for me to keep an Exact accompt of Every perticuler article which I supplied them with.

I now take Liberty to offer to your Hon[rs] Consideration some few among the many that might be offered.

The family which I undertook to provoid for Consisting of Seven at first—although I soon turned out two young men to provoid for themselves—viz. Samuel Brow [Brault] and wife being very old people, he near ninty and she Eigtey years of age and their Son above fifty, a weekly man always having a bad Cough and other infirmities, one Garil about Eighteen year old being also weekly and Exersised with Greivious Convoltion Fitts, one weekly boy, the other two were turned out to provoid for themselves—as these above being a helples family and my wife seeing what a poor hand they made of makeing there own Bread makeing so much wast of meal, Choos Reather, with some asistance from them, to make their bread for them with our own and Let them have it as they wanted it. I Let them milk one Cow at their pleasure for the most part. They had the Liberty of my orchard for aples to bake and eat with milk which they Choos. And it Lesned the Quantity of bread which I Come hardly by. So far this was to my advaintage. They had also the liberty of Gathering hearbs and roots for Saunce in my feild and Gardin. My wife was also obligd to Let them have Sope to was their Cloths with or they wood have filled my family with Lice.

Thes Articles, Gentlemen, I never Expect to be able to Give any better accompt for. Neither do I Expect to have the value of them. I am Senceble, Gent[m], you will Conclood by the acount I have given of the Circomstances of thes people that they Eat but Lettle but I must tell your Hon[rs] that they are very foody people for I was abligd to bring them to Lowance as to meet for which I am the best able to accompt for, for I Delivered that to them by weight for the most part. On they woold ofen Complain. The Quantaty of Beef and Salt fish which I supplid them with was one pound to Each person per day which amunted to thirty-five pounds p[r] weak. When I gave them pork, Something Less woold answer. As to wood I Cannot say how much, my trade being a Wheelwright, affounded a Supply of Chips which I Coold not measure by the Cord.

I Shoold have sed before that this family Lived in one room in my house which I Dwell in they year past which mad it more Dificult to accompt for Every Sone article.

Thus, Gent[m], I have Supplied these peoples as I think. Your Hon[rs] must be Senceble to my Damaige as I have had the Care of them from the first, the most of any one man in this town. I have been much Concearnd on account of the Charge which I see woold by these people arise. I have Encoureged people to imploy those that provoided for themselves and taken Cair that they were not Defrauaded in there wages for which I have Charged nothing for otherwaies then at the foot of the accompt which we have presended to your Hon[rs] in that article of the Selectmen's trouble.

We have found and Do Still fiend by Experiance that 2/8. p^r weak is the Cheepest Lay that we Could Supply them. However, Gentlemen, we shall, I beleve, never troble your Hon^{rs} with any more Such accompts.

I am Senceble that the burden is Great upon the provins. Your honnours are, I Doubt not, Sencebale it must be more so upon a few particuler men.

I have Said too much already but Considering I have had not one farthing for almost fifteen months and the burthen Still Lieing upon me Constrains me to apply myself to your Honnours. I Know it is in your power only and if it be your pleasure to Grant me my Due, I shall be glad to Know it. I can hardly Call myself a baggar in this Case, but Sure I am I must begg my bread at this Rate.

> I am, Gentlemen,
> Your Hum^{le} Ser^t
> Jon:^{a} Allen

Braintree, Jan:^{r}
  the 23^d 1758

To the Hon^{le} Gentleman Committy
appointed to Exammin the accompts
of the Charge of the inhabatents Nova Scotia.

Later records suggest that conditions improved somewhat in the following years,[61] but Thayer's wheedling and self-serving account indicates that initially the Brault family survived on a meager diet. Also, wood scraps were all they had for a fire to ward off the icy blasts of winter.

Pierre's fifty-one-year-old son evidently recovered his health, for he was bonded out to Hingham in 1760 with his two sons. Pierre and his spouse were still living in that year as they are known to have moved to Boston.[62] Pierre may have died there shortly afterward. His widow Anne lived on until 1763; also at this time Joseph's son Amand now twenty-three, was listed as married to Madeleine Dupuis. At least one child, Amand-Damien, was born to the couple in Massachusetts.

In 1760 the general court shifted the burden of providing for the Acadians from the province to the counties, at the same time redistributing the families. All Acadians able to support themselves were henceforth allowed to live anywhere they wished in Massachusetts. Work was increasingly hard to find at this time, and the deportees began to crowd into Boston, expecting to be permitted to leave soon. However, their exile was only half over. In the following years, their hopes were repeatedly dashed as petition after petition to emigrate—to France, to the islands of St. Pierre and Miquelon off Newfoundland, or to San Domingo (Haiti)—was turned down. Throughout these negotiations, the English were reluctant to augment the number of colonists in French possessions in the Western Hemisphere. In 1764 Pierre Brault's three sons, Amand, Joseph, and Pierre, and their families were living at Nantasket.[63]

On March 1, 1765, James Murray, governor of Canada, issued a proclamation offering to receive the Acadians in his province. In Massachusetts, 890 Acadians expressed a desire to accept his invitation. When, in 1766, they were finally allowed to leave, only one Acadian family elected to remain behind in that colony.[64] Individual towns contributed funds to help move their former residents, and in March 1767 the general court responded to appeals from Acadians in Massachusetts still unable to afford transportation to Canada—now numbering fewer than a hundred—and paid their way.

According to tradition, a group of two hundred families set out on foot from Boston, traveling along the coast of Maine to New Brunswick, across the Chignecto Peninsula, and eventually to the southern tip of Nova Scotia, leaving settlers in various localities encountered in this odyssey. Another large group is said to have trekked to Lake Champlain—possibly along the Mohawk Trail—and from there down the Richelieu River to Bécancour, Iberville, Montcalm, and St. John counties. Some of the Braults may have been among them. However, most of the Acadian exiles in Massachusetts probably reached the Maritime Provinces and Quebec by ship. For example, two schooners transporting Acadian exiles are known to have reached Quebec City in early September 1766.[65]

Many Acadians who returned to Canada founded communities, especially in certain areas of New Brunswick, that have remained distinctive to this day.[66] In Quebec, it is more difficult to differentiate persons descended from the Acadians from the rest of the French-speaking population. However, a few Quebec villages, among them L'Acadie, are proud of their Acadian heritage.

L'Acadie, Quebec

Although many extended families had managed to stay together during their exile in Massachusetts, now in Quebec they tended to settle in scattered communities where other Acadians could be found.[67] Pierre Brault's sons Joseph and Pierre were living at L'Assomption, west of Montreal, in 1767; a third son, Paul, was at nearby Saint-Jacques-de-l'Achigan about the same time; and a fourth son, Amand, was at St. Ours on the Richelieu River in 1766. Meanwhile, Joseph's sons and their families located a short distance away on the southern shore of the St. Lawrence River: Amand and Joseph at La Prairie, in 1767, and Jean-Anselme at Chambly (on the Richelieu). A cousin, Alexis Brault, was also living at La Prairie about this time. By 1783 the latter and Joseph's son Amand had moved to L'Acadie.[68]

L'Acadie, a village situated southeast of Montreal between La Prairie and St. John, was first settled by French Canadians about the middle of the century, before the Acadian deportation. They were joined in 1764 by an Acadian named Jean-Baptiste Cyr and, beginning in the spring of 1768, by hundreds of Acadian deportees. Like other villages in the province colonized by repatriated Acadians, the community became known as La Cadie, La Nouvelle Cadie, and La Petite Cadie. The designation La Cadie—now spelled L'Acadie—eventually won out.[69]

In 1782 the bishop of Quebec granted a petition by the inhabitants of this village to build a church and a rectory, and to lay out a cemetery on seventeen arpents of land donated by Jacques Hébert. The parish was dedicated to Saint Marguerite of Blairfindie in honor of Capt. David Alexander Grant of Blairfindie, Scotland. The British officer had married, the preceding year, the French-Canadian heiress on whose seigneurie (Longueuil) a part of the parish was located.

Today, L'Acadie is known to tourists and art historians for its second parish church.[70] Work on this remarkable stone edifice was begun in 1800 and finished the following year. Built according to a simple plan devised by Father Pierre Conefroy of Boucherville, the structure has a high-pitched roof and an elegant wooden steeple rising from the gable over the main portal. A bell purchased in 1790 hangs in the lower of the two lanterns, or openings, in the tower.

Inside, the basket-handle vault, the walls, and the apse are richly ornamented with contemporary wood sculptures carved and gilded by Jean Georges Finsterer, a native of Switzerland, and his son David, both residents of L'Acadie. The main altar, tabernacle, altarpiece, pulpit, and organ loft were also carved and decorated by them. The pews—with doors to keep out icy drafts that occurred when parishioners entered or left the building in the winter—were built in 1850–51. Tasteful restoration of the interior and exterior of the church was accomplished in 1955 and 1969. The church and nearby stone presbytery (1821) and schoolhouse (1828) have been designated as historical landmarks. No tombstone earlier than 1832 survives in the parish cemetery, where more than seven thousand persons are buried.

Born in 1740 at Rivière aux Canards, Amand Brault was fifteen years old when the deportation began. He married Marie-Madeleine Dupuis in Massachusetts about 1764. The couple eventually had seven children; two of them—Amand-Damien and Pierre-Benjamin—were born during the exile. In 1783 Amand was one of the signers of the petition to establish a new parish at L'Acadie, and the following year he was one of the first three marguilliers elected by this congregation. After Marie-Madeleine died in 1793, Amand married Marie Jeannotte (1795) and a daughter was born of this union. Amand died at L'Acadie in 1810.[71]

Between the Treaty of Paris in 1763 and the great emigration to New England that began a century later, a swirl of events relative to the American Revolution,[72] the War of 1812, and the Patriote Rebellion of 1837–38 occurred in the strategic Richelieu Valley in and around L'Acadie. Three generations of Braults who lived there were no doubt affected by these developments and perhaps even involved in them. However, nothing is known about these obscure individuals except their names, the record of their births, marriages, and deaths, and that they were ordinary farmers living in a troubled period of history.

Amand Brault's son Amand-Damien, born in Massachusetts in 1765, married Elisabeth Jacques at Contrecoeur in 1786 but spent his life at L'Acadie.[73] The couple raised ten children, all of whom were baptized in this parish. Amand-Damien died there in 1821. Although all his children except one were married at L'Acadie, several established themselves a few miles to the south in the new parish of Saint Cyprien, founded in 1822, in an area known today as Napierville.

The parish registry indicates that Amand-Damien's sons had moved to Napierville by the following years: 1824, François; 1827, Jean-Anselme; 1828, Amand; and 1832, David. Amand-Damien's son Amand, born at L'Acadie in 1791, married Josephte Granger there in 1814. Six of their eight children were born in that parish, but Cyprien was baptized at Napierville in 1828, Jean-Baptiste in 1833. Other entries show that Amand returned to L'Acadie after 1843 and no later than 1845, and that he died there in 1861.[74]

Dwellings constructed in L'Acadie about this time resembled those built in other rural Quebec communities throughout the eighteenth century. The Roy home, erected in 1825, is a good example of this architectural style.[75] Whether made of wood or fieldstone—the latter building material was increasingly being used—the houses were small by modern standards, averaging about twenty square feet of floor space, and were dwarfed by high-pitched roofs (fifty to sixty degrees) often two-thirds of their elevation. The steep angle prevented any heavy accumulation of snow. Windows were small and none faced the northeast, the direction of prevailing winds. A ladder was usually affixed to the roof to provide quick access to smokestacks in case of chimney fires. Exterior stone walls were often covered with white plaster.[76]

Early eighteenth-century homes had no basements and were simply built on the ground. About 1780, structures began to be erected on a stone foundation as a protection against humidity and seepage. An over-hang (*larmier*) eighteen to twenty-eight inches wide and a porch three to five inches above the ground were also added for this purpose, and the angle of the roof was reduced by about ten degrees. A summer kitchen was sometimes attached. With rare exceptions, Quebec farmsteads consisted of scattered buildings and were not characterized by the connected architecture that was widespread in New England during this period.

Thompsonville, Connecticut

My great-grandfather, Julien Brault, born at L'Acadie in 1819, was about nine years old when his father, Amand, moved to Napierville. Julien was a day laborer when he married Domitille Cyr there in 1841.[77] The couple had no offspring for ten years, then nine children beginning in 1851. In that year Julien became a farmer, but evidently he did not prosper for by 1865 he was once again listed as a day laborer. This was still his occupation in later years. Meanwhile, his family was growing—Philias, his last child, was born in 1869—and, probably, in dire straits.[78]

In 1870 three of Julien's daughters—Euphémie, eighteen, and the twins Célina and Délima, sixteen—were living together in a boarding house in Thompsonville, a section of Enfield, Connecticut.[79] The reason that the three Brault girls emigrated to this particular community is clear: they came to work in the carpet mills established there by Orrin Thompson in 1828.[80] This was their occupation according to the 1870 United States census. They probably learned of this employment opportunity through relatives or friends.

By 1860 Enfield had a population of five thousand, including several families of French-Canadian immigrants. Among these was Moïse Beaulac, a brewer; Frédéric Hélie, a merchant; Joseph Pépin, a cooper; Félix Raiche, a laborer; Louis Rodier, a machinist; and several employees—Adolphus and Louis Descôteaux, Martin Dufficy, and Abraham, Joseph, and Otha Manseau—at the powder works in Hazardville, another section of Enfield.[81] Thompsonville's French Canadians frequented Saint Patrick's Church, founded in 1863. Their numbers grew steadily so that, according to one source in 1908, the nine o'clock service was a French mass.[82] Saint Patrick's Franco-Americans never had their own priest, but the parish registry reveals a clear pattern of endogamy and socialization among this group.

According to family tradition, a fourth Brault daughter, Dorilda, twelve, joined her sisters in Thompsonville about 1872. By the time of the 1880 census, Julien, age sixty-one, and his wife Domitille, fifty-five, were living with their daughter Euphémie, now a dressmaker, and younger children,

Dorilda, twenty, Napoléon, seventeen, and Philias, ten. The three youngest worked in the carpet factory. Meanwhile, Julien's twin daughters, Célina and Délima, had married French Canadians in Saint Patrick's Church in 1874 and 1872, respectively.[83]

Julien never learned to read or write and spent the rest of his life in Thompsonville. He died there in 1892 at the age of seventy-four, the same year his daughter Euphémie, thirty-eight, passed away. His wife, Domitille, moved a short distance to Chicopee Falls, Massachusetts, to be near her daughter Dorilda, now married to Luc Roux, and died there in 1911. Julien, Domitille, and Euphémie are buried in the same plot in Saint Patrick's Cemetery at Thompsonville.

When my great-grandparents and four of their children emigrated from Napierville, Quebec, to Thompsonville, Connecticut, their eldest son, Julien fils, born in 1851, remained behind. As a youth, Julien fils—my grandfather—was apprenticed to a shoemaker in nearby Lacolle. By the time he was twenty, in 1871, he was plying his trade there. In that year he married Agnès Laroche in Saint Bernard parish at Lacolle.[84] By 1885 my grandparents had seven children. Not long afterward, and in order to pay off the mortgage on property acquired in 1875 for $245, they too moved to Thompsonville. According to family tradition, they stayed there ten years (1887–96?), saving $10,000 from earnings my grandfather made as a cobbler and from wages brought in by the eldest children who worked in the carpet factory. My father, Philias, and his brother, Philippe, were born in Thompsonville in 1889 and 1894, respectively; their younger sister, Yvonne—the last of ten children—was born in Lacolle in 1897, after the family had returned home.[85] Only one child, Arthur, remained in Connecticut. He was employed as an iron worker in nearby Hartford for forty years before he died there in 1936.

Lacolle, Quebec

Lacolle, a name given to certain hills (cf. *colline*) and streams in the south of France,[86] designates a creek that flows into the Richelieu River a few miles north of the present-day Quebec–New York State border. It indicated one of the last seigneurial grants (1733) made during the French regime.[87] First settled by French colonists as early as 1750, the concession remained sparsely populated until after the British Conquest.[88] During the American Revolution, Lacolle was the site of a sawmill (1778) that supplied boards and heavy timbers for the construction of a line of British blockhouses south of Montreal. (The wooden structure at Lacolle, erected about 1781, figured in two skirmishes during the War of 1812 and was listed as a historical monument in 1955. It houses a small museum today.)[89]

The area was chiefly developed by Loyalists from New York State, including Joseph Odell, in the latter part of the eighteenth century, but it also soon attracted French Canadians from Napierville and other nearby communities. By 1842 the French Canadians were still in a minority, but their number had grown to eight hundred. In that year, Saint-Bernard-de-Lacolle parish was founded, and a first church was erected a short distance from the village in 1844 (the present stone building was begun in 1865 and finished in ten years); a second parish, Notre-Dame-du-Mont-Carmel, with a church located in the village proper, was founded in 1908.[90]

At the turn of the century, the Brault family living in Lacolle consisted of my grandparents and eight of their ten children: the twins Adélina and Cordélia, Frédéric, Omer, Cléophas, Philias, Philippe, and Yvonne. (Aglore, the eldest daughter, had married Wilbrod Landry, proprietor of a small general store there, in 1898; Arthur resided in Hartford.)

At the time, the village had only two streets, Rue de l'Eglise, that is, National Highway 9A, and a side street, Rue St. Bernard. The house on Rue St. Bernard (now designated as 49, rue Van Vliet) once occupied by my grandfather and the smaller edifice adjacent to it that he used as a shoemaker's shop have been remodeled in recent years but still retain their nineteenth-century lines.

The Brault family's ties with Thompsonville, Connecticut, remained strong as is apparent from a photograph album that belonged to my grandparents about this time and that is now in my possession. Eight of the more than three-score family pictures it contains—none of them labeled and most, consequently, unidentifiable—bear the names of Thompsonville studios.

Three family members figure in a large composite photograph of Lacolle notables in 1909: my grandfather Julien (cobbler) and his two sons Frédéric (blacksmith) and Omer (tailor). Wilbrod Landry (storekeeper) and Alfred Boivin (butcher), who married Julien's daughter Aglore (1898) and Adélina (1906), also appear in this who's who. My father's future father-in-law, Gédéon Rémillard (butcher), can be seen in the photograph as well.

My maternal grandfather, Gédéon, was descended from François Hyacinthe Rémillard, a French Canadian—not an Acadian—who settled at L'Acadie at the end of the eighteenth century. (There he married Marie Amable Bourgeois, and then Charlotte Lamoureux, in 1796 and 1802 respectively).[91] Gédéon was born in nearby Stottsville (Saint-Valentin parish) in 1865 and took Virginie Thibodeau for a wife at Napierville in 1886.[92]

Lured away from country life by tales of high wages—according to family tradition, a relative on his wife's side, who worked in the industrial Northeast, created a great impression when he flashed a roll of bills—at the turn of the century Pépère Rémillard sold his house and nearly all his belongings and moved his family first to Cohoes, New York, then to Central Falls, Rhode Island, where some of his in-laws already resided. However, he was unhappy as a laborer, soon lost his illusions of making easy money in the States, and returned to Canada, settling in Lacolle.

The Rémillards now experienced further hardships. Like many other rural Quebec families of the day, they lost several children. Alexis, born in 1894, was kicked by a horse and succumbed to this injury at about the age of five; Alexandre (1901) and Méville Marcel (1906) did not survive a year; Aimé died in 1911 not far short of six.[93] Always frail, Mémère had to be cared for at home for years (she passed away in 1935 at the age of sixty-seven). Pépère spent his remaining years in Lacolle—the family home was on Rue de l'Eglise, across the street from Notre-Dame-du-Mont-Carmel Church—remarried in his seventies to Marie Godin, and died in 1947 at the age of eighty-two.

Only one of the six surviving Rémillard children, the eldest, opted for country living: Zénaïde married Eugène Hébert, a blacksmith, at Napierville in 1906. (Both died at the age of fifty-four in 1942 and 1939, respectively.) Three emigrated to the United States: Joseph to Albany, New York; Aline (my mother) to Chicopee Falls, Massachusetts; and Albert, briefly, to Chicopee, Massachusetts. After initially following in his father's footsteps and becoming a butcher in Lacolle, Albert settled for a few months in Chicopee in 1928–29. With the onset of the Great Depression, however, he returned home. Much later, in 1942, he began working for the Canadian immigration service at the United States border a few miles away, and in 1946 he moved to Lachine, on the outskirts of Montreal. The two remaining daughters, Blanche, who married Victor Julien in 1914, and Jeannette, who became Alfred Hébert's wife in 1919, also located in Montreal.

Today, Lacolle is a world away from the turn-of-the-century sleepy village with unpaved streets.[94] A flourishing community, it boasts small plants—Collins and Aikman (automobile carpeting), Finnie Manufacturing Company (work clothes, canvas products), North American Rockwell (automobile springs)—housing developments, and, on Rue de l'Eglise, a stylish new restaurant, La Porte du Ciel (a former Protestant church). Homes, offices, and stores have been refurbished, and there are late model cars everywhere. Several new streets have been opened, and all road surfaces are paved. There are still many farms in the area, but few residents in the village now use their property for agricultural purposes (farm equipment and outbuildings have all but disappeared here). For generations, enterprising young people moved away from Lacolle to the city. Nowadays, such individuals often work in local industries or commute to Montreal, easily reached via a superhighway that passes nearby, and enjoy the advantage of semirural living in a prosperous and rejuvenated Lacolle.

Manchester, New Hampshire

My father, Philias Brault, attended a one-room schoolhouse in Lacolle until he was thirteen, receiving the equivalent of a fourth-grade education. He was apprenticed for four years to Jules Girard and learned the carpenter's trade. (Throughout his life he was proud of the woodworking skills he had mastered as a youth.) His first jobs were in and around Lacolle where he also served a brief stint on a railroad gang. Since he had learned a bit of English, he was able also to find work as a store clerk across the border, a few miles away in Alburg, Vermont, and Plattsburgh, New York. But, like his father before him, he knew that the New England factory towns offered much better employment opportunities. So in 1910, shortly before his twenty-first birthday, he moved to Manchester, New Hampshire, where he was hired as a tentering machine hand, then as a trucker, in the huge Amoskeag Textile Mills.[95]

Philias lived on the west side of town, where most French Canadians of the day resided, and at first boarded with his uncle Marcellin Allard's family. He worked six days a week at the mill, from 6:00 A.M. to 6:00 P.M. But after mass on Sundays he enjoyed watching baseball games and strolling in the city's parks. He was a member of Saint Mary's parish and, in 1911, married Bernadette Corbière there.[96] She was a native of Napierville and, together with her mother, had come to live in Manchester. Philias had known them for some time as all three appear in a group photograph taken at his brother Frédéric's wedding at Lacolle in 1908. Philias's younger brother, Philippe, also moved to Manchester and was employed by Amoskeag about this time.

The newlyweds set up housekeeping at 393 Rimmon Street and in 1912 had a son, Roland. Things seemed to be going well enough when Philias's world began coming apart. A second son, Paul, born in 1915, lived only two days. The following year, Bernadette died of tuberculosis before reaching her twenty-fifth birthday. Plunged into grief, Philias returned to Lacolle. Four years later, his son Roland, who was only seven, passed away.[97]

Philippe remained in Manchester until he was called up in 1917. He served with the United States Army in France, was awarded the Purple Heart, and returned to Manchester where he married Rose Dionne in 1920.[98] Two of their children's names, Roland and Paul, recall this episode in Philias's life. Philippe and his family eventually settled in Aldenville (Chicopee), Massachusetts.

Chicopee Falls, Massachusetts

Meanwhile, in Lacolle, Philias, age thirty-one, seemed to be getting nowhere. Then things suddenly took a turn for the better. Uncle Luc Roux— Dorilda Brault's husband—had started out as a carpenter in Thompsonville but was now in business with his brothers as a small-time contractor in nearby Chicopee Falls, Massachusetts. He had done well in the boom years before and during World War I, and had acquired four separate properties, including tenements that he had helped to build. Thanks to him, Philias was able to make a fresh start in life.

Mon oncle Luc, who had no children of his own, offered to let his wife's nephew take over the mortgage of one of his properties. Philias could live rent free in one of his own tenements—initially at 146 East Main Street— and, by investing some of the money he would earn working in a factory, he would eventually own the property. Philias accepted the challenge.

He found a job at the Fisk Tire Company (he would soon discover that employment at the J. Stevens Arms was more to his liking) and, after settling in to the new routine, returned briefly to Lacolle and proposed to Aline Rémillard. On their wedding day, in 1921,[99] the couple boarded the train for Albany, New York. After an overnight stay with Aline's brother Joseph and his wife Bernadette, they continued their way to Chicopee Falls where they were to spend the rest of their lives.

The drudgery of holding down a full-time job in a factory while keeping up twenty tenements at the corner of Broadway and East Main Street was alleviated when, encouraged and at times assisted by his wife, Philias went into business for himself as an automobile and fire insurance agent. However, he continued to spend many evenings and Saturdays painting and wallpapering his tenements, disposing of trash, making small repairs, and collecting the rent.

The Braults spent twenty-four years and raised their four children in a part of Chicopee Falls that was predominantly French-Canadian. They were active members of Saint George's parish, and the children attended its school. Most of Philias's clients and, for years, practically all the family's acquaintances were Franco-American.

Philias maintained an office in his home at 1 Broadway before moving his business next door to 136½ East Main Street. In time he became a general agent of the General Accident Insurance Company. Like her husband, Aline was frugal and hardworking. She managed the household efficiently, saw to it that every room was clean and tidy, cooked all the meals, and kept a close watch on her children. She stayed up many nights sewing clothes for her three little girls.

The family had many good times. National and religious holidays as well as birthdays were cause for celebration. Many Sunday afternoons were spent at the movies or, after business began to boom during World War II, dining out. In the summertime there were picnics and outings to the beach. As the children grew older, traveling to local points of historical interest became a favorite family pursuit.

My parents lived according to strict precepts and strove to instill traditional values in their children. They loved their adoptive country but also taught their offspring to be mindful of their French-Canadian heritage. In the 1930s and during World War II, annual trips to Lacolle were an important part of this upbringing.

Leaving Chicopee Falls, we would drive northwest, then north, to Pittsfield, North Adams, and Williamstown, Massachusetts, then to Glens Falls, New York. There we would follow Route 9 north: Lake George, Ausable Chasm, Plattsburgh, Champlain, and, eventually, Rouses Point, New York.[100] Excitement began to mount when, at the end of this day-long journey, we finally reached Lacolle.

Driving down the unpaved main street was like entering another world. Grandparents, aunts, uncles, and cousins would come running out of their homes to greet us. Neighbors and other villagers would stop dead in their tracks and stare at us. We were *la grande visite des Etats!*

In Lacolle, very little ever seemed to change. We considered our grandparents' style of living dreadfully backward, dull, and rustic, and our own citified ways infinitely more modern and sophisticated. We were also acutely aware of farm smells and proud of our car and new clothes. Yet even as children we could appreciate the uncomplicated joys of rural existence and the warm feeling engendered by extended family relationships. On the other hand, language was a touchy subject, especially our interest in maintaining French.

Our first call was always at the Rémillards. Pépère, a tall, broad-shouldered man with a majestic bearing, was a jovial figure when I knew him in his old age; the calamities that filled his earlier years were completely unsuspected by his grandchildren. The parlor in the Rémillards's modest Victorian house was separated from the dining room by a beaded curtain. At the rear of the building, an attached stable sheltered a horse and buggy. A short bareback ride or a tour of the village in the horse-drawn carriage high-lighted our visit.

At Pépère Brault's more old-fashioned house, meals were taken in the kitchen around a long table, and to go to bed at night, the children were escorted to the loft by an aunt or uncle holding a lighted kerosene lamp. (Electricity came to Lacolle in 1927 but the Braults never felt the need to have it installed in their home.)[101] In the outhouse, catalog pages hung from the wall, pierced through by a nail. At some point, Pépère would take the children across the yard to his shop to show us the crude awls, lasts, and mallets of his trade, and the worn cobbler's bench. As he puttered around the barn, we would romp in the hay or stand amazed before the cows and pigs. Later, Pépère would ceremoniously set up his famous cro-quet game, and the grown-ups and children would have epic matches together.

Another stop in the round of visits at Lacolle was at mon oncle Fred's. It was exciting to enter his blacksmith shop and to watch him at work. The clangor of the metal tools on the anvil, the roar of the bellows, the bright red glow and the powerful odor of burning charcoal and hooves, the clouds of sizzling steam, and the virile grunts and movements of my lean and sinewy uncle grasping a horse's leg backwards between his knees and pounding nails through a horseshoe were unforgettable sights, smells, and sounds. The smithy is gone today but the house remains on Rue de l'Eglise. Like all the homes I knew in Lacolle, it has been remodeled inside and out. My cousin Conrad—mon oncle Fred's son—and his wife Thérèse live there now, my last remaining contact with Lacolle. Conrad is a retired customs officer and raises thoroughbred hunting dogs as a hobby.

When in Lacolle, we always visited with mon oncle Albert and his fam-ily, too. Each of my three sisters had a favorite cousin; mine was Albert's son Louis who was approximately my age. When Louis's mother, Clor-inde, died suddenly in 1936 at the age of thirty-two, my cousin spent two summers with us in Chicopee Falls; we have always been close. Louis is an English teacher in Montreal today.

We sometimes made brief side trips to Montreal where other relatives lived. Mama had a special devotion to Saint Joseph, so the journey to Quebec's metropolis always entailed a stop at the Oratoire Saint-Joseph. Mama would climb the long staircase in front of the shrine on her knees, saying a Hail Mary at each step. We all knew the story of Frère André—he was pictured on the calendar hanging in our kitchen—and the humble be-ginnings of this place of worship. Born at Saint-Grégoire d'Iberville in the Richelieu Valley, Alfred Bessette (1845–1937) was nineteen years old and an orphan in 1863 when he began working in textile mills in Hartford, Moosup, and Plainfield, Connecticut. Three years later, discouraged and penniless, he returned to St. Césaire in the eastern townships. In 1872 he entered religious life and, as a lowly brother, was assigned the duty of tending the door at the Collège Notre-Dame in Montreal, a task he fulfilled for forty years. Illiterate but extremely devout, he acquired an extraordinary reputation for healing diseases through the intercession of Saint Joseph. Although he tended to be gruff, especially with women, spent only two or three minutes with each visitor, and steadfastly denied being anything but *le petit chien de Saint Joseph,* hundreds beat a path to his door even during his annual vacations in West Warwick, Rhode Island, at the home of his sister Léocadie Lefebvre. The tiny wooden chapel he erected atop Mont-Royal in 1904 eventually grew into the Oratoire Saint-Joseph, one of the world's greatest shrines. Known to French Canadians and their descendants by his name in religion (le frère André), Alfred Bessette was beatified in 1982.[102]

We would gaze up at the shrine's unfinished copper-colored dome, proud to know that donations from ordinary French Canadians and Franco-Americans like Papa and Mama were helping to erect it; then we would stand in awe before the banks of red votive lights and the panoply of braces, canes, and crutches left by the healed.

Once, we visited Trois-Rivières and Quebec City. Many Franco-Americans are particularly devoted to the Blessed Virgin or to Saint Anne, and make regular pilgrimages to Cap de la Madeleine or Sainte-Anne-de-Beaupré near these two cities. For years my wife's uncle, Emile Douville, and his family made the trip from Hartford, Connecticut, arriving at Beaupré on July 26, the Feast of Saint Anne.[103] My wife's only visit as a girl to the Douville homestead in Sainte-Anne-de-la-Pérade near Trois-Rivières was occasioned by one such journey, in 1941, with her Uncle Emile.

The house in Chicopee Falls where I was born in 1929, which was the Brault residence until 1945, was at the corner of Broadway and East Main Street. A plain, two-story brick building attached to a row of others just like it, it resembled many tenements in the area except that its situation at the bottom of a hill allowed space at street level for a small business establishment (Max Bregman's tailor shop, then Gélinas's variety store, and, finally, Guérin's ice cream parlor).

When I think of my old neighborhood, however, I generally visualize the backyard, that is, the wide space, eventually paved, between our row of houses on Broadway and the next on East Main Street. The yard faced, across the street, a vacant lot, the Royal Theatre (long abandoned), and a line of small stores.

Located near the bridge over the Chicopee River—predecessor of the present Deady Memorial Bridge, built after the hurricane of 1938—at the edge of the commercial district concentrated along Main Street, the neighborhood was part of a wedge-shaped city block formed, at the tapering end, by our corner and, at the wide end, by Belcher Street, site of Saint George's Church. (An angle in Belcher Street explains why we used to refer to a circuit of this area as "going around the square".)

The Dufaults lived next door to us on Broadway, the Parents a little further up Broadway, and the Hurds across the yard on East Main Street. Many other families resided in this neighborhood, but my childhood friends, especially in the summertime, were Hervé Dufault, Raymond Hurd, and Jean-Paul and Leo Parent, all a bit older than I. (During World War II, they all served in the armed forces; Hervé participated in the paratroop operation that recaptured Corregidor in 1945.)

The neighborhood was a microcosm of downtown Chicopee Falls—a patchwork of tenements, modest homes, and small businesses that came into being after cotton manufacturing was established here in the 1820s and 1830s. Large numbers of French Canadians and Polish—also, many Irish—were initially drawn to Chicopee Falls by the cotton mills, the J. Stevens Arms and Tool Company, and the Fisk Tire Company. The most crowded quarter was the group of pre–Civil War row houses known as Chinatown that was erected on Grove Street by a textile mill, the Chicopee Manufacturing Company, to house its employees. Its residents were mostly French Canadians and Poles.

In 1938 Ernst Halberstadt painted a handsome mural depicting local history from 1637 to 1937 in the newly constructed Chicopee Falls, Massachusetts, post office. One of approximately three hundred such works of art throughout the United States, the mural was part of a New Deal project to engage the services of unemployed artists in decorating federal buildings.[104]

To the left of the postmaster's door are scenes showing Chicopee Falls's colonial and rural past; to the right, the covered bridge that once spanned the Chicopee River at about the site of the present structure, and a few early buildings. The lower register on the right shows two shirt-sleeved men entering the main gate of the Chicopee Manufacturing Company, a textile mill, and a view of a street in Chinatown looking toward the Fisk Tire Company.

At the top of the hill, on the corner of East Main and Belcher streets, stands Saint George's Church, an imposing brick edifice in Norman gothic style built in 1924. (The parish, founded in 1893, was originally called Saint Joachim.)[105] My three sisters, Irene, Evelyn, and Cecile, my neighborhood companions, and I—also many family friends, for example, the

Chevaliers, who loved the outdoors and whom we enjoyed visiting on Montgomery Street, across the river—all attended Saint George's parochial school on Maple Street.[106]

The school opened in 1928 and was conducted by the Sisters of the Assumption whose mother house was at Nicolet, Quebec. The order had already founded eighteen similar educational establishments at other locations throughout New England, the first at Southbridge, Massachusetts, in 1891 (also at Glens Falls, New York).[107] The first graduation at Saint George's was in 1932; my sisters and I received our diplomas in 1936, 1938, 1942, and 1946, respectively.

Saint George's corresponded perfectly to my parents' ideas about what a primary school should be: an institution where their children would learn the basic skills and subjects needed to get ahead in life but would also get an insight into their Catholic and French-Canadian heritage. With complete confidence Mama and Papa put their offspring in the hands of the sisters. My parents saw to it that their children did their homework and learned their lessons, they attended all functions to which they were invited—there was no parent-teacher assocation at Saint George's—and they made generous contributions whenever funds were being raised for the school. They were supremely happy with the result. In light of such satisfaction, it was some time before I was in a position to assess properly this education.

Some of the sisters worked hard to teach subjects for which they lacked sufficient schooling. Children were not encouraged to ask questions and tended to learn by rote. Dissent, however mild or tentative, was rarely tolerated. There was no school library. These and other deficiencies were not unique, of course, to Saint George's; they were found in many public as well as parochial schools of the day.

On the other hand, Saint George's did an excellent job of teaching the fundamentals. A number of sisters—Soeurs Cécile de Milan, Jeanne de Reims, and Marie de l'Ange Gardien come readily to mind—rank among the finest teachers I ever had. Their breadth of knowledge, good-heartedness, patience, and wit made it a joy to learn many different subjects. Finally, Saint George's unquestionably succeeded in fostering lasting Catholic and Franco-American beliefs and values.

The decline that affected many New England factory towns after World War I, the depression, and the economic disruptions following World War II created serious problems in Chicopee Falls. Housing, once considered tolerable and even relatively comfortable, deteriorated; many downtown areas became eyesores.[108]

In 1945 the Braults moved to 34 Theodore Street, but my father maintained his office on East Main Street until his retirement in 1965. The P. J. Brault Insurance Agency was purchased by Guy A. Lamarche and is now located at 94 Pine Street.

Saint George's Church and School continue to serve Chicopee Falls's Franco-Americans. However, the buildings that once housed the factories and the tenements, and nearly all the other structures in an eighty-two-acre area that included my old neighborhood, were razed in 1968 during urban renewal. Downtown Chicopee Falls has been completely transformed and now consists of moderate-income apartments and elderly housing, public and semipublic facilities, and a few businesses.

My parents, especially my mother, valued education. Mama acquired much knowledge on her own by teaching herself to read English-language newspapers. The many hours she spent reading children's adventure stories aloud eventually awakened in me an interest in learning that should last all my life. But Mama was also keen on leaving her children a French-Canadian legacy.

In 1942 I entered Assumption High School in Worcester, Massachusetts. From the age of twelve until I graduated from college there in 1950, I spent nine months of every year away from Chicopee Falls. I went on to Laval University in Quebec City, then, after fulfilling my military obligation, married Jeanne Lambert Pepin at Assumption parish church in Chicopee on January 23, 1954, and left my hometown for good.

None of the other Brault children initially remained in Chicopee Falls. Irene married in 1943 and, after living in various parts of the country and also abroad, settled in Seattle, Washington. Evelyn joined the Sisters of the Assumption and spent thirty years as a missionary in Japan before returning to the United States in 1985, where she is now provincial superior of her religious order in New England and New York State. My younger sister Cecile taught French for many years in different secondary schools in New England, looked after my parents in their old age, and, after they passed away—my mother in 1978 at the age of eighty-two, my father in 1983 at the age of ninety-four—retired and is now living in Chicopee Falls.

Assumption High School and College

An experiment in homogeneous grouping at Assumption High School led to the sectioning of my class into Eléments A, B, C, and D, a plan that was adhered to throughout our four years on the Greendale campus; at the college level, premed students followed a different track part of the time. Basically, however, everyone received the same liberal arts education, with great importance attached to French and to the teachings of the Catholic church.

In high school, the daily routine was always the same. Everyone moved from dormitory to chapel to refectory; then, with short recesses before and after, to morning classes followed by study hall and lunch. Afternoons were similarly organized but with longer recesses before and after dinner. The day ended with study hall, chapel, and dormitory. Classes were held on Saturday morning, but in the French style Thursday and Saturday afternoons were free. Everything was accomplished by class and by the numbers, down to the collection of daily written tasks at the end of each morning and afternoon study period. An electric bell signaled the beginning or end of each phase in the day.

Leaving the campus was strictly forbidden (special permission was granted to go into town once or twice a year, on school holidays), and no one was allowed to cut chapel, class, meals, or study hall. Except during meals and recess, silence was de rigueur. Any infraction of rules noticed by Argus-eyed monitors (*surveillants*) resulted in demerits and a public dressing down. Major transgressions were reported to the dean of men (*préfet de discipline*) who, like a first sergeant, had the capacity to make one's life miserable. Punishments ranged from copying a page of *Larousse*, the French dictionary, to being restricted to campus over holidays. (Father Louis-Robert Brassard, class of 1935, ruled with a firm hand but also had a well-deserved reputation for reasonableness.)

Dormitories were large, plain rooms with long rows of beds covered with uniformly white bedspreads. Steamer trunks in different shapes and sizes at the head of each bed were the only feature relieving the monotony. As these rooms were only for sleeping, there was little privacy.

The routine in college was less austere, one of the main reasons being the availability of private two- and three-person rooms. However, bed checks continued to be part of the established procedure, everyone had to be in his own room during study periods (live-in religious could enter without knocking at any time), and students were still not allowed to leave the campus. My college roommate for four years was Albert E. Bouley of Plainfield, Connecticut (Michael C. Carey resided with us the first two years). The camaraderie and sharing of a unique educational experience promoted the growth of many lifelong friendships. For example, Jeanne and I still receive visits from and go to see Al and his wife Janet regularly.

Students engaged in a variety of indoor and outdoor recreational activities during recess (e.g., cards, handball, ping-pong). A peculiar early afternoon or evening ritual, weather permitting, found many groups of four, five, or more students walking up and down favorite paths or around the track, peripatetic style, a custom doubtless derived from seminarians' habits.

Free afternoons were often spent playing pick-up basketball in the gymnasium (built in 1926), softball, tennis, or touch football outdoors. Intramural basketball was popular and generally scheduled in the early evening.

Within a few years of its foundation in 1904, Assumption had an orchestra and, not long afterward, a glee club which gave annual concerts at Mechanics Hall in Worcester and in other Franco-American population centers.[109] French and English plays and operettas were produced. Students also published a newspaper and a yearbook.

Varsity baseball and basketball date back to the 1920s at Assumption.[110] By the 1940s high school and college tennis and track (also high school football) teams had been organized. Many students developed into fine athletes, excelling in several sports. But from the time the gym was first opened, basketball was king at Assumption, and the entire faculty and student body turned out to cheer the team on at home games. Al Banx, a cartoonist for the *Worcester Telegram and Gazette*, created the school mascots, Télesphore, a greyhound, and Pierre, a French-Canadian lumberjack.

Assumption had its share of dull or eccentric teachers but also a number of gifted ones. Among those who made the most favorable impression upon me were Fathers Olivier Blanchette (English), Emile Brochu (religion), Ulric Charpentier (algebra), Engelbert Devincq (French literature), and Marius Dumoulin (Latin); also the laymen Albert R. Lacroix (English), Raymond J. Marion (history), and Cuthbert Wright (English literature).

Raymond Marion was a favorite teacher with many of us. (He was also my basketball coach.) During the war, word got back to Assumption that Marion (class of 1942) had been wounded at Tarawa. The assault on this tiny atoll in the Pacific, November 20–23, 1943, "the toughest fight in Marine Corps history," according to Vice Adm. Raymond A. Spruance, cost the U.S. Second Marine Division 913 killed and missing, and 2,037 wounded.[111] Years later I learned that Marion, a first lieutenant in the Second Marine Division, had subsequently been awarded the Silver Star medal for gallantry in action in the battle for Tinian in the Mariana Islands (1944).

At Assumption, an oral examination before a panel of three professors—Marion was one of my questioners—was the culmination of eight years of study. Ninety-odd philosophical topics, or theses, were announced early in the year, and each student was on his own to find out what he could about them. A written dissertation in French on a similar subject was also required. (By 1950 the thesis could be written in English.)

A Saint George's School classmate and close friend from Chicopee Falls, Richard J. Deslauriers, spent eight years with me at Assumption. The son of Joseph A. Deslauriers (1898–1966), a prominent dentist who was active in local Franco-American circles,[112] Richard now has a dental practice himself in Chicopee Falls.

In Worcester, I also became acquainted with Charles J. Beauchamp (class of 1950) and his brother Eugene W., Jr. (class of 1949). The Beauchamp family is a legend in Chicopee. Grandfather Joseph O. Beauchamp (1868–1953), born at St. Roch, Quebec, was awarded a medical degree from Laval University at Montreal in 1894 and emigrated to Chicopee the same year. In 1908 he was elected mayor, the first Franco-American in Massachusetts, the second in New England, to hold this office.[113] His son Eugene W. Beauchamp, Sr. (class of 1919, awarded an honorary Doctor of Science degree in 1954), one of the area's leading surgeons, was dedicated to the Franco-American cause. The latter's four sons all graduated from Assumption College: Eugene W., Jr., and Charles J., mentioned above, David T. (class of 1955), and Joseph O. (class of 1960). All went on to become doctors of medicine (Eugene W., Jr., is a surgeon in nearby Springfield).

The adjustment to communal life and long hours of supervised study was difficult, but the discipline and seclusion created an atmosphere conducive to building character and molding the mind in accordance with Assumptionist ideals. However, the eight-year program was uneven and, except in the premedical course, probably made its greatest intellectual demands upon students in the early years and in certain philosophy courses. Although controlled, exposure to the classics, to the great works of American, English, and French literature, and to philosophy was impressive. Most gratifying, perhaps, the Assumptionist Fathers succeeded in making us love learning about French, French-Canadian, and Franco-American culture. (The French-born professors routinely spoke their native standard French while the rest of us strove to improve our cultivated Canadian French. Each group, I believe, grew to respect the other's speech variant, which, in point of fact, was not all that different.) Some of us worried a bit, especially upon leaving Assumption, about the possible imbalance of an education that favored French language and culture; however, few graduates of the day, whatever their calling, would not later find that, on the contrary, it enriched their lives significantly.

While studying for my master's degree in French at Laval University, I discovered that my background and education had given me a decided advantage. A year's residence in Quebec City helped me further develop my fluency in French and experience French-Canadian life in a modern, urban setting. Military service—affording me an opportunity to spend a year in France, where I visited many of the places I had heard and read about all my life—strengthened my decision to become a French professor. I also found that French officials, with whom I came into contact in the course of my duties as a special investigator with the U.S. Army Counter Intelligence Corps, were often curious about my Franco-American background and that discussing it was a good icebreaker. (My wife and I had this pleasant experience many times while traveling in France.)

When I began studying for a doctorate at the University of Pennsylvania, I soon realized that while Assumption and Laval may not have taught me to research literary problems, they did give me an excellent start on my career in many other ways. For this foundation I shall always be grateful.

The Pepins and the Douvilles

Getting to know my wife's family—I first met Jeanne in August 1946—heightened my awareness of what it means to be Franco-American.

Amédée Edouard Pepin, Jeanne's grandfather, was born at L'Epiphanie, near Montreal, in 1864. A descendant of Guillaume Pepin, one of the early settlers of Trois-Rivières, he emigrated first to Clinton, Massachusetts, in the late 1870s, then to Fitchburg, Massachusetts, about 1886. Ed, as Amédée was known, operated a barbershop on Prichard Street, then on Oliver Street in Fitchburg until his death in 1927.

His wife Eveline, whom he married in Fitchburg in 1891, was born at Mooers Forks, New York, just south of the Quebec border, in 1872. Her parents, François P. Lambert and Rosina Ashline,[114] moved to Fitchburg when Eveline was five years old and helped establish Immaculate Conception parish in 1886. Frank was a harness maker by trade and the proprietor of a grocery store at the corner of Water and First streets. Eveline was organist at Immaculate Conception for thirty-five years and played at the first high mass celebrated in that church on December 8, 1887.[115] Her parents later moved to Franklin, Massachusetts.

One day, Eveline was walking down the street when the director of a local theatrical group spotted her and exclaimed: "There's my Evangeline!" The director was casting a "grand spectacular presentation" of Longfellow's poem and was searching for a young woman with just her looks. Eveline agreed to play the title role, and the show, performed on January 14, 1898, at the Whitney Opera House was a great success. Dozens of costumed actors and actresses, including Eveline's daughter Alice who had just turned five, mimed key scenes in a series of moving tableaux while the poem was recited and musicians provided accompaniment.

Amédée and Eveline, who died in 1958, had four children: Alice Rosina (1893–1980); Carl Edward, born in 1894, lived only eight months; Arthur Lambert (1900–1975), my wife's father; and Esther Marie, born in 1902, taught at Warren Junior High School in Newton, Massachusetts.

Of the three surviving Pepin children, Alice took the greatest interest in her French heritage. A teacher of various subjects at Fitchburg High School—in 1911, at the age of eighteen,[116] she was the first Franco-American on the faculty—Alice kept up her French in many ways, for example, by reading novels and, in 1918, by corresponding with a French soldier at the front as part of the Mon Soldat program. She also collected memorabilia about her family, including a genealogy, and traveled to France in 1926.

Arthur graduated from Wentworth Institute of Technology in Boston in 1920. At first, he was employed by the architectural firm of Andrews, Jones, Viscoe, and Whitmore in that city. In 1925 he married Beatrice Marguerite Douville in St. John the Baptist parish, Manchester, New Hampshire. The couple resided in Jamaica Plain, a suburb of Boston.

When the depression came, the Pepins returned to Fitchburg in 1932 with their two small children, Edward Lawrence and Jeanne Lambert. Now widowed, Mémère Pepin provided an apartment for the family in her roomy home at 92 Charles Street. (To make ends meet, Mémère also took in boarders.) A letter in my wife's possession conveys the anxiety of that time but also speaks of this family's courage and solidarity.

Fitchburg, June 18, 1932

Dear Arthur,

I have been "planning" my head off for the last two weeks and now I have decided to put a stop to it all. So here I am.

Thinking over your situation and ours here, I have this suggestion to make, and I want you and Bea to give it serious thought and abide by it, if you can see it the way I do.

You say you can carry on until the first of September, so I say why not break up *now* before your money is all gone? Why not move up here *now,* by the first of July? There is nothing for you or anybody else to do this summer, so it shouldn't make any difference.

I can offer you and your family a home until you can see your way clear, for it must break soon. You can do a lot around that would help and I am sure Bea and Alice, Esther and I can get along very happily together. And really, it would be a treat to have somebody get the dinner once in a while. I know we shall enjoy the children, and after they get used to the change, they will be all right and happy.

Now Arthur, don't hesitate one second to accept this. We will be very comfortable and, if you should land a job at this end, I would be so glad to arrange this home so as to give you an apartment for yourself.

The work here is becoming harder and harder for me to do and I would appreciate a smaller place.

You can store your things in the barn and there may be a few pieces that you would like around the house which would be all right to have that way.

Now we will pay your moving expenses and help you in any way possible.

It seems much cooler today but the boys are watching the cherry tree just the same.

Let me hear from you *right now.*

Lovingly,
Mother

Arthur designed and oversaw the construction of scores of buildings in the Fitchburg area; he also worked as an estimator for the F. M. Johnson Company for about six years. In 1941 he accepted a position with the J. G. Roy Lumber Company in Chicopee and eventually became a self-employed architect in that city, with an office in his home at 171 Rimmon Avenue. Although he understood French, Arthur was not comfortable speaking it. He was a loyal member of Assumption parish but chose to become active in the local Elks Lodge and Kiwanis Club rather than in Franco-American organizations. On the other hand, he was quite taken with his in-laws who lived and are still living their French-Canadian heritage.

Arthur's wife Beatrice, her older brother Emile Douville, and her younger sisters Jeannette (Dupont), Gilberte (Manseau), and Rachel—a fourth sister died as a child—have always maintained close family ties with relatives in New England as well as in Canada, and typify Franco-American bonhomie.

My wife's grandfather Donat, the son of Edouard Douville and Adéline Rouleau, was born in 1872 at Sainte-Anne-de-la-Pérade, near Trois-Rivières, in a venerable farmhouse that has been continuously inhabited by his family since 1818.[117] In November 1888, when Donat was sixteen, his family, including seven brothers and sisters (four others did not survive) and their octogenarian grandfather Pierre Douville, moved to Manchester, New Hampshire, where Edouard's sister, Elisabeth, and her husband, Célestin Lefebvre, already resided. The Douvilles lived at 608 Main Street.

Three years later, in 1892, Donat's parents returned to Sainte-Anne with their younger children, including Alphonse who would later inherit the farm. (Grandfather Pierre died at Manchester in 1889 and was buried there.) Donat was one of those who remained in Manchester (also his brother Charles, who became a mailman). In 1897 he married Alice Saint-Laurent who had emigrated there as a child from Saint-David-de-Lévis, near Quebec City. Donat, who became a truck driver, lived at 553 Montgomery Street until he passed away in 1933. Mémère Douville survived him until 1946.

After World War II, many Franco-Americans began to lose contact with their French-Canadian cousins. They were increasingly uneasy about speaking French and, naturally, felt they had more in common with their friends and relatives in the United States. But not the Douvilles. They liked to use French from time to time among themselves or with Franco-American acquaintances at social gatherings, for example at Association Canado-Américaine functions in Manchester. They also enjoyed making trips to Quebec and entertaining Canadian relatives at home. Paul-Edouard Tessier, his wife Catherine (Crète), and his sister Georgette were among the cousins with whom they remained close; also Aunt Vénérande Veillet, and Cousin Raymond Douville and his wife Bella. All have, or had, a great attachment to Sainte-Anne-de-la-Pérade (ma tante Vénérande died in 1976).

Best known perhaps as the ice-fishing capital of Quebec—the tomcod (*poulamon,* or *petit poisson des chenaux*) attracts hundreds of anglers every winter[118]—Sainte-Anne, settled in 1667,[119] was also part of a seigneurie whose proprietress in the first half of the following century was the indomitable Madeleine de Verchères.[120] At the age of fourteen, in 1682, Madeleine won fame for her week-long defense of the nearby fort of Verchères, across the river from Montreal, against marauding Iroquois. She was also a thorn in the side of administrators on both sides of the Atlantic and was constantly involved in legal wrangles with her neighbors.

As for the Douville cousins, Paul-Edouard Tessier, a physician, is a pillar of the nearby rural community of St. Casimir. Catherine, who before her marriage in 1953 taught school in the local école de rang, performs the many duties expected of the wife of a country doctor. Georgette was a nurse in Montreal before retiring to Sainte-Anne; over the years, she contributed much to keeping the members of the Douville clan on both sides of the border in touch with one another. Vénérande was a schoolmarm for four years before she married; she was seventeen and fresh from convent school when she met her first class in 1900. In 1972, at the age of ninety, she wrote her memoirs which were published the following year in three separate pamphlets by the local historical society, Les Amis de l'histoire de La Pérade.[121] Raymond is an amateur historian of the first order and a prolific author. He had a long career in journalism and served as under secretary of the province of Quebec in the administration of Maurice Duplessis.

During the six months my wife and i spent in Quebec City in the winter of 1984, we were given an enthusiastic welcome by these and other relatives. The warmth of their reception is a tribute to the remarkable solidarity that characterizes many French-Canadian and Franco-American families.

Continuity and change

Geography has impeded but by no means blocked the forging of unity among the younger Braults and Pepins who, along with the qualities and traits associated with their family names, have also inherited the Douville spirit. How much of this spirit is French-Canadian or Franco-American is difficult to say, but nationality cannot be ruled out as a factor. In any event, it is clear that a pattern of convivial gatherings existed early on in the Douville family and that it was developed by them in Manchester and by Arthur and Beatrice Pepin in Chicopee.

Like most such reunions, they involved rituals, in this case the highball or glass of sherry on arrival; the hearty meal seated around the dining room table (or, in peak years, around two tables) with fine china, silver, and linen; the cleanup afterward in the kitchen; the snack before departure; the fond farewells.

Often but not always associated with holidays, the get-togethers in Chicopee necessitated travel from distant points—Mémère and Aunt Alice Pepin from Fitchburg; Aunt Esther from Needham; Aunts Jeannette and Rachel, Uncle Lou Dupont, and Roger and Gillie Manseau from Manchester; Ed and his wife Catherine (Rouillard)[122] from Bloomfield, Connecticut; Jeanne and I from Brunswick, Maine, or Philadelphia, Pennsylvania—with its accompanying concerns about weather and road conditions.

The involvement in these get-togethers of several generations was a key ingredient, culminating in the late 1950s and early 1960s with the participation of Ed and Cathy's children (Joan, Carol, Edward, and Catherine) and ours (Francis, Anne-Marie, and Suzanne). In 1968 the locale shifted to Bloomfield where Ed and Cathy served as hosts at summer gatherings for seven years in a row.

Christenings, graduations, weddings, and funerals, with their attendant joys and sorrows, continue to punctuate our family history; but of major significance, too, are the visits to and from our children—now grown and residing in various sections of the Northeast and in Kentucky—and relatives. There are two highlights, an annual Brault-Pepin reunion at a summer home rented by Ed and Cathy at the shore in Rhode Island and a dinner held at Christmastime each year since 1978 at a restaurant in Port Jervis, New York, roughly midway between farthest points. Cathy and Jeanne have been prime movers in all these undertakings.

The Brault children were exposed to the French language while growing up, attending school, and enjoying a one-year stay in France in 1968–69 (plus additional trips to France and Quebec), and speak it with varying degrees of fluency. All their lives they have heard about their heritage and have seen it in the mementoes that are part of our home furnishings.

A Brault family Christmas Eve liturgy, composed in 1968 and read and sung faithfully by us at home every year since then, underlines our French-Canadian past and includes traditional carols in French. This tradition is followed by midnight mass and a réveillon.

Every New Year's Day since 1984, my children have perpetuated a family tradition that stretches back to my early childhood and had existed on my mother's as well as on my father's side. In danger of being lost with the death of my father in November 1983, the custom calls for the children to ask and receive their father's blessing.

Over the past few years, my wife and I have traveled thousands of miles to relive the principal events of our families' history. In France we visited La Chaussée and were warmly welcomed by Mayor René Gigon and his family, who reside a stone's throw from the church where Vincent Brault worshiped. We spent a delightful two hours at the nearby Château de Brault where Mme. Guy Brémaud kindly gave us a tour of the estate that bears our family's name. We walked along the streets of La Rochelle and explored its old port. In Canada we stood on the dikes at Rivière aux Canards, some of which were doubtless built by Pierre Brault and his sons. We read their names on the framed copy of the list of deportees from 1755 that hangs in Saint Charles Church at Grand Pré.

On June 27, 1982, my sister Evelyn, home from Japan for a visit, my wife, and I participated in the two hundredth anniversary celebration of the foundation of Saint Marguerite of Blairfindie, the historic parish at L'Acadie, near Montreal, where Amand Brault settled.[123] A descendant and distant cousin, Pierre Brault, whom I had met there on an earlier visit, still resides at L'Acadie and helped organize the family reunion attended by three hundred Braults. His impressive *Histoire de L'Acadie* was published to coincide with this memorable occasion.

Jeanne and I have seen many times in recent years the neighborhoods of the mill towns of New England which our great-grandparents, grandparents, and parents knew and where we ourselves grew up: Thompson-ville, Connecticut; Manchester, New Hampshire; Fitchburg, Chicopee, and Chicopee Falls, Massachusetts. We have also visited many other sites in Quebec associated with the Brault, Douville, Pepin, and Rémillard families.

In many of these places time has erased all trace of their presence. But their names, preserved in dusty parish registers and other records of which they were scarcely aware, enable us to piece together bits of their story, which enrich our lives today.

A Brault family quilt

From January to June 1984 my wife, Jeanne Pepin Brault, designed, appliquéd, and stitched by hand a twenty-square, 72″ × 48″ cotton quilt that depicts the main events described in this chapter. The principal colors, blue and white, and the fleurs-de-lis in the four corners (squares 1, 4, 17, and 20) were inspired by the flag of Quebec. The remaining squares portray, from left to right, top to bottom, the following images:

2. The *coq gaulois,* or rooster symbol of France. "V.B. c. 1652" is the approximate date of Vincent Brault's departure for Acadia.

3. A seventeenth-century sailing vessel.

5. The maple leaf, emblem of Canada.

6. Acadian farm girl. "Savez-vous planter des choux?" is a traditional round.

7. French-Canadian habitant, with tuque and ceinture fléchée, collecting sap for maple syrup.

8. Map of Quebec, "La Belle Province."

9. Roadside cross, indicating the importance of faith in the French-Canadian heritage.

10. The church at L'Acadie, Quebec. "A.B. 1782" is for Amand Brault, one of the first marguilliers.

11. Shoemaker's sign, designating Julien Brault and his trade.

12. Four embroidered fleurs-de-lis with the motto of Quebec, "Je me souviens," I remember.

13. Locomotive, recalling the chief way French Canadians emigrated to the United States.

14. Map of New England.

15. The Amoskeag Manufacturing Company. "P.J.B. 1910" records Philias J. Brault's arrival in Manchester, New Hampshire.

16. Three-decker tenement, typical of those found in the Little Canadas of New England.

18. Assumption College, Worcester, Massachusetts. "G.J.B. '46 and '50" are the years I graduated from high school and college there.

19. An autograph square with the date of the quilt.

Sashes between the squares are quilted in a wavy pattern that underscores the significance of rivers in the lives of the French Canadians of Quebec and New England. The small squares where the sashes intersect are quilted with fleurs-de-lis. Some pictures were adapted from illustrations, patterns, and photographs; the others are original designs. A blue and white cotton calico backing carries out the color theme.

5

THE FRANCO-
AMERICANS TODAY

World War II ushered in a new era of vast social and economic change which affected all American ethnic groups. Although their reaction to developments in the 1960s commanded relatively little attention in the news media, Franco-Americans took advantage of the opportunities by bolstering their efforts to preserve their linguistic and cultural heritage. The current revival is in part due to these initiatives.

Federal, state, and local subsidies, or aid from the government of Quebec, would be unavailing were it not for effective Franco-American leadership and genuine interest at the grass roots in preserving this legacy. One of the most encouraging signs has been the growth in the number of Franco-American conferences and colloquia with serious academic content; courses and lecture series about Franco-Americans are also being offered at institutions of higher learning. The results have not always been immediately apparent, but fewer activities have greater potential for stimulating interest in Franco-Américanie in the long run, not only among members of the group but also among others as well.

Social and economic characteristics

Franco-Americans have long been perceived by others—and, at times, by themselves—as having attained lower educational and occupational status than the population at large and certain other ethnic groups. The available evidence, marshalled by specialists in study after study over the years, bears out this impression. However, Franco-Americans have made enormous strides in this century and are well represented in all the professions. Also, many have unquestionably achieved wealth and high social status.

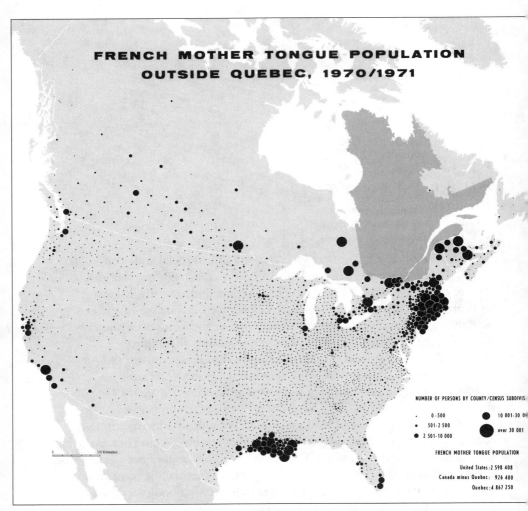

Map 3. Persons who claim a French mother tongue are mainly clustered in the six New England states and in Louisiana. The vast majority are descendants of Quebecois or Acadians. (Source: U.S. Census 1970 and Census of Canada 1971; Louder and Waddell, *Continent perdu*, p. 29, fig. 1. Courtesy Laboratoire de cartographie, Département de géographie, Université Laval, Ste-Foy, Québec.)

According to the 1950 census, second-generation Franco-Americans had fallen behind Irish, Italian, and Polish-Americans in their level of education, average income, and occupational status, and had lost the slight advantage held by the first generation in this respect.[1] (See Appendix B, tables 9–11.)

Referring to the socioeconomic status in New England in 1950 of the ethnic groups mentioned previously, one observer, a French-Canadian demographer, concluded that the slower advances made by Franco-Americans were a consequence of "voluntary segregation":

> The French-Canadian lag is probably due to the parents' desire to maintain French tradition in the family. Once the children had completed their studies at French parochial schools, their parents feared they would lose their language, their culture and their religion if they attended public secondary schools. French secondary schools were indeed rare in New England; those with the means sent their children to the classical schools in the province of Quebec. Many families took their children away from their studies to put them to work in the textile factories.[2]

An analysis of 1970 census figures shows that French mother tongue persons in New England worked in blue collar occupations more often than did English mother tongue persons.[3] (For more information, see Appendix B, table 12.)

In a predominantly Franco-American inner-city residential district of Woonsocket, Rhode Island, only 20.4 percent of the population twenty-five years and older had completed high school in 1970. The median family income was $7,444 (22.3 percent of families had incomes under $4,000.)[4] In Maine, 42.9 percent of the French mother tongue population twenty-five years and over had a grade school education or less as contrasted with 17.6 percent of English mother tongue persons, a 25.3 percent difference. The disparity among college graduates was 4.1 percent contrasted with 9.4 percent.[5] In 1979 a study by the New Hampshire Civil Liberties Union revealed that the incomes of Franco-Americans in that state were about average but that there was a low incidence of French-surnamed persons among the banking, educational, and industrial elite. The percentage of French mother tongue college graduates was again lower than that of the English mother tongue population.[6] In 1983 a report of the Vermont Advisory Committee to the U.S. Commission on Civil Rights indicated similar educational and occupational differences between the two groups.[7]

Historical factors (including prejudice and discrimination against Franco-Americans) and, possibly, cultural traits have produced this situation.[8] In any event, the problem seems to reside in education and English-language ability, generally viewed as the key to upward mobility in the United States.

It must be stressed, too, that specialists and nonspecialists alike do not agree about the reliability and significance of such statistics. Many Franco-Americans are convinced that the group's relative gains, especially in recent years, will soon close any existing gap.[9] They are also understandably sensitive about the cultural and political implications of any lag.

Politics

Although no comprehensive and up-to-date study confirms these results, Franco-Americans have tended to vote Democratic in presidential elections since 1928 (Alfred E. Smith); however, in 1952 and 1956 they favored Dwight D. Eisenhower, the Republican nominee. In the 1928 and 1960 (John F. Kennedy) elections, religion was an important consideration for many Franco-Americans, who sought to counter widely publicized anti-Catholic sentiment against the two candidates.[10]

The group has successfully backed an impressive number of Franco-American mayors and state legislators, with some five hundred of the latter elected in Maine alone over a hundred-year period.[11] In fact, from a political standpoint, several New England communities are regarded as Franco-American preserves. On the other hand, Franco-Americans have enjoyed only limited success in electing one of their own to the positions of United States senator, governor, or congressman, except in Rhode Island:[12]

United States Senator
    Felix Hébert (Rhode Island), 1929–35

Governors
    Aram J. Pothier (Rhode Island), 1909–15, 1925–28
    Emery J. San Souci (Rhode Island), 1921–23
    Philip W. Noel (Rhode Island), 1973–77

United States Representatives
    Louis Monast (Rhode Island), 1927–29
    Aimé J. Forand (Rhode Island), 1937–39, 1941–61
    Alphonse Roy (New Hampshire), 1938–39
    Fernand J. St. Germain (Rhode Island), 1961–
    Norman E. D'Amours (New Hampshire), 1975–84

Most Franco-Americans today are Democrats, but in certain areas, notably New Hampshire and Vermont, many are dyed-in-the-wool Republicans. Historically, this difference in party affiliation reflects that, at the local level, Franco-Americans, presented with the dilemma of an Irish-dominated Democratic party and a Yankee-controlled Republican organization, sided with the group perceived as being less inimical to their interests.[13] Today, many routinely support Franco-American candidates, splitting their vote when necessary; however, in no way does this voting pattern constitute blind loyalty. For example, in June 1982, Georgette Bérubé of Lewiston, a popular member of the Maine legislature, was defeated in the Democratic primary in which she opposed the incumbent governor, faring poorly in Franco-American communities and even failing to carry her own hometown.[14]

In short, Franco-Americans have at times voted as a bloc—this has certainly been the case in several presidential elections and frequently in local contests—but they have tended to do so chiefly when they felt their economic well-being or religious values were at stake.

Although not exclusively political in orientation, the Association of Franco-Americans (Assemblée des Franco-Américains), founded in 1980, is an organization that seeks to rally all persons of French extraction in the United States, a group said to number 10 million.[15] Attorney Walter J. Landry of Lafayette, Louisiana, has been instrumental in developing its political agenda, which includes coalition work with other organized American linguistic heritage groups, especially Hispanics.[16]

Ideology

Today, most Franco-Americans are acculturated to mainstream America, yet a surprisingly large number still adhere to attitudes and values that have been influenced by an ideology elaborated during an earlier phase of their history.

Older Franco-Americans may view the world beyond the group with less suspicion, but many feel a loss in the declining use of French, the evolution of the parochial school system, and the drop-off in attendance at church and other organized ethnic functions. The struggle against a largely Irish church hierarchy once perceived as insensitive and, at times, hostile to Franco-American interests is not forgotten, but it is considered to be a thing of the past.

Often it is said that the third generation in America—the grandchildren of immigrants—cultivates an ethnic identity that the second generation was eager to lose.[17] This holds true for many Franco-Americans. For some, ethnic values are an antidote to alienation, preoccupation with consumer goods, drugs, sex, technology, or other ills that affect modern society. Many discover for the first time what it means to belong when they begin to frequent Franco-American circles, attend family gatherings in New England or French Canada, or learn of the hardships and indignities experienced by their parents or ancestors.

Franco-Americans who approach their ethnicity selectively are another recent phenomenon.[18] Genuinely interested in certain elements of their heritage—for example, its customs, folklore, or history; genealogy is another popular subject—they may pay little or no attention to other facets of their culture, in particular the French language and the Catholic faith. Informed observers point out that other American ethnic groups—for example, Greeks and Jews—have a highly developed sense of pride or solidarity that does not necessarily depend on language loyalty or religious affiliation.[19] Franco-Americans may reject many of the values the group holds dear yet continue to exhibit a strong attachment to the milieu from which they sprang or to their French-Canadian forebears. Jack Kerouac was a good illustration of this paradox. Novel and varied as it may seem, this kind of awareness or identification with the Franco-American group should not be dismissed as token or symbolic ethnicity.

However, these aspects of ethnicity create an interesting dynamic in the relations between Franco-Americans and Quebecois. Since the 1950s, the Quebecois have experienced remarkable changes in religious attitudes and observances and have been won over by many modern ideas. Consequently, Quebecois have little difficulty understanding that similar developments have occurred in Franco-Américanie; indeed, many consider that they themselves have undergone a greater transformation than have the Franco-Americans, for example, in the religious sphere or in their reverence for tradition. On the other hand, Quebecois are usually dismayed when Franco-Americans show indifference to the language question, which French Canadians consider to be an absolutely essential concern.

Bishops

The lack of Franco-American bishops in New England, often remarked in the period between the two world wars, has been compensated for of late. Ernest J. Primeau was bishop of Manchester, New Hampshire, from 1960 to 1974. He was succeeded, in 1975, by Odore J. Gendron. Meanwhile, Louis A. Gelineau was installed as bishop of Providence, Rhode Island, in 1972. A fourth Franco-American bishop, Amédée W. Proulx, was consecrated auxiliary bishop of Portland, Maine, in 1975. Each appointment occasioned demonstrations of pride and satisfaction in the Franco-American community.

A Franco-American flag

Over the years, many Franco-American organizations have developed identifying symbols that often incorporate the flags of Canada, France, Quebec, and the United States, or elements thereof, for example, a cross, fleur-de-lis, maple leaf, or star. One such combination is found in the official seal, adopted in 1900, of the Union Saint-Jean-Baptiste d'Amérique. (A stylized version of this emblem, designed in 1972, was phased out beginning in 1981 in favor of a logo consisting mainly of the society's initials.) [20]

At a conference held at Saint Anselm's College in Manchester, New Hampshire, on May 27–29, 1983, some Franco-American leaders adopted a flag to represent the group. It has a blue field with a white fleur-de-lis superimposed on a white five-pointed star. Although initially intended for Franco-Americans in the Northeast only, the flag was approved, on August 5 of the same year, by the Association of Franco-Americans as a symbol for all Americans of French descent. It remains to be seen whether this banner will catch on. The flag in question is the latest in a series of devices representing Francophone groups in North America.[21]

Literature

Two Franco-American authors who burst onto the American scene in the mid-1950s anticipated the rebellious spirit that is often associated with the 1960s. Initially belittled by most critics, their works are now considered to have had far-reaching consequences. A second look also discloses that their specifically Franco-American content is far from negligible.[22]

Jean-Louis, or Ti-Jean Kérouac (1922–69) was born in Nashua, New Hampshire, but as a child moved with his family to Lowell, Massachusetts.[23] He left Lowell at the age of seventeen profoundly marked by his experiences there. Jack Kerouac's first novel, *The Town and the City,* published in 1950, was three years in the writing. Not so *On the Road,* a free-flowing memoir of his travels across America with his friend Neal Cassady in the late 1940s. The book was typewritten in twenty days in 1951 on a single 250-foot roll of paper. This novel, first published in 1957, made him an instant celebrity and a cult figure of the beat generation. Kerouac's nineteen books are replete with exotic philosophizing and constitute a paean to values and mores that run counter to those of contemporary culture. Identified early on with unconventional behavior and experimentation with drugs and sex, Kerouac is appreciated in certain quarters today more as a stylistic innovator and as an apostle of liberation and self-expression.

Kerouac was proud of his French-Canadian and Lowell origins, and snatches of French are found throughout his work.[24] Many Franco-Americans continue to be embarrassed that the dark and tormented side of his personality, as revealed, for example, in *Doctor Sax* (1959), *Maggie Cassidy* (1959), *Visions of Gerard* (1963), and *Vanity of Duluoz* (1968), is sometimes explained in terms of their culture and milieu. However, others take pride in affirming that his zest for life and mysticism sprang from the same fertile soil.[25]

Kerouac still has many devotees.[26] His works remain in print, and in 1984 an association seeking to establish closer cultural ties between French-Canadians in Quebec and New England was called Le Club Jack-Kérouac.[27]

Grace (DeRepentigny) Metalious (1924–64) was a native of Manchester, New Hampshire, and, like Kerouac, raised in a Franco-American milieu.[28] She was a housewife living with her husband and three children in Gilmanton, New Hampshire, when her steamy first novel, *Peyton Place*, appeared in 1956 and shocked America.[29] The book was a runaway best-seller (8 million copies were sold in paperback alone), and its fictitious locale entered the American language as a metaphor for a small town whose surface serenity masks an ugly underside. *Peyton Place*, which has feminist overtones and may also have helped bring about more frankness about sex, was made into a motion picture in 1957 starring Lana Turner and a television series featuring Mia Farrow, which ran for 514 episodes from 1964 to 1969.

Two of Metalious's three other novels, *The Tight White Collar* (1960) and *No Adam in Eden* (1963) deserve special note here because they concern her Franco-American roots.[30] In the first of these two works set in a northern New England factory town, Lisa St. George, the daughter of a French-Canadian mill hand, longs to rise above her working-class situation and, like the author, marries a Greek-American schoolteacher. However, the autobiographical elements in *No Adam in Eden* are even more numerous. The grim and often lurid story of three generations of French Canadians living in Quebec and Livingstone (that is, Manchester), New Hampshire, it focuses on women who resemble the author's grandmother, mother, and sister. Lesley de Montigny, who marries a truck driver and finds the sort of domestic bliss idealized in the 1950s, is modeled on the writer. The drudgery of mill work and prejudice against Franco-Americans are important themes in this novel.

Like Kerouac, Metalious had great difficulty coping with sudden fame and often seemed bent on self-destruction. She died of cirrhosis of the liver at the age of thirty-nine, five years before Kerouac, a burned-out man at forty-seven, succumbed to alcoholism.

Less celebrated than these two tragic figures and presenting a different view of Franco-American life, Robert Cormier and Gérard Robichaud published their first novels in the 1960s. *Now and at the Hour* (1960), *A Little Raw on Monday Mornings* (1963), and *Take Me Where the Good Times Are* (1965) are all set in Robert Cormier's home town, Leominster, Massachusetts, and depict Franco-Americans dealing with such problems as abortion, old age, suicide, widowhood, and widowerhood. Catholicism and ethnicity are recurrent themes but are treated in complex fashion. In *8 plus 1* (1980), a collection of short stories set in the depression, Cormier moves away from specifically Franco-American characters.[31]

Gérard Robichaud's *Papa Martel* (1961) is an appealing and wholesome tale of a Franco-American family living in a small, fictitious Maine town (Groveton). Although the author does not view the interaction of family members through rose-colored glasses—mother and father quarrel frequently, a daughter rejects her parents' ideal of a large family—he nevertheless succeeds in showing how loving relationships inside the home and the French-Canadian legacy of common sense, courage, and respect for others helps each individual adjust to the outside world. No other Franco-American novel portrays bilingualism in such a favorable light or captures so well the group's joie de vivre. The story also shows how Franco-Americans carried on many customs and traditions of their ancestors in their adoptive land. *The Apple of His Eye* (1965) tells of a week in the life of Michel Dumont, a young orphan, and his uncle Victor in the same Maine community.[32]

One of the most prolific Franco-American novelists, David Plante is the author of nine novels, four of which—*The Family* (1978), *The Country* (1981), *The Woods* (1982), and *The Foreigners* (1984)—deal with the adolescent experiences of Daniel Francoeur who, like the author, grew up in a large working-class Franco-American family in Providence, Rhode Island. Thus far, the Francoeur narratives have covered school years, a summer vacation on a small island off the New England coast, and a trip to France and Spain. Readers learn more about the intricacies of Daniel's mind than about Franco-Americans. Plante achieved considerable notoriety in 1983 with the publication of *Difficult Women,* a memoir of his relationships with Jean Rhys, Sonia Orwell, and Germaine Greer.[33]

Robert B. Perreault of Manchester, New Hampshire, has the distinction of being the only Franco-American to have published a French-language novel since 1938. *L'Héritage* (1983) relates how a young woman discovers her Franco-American past while going through mementoes left by her grandmother. Perreault, who was librarian at the Association Canado-Américaine for many years beginning in 1975, has also published several other works, including the useful survey along the lines of the present book, *One Piece in the Great American Mosaic: The Franco-Americans of New England* (1976), and *Joseph Laferrière* (1982), the story of a French Canadian who emigrated to Lowell, Massachusetts, in 1901 and, although blind from the age of thirty-six, continued to write poetry.[34]

Many present-day Franco-Americans have composed verse in French, the best-known active poets perhaps being Paul P. Chassé and Normand C. Dubé.[35] Among the most recent French-language plays, Grégoire Chabot's *Un Jacques Cartier Errant,* published in 1977 but performed earlier, is probably the most memorable. It offers wry comments on Franco-

American attitudes and culture today through a conversation between two habitués of a bar and an unexpected visitor in period costume, the famed French explorer who discovered the St. Lawrence River in 1535.[36]

A small Franco-American writers' workshop was held in conjunction with the Lewiston Festival in 1982. An informal support group known as the Rassemblement des Artistes Franco-Américains has held annual gatherings of artists and musicians as well as creative writers since 1982. Some fifty participants attended the third such get-together on June 15–17, 1984, at Assumption College in Worcester, Massachusetts.[37]

Folk artists and musicians

The best-known Franco-American wood-carver is perhaps Adelard Coté (1889–1974).[38] (He never accented the first *e* and the *o* in his name.) Born in St. Sophie, Quebec, he emigrated to the United States in his early twenties and settled in Biddeford, Maine, where he maintained a blacksmith shop for thirteen years. He later moved to a farm in nearby Saco. He began whittling in the 1940s, eventually producing hundreds of carvings, many of them elaborate pieces with moving parts.

Folk artists often have more than one talent. For example, Omer Marcoux of Concord, New Hampshire, was a well-known fiddler and wood-carver.[39] Sometimes an entire family will have musical aptitude, as in the case of the Beaudoins of Burlington, Vermont.[40]

Franco-American artists and musicians are fixtures at fiddling contests and folk festivals throughout New England, for instance, at Celebration Northeast held at Dartmouth College in Hanover, New Hampshire, on July 22–23, 1977, and, of course, at Franco-American ethnic fairs. Gilbert O. Roy (1877–1947) of Maine's St. John Valley achieved local fame as a Franco-American folk painter.[41]

Finally, the term *folksinger* is often used today for a person with a trained voice, such as Joan Baez, who sings folk songs. Lilianne Labbé, an admirable Franco-American performer, fits this designation.[42]

Celebrities

Two Franco-Americans and their achievements in the fields of sports and entertainment are well known to the American public today.

Joan Benoit, born in 1957, is a resident of Freeport, Maine. Twice victorious in the Boston Marathon in 1979 and 1983, her time in the latter race (2 hours 22 minutes 43 seconds) was the fastest ever by a woman. She qualified for the United States olympic team on May 12, 1984, only seventeen days after undergoing arthroscopic surgery to remove restrictive fibers from her right knee. Benoit went on to win a gold medal in the first women's olympic marathon in Los Angeles on August 5 of that year. She also holds the American women's record for 10 kilometers, 10 miles, the half-marathon, and 25 kilometers.

Robert Goulet was born in Lawrence, Massachusetts, in 1933 and made his Broadway singing debut in the Lerner and Loewe musical *Camelot* (1960). Since 1964 he has had starring, dramatic roles in many Hollywood films. He has also made numerous guest appearances on television. His performance in the musical version of Robert Fontaine's *The Happy Time* (1968) earned him a Tony award.

Perception of Franco-Americans by others

Franco-Americans often feel that their group lacks visibility, that its achievements and very existence are rarely accorded proper recognition.[43] The role of French explorers in North America, the rivalry between French and English colonists for control of the continent, and the contributions of Revolutionary War patriots of French Huguenot extraction are widely recognized, but present-day Franco-Americans are seldom mentioned in textbooks.[44] In motion pictures or television situation comedies set in New England, one infrequently encounters a Franco-American character or even hears a Franco-American name.

The group's small size when compared with the total population of the United States is perhaps the main reason for this neglect, at least at the national level. Also, a minority's prestige is enhanced or diminished by the fame or notoriety of individuals identified with it, and it is true that relatively few Franco-Americans have attained prominence in the arts, literature, politics, or science, or celebrity status in the fields of entertainment or sports.

Historically, it appears that greater hostility was shown toward other nationalities arriving in New England, particularly the Irish, Italians, and Jews, and that negative stereotypes of Franco-Americans began fading at the turn of the century. However, over the years the group has suffered its share of abuse and discrimination, and highly standardized impressions of its cultural traits persist in certain quarters. Positive statements are often heard, but caricatures, such as those found earlier in this century in the works of Robert Pike or Rowland Robinson,[45] nicknames—Canuck, Frenchy, Frog—and jokes in which Franco-Americans are ridiculed are still in circulation and are degrading.

Scientific studies of Franco-American attitudes and values

The preceding views, while historically important, paint a distorted or oversimplified picture of Franco-Americans. Using a variety of tests based on empirical data, anthropologists and sociologists have sought to provide more reliable information about the group's characteristic outlook on life.

One study, based on data collected in the late 1950s from 427 pairs of mothers and their sons (from eight to fourteen years of age) residing in the Northeast, found that Franco-Americans—62 pairs were interviewed— had significantly lower achievement motivation and lower educational and vocational aspirations than Greek-Americans, Jewish-Americans, and white Protestants of the same social class. Achievement orientation was determined by analyzing (1) stories the boys told about four ambiguous pictures (Thematic Apperception Test), and (2) responses given by the mothers to a series of standardized questions, for example, "At what age do you expect your son to make decisions like choosing his own clothes?", "How far do you intend for your son to go to school?", and "Do you agree or disagree with the following statement: 'Nothing is worth the sacrifice of moving away from one's parents'?"[46] (See Appendix B, table 13.)

It would appear from the statistics that Franco-American parents lay more stress on self-reliance than achievement when training their children—they tend to emphasize doing things on one's own more than doing things well—and that they play down the importance of planning, working hard, making sacrifices, and being physically mobile for the sake of achieving status. The key, the author suggests, may be that Franco-Americans, like Italian-Americans who have similar attitudes in this respect, came from rural areas where opportunities for achievement were limited and habits of resignation, reinforced by Catholic teachings, prevailed.

In the late 1960s, a random sampling of third-generation working-class or lower-class Franco-American and Italian-American housewives determined that more than half of both groups felt generally unhappy and inadequate in their personal lives. The Franco-American respondents were more inclined than their counterparts to seek help from their spouses than from parents, relatives, and friends, on the one hand, and from priests rather than from lay professionals, on the other. The 108 Franco-Americans who participated in this mental health study resided in Woonsocket; the 102 Italian-Americans were inhabitants of nearby Providence, Rhode Island.[47]

Some tentative findings about Franco-American schoolchildren and their parents in rural northeastern Vermont have also been published. Using a questionnaire based on a modification of the Stoudtbeck-Kluckhohn Value Orientation Model, the researcher concluded that parochial school boys were more traditional, cautious, and reserved than girls, who were more oriented toward the future and change. Boys and girls were both self-reliant, but boys were more independent when the authority figure was a parent, girls when the person making decisions was an older brother or sister. As opposed to Yankee neighbors, who were also queried, Franco-American parents were more reserved about personal matters, for example were reluctant to seek help and advice from others. Answers furnished by a total of thirty-nine third- and fourth-grade parochial and public school children and by seventeen parents were analyzed in this survey conducted in 1972.[48]

In these investigations, the reliability of the sampling procedures, the tests, and the controls for such factors as social class varies a good deal. Also, it should be emphasized, none of these studies has yet been replicated. Obviously, Franco-Americans are not all alike in any one of these respects and, like other minorities, are constantly changing.

Franco-American speech

Languages vary from region to region and according to social milieu. Everywhere in the world that French is spoken, one recognizes distinct sounds, vocabulary, and grammar as well as variations depending on social level and circumstances.

Canadian French is a dialect of French, that is, it is a regional variety of the language.[49] The French spoken by most people in Canada differs somewhat from that used by many Acadians in the Maritime Provinces.[50] In Quebec, one also sometimes hears slight variations in Montreal as opposed to Quebec City French, for example, in the way the r is pronounced.[51] Franco-American speech is an extension of Quebecois except in certain areas, notably Maine's St. John Valley, where an admixture of Acadian can at times be discerned.

Today, most Canadian-born living in the northeast United States have spent the greater part of their lives in their adoptive country. A growing majority of second-, third-, and fourth-generation Franco-Americans speak French only as a second language. Naturally, a group that has been separated from the motherland for so long and that has become bilingual has developed differences in its speech. However, the proximity to Canada, the concentration of Franco-Americans in certain areas, and the extraordinary effort made to maintain French have resulted in fewer changes than might have been expected.

Isolation from Canadian linguistic changes

During World War II and the years that followed, the rapid industrialization of Quebec set in motion the social transformation known as the Quiet Revolution. Major economic, educational, political, and religious changes in the 1960s metamorphosed a conservative, introverted people living for the most part in rural villages into an urban society with one of the highest living standards in the world.

A revitalization of Canadian French accompanied the modernization of Quebec. A growing cosmopolitanism resulted in increased contacts with France, and the distance between cultivated Canadian French and standard French diminished greatly. However, certain differences in pronunciation still persist, and Canadians also tend to produce indigenous terms and expressions. Moreover, public opinion, reinforced by nationalistic voices, considers that Quebecois is a perfectly acceptable variety of French.[52] These factors suggest that Canadian French will continue to maintain most of its distinctive features in the future.

Except perhaps for those who reside near the Quebec border, Franco-Americans have not been affected by the evolution of Canadian French. Increasingly acculturated to American life, they are scarcely more knowledgeable about events across the border than are their fellow citizens.

New England French is still well suited for ordinary conversational use, but it is outmoded and constantly gives way to anglicisms as the modern world presents new situations to which it must adapt.[53] Many of the same English loanwords are found in other foreign languages spoken by American immigrants and their descendants. On the other hand, some modern French anglicisms are not heard in New England.

The generation gap

Canadians who have spent nearly all their lives in small communities but later move to an urban center like Montreal maintain language patterns that are not present in the speech of relatives born and raised in the city. But the younger and older Franco-Americans often exhibit even greater disparity in speech patterns, not just because of differences in education and environment but also because of variations in fluency. Young Franco-Americans may have had the advantage of more schooling in French, but they have had less occasion to speak it or less opportunity to work or associate with members of the same ethnic group. Mixed marriages are more common today, and English is heard more often at home, whether the parents are Franco-American or not. Even older couples often find it easier to attend a church that is closer to home than to travel back and forth to the parish to which they belong.

Many Canadian-born Franco-Americans prefer to use their mother tongue but do not hesitate to use English words and expressions for practical purposes and switch to that language when, for example, they quote someone or follow a characteristically American train of thought.[54] Most parents, even those who customarily speak French at home, do not object to having their children address them in English.

Perfect bilinguals are rare in any culture, and Franco-Americans are no exception to this rule. The English they speak reflects the variety heard in the area of New England where they live. They sometimes use French words and phrases, especially in conversations with little children or in jest, but rarely with persons who are not members of the group.[55] Franco-Americans (and French Canadians) who speak English with an accent do not sound like French people. For example, the former tend to pronounce *th* as in *this* like *d*, the latter like *z*. The French nasalize English vowels a good deal more (e.g., *abandon*). Also, French Canadians and their New England cousins routinely approximate the sound of American and English proper names (*le Maine*), which is generally not the case with French speakers. Finally, neither French Canadians nor Franco-Americans use French gestures.[56]

Influence of schools

Parochial schools exerted a major influence on Franco-American speech, particularly between the two world wars. Most teachers spoke cultivated Canadian French—at least in formal conversation and when providing instruction about correct French usage.[57] Whether any other kind of French, including standard French, should be taught in the schools was never broached or even considered before the 1960s.[58]

Graduates of Franco-American parochial schools often encountered open hostility from French language teachers at the secondary school level (the situation was the same in Catholic as well as public schools). Their initial confidence vanished when instructors insisted from the outset, often sarcastically, on "Parisian French" pronunciation and vocabulary. Parents were confounded by this uncompromising and unsympathetic attitude and frequently did not object when their children decided to drop French. To their credit, many young Franco-Americans overcame this obstacle and went on to achieve distinction in the field. When, toward the end of the 1950s, high school teachers began to acquire greater competence in linguistics, pedagogy, and Francophone culture, many changed their attitude.[59] (However, there is still great reluctance on the part of most teachers in America to accept any French that varies from the standard form.) Meanwhile, a splendid opportunity had been wasted to help Franco-Americans maintain their mother tongue.

Sooner or later every Franco-American must answer the question What good is French anyway? Mother tongue loyalty, especially among the young, is affected by how much others value knowledge of a foreign language. Except in the late 1950s and early 1960s, language learning has never been popular in the United States.

An astonishing number of Americans do not value foreign languages or ethnic cultures. Many are convinced, for example, that English is superior to all other languages and that everyone in the world should be made to learn it.[60] Such chauvinism is often associated with a low opinion of and even hostility toward ethnicity.

English is the de facto official language of the United States, unifies this nation, and must be mastered by anyone expecting to get along and, certainly, to get ahead here. Still, fluency in foreign languages has many practical advantages in today's shrinking world and can lead to a better understanding of other cultures. People have a deep attachment to their mother tongue and way of life, and consideration for those who do in this country is the key to an appreciation of the great diversity that exists in American life.

In the 1960s, those seeking to convince young Franco-Americans to take French courses in high school found their efforts undercut when many universities decided to abolish language entrance and degree requirements. Classic reasons for developing or maintaining fluency in French— its beauty, its prestige throughout the world, its utility as a discipline—no longer seemed valid, and new justifications—it is needed for business and travel abroad, improved foreign relations, and national defense—left many skeptical. Often the desire to get ahead impelled second- and third-generation Americans to disassociate themselves from a low-status ethnic group and its betraying accent.

Although the foreign language crisis in the United States is far from over, in recent years things appear to have taken a turn for the better, due in large measure to growing foreign business and travel opportunities. This trend could have a significant impact on the Franco-American situation.

Mother tongue maintenance

Experienced observers agree that fewer Franco-Americans than ever before use French in their daily lives or are even fluent in the language. To what extent can this decline be measured?

In July 1975 the Bureau of the Census conducted a survey that included two questions designed to ascertain foreign language usage in the United States: "What language was usually spoken in this person's home when he was a child?" and "Does this person often speak another language?" The sample was unusually large: data concerning 110,000 households and 440,000 individuals were collected. (Most public opinion polls in this country query 2,000 people or less.)[61]

Detailed analysis suggested that (1) "Non-English languages (minority languages) in this nation are following the pattern of previous immigrant languages," and (2) "While first-generation newcomers speak their native language and learn some English, their offspring are likely to learn English first. The parents' native language, having been eroded, is seldom used by the majority of the subsequent generations."[62] Distinctions were drawn between age groups, foreign- and native-born, regions, and monolingual and bilingual individuals.

According to this survey, 70.8 percent of the foreign-born French mother tongue population of New England either customarily uses French or speaks it frequently; among the native-born, the percentage drops to 52.9. However, two-thirds of these individuals are forty years of age or over, and, in both instances, the percentages are significantly lower in southern New England.[63] (See Appendix B, tables 14–16 and figures 2–3, for more information.)

Critics are quick to point out that samplings based on self-reporting are unreliable. Also, the north-south partition of New England obscures the fact that maintenance of French seems to be greater in cities and towns where Franco-Americans are preponderant, for example, in Woonsocket, Rhode Island.

It is generally agreed that factors favoring mother tongue retention among American ethnic groups include the following: (1) high concentration in a given area; (2) continued arrival of new immigrants; (3) marriage within the group; (4) proximity of the motherland; (5) identification of mother tongue with religious values; and (6) effective educational and institutional support.[64]

Because of improved roads and means of transportation, Franco-Americans are arguably closer today than ever before to their country of origin. Of the other elements that once fostered French language maintenance among this group, the first—high concentration in a given area—may have eroded the least.[65] There is, nonetheless, considerably more dispersion within the New England region, and Franco-American residential segregation is decidedly on the wane.

Signs of a cultural revival in Franco-Américanie

World War II and its aftermath brought about a profound transformation of American society which affected all major ethnic groups. In the

1950s and early 1960s it sometimes seemed that the very fabric of Franco-American life was unraveling. The Comité de Vie Franco-Américaine, founded in 1947, was concerned. Parish priests, once the stoutest advocates of survivance, began to use English in all religious ceremonies; Franco-American elementary and secondary schools consolidated or closed permanently as enrollments dropped precipitously; French, formerly the language of instruction in half the curriculum, was reduced to an hour a day or less in the surviving establishments;[66] membership in various organizations plummeted. Vatican II introduced far-reaching changes in the Catholic church, too little and too late in the opinion of some members, too many and too fast to suit others. The troubled 1960s ushered in a series of crises that produced an effect upon the young in particular. Yet the 1960s also witnessed the beginnings of a remarkable turnabout in ethnic consciousness whose fountainhead was Sputnik and the civil rights movement.

Causes of the cultural revival

Reacting to spectacular Soviet technological achievements, Congress in 1958 passed the National Defense Education Act (NDEA), which fostered major educational reforms in the United States. The new law stressed the importance of foreign language instruction and funded numerous programs designed to improve and develop this study.

On a different front, the black civil rights movement was soon emulated by other minorities seeking recognition and redress.[67] The so-called New Ethnicity, characterized by greater assertiveness on the part of white minorities, resulted in the Ethnic Heritage Studies Program established by Congress in 1972 and, more significant insofar as Franco-Americans are concerned, in novel bilingual education programs under Title VII of the Elementary and Secondary Education Act (ESEA) and the Emergency School Aid Act (ESAA), also enacted in 1972.

About this time two other developments had a great impact on Franco-Americans. In 1976 the American Revolution Bicentennial Administration reported that some 11,700 communities throughout the United States celebrated the nation's birthday. Thousands of cultural and educational programs, funded by private contributions and by federal, state, and local grants, took official cognizance of the key role that ethnic groups played and continue to play in American life. Efforts were made by Franco-Americans in many communities to draw attention to the group's achievements through various festivities, local history projects, and textbooks.

Alex Haley's best-selling *Roots* appeared the same year.[68] Haley recounted his own family's story but also succeeded in capturing the essence of black America's rich cultural heritage. The eight-part television dramatization, first aired in January 1977, created a sensation and inspired thousands to become interested in family history.

These developments rekindled ethnic pride and encouraged minority groups to turn to government at all levels for help in maintaining their cultural heritage and mother tongue. However, Franco-Americans also benefited from the sudden economic and social transformation of Quebec in the 1960s, known as the Quiet Revolution, and from the Parti Québécois's dramatic accession to power in 1976. Many recent changes in Franco-Américanie can be linked to these specific developments. It should be noted, too, that new Franco-American leaders have played an important role in shaping these events.

Federal subsidies

In 1960 I was awarded an NDEA research contract to prepare pedagogical materials designed to help Franco-Americans maintain and enhance their command of French.[69] In 1961, 1962, and 1964 I directed three NDEA summer institutes at Bowdoin College in Maine and at Assumption College in Massachusetts for Franco-American teachers of French, most of whom were engaged in providing instruction to large numbers of Franco-Americans. These programs imparted advanced training in French but also dealt with the many special problems involved in teaching Franco-Americans their mother tongue.[70] Each summer the six-week institute for forty participants included required courses in Franco-American speech and culture as well as a demonstration class made up of local Franco-American children. The 1960 contract marked the first time ever an American ethnic group was granted federal support to help preserve its linguistic and cultural heritage.[71] In 1963 a team of specialists I brought together, again with NDEA funding, wrote a textbook that was used to teach Franco-American students throughout New England.[72] Many of the 120 graduates of these summer institutes played an important role in the revival that came afterward.

Under Title VII of the Elementary and Secondary Education Act of 1972, a National Materials Development Center for French and Creole was created in 1975 in Bedford, New Hampshire. Over a period of seven years the center was awarded $3 million. It published an impressive number of Franco-American documents and texts: reprints of ten novels, a nine-volume anthology of prose and poetry, an original novel, volumes dealing with artists, cooking, genealogy, and so forth. Budget cuts in 1980 sharply curtailed the center's activities and finally forced it to shut down in September 1982. The remaining stock of materials was transferred to the

Department of Media Services at the University of New Hampshire, where they are still available for purchase.[73] These publications were not always of the highest quality from the point of view of typography and content, but together they form a precious collection of pedagogical and research material. Much of the credit for this achievement goes to the center's director, Normand C. Dubé, a prolific poet and one of the most active new leaders on the Franco-American scene.

Other ESEA undertakings in the 1970s and early 1980s include bilingual elementary school programs in Caribou, Lewiston, and the St. John Valley, Maine; Berlin and Greenville, New Hampshire; and Canaan-Norton, Derby, Highgate-Sheldon, and Richford, Vermont. Some programs (e.g., Derby and Lewiston) were short-lived, others were funded for five or six years, and one, the St. John Valley program, received federal support for ten years. Funds were also made available for special teacher training programs at Boston State College, Boston University, and the University of Vermont.[74]

Bilingual education is not without its critics. When the U.S. Supreme Court ruled in 1974 in *Lau v. Nichols* (414 U.S. 563) that public schools must offer special education programs, bilingual if necessary, wherever twenty or more children speak a non-English mother tongue, the Department of Education issued guidelines that were promptly challenged. In December 1980 the department's ruling concerning the Fairfax County, Virginia, school district meant that henceforth non-English-speaking pupils could be taught by means other than bilingual classes. The following year the Reagan administration began reducing federally funded bilingual education programs. Local politics also contributed to the rise and fall of these endeavors. Franco-American parents were divided, too, over the value of bilingual education: many feared their children would fall behind in their other studies if more time were spent developing French skills.[75]

Two kinds of public school programs have been designed to aid non-English-speaking children learn English: (1) bilingual education in which pupils gradually learn English while being taught other subjects in their mother tongue, and (2) immersion, consisting of English as a Second Language (ESL), an intensive course in English taken by students who attend regular classes the rest of the school day.

When properly used by competent teachers, both approaches work, but there is a trade-off to be considered in each case. Critics of bilingual education assert that it is a costly scheme designed to enhance mother tongue retention and delays the process of learning English. Opponents of ESL find fault with a "sink or swim" method that tends to make children feel self-conscious and reject their mother tongue and values. The debate often comes down to the importance or worth one assigns to maintaining ethnic languages and culture.[76]

Government grants to foster interest in an ethnic group's cultural heritage have been less controversial. In 1973 Anne Kempers and Beatrice Maltais of Waterville, Maine, received Title III ESEA support to produce materials entitled "Your Franco-American Heritage." These were distributed locally. A larger Title IX ESEA award was made in 1976 to Assumption College in Worcester, Massachusetts, to implement a Franco-American Heritage Studies Program. Twelve units in both French and English, covering a wide range of topics (e.g., arts and literature, church, education, family, media, traditions), were supplied to one hundred communities. The project was directed by Claire Quintal of Assumption College, who was assisted by Paul P. Chassé of Rhode Island College.

A number of television programs and films in this field have also been produced in recent years. Two series intended for Franco-American children were made possible by Title VII ESEA grants to the Maine Public Broadcasting Network in 1974 and to New Hampshire Public Television in 1978. The first of these, "La Bonne Aventure," featured French-speaking puppets; the second, "The Franco File," a ten-part series set in a fictional New England mill town, introduced the old bookseller Monsieur Beausoleil who spoke of his heritage. One episode of the latter program won an Emmy award from the New England chapter of the National Academy of Television Arts and Sciences.

The Maine Council for the Humanities and Public Policy and the National Endowment for the Humanities also funded the Maine Public Broadcasting Network's "Reflets et Lumière," a series of monthly half-hour television programs in a magazine format which began in the fall of 1979.

The Ethnic Heritage Studies Program sponsored the film "Emigration" by Gary Samson of the University of New Hampshire in 1981. Other video films about Franco-Americans include "Soirée franco-américaine" (1976) by David Whittier, WGBH-TV, Boston, and "Milltown" (1977) by Gary Samson and Denise Arel. Perhaps the best-known film, however, is "Bien des choses ont changé: Les Franco-Américains de la Nouvelle-Angleterre," a fifty-nine-minute documentary produced for Canadian television by Daniel Louis of Montreal. The film premiered on June 28, 1982, at the annual meeting of the American Association of Teachers of French held at Quebec City.[77]

One of the most ambitious educational undertakings, the Canadian/Franco-American Studies Project at the University of Maine at Orono, was funded by a three-year grant (1979–81) from the National Endowment for the Humanities. It involved several faculty seminars, a summer institute for fifty secondary school teachers, support for four faculty members, regional workshops in five New England states, and a three-day international congress, in August 1981, entitled "Etre Français en Amérique—The French in North America."[78]

State cultural commissions

One of the first signs of growing Franco-American political assertiveness was the creation of state cultural commissions. These groups are generally made up of Franco-American legislators and prominent civic leaders who seek ways to advance the group's welfare, usually by symbolic acts such as official proclamations, banquets, and ceremonial visits by French and Quebecois dignitaries. (From the turn of the century, Franco-American leaders have always had good rapport with French envoys in the area.) The first such body was the American and Canadian French Cultural Exchange Commission established by the Massachusetts General Court in 1968.[79] Similar agencies were later created in Connecticut, New Hampshire, Rhode Island, and Vermont. A bill for such a commission is currently pending before the Maine legislature.

Public events

Another analogous phenomenon is the designation of a Franco-American day or week. French Canadians have been celebrating the feast of Saint John the Baptist since 1834. Such commemorations have been held annually without interruption since 1868 in Lowell, Massachusetts,[80] and more or less regularly in several other Franco-American centers. In 1982, for example, noteworthy celebrations were held in Fall River, Lowell, New Bedford, and Springfield, Massachusetts; Manchester and Nashua, New Hampshire; and Central Falls and Woonsocket, Rhode Island.[81] Usually such events take the form of a French mass and a banquet. Sometimes a plaque or a monument is unveiled. At the turn of the century and in the decades that followed, elaborate parades were organized as they still are in French Canada today, but the custom died out in New England. However, beginning in 1971 Lowell has had an annual Franco-American Week; Manchester has had one since 1981; Nashua since 1982. In 1976 the American and Canadian French Cultural Exchange Commission organized a French Ethnic Week in Boston; in 1978 a Franco-American Night was held in Waterville, Maine, with one thousand persons in attendance; a similar event was held in Leominster, Massachusetts, the same year. In 1981 the Vermont legislature adopted a resolution proclaiming that henceforth the Sunday nearest June 24 (the feast of Saint John the Baptist) would be Franco-American Day. In 1982 the governors of Maine and New York issued similar proclamations but for that year only.

Ethnic fairs

Franco-American fairs are a related development. In 1977 Lewiston, Maine, had its first annual Festival.[82] Similar celebrations have been held annually in Biddeford and Old Town, Maine; in the Chicopee-Holyoke and Salem, Massachusetts, areas; and in northern Vermont.

Commercial fairs have long been a part of the American scene. Churches, too, have often held bazaars or carnivals for charitable purposes or to pay off debts. Many ethnic fairs today, including Franco-American festivals, are an outgrowth of this religious tradition. But they are also related to business ventures that have sprung up in cities and towns everywhere since the 1950s, touting local customs or products and seeking to attract tourists. In many instances, business and ethnic leaders have found it mutually advantageous to come together in a common undertaking.[83]

Many such festivals soon become artificial and institutionalized, but the better ones protect and sustain ethnic culture and group feeling. Much of the spontaneity of these fairs depends on the enthusiastic participation of persons of all ages. Ideally, such occasions are an entertaining and educational experience for everyone involved.

It is not surprising, then, to learn that some Franco-Americans view such events as a mixed blessing: they applaud these manifestations of new-found pride and the high quality of certain artistic displays and performances but also decry some of the tawdriness and beery atmosphere. The fear is that these fairs may turn into essentially commercial ventures without much genuine cultural content.[84] However, on balance, Franco-American fairs clearly effect their purpose, which is to provide occasions for socializing and for demonstrations of solidarity, and for heightening public awareness of the group's vitality and cultural activities.

Role of the Quebec government

The government of Quebec actively supports such cultural manifestations by providing grants and by maintaining an official presence in the area. After the Quebec Ministry of Cultural Affairs was established in 1961, preliminary contacts were made with Franco-American leaders but plans remained tentative.[85] The situation changed dramatically after the Parti Québécois came to power in 1976. The Ministry of Intergovernmental Affairs (called the Ministry of International Relations since March

1984) now devoted serious energy to strengthening ties with Franco-Americans.[86] One major undertaking in 1977, 1978, and 1980 has been the Festival de la Jeunesse in Quebec City. Groups of Franco-American youths were afforded a free trip to the capital paid for with contributions from the Quebec government and Franco-American organizations.[87]

In another significant development, in July 1981 ActFANE (Action for Franco-Americans of the Northeast) was established with Quebec government funding to help coordinate Franco-American activities of all sorts and to disseminate information through a quarterly newsletter (current circulation, 4,000). ActFANE, whose secretary is Paul M. Paré, has the potential for becoming the nerve center of the current revival. It has already provoked significant changes in many Franco-Americans' conception of themselves or their role.[88]

Quebec's efforts to maintain good rapport with Franco-Americans make excellent economic sense. The value of Quebec's exports to the United States has grown rapidly in recent years ($10.5 billion in 1981, a 17.5 percent increase over the preceding year).[89] Energy and tourism are two sectors of Quebec's economy in which New England plays a prominent part. In March 1983 sixty-four companies in the New England Power Pool signed an eleven-year contract, known as "phase one," with Hydro-Quebec for the sale of 33 billion kilowatt-hours of electricity to begin in 1986.[90] In June 1984 a second accord, "phase two," involved the importation of an additional 7 billion kilowatt-hours per year, worth about $2.5 billion in the 1990s. Also, each year seven hundred thousand New England tourists travel to Quebec.[91]

The political implications of this policy are less clear. In 1982 George Jaeger, U.S. consul general in Quebec, repeatedly cautioned Quebec officials, notably Jacques-Yvan Morin, minister of intergovernmental affairs, against activism in their dealings with Franco-Americans. Jaeger reportedly believed these officials were seeking to influence the United States to favor Quebec's efforts to achieve independence; he considered this pressure an intrusion in American affairs. These warnings are said to have produced the desired effect.[92]

Certain Franco-American militants support independence for Quebec. However, on the whole, Franco-Americans appear ambivalent about current political issues north of the border.[93]

Fraternal societies

Many Franco-Americans belong to one of three fraternal benefit societies: the Association Canado-Américaine, the Société L'Assomption (since 1969 officially designated L'Assomption compagnie mutuelle d'assurance-vie), and the Union Saint-Jean-Baptiste d'Amérique. (The Société L'Assomption has its headquarters in Moncton, New Brunswick, recruits mainly among Acadians, and will not be discussed here.)

The most influential of the nonprofit insurance groups for Franco-Americans is the Union Saint-Jean-Baptiste d'Amérique founded in 1900 at Woonsocket, Rhode Island, site of its present-day home office. USJB councils—115 throughout New England and one in New York City—are found wherever Franco-Americans reside in great numbers, and the status of individual branch organizations is often an accurate barometer of local Franco-American vitality. The society publishes a newsletter six times a year and owns an important collection of Franco-Americana purchased in 1908 from the estate of Civil War major Edmond Mallet.[94]

In former times, USJB council meetings once a month tended to be occasions for socializing and raising funds for a parish church or school. Though the USJB was often represented in hometown parades by a band or a drill team, council activities were mostly private affairs. Emulating the efforts of other minority organizations, local councils, in recent years, have become increasingly publicity conscious and community oriented.

At headquarters and at annual conventions, change is even more apparent. The USJB became officially bilingual—that is, not exclusively French—in 1966, its newsletter in 1972. In what was perhaps the greatest departure from tradition, non-Catholics were permitted to join in 1982. An extensive modernization of the home office was undertaken in 1975, and the following year the USJB took an active part in Bicentennial celebrations in fifteen different localities. Edgar J. Martel's accession to the presidency in 1975 marked the beginning of a new era characterized by growth and greater visibility of the organization.[95] The USJB's Project FAITH—an acronym for Franco-American Interest in the Handicapped—begun in 1977, is a typical activity in the new style.[96]

The Association Canado-Américaine, founded in 1896, is a bit more conservative but has recently experienced a similar renewal.[97] When Eugène A. Lemieux became president in 1981, the number of ACA policyholders had dwindled to 25,731, and several possible mergers had been seriously discussed.[98] The association, whose home office is in Manchester, New Hampshire, has forty-two councils—called *cours,* or courts—in New England. It is strongest in New Hampshire (thirteen councils, six in Manchester alone). As opposed to the USJB, the association is also firmly established in Quebec, with half as many councils located there.

The ACA welcomes scholars to its excellent research library housing some fifty thousand items.[99] The nucleus of this priceless collection of Franco-Americana was assembled by Adélard Lambert, who sold it to the

ACA in 1921. Well indexed and considerably augmented through the efforts of Adolphe Robert, scholarly president of the ACA from 1936 to 1956, and Monsignor Adrien Verrette (born 1897), one of the greatest authorities on Franco-American history, this library is rightly called the Archives Franco-Américaines.[100] The librarian is Dr. Robert A. Beaudoin.

The ACA publishes a quarterly newsletter, which recently began to look a good deal slicker with many lively articles and a more stylish format. It also sponsors many activities under the guidance of its able social director, Julien Olivier. The ACA also provides office space for two promising new endeavors, ActFANE and the American-Canadian Genealogical Society.

Other New England organizations

A large number of other Franco-American associations have always existed at the parish, city, state, and regional levels; but except in a few cases, public awareness of their activities and even, at times, of their existence was slight. Two organizations have done much to draw attention to the group and, by example and support, have injected new life into local Franco-American organizations.

The Fédération Féminine Franco-Américaine, a coalition of Franco-American women's clubs, was founded in 1951 and now has ten thousand members throughout New England. The "Fédé" organizes contests, concerts, excursions, and the like, publishes a newsletter, and holds highly publicized biennial conventions.[101] Its current president is Marthe Biron-Péloquin.

Richelieu service clubs have also become a fixture in New England. Modeled on Rotary International, the Richelieu was founded at Ottawa in 1944 and spread rapidly throughout Canada. The first such club in New England was established in Manchester, New Hampshire, in 1955. There are now fourteen more clubs in the area: Hartford, Connecticut; Biddeford and Lewiston, Maine; Fall River, Lawrence, Lowell, New Bedford, Salem, and Springfield, Massachusetts; Nashua, Pinardville, Rochester, and Suncook, New Hampshire; and Woonsocket, Rhode Island. Although the society's constitution does not exclude women, the first female members were not admitted until 1982. Also, in 1984 all-women Richelieu clubs were founded at Salem and Woonsocket. Clubs meet every week or two, conduct all business in French, and engage in numerous humanitarian activities, notably charity drives benefiting disadvantaged children.[102]

A very great need exists for a Franco-American museum. Important collections are housed in the headquarters of the Association Canado-Américaine and the Union Saint-Jean-Baptiste d'Amérique, but no institution is devoted entirely to this purpose. Perhaps the most interesting local display is in the Centre d'Héritage Franco-Américain at the Lewiston-

Auburn Center of the University of Maine. The center was founded in 1970 and sponsors various activities of a cultural nature.

Academic involvement

Franco-Americans have long enjoyed a special relationship with certain Catholic institutions of higher learning in New England, notably Assumption College in Worcester, Massachusetts (founded in 1904); Rivier College in Nashua, New Hampshire (1933; a college-level program was actually started ten years earlier at the boarding school operated by the Sisters of the Presentation of Mary in Hudson, New Hampshire); Anna Maria College in Paxton, Massachusetts (1946); and Notre Dame College in Manchester, New Hampshire (1950). All are now coeducational and no longer focus their recruiting efforts on Franco-Americans. Assumption (current enrollment of about fifteen hundred undergraduates, about one-third of whom are Franco-Americans) remains most involved with the group. Its attractive library and conference center—La Maison Française—was a gift of the Union Saint-Jean-Baptiste d'Amérique.

Following World War II, the Comité de Vie Franco-Américaine sponsored every other year or so a Congrès des Franco-Américains that strove to address current issues. Long on rhetoric and fine resolutions, these meetings had mixed results. However, at the eleventh congress in 1974, at a small but important conference organized in 1975 by Donald Dugas at the University of Massachusetts at Amherst, then at a similar gathering the following year sponsored by the National Materials Development Center at Bedford, New Hampshire,[103] different voices began to be heard. Younger, less conservative individuals were now participating, new leaders were emerging, many with academic connections and accustomed to turning to the government for support. The trend continued at a public conference at the University of Lowell in 1977 and at a major colloquium organized by Raoul Pinette and funded by a grant from the Maine Council for the Humanities and Public Policy held at Bates College in Lewiston, Maine, in 1978.

In perhaps the most significant development, Assumption College founded its French Institute directed by Claire Quintal in 1979. Each spring, the institute has sponsored a highly successful bilingual conference on Franco-American studies. The caliber of the papers has been uniformly high, and the proceedings have all been printed within a year of each occasion.[104] Equally remarkable, of the more than two hundred persons who have attended the annual event, a substantial number are not academics but simply interested Franco-Americans. Many of the invited speakers have been products of the NDEA generation, that is, scholars who received fellowships (while earning their Ph.D.s) or postdoctoral research grants from

the federal government. Others became interested in the field as a consequence of the Quiet Revolution in Quebec. The institute is currently involved in a million dollar fund-raising campaign.[105]

Meanwhile, courses in Franco-American language and culture have begun to be offered throughout the Northeast, notably in Maine: as part of
the adult education program at Waterville High School in 1973; at the
University of Maine at Augusta in 1977; at the University of Maine at
Orono in 1980; at Cohoes, New York, in 1981 and 1983; at the University
of Massachusetts and at the University of Maine at Presque Isle in 1981; at
the University of Maine at Fort Kent in 1982.

The Franco-American and Quebec Heritage Series, directed by
Eloise A. Brière of the Department of French, State University of New
York at Albany, is a particularly successful undertaking. Begun as an informal seminar at Saint Joseph's parish hall in Cohoes, with modest support
from the Capital District Humanities Program but developed by Brière, an
exceptionally effective and resourceful teacher, the combination of lectures
and activities exploring Franco-American life, language, and literature has
since received funds from the National Endowment for the Humanities
and the governments of Canada and Quebec.

Finally, papers on Franco-American topics have been given at meetings
sponsored by many professional associations, including the Middle Atlantic Conference for Canadian Studies, the Modern Language Association
of America, the Northeast Conference on the Teaching of Foreign Languages, the Northeast Council for Quebec Studies, and the Northeast
Modern Language Association.

FAROG

In 1972 the Franco-American Resource Opportunity Group was established at the University of Maine at Orono.[106] The acronym FAROG was a
deliberate attempt to co-opt a familiar ethnic slur. Yvon Labbé has transformed what was initially a modest support group into a force to be reck-
oned with. Labbé organizes ten to twenty student volunteers, who engage
in a variety of activities not only on campus but locally. For example, they
work with the elderly and with hearing-impaired children.[107] The group
publishes a monthly bilingual tabloid, FAROG Forum, a sassy, irreverent,
let-it-all-hang-out newspaper with a circulation of forty-five hundred. In
addition to covering the Franco-American scene—the focus is New England, especially Maine, but the term is often applied here to all Francophones in the United States—and developments in French Canada, students and guest feature writers contribute articles, often in so-called [St.
John] Valley French, about their frustrations, gripes, and personal experi-

ences of discrimination. FAROG has also sponsored the "Blé d'Inde Contraband," a country music group that played a combination of French-Canadian folk music and popular songs, and soirées featuring authentic Franco-American cuisine and entertainment conducive to good fellowship.[108] FAROG is at times a thorn in the UMO administration's side, but it is one of the most refreshing Franco-American phenomena in years.

Media

Programs on public television and on the radio in a few localities in New England,[109] as well as the newsletters of ActFANE, the Association Canado-Américaine, the Fédération Féminine Franco-Américaine, and the Union Saint-Jean-Baptiste d'Amérique inform Franco-Americans about current activities and issues but are no substitute for a first-rate newspaper. *FAROG Forum, Le Journal de Lowell,* and *L'Unité* all strive to fill this gap but have limited budgets and staffs.[110] It remains to be seen whether one or more of these undertakings will succeed in reaching the mass readership they deserve.

La Librairie Populaire, a bookshop specializing in French-language publications and records, as well as works about France, Franco-Americans, and French Canada, has been in existence since 1962. Owned and operated by Roger Lacerte, the store was first established in Lowell, Massachusetts. From 1977 to 1979 the proprietor managed identically designated businesses in Manchester, New Hampshire, and Lowell; since the latter date, La Librairie Populaire has had one location only in Manchester.[111]

Genealogy

Franco-American interest in genealogy and family history has grown by leaps and bounds in recent years. The American-Canadian Genealogical Society, founded in Manchester, New Hampshire, in 1973 has fifteen hundred members. Acadians also have a separate organization, the Acadian Genealogical Historical Association, Inc., with headquarters in Fitchburg, Massachusetts.[112] Another group, the American-French Genealogical Society, established in 1978, is based in Pawtucket, Rhode Island.[113]

Large family gatherings, many of them held in Quebec on some anniversary—for example, the bicentennial or tricentennial of a city, the foundation of a parish—in communities associated with an ancestor, parallel this development.

Soft spots can be found in this cultural revival—the disappearance of parochial schools in many areas and the decline in French-language usage and media are grave matters.[114] Also, this revival primarily affects the middle class and should not be exaggerated. But many Franco-Americans currently feel more optimistic about maintaining their culture than they have since the period of its greatest vigor half a century ago.

Conclusion

French Canadians have lived in New England in large numbers for a relatively short time period—not much longer than the span of a person's life—but they have undergone a profound change. Heirs to a proud tradition nearly four centuries old, they have also embraced that of the American people with whom they have become integrated. The current cultural revival suggests that Franco-Americans hold their distinctive beliefs and values to be fundamentally sound and enriching, hence worth preserving. This pluralistic view of American society is shared by many other ethnic groups today.

Although some uninformed individuals still equate ethnicity with conflicting loyalties, one can only hope that public campaigns against so-called hyphenated Americans are a thing of the past. Most Americans, especially since the 1960s, respect or at least tolerate ethnic pride. Franco-Americans have proved their patriotism by serving with distinction in the U.S. armed forces in several wars and in peacetime, and are second to none in discharging their other civic duties.

Loyalty to the French language and to Roman Catholicism are still regarded as key elements in Franco-American culture, but members of the group are finding increasing fulfillment in their other achievements in New England, in their social development, and in their contributions to American life and thought. French-language usage is declining; however, a not inconsiderable number continue to cherish their ancestral language and to find it practical. As before, Franco-Americans aspire to have their voice heard in the Francophone world; but more and more, too, they wish to be considered as people who make important contributions to the region they inhabit and to the nation.

In the face of gloomy forecasts about the group's future, Franco-Americans can take heart in the remarkable success Quebecois have achieved in modernizing and reinvigorating their own culture.[115] If the current revival in New England is to grow in momentum and scope—and I am confident that it will—Franco-Americans must continue to innovate without losing sight of what is tried and true in their heritage. Above all, they will need to develop a better appreciation of the quality and strength of their survival, which, all things considered, are far greater than many may realize.

APPENDIX A

Size and percentage of the Franco-American population in selected urban areas in central and southeastern New England

A. High Franco-American population (more than 5,000) and high percentage of the total population (more than 20 percent)

*Biddeford-Saco, Maine
Central Falls, Massachusetts
Fall River, Massachusetts
Fitchburg, Massachusetts
Holyoke, Massachusetts
*Lewiston-Auburn, Maine
Lowell, Massachusetts

*Manchester, New Hampshire
Nashua, New Hampshire
New Bedford, Massachusetts
Salem, Massachusetts
Southbridge, Massachusetts
Warwick, Rhode Island
*Woonsocket, Rhode Island

B. Medium-sized Franco-American population (1,500–5,000) and high percentage of the total population (more than 20 percent)

Adams, Massachusetts
Berlin, New Hampshire
Brunswick, Maine
Burrillville, Rhode Island
Chicopee, Massachusetts
Claremont, New Hampshire
Coventry, Rhode Island
Danielson, Connecticut
Gardner, Massachusetts
Grafton, Massachusetts
Killingly-Brooklyn, Connecticut
Laconia, New Hampshire
Lincoln, Rhode Island
Marlboro, Massachusetts
Millbury, Massachusetts
North Adams, Massachusetts
Old Town, Maine

Palmer, Massachusetts
Plainfield, Connecticut
Putnam, Connecticut
Rumford, Maine
Sanford, Maine
Skowhegan, Maine
Somersworth, New Hampshire
Spencer, Massachusetts
Suncook, New Hampshire
Sutton, Massachusetts
Thompson, Connecticut
Ware, Massachusetts
Warren, Rhode Island
Waterville, Maine
Webster-Dudley, Massachusetts
Westbrook, Maine
Willimantic, Connecticut

*Very high Franco-American population and very high percentage of the total population.

C. Medium-sized Franco-American population (1,500–5,000) and low percentage of the total population (less than 20 percent)

Augusta, Maine
Brockton, Massachusetts
Cambridge, Massachusetts
Concord, New Hampshire
Hartford, Connecticut
Leominster, Massachusetts
Lynn, Massachusetts
Meriden, Connecticut
Northampton, Massachusetts
Pittsfield, Massachusetts
Taunton, Massachusetts
Waterbury, Connecticut

D. High Franco-American population (more than 5,000) and low percentage of the total population (less than 20 percent)

Boston, Massachusetts
Haverhill, Massachusetts
Lawrence, Massachusetts
Pawtucket, Rhode Island
Providence, Rhode Island
Springfield, Massachusetts
Worcester, Massachusetts

Source: Gerard J. Brault, "Etat présent des études sur les centres franco-américains de la Nouvelle-Angleterre," *CIF* 1, 9–10 (but see Introduction, n. 10).

Selected Franco-American parishes

Connecticut
   Baltic, Immaculate Conception
   Bristol, St. Anne
   Hartford, St. Anne
   Meriden, St. Laurent
   New Britain, St. Peter
   North Grosvernordale, St. Joseph
   Plainfield, St. John
   Putnam, St. Mary
   Taftville, Sacred Heart
   Waterbury, St. Anne
   West Wauregan, Sacred Heart
   Willimantic, St. Mary

Maine
   Ashland, St. Mark
   Auburn, Sacred Heart
   ——, St. Louis
   ——, St. Philip
   Augusta, St. Augustine
   Biddeford, St. André
   ——, St. Joseph
   Brunswick, St. John the Baptist
   Caribou, Holy Rosary
   ——, Sacred Heart
   Chisholm, St. Rose of Lima
   Daigle, Holy Family
   Dexter, St. Anne
   Eagle Lake, St. Mary
   Fairfield, Immaculate Heart of Mary

Fort Kent, St. Louis
Gorham, St. Anne
Grand Isle, St. Gerard
Hamlin, St. Joseph
Keegan (Van Buren), St. Remy
Lewiston, Holy Cross
——, Holy Family
——, St. Mary
——, SS. Peter and Paul
Lille (Lower Grand Isle), Notre Dame
Lisbon, St. Anne
Madawaska, St. David
——, St. Thomas Aquinas
Madison, St. Sebastian
Mexico, St. Theresa
Oguossoc, Our Lady of the Lakes (mission)
Old Orchard Beach, St. Margaret
Old Town, St. Joseph
Presque Isle, St. Mary
Rumford, St. Athanasius and St. John
Saco, Notre Dame
St. Francis, St. Charles
St. John Plantation (Fort Kent), St. John the Baptist
Sanford, Holy Family
——, St. Ignatius
Sinclair, St. Joseph

Skowhegan, Notre Dame
South Berwick, St. Michael
Springvale, Notre Dame
Upper Frenchville, St. Luce
Van Buren, St. Bruno
Waterville, Notre Dame
———, St. Francis de Sales
Westbrook, St. Hyacinth
Winslow, St. John the Baptist

Massachusetts
Acushnet, St. Francis Xavier
Adams, Notre Dame
Agawam, St. Theresa
Amesbury, Sacred Heart
Athol, Our Lady Immaculate
Attleboro, St. Joseph
Bellingham, Assumption
Beverly, St. Alphonse
Brockton, Sacred Heart
Cambridge, Our Lady of Pity
Chelsea, Our Lady of the
  Assumption
Chicopee, Assumption
Chicopee (Aldenville), St. Rose of
  Lima
Chicopee (Chicopee Falls),
  St. George
Chicopee (Fairview), St. Anne
Chicopee (Willimansett), Nativity
  of the Blessed Virgin Mary
Dracut, St. Theresa
East Blackstone, St. Theresa
Easthampton, Our Lady of Good
  Counsel
Fairhaven, Sacred Heart
Fall River, Blessed Sacrament
———, Notre Dame de Lourdes
———, St. Anne
———, St. John the Baptist
———, St. Matthew
Fitchburg, Immaculate
  Conception
———, St. Francis of Assisi
———, St. Joseph
Gardner, Our Lady of the Rosary
Haverhill, St. Joseph
Holyoke, Immaculate Conception
———, Our Lady of Perpetual
  Help
———, Precious Blood
Hudson, Christ the King
Indian Orchard, St. Aloysius (St.
  Louis de Gonzague)

Ipswich, St. Stanislaus
Lawrence, Sacred Heart
———, St. Anne
Leominster, St. Cecilia
Linwood, Good Shepherd
Lowell, Our Lady of Lourdes
———, St. Joan of Arc
———, St. John the Baptist
———, St. Louis de France
———, St. Mary
Ludlow, St. John the Baptist
Lynn, St. John the Baptist
Manchaug, St. Anne
Marlboro, St. Mary
Methuen, Our Lady of Mount
  Carmel
Millbury, Our Lady of the
  Assumption
New Bedford, Our Lady of the
  Holy Rosary
———, Sacred Heart
———, St. Anne
———, St. Anthony of Padua
———, St. Joseph
———, St. Theresa
Newburyport, St. Aloysius (St.
  Louis de Gonzague)
North Adams, Holy Family
———, Notre Dame
Northampton, Sacred Heart
North Attleboro, Sacred Heart
Northbridge, St. Peter
Pittsfield, Notre Dame
Salem, St. Anne
———, St. Joseph
Shirley, St. Anthony of Padua
Southbridge, Notre Dame
———, Sacred Heart
South Grafton, St. James
Spencer, St. Mary
Springfield, St. Joseph
———, St. Thomas Aquinas
Springfield (West Springfield),
  St. Louis de France
Swansea, St. Louis de France
Taunton, St. James
Three Rivers, St. Anne
Turners Falls, St. Anne
Waltham, St. Joseph
Ware, Our Lady of Mount Carmel
Webster, Sacred Heart
West Warren, St. Thomas Aquinas
Williamstown, St. Raphael

Worcester, Holy Name of Jesus
——, Notre Dame des
Canadiens
——, St. Anthony
——, St. Joseph

New Hampshire
Berlin, Guardian Angel
——, St. Anne
——, St. Benedict
——, St. Joseph
Colebrook, St. Brendan
Concord, Sacred Heart
Dover, St. Charles Borromeo
Gonic, St. Leo
Gorham, Holy Family
Greenville, Sacred Heart
Groveton, St. Francis Xavier
Laconia, Sacred Heart
Manchester, Blessed Sacrament
——, Sacred Heart
——, St. Anthony of Padua
——, St. Augustine
——, St. Edmund
——, St. George
——, St. John the Baptist
——, St. Mary
——, St. Theresa
Nashua, Holy Infant Jesus
——, St. Aloysius (St. Louis de
Gonzague)
Newmarket, St. Mary
Rochester, Holy Rosary
Rollinsford, St. Mary
Somersworth, St. Martin of Tours
Suncook, St. John the Baptist
West Stewartstown (Beecher Falls,
Vt.), St. Albert

Rhode Island
Albion, St. Ambrose
Arctic (Centreville), St. John the
Baptist
Arctic (West Warwick), Christ the
King
Central Falls, Notre Dame (Our
Lady of Sacred Heart)
——, St. Matthew
Cumberland, St. Joan of Arc
Manville, St. James
Mapleville (Oakland), Our Lady
of Good Help
Nasonville, St. Theresa
Pascoag, St. Joseph

Pawtucket, Our Lady of
Consolation
——, St. Cecilia
——, St. John the Baptist
Phenix (West Warwick), Our Lady
of Good Counsel
Providence, Our Lady of Lourdes
——, St. Charles Borromeo
Warren, St. John the Baptist
Woonsocket, Holy Family
——, Our Lady of Victories
——, Our Lady Queen of
Martyrs
——, Precious Blood
——, St. Agatha
——, St. Aloysius (St. Louis de
Gonzague)
——, St. Anne
Woonsocket (Chipman's Corners),
St. Joseph

Vermont
Alburg, St. Amadeus
Barton, Conversion of St. Paul
Bennington, Sacred Heart
Burlington, St. Joseph
Canaan, Assumption
Derby Line, St. Edward
Enosburg Falls, St. John the
Baptist
Gilman, St. Theresa
Highgate Center, St. Louis
Hyde Park, St. Theresa
Island Pond, St. James
Johnson, St. John the Baptist
Newport, St. Mary Star of the Sea
North Troy, St. Vincent de Paul
Orleans, St. Theresa
Orwell, Commemoration of
St. Paul
Richford, All Saints
Rutland, Immaculate Heart of
Mary
St. Albans, Guardian Angels
St. Johnsbury, St. John the
Evangelist
Sheldon Springs and Franklin,
St. Anthony and St. Mary
South Hero, St. Rose of Lima
Swanton, Nativity of the Blessed
Virgin Mary
Troy, Sacred Heart
Winooski, St. Francis Xavier

Sources: This list represents information I obtained in a mail survey, conducted in 1972 and 1975, requesting from individual pastors the number of parishioners and percentage of Franco-Americans in each parish. Only parishes specifying 50 percent or more Franco-Americans have been entered here. I compiled the mailing list from parishes that, in the *Official Catholic Directory* (New York: Kenedy, 1972), listed priests having French surnames; from indications in the *Guide officiel franco-américain* (Woonsocket, R.I.: Sansouci, 1946); and from localities mentioned by James P. Allen, in "Catholics in Maine: A Social Geography," Ph.D. diss., Syracuse University, 1970, tables 14, 15. Names of parishes are given here according to the style found in the 1984 edition of the *Official Catholic Directory*. For a slightly different list, see Paul P. Chassé, *Church,* Franco-American Ethnic Heritage Studies Program, Title IX (ESEA) grant (Worcester, Mass.: Assumption College, 1976), appendix.

Some early Franco-American parishes

1838 Van Buren, Maine—St. Bruno
1843 Upper Frenchville, Maine—St. Luce
1850 Burlington, Vermont—St. Joseph
1858 Alburg, Vermont—St. Amadeus
1867 Pittsfield, Massachusetts—St. Joseph (later Notre Dame)
1868 Lowell, Massachusetts—St. Joseph (later St. John the Baptist)
      Winooski, Vermont—St. Francis Xavier
1869 Fall River, Massachusetts—St. Anne
      Holyoke, Massachusetts—Precious Blood
      Rutland, Vermont—Immaculate Heart of Mary
      Worcester, Massachusetts—Notre Dame des Canadiens
1870 Biddeford, Maine—St. Joseph
      Fort Kent, Maine—St. Louis
      Marlboro, Massachusetts—St. Mary
      North Adams, Massachusetts—Notre Dame
      Webster, Massachusetts—Sacred Heart
1871 Augusta, Maine—St. Augustine
      Haverhill, Massachusetts—St. Joseph
      Lawrence, Massachusetts—St. Anne
      Lewiston, Maine—St. Peter (later SS. Peter and Paul)
      Madawaska, Maine—St. David
      Nashua, New Hampshire—St. Aloysius (St. Louis de Gonzague)
1873 Agawam, Massachusetts—St. Theresa
      Central Falls, Rhode Island—Notre Dame
      Indian Orchard, Massachusetts—St. Aloysius (St. Louis de Gonzague)
      Newport, Vermont—St. Mary Star of the Sea
      Salem, Massachusetts—St. Joseph
      Springfield, Massachusetts—St. Joseph
      Suncook, New Hampshire—St. John the Baptist
      Woonsocket, Rhode Island—Precious Blood
1874 Arctic (Centreville), Rhode Island—St. John the Baptist
      Fall River, Massachusetts—Notre Dame de Lourdes
      Manville, Rhode Island—St. James
      Providence, Rhode Island—St. Charles Borromeo
1877 Brunswick, Maine—St. John the Baptist
      New Bedford, Massachusetts—Sacred Heart
      Taftville, Connecticut—Sacred Heart
      Warren, Rhode Island—St. John the Baptist
      Westbrook, Maine—St. Hyacinth

1879 Caribou, Maine—Sacred Heart
1880 Boston, Massachusetts—Our Lady of Victories
       Manchester, New Hampshire—St. Mary
       Meriden, Connecticut—St. Laurent

Sources: Father Edouard Hamon, *Les Canadiens-français de la Nouvelle-Angleterre* (Quebec City: Hardy, 1891); and Robert Rumilly, *Histoire des Franco-Américains* (Montreal, 1958). Verified in survey described in Appendix A, "Selected Franco-American Parishes."
Note: For some early parishes in New York State, see Rumilly, *Histoire des Franco-Américains*, pp. 26, 32, 43, 44.

APPENDIX B

Table 1. French mother tongue population of New England, 1970

State	Total population	French mother tongue
Connecticut	3,031,705	142,118
Maine	993,663	141,489
Massachusetts	5,688,903	367,194
New Hampshire	737,681	112,559
Rhode Island	948,844	101,270
Vermont	444,330	42,193
New England	11,845,126	906,823

Sources: Gerard J. Brault, "Le français en Nouvelle-Angleterre," in *Le Français hors de France*, ed. Albert Valdman (Paris: Champion, 1979), p. 80, based on U.S. Department of Commerce Bureau of the Census, *Census of the Population: General Social and Economic Characteristics* (Washington, D.C.: Government Printing Office, 1972). Madeleine Giguère, a sociologist at the University of Southern Maine, South Portland, Maine, is the foremost expert on Franco-American population data that can be determined from the 1970 and 1980 censuses. French mother tongue statistics (1970) for individual New England cities and towns compiled by Giguère are listed in Dyke Hendrickson, *Quiet Presence: Dramatic, First-Person Accounts—The True Stories of Franco-Americans in New England* (Portland, Maine: Guy Gannet Publishing Co., 1980), Appendixes D–O.

Table 2. Franco-American population of New England, 1970

State	French	Franco-American
Connecticut	8,388	133,730
Maine	1,052	140,437
Massachusetts	12,342	354,852
New Hampshire	1,265	111,294
Rhode Island	3,261	98,009
Vermont	759	41,434
New England	27,067	879,756

Source: Brault, "Français en Nouvelle-Angleterre," p. 81.

Table 3. New England population of French ancestry, 1980

State	Single	Multiple
Connecticut	107,346	219,101
Maine	147,058	119,016
Massachusetts	312,497	525,978
New Hampshire	112,093	125,044
Rhode Island	77,045	101,660
Vermont	57,160	87,368
New England	813,199	1,178,167

Source: U.S. Department of Commerce, Bureau of the Census, *1980 Census of the Population: Ancestry of the Population by State* (Washington, D.C.: Government Printing Office, 1983), tables 3a, 3b.

Table 4. New England population of French-Canadian ancestry, 1980

State	Single	Multiple
Connecticut	42,821	14,168
Maine	26,205	4,624
Massachusetts	118,844	41,405
New Hampshire	37,873	9,407
Rhode Island	27,835	5,694
Vermont	15,612	4,351
New England	269,190	79,649

Source: See table 3.

Table 5. Estimated net migration of French Canadians to New England, 1840–1900

	1840–50	1850–60	1860–70	1870–80	1880–90	1890–1900
Conn.	250	1,550	5,600	6,400	5,300	6,600
Maine	600	2,750	5,400	7,100	10,300	11,300
Mass.	2,000	3,950	22,900	28,800	54,700	55,500
N.H.	250	1,350	4,700	15,100	18,800	16,400
R.I.	200	1,300	6,100	8,300	10,800	13,100
Vt.	5,500	1,700	8,000	50	2,900	3,400
Total	8,800	12,600	52,700	65,750	102,800	106,300

Source: Ralph D. Vicero, "Immigration of French Canadians to New England, 1840–1900: A Geographical Analysis," Ph.D. diss., University of Wisconsin, 1968, tables 5, 13.

Table 6. Estimated French-Canadian population of New England, 1850–1900

	1850	1860	1870	1880	1890	1900
Conn.	250	1,980	8,600	18,500	28,000	39,000
Maine	3,680	7,490	15,100	29,000	52,000	77,000
Mass.	2,830	7,780	34,600	81,100	162,000	275,000
N.H.	250	1,780	7,300	26,200	49,000	76,000
R.I.	300	1,810	8,900	19,800	36,000	61,000
Vt.	12,070	16,580	29,000	33,500	38,000	45,000
Total	19,380	37,420	103,500	208,100	365,000	573,000

Source: Vicero, "Immigration," tables 7, 17.

Table 7. Franco-American parochial schools and enrollment, 1938

State	Franco-American population	Franco-American parochial school children	Franco-American schools
Connecticut	79,000	7,800	16
Maine	132,000	17,269	32
Massachusetts	378,000	44,712	81
New Hampshire	138,000	17,300	41
Rhode Island	142,000	13,413	19
Vermont	65,000	4,150	9
New England	934,000	104,644	198

Source: *Guide officiel des Franco-Américains 1938*, ed. Albert A. Bélanger (Providence, R.I.: Guide Franco-Américain, Inc., 1938), [p. ii].

Table 8. Selected French provincial origins of French-Canadian colonists, 1608–1765

Provinces	Percentage of total colonists
Seventeenth Century	
Normandy	18.5%
Ile-de-France and Paris	14.7%
Poitou	10.9%
Aunis, Ile de Ré, Ile d'Oléron	10.6%
Brittany	3.5%
Eighteenth Century	
Ile-de-France and Paris	12.2%
Normandy	10.9%
Brittany	8.2%
Poitou	6.0%
Guyenne and Agennois	5.8%
Aunis and Ile de Ré	5.6%
Languedoc	5.2%

Source: Father Archange Godbout, "Nos hérédités provinciales françaises," *Archives de Folklore* 1 (1946), 26–40.
Note: These percentages do not include Acadian colonists.

**Table 9. Median number of years of education completed
by the New England population aged 14 years and over, 1950**

Ethnic group	Born abroad	Born in the U.S. of foreign and mixed parentage	Increase
French-Canadian	7.6	8.8	+1.2
Irish	8.3	11.4	+3.1
Italian	5.2	10.5	+5.3
Polish	4.8	10.5	+5.7

Source: Léon F. Bouvier, "La stratification sociale du groupe ethnique canadien-français aux Etats-Unis," *Recherches Sociographiques* 5 (1964), 371–79.

**Table 10. Median income of the U.S. population
aged 14 years and over, 1950**

Ethnic group	Born abroad	Born in the U.S. of American parents and mixed couples	Increase
Total white population	$2,181	$2,314	+$133
French-Canadian	1,958	2,010	+52
Irish	1,970	2,309	+339
Italian	2,301	2,293	−8
Polish	2,267	2,476	+209

Source: See table 9.

Table 11. Occupational status of selected New England ethnic groups, 1950

Ethnic group	Born abroad	Born in the U.S. of foreign parents and mixed couples	All of persons born abroad
French-Canadians	452	464	463
Irish	408	539	526
Italians	414	486	478
Poles	464	485	481

Source: See table 9.

Table 12. Occupations of the New England French and English mother tongue population, 1970 (percentage)

MALE

	Conn.		Maine		Mass.		N.H.		R.I.		Vt.	
	Fr.	Eng.	Fr.	Eng.	Fr.	Eng.	Fr.	Eng.	Fr.	Eng.	Fr.	Eng.
White collar	26	47	25	32	26	44	27	37	26	42	30	36
Clerical and sales	11	16	11	11	10	18	11	12	11	16	12	12
Blue collar	67	43	62	14	64	43	63	56	64	45	44	46
Semiskilled	27	16	27	22	26	17	28	19	29	19	20	16
Service workers	7	9	10	8	9	12	10	10	10	12	14	10
Farm workers	—	1	3	6	1	1	1	2	—	1	13	9

FEMALE

	Conn.		Maine		Mass.		N.H.		R.I.		Vt.	
	Fr.	Eng.	Fr.	Eng.	Fr.	Eng.	Fr.	Eng.	Fr.	Eng.	Fr.	Eng.
White collar	49	69	40	48	43	67	36	55	38	67	48	56
Clerical and sales	37	47	30	32	31	48	27	38	29	42	37	37
Blue collar	33	15	35	26	38	15	42	22	49	24	20	15
Semiskilled	30	13	30	22	34	13	39	20	45	20	18	22
Service workers	16	15	24	23	19	18	23	20	13	17	31	27
Farm workers	—	1	2	3	—	—	—	0.7	—	—	—	1

Source: Madeleine Giguère, "The Franco-Americans: Occupational Profiles," in *The Quebec and Acadian Diaspora in North America*, ed. Raymond Breton and Pierre Savard (Toronto: Multicultural History Society of Ontario, 1982), pp. 70–71, table 3.

Table 13. Achievement orientation of selected northeastern ethnic groups

Ethnic group	Mean achievement motivation scores	Mean achievement value orientation scores	Rank vocational aspiration
Greeks	10.80	5.08	2
Jews	10.53	5.54	1
Protestants	10.11	5.16	3
Italians	9.65	4.17	4
French-Canadians	8.82	3.68	5
Blacks	8.40	5.03	6

Source: Bernard C. Rosen, "Race, Ethnicity, and the Achievement Syndrome," *American Sociological Review* 24 (1959), 47–60, tables 2, 3, 4.

Table 14. French usual language by age group and region, 1975

Age group	Northern New England[a]	Southern New England[b]
0–9	2.3	1.8
10–19	8.4	4.0
20–29	9.4	8.0
30–39	15.0	10.1
40–49	17.2	18.6
50–59	18.8	22.0
60–69	14.4	17.7
70 and over	14.4	17.7
Total	100.0	100.0

Source: Calvin J. Veltman, "Le sort de la francophonie aux Etats-Unis," *Cahiers Québécois de Démographie* 9, no. 1 (1980), 48, table 1.
[a]Maine, New Hampshire, and Vermont.
[b]Connecticut (except Bridgeport and New Haven), Massachusetts, and Rhode Island.

Table 15. Percentage of persons of French mother tongue with English and French usual language, foreign born, New England, 1975

Usage	Northern New England	Southern New England
English usual language		
Bilingual[a]	32.1	48.1
Monolingual[b]	18.5	33.5
Subtotal	50.6	81.5
French usual language	49.4	18.5
Total	100.0	100.0

Source: Veltman, "Sort de la francophonie," p. 49, table 2.
Note: For definitions of northern and southern New England, see table 14.
[a]Those who speak French often.
[b]Those who do not speak French often.

Table 16. Percentage of persons of French mother tongue with English and French usual language, native born, New England, 1975

Usage	Northern New England	Southern New England
English usual language		
Bilingual[a]	43.9	34.3
Monolingual[b]	40.0	60.9
Subtotal	83.9	95.2
French usual language	16.1	4.8
Total	100.0	100.0

Source: Veltman, "Sort de la francophonie," p. 50, table 3.
Note: For definitions of northern and southern New England, see table 14.
[a]Those who speak French often.
[b]Those who do not speak French often.

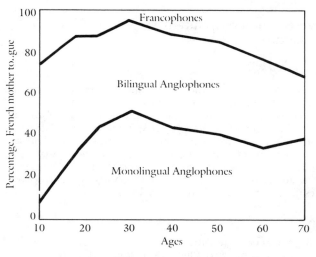

Figure 2. Percentage distribution by age group, native born, northern New England, 1975. (Source: Veltman, "Sort de la francophonie," p. 52, fig. 1.)

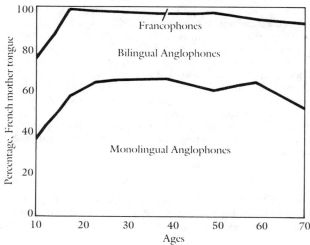

Figure 3. Percentage distribution by age group, native born, southern New England, 1975. (Source: Veltman, "Sort de la francophonie," p. 54, fig. 2.)

APPENDIX C

The Study and preservation of traditional French-Canadian culture

Ministry of Cultural Affairs

Created on March 24, 1961, Quebec's Ministry of Cultural Affairs sponsors and coordinates a host of activities designed to foster the development of arts and letters in French Canada and supports preservation of the French-Canadian heritage.[1] It administers public archives, conservatories, libraries, and museums; awards numerous grants and prizes; maintains a list of historical monuments and sites; and subsidizes major restoration projects, for example the complex of buildings in Quebec City's Lower Town known as Place Royale. In 1984 the ministry employed 917 persons and had a budget of $144,320,700 Canadian dollars.[2] (Ministère des Affaires Culturelles, 225, Grande-Allée Est, Quebec City.)

Macro-Inventaire

From 1977 to 1983, the Service du Patrimoine, a division of the Ministry of Cultural Affairs, conducted a vast survey of Quebec's architectural, ethnographical, and religious heritage. This project, known as the Macro-Inventaire des biens culturels du Québec, produced a data bank of manuscripts and mimeographed reports (*cahiers du terrain, rapports synthèse,* and *analyses du paysage architectural*) containing basic information—history, economy, social and religious life—about 1,500 cities, towns, and villages. It includes photographs and descriptions of some 3,500 churches constructed before 1930, over 3,000 works of art, and a multitude of artifacts relating to traditional life. Buildings more than thirty years old were photographed from the ground and from the air. The aerial survey consists of low-level photographs taken at an angle of each street and road. The more than 250,000 pictures were each given a serial number and coordinated with accompanying maps. Located at the ministry, the inventory is not open to the general public but may be consulted for research purposes.[3]

Grande Ferme

Since 1979 the Ministry of Cultural Affairs has conducted an experimental program to help Quebec children become more aware of their rural cultural heritage. The program is run from a center located in the village of St. Joachim twenty-five miles east of Quebec City, near St. Anne de Beaupré, at Cap Tourmente. The one-and-a-half-day (elementary school) and four-day (junior high) sessions taught by two instructors are held in a large farmhouse built in 1866 in an area rich in traditions dating back to 1636. Students learn about rural life at the turn of the century through walking tours, slide shows, video programs, and informal talks with local resource persons. Topics covered include local folklore, daily living, and the architectural landscape. (Centre d'initiation au patrimoine, 800, chemin du Cap, St. Joachim, Montmorency, Québec GOA 3XO. In 1984, cost of the one-and-a-half-day program was $22, the four-day program was $45 Canadian dollars.)[4]

CELAT

Inspired by the pioneering work in this domain of Charles-Marius Barbeau of the National Museum at Ottawa, Luc Lacourcière and other specialists began to develop folklore studies at Laval University, Quebec City, in 1944.[5] The research center they founded, the Archives de Folklore, initially concentrated on folktales and songs, children's games, clothing, customs, dances, and music, then, beginning in 1968, also on folk arts and crafts. The center has published a journal and monograph series, *Les Archives de Folklore,* since 1946. In 1970 the Department of History accepted responsibility for the instructional program in folklore at Laval, henceforth referred to as Arts et traditions populaires.

In 1976 the Archives de Folklore fused with teams of scholars preparing the *Trésor de la langue française au Québec* and the *Atlas linguistique de l'Est du Canada,* and broadened its scope to form the Centre d'Etudes sur la langue, les arts et les traditions populaires des francophones en Amérique du Nord (CELAT). Today, this interdisciplinary institute is the most important center for folklore studies in Canada.

Among its many collections, the Archives de Folklore preserves more than 3,400 tape recordings of French-Canadian folk songs and tales, and more than 12,000 slides depicting French-Canadian arts and crafts, architecture, clothing, customs, furniture, textiles, tools, and utensils. It also owns many manuscripts and illustrations, including one of the most important collections of small-format holy pictures in the world.[6]

These collections are constantly growing. For example, in 1982–83 the Archives de Folklore acquired fifty-six new sets of materials, including eighty-nine tape recordings. After each recording is received, its contents are analyzed and cataloged before the tape is stored. More than 10,000 folktales, 100,000 folk songs, and 20,000 legends and counting-out rhymes have been identified.[7] To guard against deterioration and to ensure safekeeping, recordings—now uniformly on polyester tape—are kept in cold storage; copies are preserved in a vault of the Archives Nationales du Québec elsewhere on campus.

The Archives de Folklore is located on the fifth floor of the Pavillon De Koninck. The main office houses various catalogs and files, and provides a small work area for researchers. There is also a listening room and laboratory. The staff consists of a full-time archivist and several technicians and assistants, some of them part time.

Centre d'Etudes Acadiennes

The University of Moncton in New Brunswick, founded in 1963, houses an important collection of Acadiana in its library: manuscripts; copies of documents preserved in public and private archives in Canada, England, France, Spain, the United States, and the Vatican; books and periodicals; and folklore material. A museum displays related artifacts.[8]

NOTES

Abbreviations

ALFANA Richard R. Santerre, *Anthologie de la littérature franco-américaine de la Nouvelle-Angleterre,* 9 vols. (Bedford, N.H.: NMDC, 1980–81).

BSHFA *Bulletin de la Société Historique Franco-Américaine.*

CIF 1 "Situation de la recherche sur la Franco-Américanie," in *Premier Colloque de l'Institut Français du Collège de l'Assomption (1980),* ed. Claire Quintal, *Vie Française* (Quebec City, 1980).

CIF 2 "L'Emigrant québécois vers les Etats-Unis, 1850–1920," in *Deuxième Colloque de l'Institut Français du Collège de l'Assomption (1981),* ed. Claire Quintal, *Vie Française* (Quebec City, 1982).

CIF 3 "The Little Canadas of New England," in *Third Annual Conference of the French Institute/Assumption College (1982),* ed. Claire Quintal (Worcester, Mass.: French Institute, 1983).

CIF 4 "Le Journalisme de langue française aux Etats-Unis," in *Quatrième Colloque de l'Institut Français du Collège de l'Assomption (1983),* ed. Claire Quintal, *Vie Française* (Quebec City, 1984).

CIF 5 "L'Emigrant acadien vers les Etats-Unis, 1842–1950," in *Cinquième Colloque de l'Institut Français du Collège de l'Assomption (1984),* ed. Claire Quintal, *Vie Française* (Quebec City, 1984).

FAO 1 *A Franco-American Overview,* ed. Renaud S. Albert (Cambridge, Mass.: NADC, 1979), vol. 1.

FAO 3 *A Franco-American Overview,* ed. Madeleine Giguère (Cambridge, Mass.: NADC, 1981), vol. 3, *New England, (Part 1).*

FAO 4 *A Franco-American Overview,* ed. Madeleine Giguère (Cambridge, Mass.: NADC, 1981), vol. 4, *New England, (Part 2).*

NADC National Assessment and Dissemination Center for Bilingual/Bicultural Education.

NMDC National Materials Development Center for French and Creole.

Preface

1. *BSHFA* (1954), 21–22, 97; (1956), 26–28, 31, 174–75; (1959), 91. "Il y a déjà trente ans, nous avons souvenance d'avoir suggéré à nos aînés cette initiative qui hantait notre âme de jeune ardent de notre histoire" (We recall that, thirty years ago, we suggested this project to our elders for it preoccupied our mind as a budding devotee of our history) (Monsignor Adrien Verrette, *BSHFA* [1956], 29).

201

2. Josaphat-T. Benoît, *L'Ame franco-américaine* (Montreal: Editions Albert Lévesque, 1935); Jacques Ducharme, *The Shadows of the Trees: The Story of French-Canadians in New England* (New York: Harper & Brothers, 1943); Robert Rumilly, *Histoire des Franco-Américains* (Montreal: Robert Rumilly [under the auspices of the Union Saint-Jean-Baptiste d'Amérique], 1958); Robert B. Perreault, *One Piece in the Great American Mosaic: The Franco-Americans of New England* (Manchester, N.H.: Association Canado-Américaine, 1976). Special issue of *Canado-Américain* 2, no. 2 (1976). Rumilly's indispensable work has no notes.

3. See, for example, "Autour des conférences Podea-Wade," *BSHFA* (1950), 68– 71; and Normand C. Dubé's reaction to Robert A. Fischer's paper, *CIF* 1, 61–63; see also chap. 3, n. 9 in this volume.

4. This paragraph and the two that follow are adapted from Gerard J. Brault, "New England French Culture," *French Review* 45 (1972), 837.

5. Claire Bolduc, "Les Franco-Américains eux-mêmes, veulent-ils d'une renaissance culturelle?" in *Les Franco-Américains: La promesse du passé, les réalités du présent. Colloque 1976* (Cambridge, Mass.: NADC, 1976), p. 104: "Il ne suffit pas d'offrir une histoire romancée des exploits des Franco-Américains. Il nous faut la vérité . . . la vérité est que nous sommes un petit peuple méconnu, doué d'une énergie impressionnante; nous ne sommes que des humains parmi d'autres. . . . Mais nous ne sommes pas moins que cela."

Introduction

1. U.S. Department of Commerce, Bureau of the Census, *1980 Census of Population: Ancestry of the Population by State.* Supplementary Report, PC 80-S1-10 (Washington, D.C.: Government Printing Office, 1983), p. 2. This list combines totals for persons reported as being solely or partly of a specific ancestry.

2. Robert G. LeBlanc, "Les migrations acadiennes," in *Du Continent perdu à l'archipel retrouvé: Le Québec et l'Amérique française,* ed. Dean R. Louder and Eric Waddell (Quebec City: Les Presses de l'Université Laval, 1983), pp. 137–62; Eric Waddell, "La Louisiane: Un poste outre-frontière de l'Amérique française ou un autre pays et une autre culture?" in *Continent perdu,* pp. 195–211; Roland J.-L. Breton and Dean R. Louder, "La géographie linguistique de l'Acadiana, 1970," in *Continent perdu,* pp. 213–34.

3. Robert A. Beaudoin, "Le nom 'Franco-Américain,'" *BSHFA* (1967), 151–54.

4. Ralph D. Vicero, "Immigration of French Canadians to New England, 1840– 1900: A Geographical Analysis," Ph.D. diss., University of Wisconsin, 1968; Yolande Lavoie, *L'Emigration des Québécois aux Etats-Unis de 1840 à 1930* (Quebec City: Editeur officiel du Québec, 1979).

5. Jacques Portes, "Le réveil des Franco-Américains," *Le Monde,* 29 November 1981 (the English translation that appeared in the *Manchester Guardian,* 3 January 1982, was reprinted in the *Boston Globe,* 21 February 1982); Chris Chinlund, "A Renaissance of French Pride," *Boston Globe,* 6 February 1983; Daniel Golden, "Franco-Americans in Search of Roots," *Boston Globe,* 30 May 1983.

6. Gerard J. Brault, "Etat présent des études sur les centres franco-américains de la Nouvelle-Angleterre," *CIF* 1, 9–12, referring to Vicero.

7. James P. Allen, "Catholics in Maine: A Social Geography," Ph.D. diss., Syracuse University, 1970.

8. No up-to-date study exists of Franco-Americans in upper New York State. Some localities are identified in Father Edouard Hamon, *Les Canadiens-français de la Nouvelle-Angleterre* (Quebec City: Hardy, 1891), pp. 451–52, and in the vari-

ous Franco-American guidebooks, e.g., *Guide officiel des Franco-Américains 1931* (Auburn, R.I.: Albert A. Bélanger, 1931), pp. 259–76.

9. Brault, "Etat présent," pp. 9–10. On the rate of assimilation of American ethnic groups, see James W. Vander Zanden, *American Minority Relations,* 4th ed. (New York: Knopf, 1983), pp. 282–84.

10. Brault, "Etat présent," pp. 11–12, projected from data relative to the situation in 1900 according to Vicero.

11. Gerard J. Brault, "Le français en Nouvelle-Angleterre," in *Le Français hors de France,* ed. Albert Valdman (Paris: Champion, 1979), p. 80, citing *Family Almanac '72,* ed. Morris Harth and Theodore M. Bernstein (New York: New York Times, 1971), p. 146.

12. Adolphe Robert and Father Thomas-M. Landry, "Les catholiques américains de langue française en Nouvelle-Angleterre," in *Notre Vie franco-américaine* (Manchester, N.H.: L'Avenir National [for the Comité d'Orientation Franco-Américaine], 1949), pp. 18–21. On the problem of identifying Franco-American national parishes, see Father Clarence J. d'Entremont, "The Franco-Americans and Louisiana," in *The 20th-Century Franco-American* (Comité de Vie Franco-Américaine, 1976), pp. 53–55.

13. Monsignor Adrien Verrette, "Les Acadiens aux Etats-Unis, 1755–1955," *BSHFA* (1955), 79; Rumilly, *Histoire des Franco-Américains,* pp. 42, 189; Vicero, "Immigration," p. 241, n. 5. The most informed discussion is by Father Clarence J. d'Entremont, "La survivance acadienne en Nouvelle-Angleterre," *CIF* 5, 8–25, listing additional localities.

Chapter 1. The Roots of Franco-American Culture

1. Jean C. Falardeau, "Les Canadiens français et leur idéologie," in *Canadian Dualism: Studies of French-English Relations,* ed. Mason Wade (Toronto: University of Toronto Press; Quebec City: Presses de l'Université Laval, 1960), pp. 23–31.

2. Mireille Servais-Maquoi, *Le Roman de la terre au Québec* (Quebec City: Presses de l'Université Laval, 1974). For Gérin-Lajoie, see chap. 2. See also Pierre Anctil, "L'attachement à la terre et l'émigration dans certains romans du terroir québécois," *CIF* 2, 61–80. This ideology is examined in detail in Jeanne d'Arc Lortie, *La Poésie nationaliste au Canada français (1606–1867)* (Quebec City: Presses de l'Université Laval, 1975), pp. 397–446. On the role of ideology, see Jean-Paul Hautecoeur, *L'Acadie du discours: Pour une sociologie de la culture acadienne* (Quebec City: Presses de l'Université Laval, 1975), pp. 11–20.

3. M. Tremblay, "Orientations de la pensée sociale," in *Essais sur le Québec contemporain,* ed. Jean C. Falardeau (Quebec City: Presses de l'Université Laval, 1953), p. 197.

4. Edmond J. Massicotte, *Nos Canadiens d'autrefois: 12 grandes compositions* (Montreal: Granger Frères, 1923).

5. Vicero, "Immigration," p. 204; Yves Roby, "Un Québec émigré aux Etats-Unis: Bilan historiographique," in *Les Rapports culturels entre Québec et les Etats-Unis* (Quebec City: Institut Québécois de Recherche sur la Culture, 1984), pp. 105–129.

6. Louis Hémon, *Maria Chapdelaine,* ed. Nicole Deschamps and Ghislaine Legendre (Montreal: Boréal Express, 1983). On Hémon, see Alfred Ayotte and Victor Tremblay, *L'Aventure Louis Hémon* (Montreal: Fides, 1974). For a revisionist interpretation of Hémon's novel, see Nicole Deschamps, Raymonde Héroux, and Normand Villeneuve, *Le Mythe de Maria Chapdelaine* (Montreal: Presses de l'Université de Montréal, 1980).

7. The two most useful studies are still Horace Miner, *St. Denis: A French-Canadian Parish* (1939; rpt. Chicago: University of Chicago Press, 1963); and Sister Marie-Ursule, *Civilisation traditionnelle des Lavalois* (Quebec City: Presses de l'Université Laval, 1951). On the study and preservation of traditional French-Canadian culture today, see Appendix C. For Acadian traditions, see Jean-Claude Dupont, *Héritage d'Acadie* (Montreal: Leméac, 1977); and idem, *Histoire populaire de l'Acadie* (Montreal: Leméac, 1979).

8. Yves Roby, "L'évolution économique du Québec et l'émigrant (1850–1929)," *CIF* 2, 8–20.

9. Miner, *St. Denis*, chap. 3. On the rang, see Pierre Deffontaines, *Le Rang, type de peuplement rural du Canada français* (Quebec City: Presses de l'Université Laval, 1953). On the origin of rangs, see Richard C. Harris, *The Seigneurial System in Early Canada: A Geographical Study* (Madison: University of Wisconsin Press, 1968).

10. Jean-Paul Bernard, *Les Rouges: Libéralisme, nationalisme et anticléricalisme au milieu du XIXe siècle* (Montreal: Presses de l'Université du Québec, 1971).

11. Miner, *St. Denis*, pp. 57–58, 62.

12. Ibid., p. 54.

13. Ibid., p. 250.

14. Georges Gauthier-Larouche, *Evolution de la maison rurale traditionnelle dans la région de Québec (Etude ethnographique)* (Quebec City: Presses de l'Université Laval, 1974). Roof types are summarized by Michel Lessard and Gilles Vilandré, *La Maison traditionnelle au Québec* (Montreal: Editions de l'Homme, 1974), pp. 66–67.

15. Deschamps, Héroux, and Villeneuve, *Mythe de Maria Chapdelaine*.

16. Gauthier-Larouche, *Evolution*, chap. 10. Detailed description and photographs in Nora Dawson, *La Vie traditionnelle à Saint-Pierre (Ile d'Orléans)* (Quebec City: Presses de l'Université Laval, 1960), chap. 1; see also Michel Lessard and Huguette Marquis, *Encyclopédie de la maison québécoise* (Montreal: Editions de l'Homme, 1972), chap. 5.

17. Gauthier-Larouche, *Evolution*, p. 208; Dawson, *Vie traditionnelle*, pp. 33–34.

18. Dawson, *Vie traditionnelle*, pp. 31, 33, 36.

19. Ibid., p. 24.

20. Ibid., chap. 2.

21. Ibid., pp. 67–68.

22. Peggy Tyrchniewicz, *Ethnic Folk Costumes in Canada* (Winnipeg: Hyperion Press, 1979), p. 9. For other examples of modern costumes, see Madeleine Doyon-Ferland, *Jeux, rythmes et divertissements traditionnels* (Montreal: Leméac, 1980), pp. 166, 183 (photographs).

23. Dawson, *Vie traditionnelle*, p. 71.

24. Marius Barbeau, *Ceinture fléchée* (1945); rpt. Montreal: Editions l'Etincelle, 1973); Françoise Bourret and Lucie Lavigne, *Le Fléché* (Montreal: Editions de l'Homme, 1973).

25. Dawson, *Vie traditionnelle*, pp. 68, 70 (illustrations); Rose Lahaie and Irène Bilodeau, "Le costume traditionnel d'hiver de la région de Charlevoix de la fin du XIXe siècle au début du XXe," *Culture et Tradition* 4 (1979), 11–18 (illustrations). Cf. Dupont, *Histoire populaire de l'Acadie*, pp. 193–204; Jeanne Arseneault, "La survie du costume traditionnel français en Acadie," in *La Vie quotidienne au Québec*, ed. René Bouchard (Montreal: Presses de l'Université du Québec, 1983), pp. 249–52 (1905 photograph).

26. Dawson, *Vie traditionnelle*, pp. 71–72. Cf. Madeleine Doyon-Ferland, "Le costume traditionnel féminin: Documents beaucerons recueillis et présentés," *Archives de Folklore* 1 (1946), 112–20 (illustrations); idem, "Le costume tra-

ditionnel féminin (deuxième série): Documents de Charlevoix recueillis et présentés," *Archives de Folklore* 2 (1947), 183–89 (illustrations).
27. Sister Marie-Ursule, *Civilisation,* pp. 140, 141 (illustration).
28. Dawson, *Vie traditionnelle,* p. 70; Lahaie and Bilodeau, "Costume traditionnel," pp. 18–19 (illustration).
29. Dawson, *Vie traditionnelle,* pp. 71, 72, 75.
30. Miner, *St. Denis,* chap. 4, and pp. 66–68; Philippe Garigue, *La Vie familiale des Canadiens français* (Montreal: Presses de l'Université de Montréal; and Paris: Presses Universitaires de France, 1962), review of earlier scholarship, pp. 13–27.
31. Garigue, *Vie familiale,* pp. 33–45.
32. See, for example, the outing described in Hémon, *Maria Chapdelaine,* chap. 5.
33. Miner, *St. Denis,* pp. 64, 79–81.
34. Ibid., pp. 79, 82–83.
35. Dawson, *Vie traditionnelle,* pp. 128–30.
36. Vicero, "Immigration," pp. 29–30.
37. Miner, *St. Denis,* p. 141.
38. Ibid., chap. 8; Sister Marie-Ursule, *Civilisation,* pp. 136–40, 147; Dawson, *Vie traditionnelle,* chap. 5 and pp. 93–111.
39. Miner, *St. Denis,* chap. 8; Dawson, *Vie traditionnelle,* pp. 111–30.
40. Sister Marie-Ursule, *Civilisation,* pp. 140–47; Dawson, *Vie traditionnelle,* chap. 3 and pp. 111–18.
41. Miner, *St. Denis,* p. 256.
42. Dawson, *Vie traditionnelle,* p. 60 (illustration).
43. Miner, *St. Denis,* pp. 141–43; Dawson, *Vie traditionnelle,* pp. 79–81.
44. Miner, *St. Denis,* p. 165, n. 13; Sister Marie-Ursule, *Civilisation,* pp. 147–48.
45. For recipes, see Dawson, *Vie traditionnelle,* pp. 81–91. For other French-Canadian recipes, see Mireille Beaulieu, *Les Meilleures Récettes du Québec* (Montreal: La Presse, 1974); and Marielle Boudreau and Melvin Gallant, *La Cuisine traditionelle en Acadie* (Moncton, New Brunswick: Editions d'Acadie, 1975). In a different vein, see also *Vers Une Nouvelle Cuisine québécoise,* 2d ed., Institut de tourisme et d'hôtellerie du Québec (Quebec City: Editions Elysée, 1979). Among Franco-American cookbooks, two deserve special note (both are bilingual): Betty A. Lausier Lindsay, *Nothing Went to Waste . . . in Grandmother's Kitchen* (Bedford, N.H.: NMDC, 1981); and Hermanita Robert and Roseline Moore, eds., *La Bonne Croûte, livre de récettes* (Chicopee-Holyoke, Mass.: Le Festival Franco-Américain, Inc., 1983).
46. Miner, *St. Denis,* chap. 5; Nive Voisine, "Les valeurs religieuses de l'émigrant québécois (1850–1920)," *CIF* 2, 21–37.
47. Voisine, "Valeurs religieuses," pp. 22–23.
48. Ibid., p. 25. On the background of these tensions, see Jean-Pierre Wallot, "Religion and French-Canadian Mores in the Early Nineteenth Century," *Canadian Historical Review* 52 (1971), 51–94; Robert-Lionel Séguin, *La Vie libertine en Nouvelle-France au XVIIᵉ siècle* (Montreal: Leméac, 1972); Fernand Ouellet, *Le Bas-Canada, 1791–1840: Changements structuraux et crise* (Ottawa: Editions de l'Université d'Ottawa, 1976), pp. 260–68.
49. Miner, *St. Denis,* chap. 7; Jean Simard, ed., *Un Patrimoine méprisé: La religion populaire des Québécois* (Ville LaSalle, Quebec: Hurtubise HMH, 1979).
50. Miner, *St. Denis,* pp. 157–58; Sister Marie-Ursule, *Civilisation,* pp. 67–69; Michèle Paradis Croteau, "Le temps de boucherie chez nos ancêtres à St-Edouard de Maskinongé," *Culture et Tradition* 7 (1983), 87–105. For a hilarious account of hog butchering by a Franco-American family at Danielson, Connecticut, in 1945, see Théodore J. Cusson, Sr., "On va tuer un cochon! Killing a Pig—in Three Acts," *Canado-Américain* 7 (1981), 16–18.

51. Miner, *St. Denis,* pp. 158–59; Sister Marie-Ursule, *Civilisation,* pp. 69–71; Paulette Collet, *L'Hiver dans le roman canadien-français* (Quebec City: Presses de l'Université Laval, 1965), pp. 88–96; Raymond Montpetit, *Le Temps des Fêtes au Québec* (Montreal: Editions de l'Homme, 1978). For a captivating account of a family Christmas celebration in Lewiston, Maine, in 1954 as seen through the eyes of a ten-year-old Franco-American boy, see Grégoire Chabot, "Un Noël chabotant," *FAROG Forum* 8, no. 4 (1980), 3.

52. Father Anselme Chiasson, "Traditions and Oral Literature in Acadia," in *The Acadians of the Maritimes: Thematic Studies,* ed. Jean Daigle (Moncton, New Brunswick: Centre d'Etudes Acadiennes, 1982), p. 497.

53. Sister Marie-Ursule, *Civilisation,* p. 71, n. 1.

54. Sophie-Laurence Lamontagne, *L'Hiver dans la culture québécoise (XVIIᵉ–XIXᵉ siècles)* (Quebec City: Institut Québécois de Recherche sur la Culture, 1983), p. 127.

55. Lamontagne, *Hiver,* pp. 125–27.

56. Miner, *St. Denis,* p. 159.

57. Ibid., p. 160.

58. Lamontagne, *Hiver,* p. 127; Collet, *Hiver dans le roman canadien-français,* p. 97.

59. Father Chiasson, "Traditions," p. 490. For other New Year's Day customs, see Collet, *Hiver dans le roman canadien-français,* pp. 96–97.

60. Sister Marie-Ursule, *Civilisation,* p. 73; other formulas, pp. 72–73.

61. Father Chiasson, "Traditions," p. 490.

62. Lamontagne, *Hiver,* p. 127.

63. Sister Marie-Ursule, *Civilisation,* p. 75; cf. Father Chiasson, "Traditions," p. 491, and Lamontagne, *Hiver,* p. 128.

64. Sister Marie-Ursule, *Civilisation,* p. 76; Denise Rodrigue, *Le Cycle de Pâques au Québec et dans l'Ouest de la France* (Quebec City: Presses de l'Université Laval, 1983), pp. 9–37.

65. Rodrigue, *Cycle de Pâques,* pp. 58, 76.

66. Georges Arsenault, *Courir la Chandeleur* (Moncton, New Brunswick: Editions d'Acadie, 1982).

67. Sister Marie-Ursule, *Civilisation,* p. 78; Rodrigue, *Cycle de Pâques,* pp. 43–57.

68. Rodrigue, *Cycle de Pâques,* p. 60.

69. Ibid., pp. 67–70.

70. Ibid., pp. 70–85. Micheline Lachance, *Le Frère André* (Montreal: Editions de l'Homme, 1979), bibliography, pp. 411–14. Appendix 3 is by Father Benoît Lacroix, "L'Oratoire Saint-Joseph (1904–1979), fait religieux populaire."

71. Miner, *St. Denis,* pp. 164–65; Sister Marie-Ursule, *Civilisation,* p. 76; Rodrigue, *Cycle de Pâques,* pp. 161–86.

72. Photographs in Sister Marie-Ursule, *Civilisation,* p. 77.

73. Miner, *St. Denis,* pp. 165–67; Sister Marie-Ursule, *Civilisation,* pp. 78–83; Rodrigue, *Cycle de Pâques,* pp. 187–238.

74. Photograph in Miner, *St. Denis,* opposite p. 157.

75. Sister Marie-Ursule, *Civilisation,* p. 83; Rodrigue, *Cycle de Pâques,* p. 244.

76. Rodrigue, *Cycle de Pâques,* p. 237. See Conrad Laforte, *Catalogue de la chanson folklorique française* (Quebec City: Presses de l'Université Laval, 1983), vol. 6, no. 77; cf. no. 78.

77. Miner, *St. Denis,* p. 167; Sister Marie-Ursule, *Civilisation,* pp. 83–84; Rodrigue, *Cycle de Pâques,* pp. 239–66.

78. Ronald Labelle, "L'eau de Pâques: Coutume religieuse populaire," *Culture et Tradition* 2 (1977), 1–11. For modern reenactments at Saint-Jean-Chrysostome and St. Romuald near Quebec City, see Andrée Roy in *Le Soleil* (Quebec City), 24 April 1984.

79. Sister Marie-Ursule, *Civilisation,* pp. 195–98; Nicole Guilbault, *Henri Julien et la tradition orale* (Montreal: Boréal Express, 1980), pp. 99–124; Brigitte Marie Lane, "Franco-American Folk Traditions and Popular Culture in a Former Milltown: Aspects of Ethnic Urban Folklore and the Dynamics of Folklore Change in Lowell, Massachusetts," Ph.D. diss., Harvard University, 1983, pp. 203–6.

80. Sister Marie-Ursule, *Civilisation,* pp. 79–82; Dawson, *Vie traditionnelle,* pp. 133–37; and, especially, Jean-Claude Dupont, *Le Sucre du pays* (Montreal: Leméac, 1975).

81. For further information, contact the Institut International du Syrop d'Erable, 498 rue Principale, Saint-Joseph-du-Lac, Quebec, or Les Producteurs de sucre d'érable du Québec, C.P. 310, Plessisville, Quebec.

82. Sister Marie-Ursule, *Civilisation,* pp. 84–85; Monique Laliberté, "Le poisson d'avril," *Culture et Tradition* 5 (1980), 79–89 (bibliography, pp. 88–89); Rodrigue, *Cycle de Pâques,* pp. 93–110.

83. Sister Marie-Ursule, *Civilisation,* p. 85; Rodrigue, *Cycle de Pâques,* pp. 110–22.

84. Rodrigue, *Cycle de Pâques,* p. 123.

85. Marcel Trudel, *Initiation à la Nouvelle-France: Histoire et institutions* (Montreal: Editions HRW, 1971), p. 189.

86. Sister Marie-Ursule, *Civilisation,* pp. 85–86; Rodrigue, *Cycle de Pâques,* pp. 129–49.

87. Rodrigue, *Cycle de Pâques,* pp. 150–52.

88. Miner, *St. Denis,* pp. 149–50; Sister Marie-Ursule, *Civilisation,* pp. 86–87.

89. Sister Marie-Ursule, *Civilisation,* pp. 87–88.

90. Father Chiasson, "Traditions," p. 496.

91. Sister Marie-Ursule, *Civilisation,* p. 89.

92. Ibid., p. 90.

93. Miner, *St. Denis,* pp. 169–76; Sister Marie-Ursule, *Civilisation,* pp. 91–95.

94. Sister Marie-Ursule, *Civilisation,* p. 97; variant in Doyon-Ferland, *Jeux,* p. 119, and Lauraine Léger, "L'émigrant acadien et sa culture populaire," *CIF* 5, 87.

95. Sister Marie-Ursule, *Civilisation,* pp. 96–97; also provides other examples.

96. Miner, *St. Denis,* pp. 179–96; Corinne Rocheleau-Rouleau, *Laurentian Heritage* (Toronto: Longmans, Green and Co., 1948), chap. 3; Vénérande Douville-Veillet, *Souvenirs d'une institutrice de petite école de rang,* Collection "Notre Passé," no. 2 (Trois-Rivières: Editions du Bien Public, 1973); and, especially, Jacques Dorion, *Les Ecoles de rang au Québec* (Montreal: Editions de l'Homme, 1979).

97. Dorion, *Ecoles de rang,* pp. 62 and 372: "le vestibule de l'église."

98. With the creation of the Ministry of Education in 1964, Quebec's school system was modernized and the école de rang disappeared from the scene.

99. On the Feast of Saint Joseph at Sainte-Brigitte-de-Laval, near Quebec City; see Sister Marie-Ursule, *Civilisation,* pp. 78, 99.

100. Ibid., pp. 98–115 (twenty-one games listed); cf. also Doyon-Ferland, *Jeux,* pp. 115–24 (Acadian games), 125–36.

101. Doyon-Ferland, *Jeux,* pp. 23–114. Article reprinted from *Archives de Folklore* 3 (1948), 159–207.

102. Sister Marie-Ursule, *Civilisation,* p. 107.

103. Luc Lacourcière, "Comptines canadiennes," *Archives de Folklore* 3 (1948), 109–57; Doyon-Ferland, *Jeux,* pp. 120–21; Father Chiasson, "Traditions," p. 505. For Franco-American examples, see Roger Lacerte, "Du neuf sur nos comptines," *FAROG Forum* 7, no. 8 (1980), 17; idem, "Comptines et chansons grivoises de chez nous," 8, no. 6 (1981), 1, 12. For an angry reaction to the more licentious rhymes, see Louis-Israël Martel's letter to the editor, 8,

nos. 7–8 (1981), 20; also other letters, same page, with additional examples. For other Franco-American counting-out rhymes, see Lane, "Franco-American Folk Traditions," pp. 235–37.

104. Sister Marie-Ursule, *Civilisation,* pp. 99–106; Doyon-Ferland, *Jeux,* pp. 162, 184. For Franco-American examples, see Lane, "Franco-American Folk Traditions," pp. 232–34.

105. Doyon-Ferland, *Jeux,* pp. 149–69.

106. Sister Marie-Ursule, *Civilisation,* p. 116.

107. Miner, *St. Denis,* p. 83.

108. Ibid., pp. 83–84. See also Claude Galarneau, *Les Collèges classiques au Canada français (1620–1970)* (Montreal: Fides, 1978).

109. Miner, *St. Denis,* pp. 196–206; Sister Marie-Ursule, *Civilisation,* pp. 117–19.

110. Doyon-Ferland, *Jeux,* pp. 149–69, 184–90; Hélène Fournier, "Examen comparatif des quadrilles charentais et québécois," *Culture et Tradition* 6 (1982), 52–72.

111. See, for example, the thirty square dances with calls in Pierre Daignault, *En Place pour un set* (Montreal: Editions de l'Homme, 1964). Volume 1 of *Danses et costumes régionaux du Québec* (Montreal: Fédération des Loisirs-Danse du Québec, 1977) is an analysis of eighteen folk dances observed in various localities of Quebec in 1974; volume 2 describes eight examples of clothing worn in Montreal and Quebec City, 1800–50, for use by present-day dance groups.

112. Miner, *St. Denis,* pp. 207–14; Rocheleau-Rouleau, *Laurentian Heritage,* chap. 6; Sister Marie-Ursule, *Civilisation,* pp. 119–30.

113. For these and other examples, see Sister Marie-Ursule, *Civilisation,* pp. 120–22; Father Chiasson, "Traditions," p. UN 487.

114. Doyon-Ferland, *Jeux,* p. 178 (photograph, Quebec City, about 1870).

115. Sister Marie-Ursule, *Civilisation,* pp. 122, 124.

116. Ibid., p. 125.

117. Ibid., p. 126.

118. Miner, *St. Denis,* pp. 214–16; Sister Marie-Ursule, *Civilisation,* pp. 126–30.

119. Father Chiasson, "Traditions," p. 487; Sister Marie-Ursule, *Civilisation,* p. 130, n. 2.

120. Miner, *St. Denis,* pp. 215–16.

121. Ibid., p. 219; Sister Marie-Ursule, *Civilisation,* pp. 130–31.

122. Miner, *St. Denis,* pp. 219–32; Sister Marie-Ursule, *Civilisation,* pp. 131–35.

123. Ibid., p. 133; Father Chiasson, "Traditions," p. 488.

124. For a general introduction to French-Canadian folklore, see Jean Du Berger, *Introduction aux études en arts et traditions populaires, première partie: Eléments de bibliographie et choix de textes historiques* (Quebec City: Archives de Folklore, 1973). On the French-Canadian folktale, see Luc Lacourcière, "Le conte populaire français en Amérique du Nord" (Quebec City: Archives de Folklore, 1959). See also Jean-Claude Dupont, *Le Légendaire de la Beauce* (Montreal: Leméac, 1978). For Acadian folklore, see idem, *Héritage d'Acadie;* and Catherine Jolicoeur, *Les Plus Belles Légendes acadiennes* (Montreal and Paris: Stanké, 1981). For an excellent overview, see Jean-Claude Dupont, "Culture populaire de l'émigrant québécois, 1850–1920," *CIF* 2, 47–60 (bibliography, pp. 57–60).

125. Marius Barbeau, *Jongleur Songs of Old Quebec* (New Brunswick, N.J.: Rutgers University Press, 1962), pp. xviii–xix (bibliography, pp. 193–202); also Du Berger, *Introduction,* p. 243.

126. Stith Thompson, *The Folktale* (Berkeley: University of California Press, 1977), p. 18. On the prevalence of certain kinds of tales in French-Canadian folklore,

see Lacourcière, "Conte populaire français," pp. 7–9; and Dupont, "Culture populaire de l'émigrant québécois," p. 54.

127. Thompson, *Folktale*, p. 126.
128. Ibid., pp. 136, 184. Lutz Mackensen, *Der singende Knocken: Ein Beitrag zur vergleichenden Märchenforschung*, Folklore Fellows Communications, no. 49 (Helsinki: Suoamlainen tiedeakatemia, 1923). See also Eugène Monseur, "L'os qui chante," *Bulletin de Folklore* 1 (1891–92), 39–51, 89–149; 2 (1893–95), 219–41, 245–51, a study utilized extensively here. I am indebted to Luc Lacourcière, professor emeritus of Laval University, for providing me with tape recordings of fifteen French-Canadian versions.
129. Thompson, *Folktale*, p. 136; Stith Thompson, *Motif-Index of Folk Literature: A Classification of Narrative Elements in Folktales, Ballads, Myths, Fables, Mediaeval Romances, Exempla, Fabliaux, Jest-Books, and Local Legends*, revised and enlarged ed. 6 vols. (Bloomington: Indiana University Press, 1955–58).
130. Barbeau, *Jongleur Songs*, pp. 91–96.
131. Ibid., pp. 126–30.
132. Ibid., pp. 97–107.
133. Ibid., pp. 138–41, 170–72.
134. Ibid., pp. 122–25.
135. Ibid., pp. 189–91.
136. Laforte, *Catalogue de la chanson folklorique française*.
137. Jean-Claude Dupont, *L'Artisan forgeron* (Quebec City: Presses de l'Université Laval, 1979), pp. xix, 202–9.
138. Jean-Claude Dupont and Jacques Mathieu, *Les Métiers de cuir* (Quebec City: Presses de l'Université Laval, 1981), p. 9.
139. Dupont, *Artisan forgeron*, pp. 81ff., 133ff.
140. Ibid., pp. 6–9.
141. Ibid., pp. 293–94.
142. Ibid., p. 185.
143. Dawson, *Vie traditionnelle*, pp. 152–53; Dupont and Mathieu, *Métiers de cuir*.
144. Studies on related traditional crafts and skills include: Jean-Claude Dupont, *Le Pain d'habitant* (Montreal: Leméac, 1974); idem, *Le Fromage de l'île d'Orléans* (Montreal: Leméac, 1977); Hélène de Carufel, *Le Lin* (Montreal: Leméac, 1980); and Marcel Moussette, *Le Chauffage domestique au Canada des origines à l'industrialisation* (Quebec City: Presses de l'Université Laval, 1983). See also *L'Aide mémoire: Répertoire pour la mise en valeur du patrimoine québécois, Version préliminaire* (Quebec City: Télé-université, 1979).
145. Paul Carpentier, *La Croix de chemin: Au-delà du signe* (Ottawa: National Museum of Canada, 1981).
146. Einar Haugen, *Bilingualism in the Americas: A Bibliography and Research Guide*, Publication of the American Dialect Society, no. 26 (University, Ala.: University of Alabama Press, 1956), chap. 2; idem, "Bilingualism, Language Contact, and Immigrant Languages in the United States: A Research Report, 1956–1970," in *Current Trends in Linguistics*, ed. Thomas A. Sebeok (The Hague and Paris: Mouton, 1973), 10:513–20; Maurice Cagnon, "The Dialectal Origins of the French-Canadian Lexicon," Ph.D. diss., University of Pennsylvania, 1967; Edmund Brent, "Canadian French: A Synthesis," Ph.D. diss., Cornell University, 1971; Jean-Paul Vinay, "Le français en Amérique du Nord: Problèmes et réalisations," in *Current Trends in Linguistics* 10, 323–406; Gaston Dulong, "Histoire du français en Amérique du Nord," in ibid., pp. 407–21; Ernest F. Haden, "French Dialect Geography in North America," also in ibid., pp. 422–39, bibliography by Jean-Paul Vinay, pp. 441–63.

147. On the varieties of Canadian French depending on social and other factors, see Brent, "Canadian French," pp. 118–21; Danielle Forget, "Quel est le français standard au Québec?" in *Le Français parlé: Etudes sociologiques,* ed. Pierrette Thibault, Current Inquiry into Language and Linguistics, no. 30 (Edmonton, Alberta: Linguistics Research, Inc., 1978), pp. 153–61.
148. Louis-Philippe Audet and Armand Gauthier, *Le Système scolaire du Québec: Organisation et fonctionnement* (Montreal: Beauchemin, 1967), pp. 5, 25.
149. For example, *Glossaire du parler français au Canada* (Quebec City: L'Action Sociale, 1930); Mark M. Orkin, *Speaking Canadian French,* rev. ed. (Toronto: General Publishing Co., 1971), pp. 82–84; Claude Poirier, "Le lexique québécois: Son évolution, ses composantes," in *Culture populaire et littératures au Québec,* ed. René Bouchard, Stanford French and Italian Studies, no. 19 (Saratoga, Calif.: Anma Libri and Co., 1980), pp. 43–80; Sinclair Robinson and Donald Smith, *Practical Handbook of Quebec and Acadian French* (Toronto: Anansi, 1984). Specialized bibliographies include: Gaston Dulong, *Bibliographie linguistique du Canada français,* Bibliothèque française et romane, Série E: Langue et littérature françaises au Canada, no. 1 (Quebec City: Presses de l'Université Laval; and Paris: Klincksieck, 1966); and Conrad Sabourin and Rolande Lamarche, *Le Français québécois (Bibliographie analytique)* (Montreal: Office de la langue française, 1979).
150. Gaston Dulong and Gaston Bergeron, *Le Parler populaire du Québec et de ses régions voisines: Atlas linguistique de l'Est du Canada,* 10 vols. (Quebec City: Ministère des Communications, 1980). This work is referred to as the *ALEC.*
151. See Marcel Juneau, *Problèmes de lexicologie québécoise: Prologomènes à un Trésor de la langue française au Québec* (Quebec City: Presses de l'Université Laval, 1977); and, especially, Claude Poirier, "Chronique du Trésor de la langue française au Québec," *Québec Français,* March 1982, pp. 20–22. This work is referred to as the *TLFQ.*
152. Brault, "Français en Nouvelle-Angleterre," pp. 82–84, based on William N. Locke, *Pronunciation of the French Spoken at Brunswick, Maine,* Publication of the American Dialect Society, no. 12 (Greensboro, N.C.: American Dialect Society, 1949); and Sister Maris Stella, "A Note on the Pronunciation of New England French," *French Review* 32 (1959), 363–66. For more technical treatment and bibliography, see Brent, "Canadian French," pp. 18–69.

Chapter 2. The Immigration Phase, 1865–1920

1. Donald F. Putnam and Robert G. Putnam, *Canada: A Regional Analysis* (Toronto: Dent, 1970), pp. 126–27.
2. Vicero, "Immigration," chap. 1.
3. Ibid., figs. 8 and 9.
4. The statistics in this chapter relative to the French-Canadian emigration to New England are drawn from Vicero, "Immigration."
5. Robin W. Wink, "The Creation of a Myth: 'Canadian' Enlistments in the Northern Armies during the American Civil War," *Canadian Historical Review* 39 (1958), 24–40; Robert Provost, "Les Canadiens français à la Guerre de Sécession," *BSHFA* (1956), 143–55 (lists many individuals); Rumilly, *Histoire des Franco-Américains,* pp. 37–38; Vicero, "Immigration," pp. 201–3. Albert H. Ledoux, "Franco-American Veterans of the Civil War (Massachusetts Residents)," *Fleur de Lys* 2, no. 3 (1980), 3–24; no. 4, pp. 6–38, is a list of more than 650 Massachusetts veterans with French surnames. See also the list, pp. 38–39, of men with French surnames who died in the Confederate prisoner of war camp at Andersonville, Georgia, 1864–65.

6. Gabriel Nadeau, "L'oeuvre historique d'Edmond Mallet," *BSHFA* (1941), 49–60; idem, "La blessure du Major Mallet," *BSHFA* (1953), 32–40; Rosaire Dion-Lévesque, *Silhouettes franco-américaines* (Manchester, N.H.: Association Canado-Américaine, 1957), pp. 603–7; obituary in the *New York Times,* 13 April 1907.

7. Dion-Lévesque, *Silhouettes,* pp. 509–13; Eugène Lapierre, *Calixa Lavallée: Musicien national du Canada* (1936; rev. ed., Montreal: Fides, 1966); idem, "Calixa Lavallée," *BSHFA* (1970), 15–23.

8. Rémi Tremblay, *Un Revenant: Episode de la Guerre de Sécession aux Etats-Unis* (Montreal: Typographie de la Patrie, 1884); reprinted by the NMDC, 1980. See Richard R. Santerre, "Le Roman franco-américain en Nouvelle-Angleterre, 1878–1943," Ph.D. diss., Boston College, 1974, pp. 227–65. For Tremblay's poetry, see Paul P. Chassé, "Les Poètes franco-américains de la Nouvelle-Angleterre, 1875–1925," Ph.D. diss., Laval University, 1968, pp. 46–97; selections in idem, *Anthologie de la poésie franco-américaine* (Rhode Island Bicentennial Commission, 1976), pp. 23–31; and *ALFANA* 1: 242–92.

9. The novel, which was serialized in *Le Droit* (Ottawa) in 1936, was reprinted by the NMDC, 1980. See Dion-Lévesque, *Silhouettes,* pp. 476–80; and, especially, Santerre, "Roman franco-américain," pp. 199–216.

10. Evelyn H. Knowlton, *Pepperell's Progress: History of a Cotton Textile Company, 1844–1945* (Cambridge, Mass.: Harvard University Press, 1948), pp. 28–32.

11. Ibid., p. 6; Vicero, "Immigration," fig. 15.

12. Allen, "Catholics in Maine," p. 265.

13. Vera Shlakman, *Economic History of a Factory Town: A Study of Chicopee, Massachusetts,* Smith College Studies in History, vol. 20, nos. 1–4 (Northampton, Mass.: Department of History, Smith College, 1935), pp. 148–49; Vicero, "Immigration," pp. 117–79.

14. Vicero, "Immigration," p. 179.

15. Frances H. Early, "The Settling-In Process: The Beginnings of Little Canada in Lowell, Massachusetts, in the Late Nineteenth Century," *CIF* 3, 24.

16. Vicero, "Immigration," pp. 94–95, 162.

17. William N. Locke, "The French Colony at Brunswick, Maine: A Historical Sketch," *Archives de Folklore* 1 (1946), 107–10; Allen, "Catholics in Maine," fig. 10.

18. Vicero, "Immigration," p. 256, n. 129. On Salem, see Robert F. Harney, "Franco-Americans and Ethnic Studies: Notes on a Mill Town," in *The Quebec and Acadian Diaspora in North America,* ed. Raymond Breton and Pierre Savard (Toronto: Multicultural History Society of Ontario, 1982), pp. 77–88.

19. Vicero, "Immigration," pp. 217–19.

20. Allen, "Catholics in Maine," pp. 125–39 and figs. 11–14.

21. Honoré Beaugrand, *Jeanne la fileuse: Episode de l'émigration franco-canadienne aux Etats-Unis* (Fall River, Mass.: 1878); reprinted with an introduction by Roger Le Moine (Montreal: Fides, 1980) and, the same year, by the NMDC. See Santerre, "Roman franco-américain," pp. 39–69; also, on the date, see Santerre, p. 48 and n. 45. Le Moine, pp. 48–50, holds to the earlier view that the novel first appeared in serial form in 1875. For the interesting suggestion that Jeanne symbolizes survivance, see B.M.L., "Portée et signification historique du personnage de 'Jeanne' dans le roman d'Honoré Beaugrand, 'Jeanne la fileuse,'" *L'Unité* 6, no. 7 (1982), 5, 8, 9. On upper-lower and lower-middle-class Franco-Americans of the day, see Corinne Rocheleau-Rouleau, "Silhouettes et cadres franco-americains, 1880–1900," *BSHFA* (1942), 58–78.

22. Beaugrand, *Jeanne la fileuse* (rpt. Roger Le Moine), p. 254.

23. Father Hamon, *Canadiens-français,* pp. 14–16. This portion of Hamon's book (1891) appeared the preceding year in *Etudes Religieuses* (Paris).
24. Ibid., p. 20.
25. Ibid., p. 21.
26. Ibid., p. 17.
27. Emma Port-Joli (pseudonym of Emma Dumas), *Mirbah* (Holyoke, Mass.: La Justice Publishing Co., 1910–12); reprinted by the NMDC, 1979; also reprinted in *ALFANA* 4: 56–213. See Santerre, "Roman franco-américain," pp. 118–45, 178–98. Camille Lessard's *Canuck* was first serialized in *Le Messager* in Lewiston, Maine, in 1936, but was reprinted the same year in book form. Also reprinted by the NMDC, 1980.
28. Father Hamon, *Canadiens-français,* pp. 17–19.
29. Frances H. Early, "French-Canadian Beginnings in an American Community: Lowell, Massachusetts, 1868–1886," Ph.D. diss., Concordia University, 1980, pp. 138, 142–44; idem, "Settling-In Process," p. 26; idem, "The Rise and Fall of Félix Albert: Some Reflections on the Aspirations of Habitant Immigrants to Lowell, Massachusetts, in the Late Nineteenth Century," in *Quebec and Acadian Diaspora in North America,* pp. 25–38.
30. Early, "French-Canadian Beginnings," pp. 151, 155, 161.
31. Ibid., pp. 166–72, 175–77.
32. Peter Haebler, "Habitants in Holyoke: The Development of the French-Canadian Community in a Massachusetts City, 1865–1910," Ph.D. diss., University of New Hampshire, 1976, pp. 80–87; Philip T. Silvia, Jr., "The Spindle City: Labor, Politics, and Religion in Fall River, Massachusetts, 1870–1905," Ph.D. diss., Fordham University, 1973, pp. 331–42.
33. George F. Kenngott, *The Record of a City: A Social Survey of Lowell, Massachusetts* (New York: Macmillan, 1912), pp. 51, 71–86, 205.
34. *Brunswick Telegraph,* 6 August 1886.
35. Edward C. Kirkland, *Brunswick's Golden Age* (Lewiston, Maine: Loring, 1941).
36. Locke, "French Colony," p. 101.
37. *Brunswick Telegraph,* 10 September 1886.
38. Obituary in the *Brunswick Telegraph,* 7 January 1887.
39. Early, "French-Canadian Beginnings," pp. 197–98.
40. Daniel J. Walkowitz, *Worker City, Company Town: Iron and Cotton Worker Protest in Troy and Cohoes, New York* (Urbana: University of Illinois Press, 1978), p. 103. Similar data about Connecticut's Franco-Americans in 1886 cited by Vicero, "Immigration," p. 374, n. 46.
41. Early, "French-Canadian Beginnings," p. 197.
42. Vicero, "Immigration," table 31.
43. Father Hamon, *Canadiens-français,* pp. 22 (synopsis), 24–25; Early, "French-Canadian Beginnings," pp. 201–2.
44. Early, "French-Canadian Beginnings," pp. 128, 204; Father Hamon, *Canadiens-français,* pp. 28–32.
45. Tamara K. Hareven, *Family Time and Industrial Time: The Relationship between the Family and Work in a New England Industrial Community* (New York: Cambridge University Press, 1982).
46. Tamara K. Hareven, "The Laborers of Manchester, New Hampshire, 1912–1922: The Role of Family and Ethnicity in Adjustment to Industrial Life," *Labor History* 16 (1975), 249–65.
47. Allen, "Catholics in Maine," p. 221; Haebler, "Habitants in Holyoke," pp. 45, 80; Silvia, "Spindle City," pp. 361–65.
48. Anthony Coelho, "A Row of Nationalities: Life in a Working-Class Community: The Irish, English, and French Canadians of Fall River, Massachusetts,

1850–1890," Ph.D. diss., Brown University, 1980, p. 215. For other incidents in Holyoke in 1872 and 1887, see Haebler, "Habitants in Holyoke," pp. 80, 194. Additional listing in Vicero, "Immigration," p. 221.
49. Silvia, "Spindle City," pp. 358–59.
50. Coelho, "Row of Nationalities," p. 282.
51. Walkowitz, *Worker City,* pp. 220–22.
52. *Springfield's Ethnic Heritage: The French and French-Canadian Community* (Springfield, Mass.: U.S.A. Bicentennial Committee of Springfield, 1976), p. 15; Haebler, "Habitants in Holyoke," p. 197.
53. Pierre Anctil, "Aspects of Class Ideology in a New England Ethnic Minority: The Franco-Americans of Woonsocket, Rhode Island (1865–1929)," Ph.D. diss., New School for Social Research, 1980, pp. 71–75.
54. Donald B. Cole, *Immigrant City: Lawrence, Massachusetts, 1845–1921* (Chapel Hill: University of North Carolina Press, 1963), p. 184; Silvia, "Spindle City," pp. 353–54; Coelho, "Row of Nationalities," p. 279; Michael J. Guignard, *La Foi, la Langue, la Culture: The Franco-Americans of Biddeford, Maine* (1982), revision of "Ethnic Survival in a New England Mill Town: The Franco-Americans of Biddeford, Maine," Ph.D. diss., Syracuse University, 1976.
55. "Child Labor," *Funk & Wagnalls Standard Reference Encyclopedia,* 1959 ed., 6: 2025.
56. Gerard J. Brault, "Photographs of French-Canadian Children Working in New England Textile Mills by Lewis W. Hine, 1908–1916," *French-Canadian and Acadian Genealogical Review* 8, nos. 3–4 (1980), 131–40, provides a list of 193 names and street addresses for children in the following cities and towns: Bennington, Vermont (1910); Burlington, Vermont (1909); Chicopee, Massachusetts (1911); Dover, New Hampshire (1909); Fall River, Massachusetts (1912, 1916); Indian Orchard, Massachusetts (1911); Lawrence, Massachusetts (1911); Leeds, Massachusetts (1912); Lowell, Massachusetts (1911); Ludlow, Massachusetts (1911); Manchester, New Hampshire (1909); New Bedford, Massachusetts (1911, 1912); North Adams, Massachusetts (1911); North Pownal, Vermont (1909, 1910); Palmer, Massachusetts (1911); Phenix, Rhode Island (1909); Salem, Massachusetts (1911); Somersworth, New Hampshire (1909); Winchendon, Massachusetts (1911); and Winooski, Vermont (1909, 1910).
57. Early, "French-Canadian Beginnings," p. 104; Haebler, "Habitants in Holyoke," p. 68 and table 2.
58. Santerre, "Roman franco-américain," p. 93, n. 6; idem, *The Franco-Americans of Lowell, Massachusetts* (Lowell, Mass.: Franco-American Day Committee, 1972), [p. 7].
59. Maurice Violette, *The Franco-Americans: A Franco-American's Chronicle of Historical and Cultural Environment: Augusta Revisited* (New York: Vantage Press, 1976), p. 154.
60. Vicero, "Immigration," pp. 229–31. On Cartier's remark, which may be apocryphal, see p. 266, n. 201.
61. Letter to the editor of the St. Albans, Vermont, French-language newspaper, *Le Protecteur Canadien,* cited in Father Hamon, *Canadiens-français,* pp. 171–76; reference to Providence, p. 173.
62. See, for example, ibid., pp. 128–34, 143–55.
63. Mason Wade, "The French Parish and *Survivance* in Nineteenth-Century New England," *Catholic Historical Review* 36 (1950), 163–89; reprinted in *FAO* 3: 235–53. On the origins of this ideology, see idem, *The French Canadians, 1760–1967,* Laurentian Library, no. 33 (1968; rpt., Toronto: Macmillan of Canada, 1975), p. 1 and chaps. 3–6. See also Pierre Anctil, "Vie et Survie:

A Portrait of the Franco-American Press," *Société Historique Franco-Américaine*, Cahier no. 1 (1983), 37–41, especially 40–41. See also chap. 1, n. 2.

64. Wade, *French Canadians*, pp. 1, 5; Voisine, "Valeurs religieuses," p. 31.
65. Father Hamon, *Canadiens-français*, p. 105, speaks of the Franco-American parish as "la citadelle qui gardera la langue, la religion et la nationalité" (the citadel which will protect our language, religion, and nationality); cf. Monsignor Adrien Verrette, *Paroisse Sainte-Marie, Manchester, New Hampshire: Cinquantenaire 1880–1930* (Manchester, N.H.: Imprimerie Lafayette, 1931), p. i: "ces vaillantes citadelles de notre foi aux Etats-Unis" (those staunch citadels of our faith, in the United States).
66. Anctil, "Aspects of Class Ideology," chap. 3.
67. Haebler, "Habitants in Holyoke," pp. 145, 316.
68. David B. Walker, *Politics and Ethnocentrism: The Case of the Franco-Americans* (Brunswick, Maine: Bowdoin College, Bureau for Research in Municipal Government, 1961). Walker does not include any Vermont communities.
69. Ronald A. Petrin, "Culture, Community, and Politics: French Canadians in Massachusetts, 1885–1915," *CIF* 3, 66–77.
70. Silvia, "Spindle City," pp. 821, 831, 838.
71. Pothier is regarded as a hero by many Franco-Americans. For a divergent view, see Anctil, "Aspects of Class Ideology," pp. 132–38; "a bland and ineffective figure," p. 136.
72. Barbara M. Solomon, *Ancestors and Immigrants: A Changing New England Tradition* (Cambridge, Mass.: Harvard University Press, 1956); see index. On stereotyping, see Vander Zanden, *American Minority Relations*, pp. 19–21.
73. See, however, Solomon, *Ancestors and Immigrants*, p. 162.
74. Father Hamon, *Canadiens-français*, p. 29.
75. Guignard, *La Foi, la Langue, la Culture*, p. 117.
76. Rumilly, *Histoire des Franco-Américains*, pp. 96–97; Wade, "French Parish" (*FAO* 3), pp. 243–44; Pierre Anctil, "Un point tournant de l'histoire du Québec: L'épisode des 'Chinese of the Eastern States' de 1881," *Canado-Américain* 7, no. 2 (1981), 17–19.
77. Massachusetts Bureau of Statistics of Labor, *Twelfth Annual Report, 1881*, p. 469; Vicero, "Immigration," p. 356.
78. Rumilly, *Histoire des Franco-Américains*, pp. 97, 102.
79. Sister Mary-Carmel Therriault, *La Littérature française de Nouvelle-Angleterre* Montreal: Fides, 1946), pp. 81–82, n. 4; Wade, "French Parish" (*FAO* 3), pp. 244–45; Robert B. Perreault, "Survol de la presse franco-américaine," *CIF* 4, 17.
80. Vicero, "Immigration," p. 254, n. 118. On the earlier parishes, see Rumilly, *Histoire des Franco-Américains*, pp. 20, 27, 31.
81. Vicero, "Immigration," pp. 212–13, 254, n. 118.
82. Monsignor Verrette, *Paroisse Sainte-Marie*, p. 3; similar statement in Father Hamon, *Canadiens-français*, chap. 12.
83. Father Hamon, *Canadiens-français*, pp. 167–68, 188, 273, 351–52.
84. Ibid., p. 98.
85. Ibid., pp. 90–92. Bingo only dates from 1936.
86. Adolphe Robert, "L'inviolabilité de la paroisse nationale," *Vie Franco-Américaine* (1948), 115–24.
87. Father Hamon, *Canadiens-français*, pp. 261–62.
88. Ibid., pp. 313–20; and, especially, Silvia, "Spindle City," pp. 381–413. On Bédard's career, see Silvia, pp. 369–80.
89. Rumilly, *Histoire des Franco-Américains*, pp. 146–58, 163, 168–69, 175, 177–80.

90. Monsignor Adrien Verrette, "La paroisse franco-américaine," *Vie Franco-Américaine* (1948), 126.
91. Rumilly, *Histoire des Franco-Américains,* pp. 238–40, 254–55, 268–69; Michael J. Guignard, "Maine's Corporation Sole Controversy," *Maine Historical Society Newsletter* 12 (1973), 111–26. For satirical sketches, see Joseph Charlebois, *La Bêche (The Spade) ou les assimilateurs en action: Album de dessins gais* (Montreal: J. A. Lefebvre, 1911).
92. Rumilly, *Histoire des Franco-Américains,* pp. 214–15, 218–19, 374–75, 382, 388, 424, 443. Obituary in the *New York Times,* 7 August 1931. For a divergent view of Bishop Guertin's role in the Sentinelle Affair, see Robert B. Perreault, *Elphège-J. Daignault et le mouvement sentinelliste à Manchester, New Hampshire* (Bedford, N.H.: NMDC, 1981).
93. Rumilly, *Histoire des Franco-Américains,* p. 52 (Salvail); Guignard, *La Foi, la Langue, la Culture,* p. 58 (Paré, Paquet); Haebler, "Habitants in Holyoke," p. 128 (lay teachers); Father Antonin Plourde, "Cent ans de vie paroissiale, SS. Pierre et Paul de Lewiston," in *Paroisse Saint-Pierre et Saint-Paul: Centenaire, album souvenir* (Lewiston, Maine, 1971), p. 40 (Lacourse, Vidal, Bourbeau).
94. Pepperell Sheet, April 1941, p. 5. Guignard, *La Foi, la Langue, la Culture,* p. 58, claims this school had nearly four hundred students by 1881. On the Thivierges, see Dion-Lévesque, *Silhouettes,* pp. 839–49; obituary of daughter (1883–1963) in *BSHFA* (1963), 48–51.
95. Rocheleau-Rouleau, "Silhouettes," pp. 61–62.
96. Santerre, *Franco-Americans of Lowell,* [p. 3].
97. *Brunswick Telegraph,* 13 May 1887.
98. Mother Mary Lucy, principal, St. Ignatius School, Sanford, Maine, to author, 28 March 1972.
99. Father Hamon, *Canadiens-français,* p. 206, provides the dates 1869 (see also Rumilly, *Histoire des Franco-Américains,* p. 51) and 1882. See, however, Sister Hélène Chaput, *Mère Marie-du-Rosaire,* Histoire de la Congrégation des Soeurs des SS. NN. de Jésus et de Marie (St. Boniface, Manitoba: Éditions du Blé, 1982), pp. 39 and 56, n. 10. On the many tribulations of the sisters, who were opposed by the local Irish pastor, see Sister Chaput, pp. 39–44, 55–56, n. 10. I am indebted to Sister Claire Laplante, the community's archivist, for confirming these dates, which are recorded in the Rutland convent's manuscript chronicles preserved at Longueuil, near Montreal.
100. Father Hamon, *Canadiens-français,* p. 316. Auguste Viatte, *Histoire de la Congrégation de Jésus-Marie, 1818–1950* (Quebec City: Charrier and Dugal, 1952), p. 162, errs when he states that this was "la première école de langue française en Nouvelle-Angleterre" (the first French-language school in New England). Father Plourde, "Vie paroissiale," pp. 15, 24–25 (photograph), 31 (photograph).
101. See, for example, Mother Marie de Saint Jean Martin, *Ursuline Method of Education* (Rahway, N.J.: Quinn and Boden, 1946).
102. Father Hamon, *Canadiens-français,* pp. 380–81; Rumilly, *Histoire des Franco-Américains,* pp. 123, 149.
103. *Programme d'études et Directoire à l'usage des SS. de l'Assomption de la S.V. pour les écoles bilingues* (Nicolet, Quebec, 1912). Cf. *Programme d'études pour les pensionnats des Soeurs de l'Assomption* (Nicolet, Quebec, 1905).
104. "Souvenir des noces d'argent, 1904–1929," *L'Assomption,* April–May 1929 (special issue).
105. Father Hamon, *Canadiens-français,* pp. 90–96.

106. Rumilly, *Histoire des Franco-Américains,* p. 29; Vicero, "Immigration," pp. 181–82.

107. Edward B. Ham, "French National Societies in New England," *New England Quarterly* 12 (1939), 315–32; Sister Florence M. Chevalier, "The Role of French National Societies in the Sociocultural Evolution of the Franco-Americans of New England from 1860 to the Present: An Analytical Macro-Sociological Case Study in Ethnic Integration Based on Current Social System Models," Ph.D. diss., Catholic University of America, 1972.

108. Félix Gatineau, *Historique des conventions générales des Canadiens-français aux Etats-Unis, 1865–1901* (Woonsocket, R.I.: Union Saint-Jean-Baptiste d'Amérique, 1927).

109. J. K. L. Laflamme, David E. Lavigne, and J. Arthur Favreau, "French Catholics in the United States," *Catholic Encyclopedia,* 1909 ed. (reprinted in *FAO* 3: 23–35). For figure 400, see *FAO* 3: 32.

110. Guignard, *La Foi, la Langue, la Culture,* p. 79; Santerre, *Franco-Americans of Lowell,* [p. 6] (photograph).

111. *Springfield's Ethnic Heritage,* p. 26.

112. Sister Therriault, *Littérature française,* p. 67.

113. Santerre, *Franco-Americans of Lowell,* [p. 17]; photographs of 1906 parade, [p. 20].

114. Guignard, *La Foi, la Langue, la Culture,* p. 80; Monsignor Verrette, *Paroisse Sainte-Marie,* p. 309.

115. Father Plourde, "Vie paroissiale," p. 35, photograph of the Fanfare Ste-Cécile, p. 29; *BSHFA* (1965), 109.

116. Gabriel Nadeau, "Le théâtre chez les Franco-Américains," *BSHFA* (1955), 69–74.

117. Santerre, *Franco-Americans of Lowell,* [p. 2]; Félix Gatineau, *Histoire des Franco-Américains de Southbridge, Massachusetts* (Framingham, Mass.: Lakeview Press, 1919), p. 164, adding that there were some earlier productions.

118. Nadeau, "Théâtre," pp. 69, 72; Ernest B. Guillet, "French Ethnic Literature and Culture in an American City: Holyoke, Massachusetts," Ph.D. diss, University of Massachusetts, 1978, pp. 149–50.

119. Guillet, "French Ethnic Literature," pp. 146–49; see also Normand R. Beaupré, *L'Enclume et le couteau: The Life and Work of Adelard Coté, Folk Artist* (Manchester, N.H.: NMDC, 1982), p. 96, on New England tours by the Troupe Jean Grimaldi (Tizoune et Manda) in the 1940s.

120. Santerre, "Roman franco-américain," pp. 139–40; Guillet, "French Ethnic Literature," pp. 153–56.

121. Santerre, "Roman franco-américain," p. 139.

122. *Les Quarante Ans de la Société Historique Franco-Américaine, 1899–1939* (Boston: Société Historique Franco-Américaine, 1940); Sister Therriault, *Littérature française,* pp. 61–66. The Société Historique published a bulletin (*BSHFA*) on an occasional basis from 1900, then annually from 1935 to 1973. A new series was begun in 1983. Thus far, this consists of a single issue (Cahier no. 1). See chap. 3, no. 10, in this volume.

123. Sister Therriault, *Littérature française,* pp. 72–75.

124. Monsignor Verrette, *Paroisse Sainte-Marie,* pp. 307–9, 314 (photographs); Laurent Galarneau, *Histoire de la garde Lafayette, ou compagnie A, du premier régiment d'infanterie de la garde nationale de l'état du New Hampshire* (Manchester, N.H.: L'Avenir National, 1937); *BSHFA* (1957), 198–200, 390; Richard R. Santerre, "Bibliographie des imprimés franco-américains parus à Lowell, Massachusetts, de 1837 à 1968," *BSHFA* (1968), 164–65. For a sa-

tirical poem in English about 1898, see Ducharme, *Shadows of the Trees,* pp. 225–26.

125. Monsignor Verrette, *Paroisse Sainte-Marie,* p. 309.

126. *Almanach franco-américain et catholique* (1911), p. 79. See also the *Programme-souvenir du huitième congrès de la Brigade des volontaires franco-américains des Etats-Unis* (Lowell: J. E. Lambert, 1915), and *L'Avenir National,* October 1895, special issue [pp. 11–12], and 24 April 1924.

127. Rumilly, *Histoire des Franco-Américains,* pp. 299–300.

128. *BSHFA* (1969), 26.

129. Rumilly, *Histoire des Franco-Américains,* pp. 231–32; *BSHFA* (1959), 213; Paul M. Paré, "Franco-Americans and Credit Unions," *InformACTION* 3, no. 1 (1984), 4–5, 7 (see also press release, p. 1).

130. Robert B. Perreault, "Survol," pp. 9–34 (bibliography, pp. 32–34). See also Edward B. Ham, "Journalism and the French Survival in New England," *New England Quarterly* 11 (1938), 89–107; Alexandre Bélisle, *Histoire de la presse franco-américaine* (Worcester, Mass.: L'Opinion Publique, 1911). Paul P. Chassé, *La Presse chez les Franco-Américains* (Cambridge, Mass.: NADC, 1979) has full-page illustrations of numerous Franco-American news-papers. See also Robert B. Perreault, *La Presse franco-américaine et la politique: L'oeuvre de Charles-Roger Daoust* (Bedford, N.H.: NMDC, 1981).

131. Sister Therriault, *Littérature française,* pp. 94–95; Rumilly, *Histoire des Franco-Américains,* pp. 23–25.

132. Sister Therriault, *Littérature française,* p. 99 and n. 36.

133. Ibid., pp. 88–93; Dion-Lévesque, *Silhouettes,* pp. 336–40; Perreault, "Survol," pp. 13–15. On the hundredth anniversary of his birth in 1949, a statue was erected to his memory near Saint Mary's Church in Manchester, New Hampshire. See *BSHFA* (1964), 54; photograph in *BSHFA* (1970), opposite p. 64. A sculpture of him by Alfred Laliberté is also owned by the Association Canado-Américaine. See *Canado-Américain* 5, no. 4 (1979), 3.

134. Donald Chaput, "Some Repatriement Dilemmas," *Canadian Historical Review* 49 (1968), 400–412.

135. Paul M. Paré, "Les vingt premières années du *Messager* de Lewiston, Maine," *CIF* 4, 81–96.

136. Vicero, "Immigration," pp. 231–36. On repatriation, see Chaput, "Some Repatriement Dilemmas"; Robert G. LeBlanc, "Regional Competition for Franco-American Repatriates, 1870–1930," *Quebec Studies* 1 (1983), 110–29; and idem, "Colonisation et rapatriement au Lac Saint-Jean (1895–1905)," *Revue d'Histoire de l'Amérique Française* 38 (1985), 379–408.

137. Vicero, "Immigration," pp. 226, 232–33.

138. Guignard, *La Foi, la Langue, la Culture,* pp. 37, 113–14.

139. Vicero, "Immigration," pp. 2, 194–95.

140. Cole, *Immigrant City,* p. 75.

141. Town of Enfield, Connecticut, Manuscript Record of Deaths.

142. Santerre, "Roman franco-américain," p. 53 and n. 52.

143. *Jubilé d'or paroissial (1872–1922, Paroisse du Précieux Sang, Holyoke, Massachusetts* (Holyoke, Mass., 1922). In the copy preserved in the library of the Association Canado-Américaine (T-32, 1922), the list of victims, p. 15, has handwritten corrections. See also Maxime O. Frenière, "Une catastrophe à Holyoke, 1875," *BSHFA* (1961), 103–9 (list, pp. 106–7).

144. Santerre, "Roman franco-américain," pp. 133–135.

145. *New York Times,* 26 June 1914; 27 June 1914; 28 June 1914; *La Presse* (Montreal), 26 June 1914.

146. See, for example, the three hundred biographies in Dion-Lévesque, *Silhouettes*; reviewed by Gabriel Nadeau in *BSHFA* (1958), 111–13. For mayors, see Maxime O. Frenière, "Les maires franco-américains des villes des Etats-Unis, 1684–1942," *BSHFA* (1942), 109–13; additions and corrections by the author, *BSHFA* (1943), 110; see also *BSHFA* (1956), 245; (1959), 158; (1960), 85; (1964), 74; (1967), 103. Various other elected officials are listed by Josaphat-T. Benoît, "Les Franco-Américains en politique," in *Guide officiel franco-américain* (1946), pp. 157–64. For physicians, see Paul Dufault, "Notes sur la médecine franco-américaine," *BSHFA* (1943), 98–109 (list, pp. 106–9); another list in Adolphe Robert's obituary of Joseph-Euclide Mercier, *BSHFA* (1961), 38–39; for Lowell, Massachusetts, see *Le Journal de Lowell* 8, no. 1 (1982), 2; 8, no. 2, pp. 3, 4. On Franco-American judges, see Father Thomas-M. Landry, *BSHFA* (1957), 86–89 (not a listing). Lawyers in Lowell, Massachusetts, are listed by Arthur L. Eno, *Les Avocats franco-américains de Lowell, Massachusetts, 1886–1936* (Lowell, Mass.: Eno Printing Co., 1936).

147. Hélène Charbonneau, *L'Albani: Sa carrière artistique et triomphale* (Montreal: Imprimerie Jacques-Cartier, 1938); Dion-Lévesque, *Silhouettes,* pp. 468–71; obituary in the *New York Times*, "Dame Emma Albani" (she was made a Dame Commander of the British Empire in 1925), 4 April 1930.

148. Dion-Lévesque, *Silhouettes,* pp. 915–18; obituary in the *New York Times,* 7 February 1938.

149. Rumilly, *Histoire des Franco-Américains*, p. 526. For "Charette's March," composed by A. Mirault (1898), see Santerre, *Franco-Americans of Lowell*, [p. 12]; illustration of sheet music cover includes a photograph of Charette.

150. Ben Weider, *Les Hommes forts du Québec* (Montreal: Editions du Jour, 1973), pp. 73–230 (many photographs). See also Santerre, *Franco-Americans of Lowell*, [p. 16] (photograph); Lane, "Franco-American Folk Traditions," pp. 190–94. On the legendary Jos Montferrand (1802–64) also associated with New England, see George Monteiro, "Histoire de Montferrand: L'Athlète Canadien and Joe Mufraw," *Journal of American Folklore* 73 (1960), 24–34; Weider, pp. 19–22; Lane, pp. 187–89.

151. Dion-Lévesque, *Silhouettes,* pp. 460–65; Richard S. Sorrell, "Sports and Franco-Americans in Woonsocket, 1870–1930," *Rhode Island History* 31 (1972), 120–21. Obituary in the *New York Times,* 8 February 1959; also account of the funeral, 10 February 1959.

152. Dion-Lévesque, *Silhouettes,* pp. 816–19 (date of death erroneously given as 1940 on p. 816, but correctly given on p. 819); Guillet, "French Ethnic Literature," pp. 176–78. Obituary (and 1934 photograph) in the *New York Times,* 12 January 1947.

153. Santerre, "Roman franco-américain," p. 138; Albert Santerre, "The Champagne Family: Strauss of New England," *FAROG Forum* 6, no. 8 (1979), 15; Lane, "Franco-American Folk Traditions," pp. 384, 438–40, 448, n. 21; text of "L'amour c'est comme la salade," pp. 427–28.

154. Text of "Lowell March" in Lane, "Franco-American Folk Traditions," p. 390.

155. *L'Union* 82, no. 3 (1982), 1; 82, no. 4 (1982), 11; *Canado-Américain,* 8, no. 2 (1982), 14–15.

156. *100th Anniversary, St. Joseph's Church, Cohoes, New York* (1984), [p. 5] (photograph). See also photograph of the interior of Saint Mary's Church, Manchester, New Hampshire, decorated by the Quebecois artist Ozias Leduc in 1906, in *Magazine OVO* (Montreal), 12, no. 46 (1982), 37.

Chapter 3. The Middle Phase, 1920–1960

1. Richard S. Sorrell, "The Sentinelle Affair (1924–1929) and Militant 'Survivance': The Franco-American Experience in Woonsocket, Rhode Island," Ph.D. diss., State University of New York at Buffalo, 1975, pp. 157–69.
2. Benoît, *Ame franco-américaine,* pp. 77–91. On Franco-American ideology of the day, presented from a Sentinelliste point of view, see *Les Franco-Américains peints par eux-mêmes* (Montreal: Albert Lévesque [for the Association Canado-Américaine], 1936).
3. Rumilly, *Histoire des Franco-Américains,* pp. 335, 346, 347, 377; Sorrell, "Sentinelle Affair," pp. 163–68.
4. Kenneth B. O'Brien, Jr., "Education, Americanization at the Supreme Court: The 1920s," *American Quarterly* 13 (1961), 161–71; Bonnie Hume, "Education and Parents' Rights," *Religious Education* 60 (1965), 460–66, 472.
5. Edmond de Nevers, *L'Ame américaine: Les origines, la vie historique,* 2 vols. (Paris: Jouve and Boyer, 1900).
6. Bessie Bloom Wessel, *An Ethnic Survey of Woonsocket, Rhode Island* (Chicago: University of Chicago Press, 1931), pp. 244, 256–57 (bibliography).
7. Benoît, *Ame franco-américaine,* pp. 225–26; Rumilly, *Histoire des Franco-Américains,* pp. 361ff.; and, especially, Sorrell, "Sentinelle Affair," and Anctil, "Aspects of Class Ideology." Parts of Sorrell's thesis have been published as "The Sentinelle Affair (1924–1929): Religion and Militant Survivance in Woonsocket, Rhode Island," *Rhode Island History* 36 (1977), 67–80; and "La Sentinelle et la Tribune: Le rôle joué par ces journaux de Woonsocket dans l'affaire de la Sentinelle," *CIF* 4, 35–49. (To eliminate confusion, references below to Sorrell, "Sentinelle Affair," are to his 1975 dissertation only.)
8. The militants' case is presented by Elphège-J. Daignault, *Le Vrai Mouvement sentinelliste en Nouvelle-Angleterre, 1923–1929, et l'affaire du Rhode Island* (Montreal: Editions du Zodiaque, 1935). See also Perreault, *Elphège-J. Daignault et mouvement sentinelliste,* and above, n. 2. Obituaries of Daignault and Vézina appeared in the *New York Times,* 26 May 1937 and 11 March 1942, respectively.
9. Roger Brunelle, "Les remarques d'un supposé spécialiste ont déplu à l'auditoire du Colloque de la presse franco-américaine," *L'Unité* 7, no. 5 (1983), 4–5; Benoît Bourget, "Gens du pays . . . c'est à mon tour!" *FAROG Forum* 10, no. 7/8 (1983), 22.
10. Oda Beaulieu, ed., "Actes du Symposium tenu à l'occasion de l'ouverture des Archives Wilfrid Beaulieu–*Le Travailleur* sous les auspices conjoints de la Société Historique Franco-Américaine et de la Bibliothèque Publique de Boston," *Société Historique Franco-Américaine,* Cahier no. 1 (1983); Armand B. Chartier, "Wilfrid Beaulieu: L'homme et l'oeuvre," *CIF* 4, 50–80.
11. Rumilly, *Histoire des Franco-Américains,* pp. 320, 324–26.
12. Sorrell, "Sentinelle Affair," pp. 171–73.
13. "Mount Saint Charles Turns Sixty," *L'Union* 84, no. 5 (1984), 14.
14. George F. Theriault, "The Franco-Americans of New England," in *Canadian Dualism,* pp. 392–411, a summary of the author's thesis, "The Franco-Americans in a New England Community: An Experiment in Survival," Ph.D. diss., Harvard University, 1951.
15. W. Lloyd Warner and Paul S. Lunt, *The Social Life of a Modern Community* (New Haven: Yale University Press, 1941), p. 250.
16. W. Lloyd Warner and Leo Srole, *The Social Systems of American Ethnic Groups* (New Haven: Yale University Press, 1945), pp. 100–102.

17. Ibid., p. 79. For a negative assessment of the value of higher education, see Father Joseph S. Vermette, "Par l'école," in *Franco-Américains peints par eux-mêmes*, pp. 104–6. Father Vermette was pastor of Saint John the Baptist parish, Lynn, Massachusetts (p. 286).

18. Elin L. Anderson, *We Americans: A Study of Cleavage in an American City* (1937; rpt., New York: Russell & Russell, 1964), pp. 37, 54–55, 58–59, 60. The informant is identified only as "a citizen who belongs to the fourth generation of French and Irish stock and who has lived many years in the city."

19. Wessell, *Ethnic Survey*, tables 30a, 56, 62, 63. On intermarriage among Franco-Americans, 1876–1946, see Ulysee Forget, "Les Franco-Americains et le 'Melting Pot,'" *BSHFA* (1946–47), 32–49.

20. Daniel Creamer and Charles W. Coulter, *Labor and the Shut-down of the Amoskeag Textile Mills* (1939; rpt., New York: Arno and New York Times, 1971), pp. 8–37, 194–203.

21. Katherine Du Pre Lumpkin, *Shutdowns in the Connecticut Valley: A Study of Worker Displacement in the Small Industrial Community*, Smith College Studies in History, no. 29 (Northampton, Mass.: Department of History, Smith College, 1934), tables 5, 11.

22. Creamer and Coulter, *Labor and Shut-down of Amoskeag*, pp. 68, 299, 306, 310, table G-6.

23. Lumpkin, *Shutdowns in the Connecticut Valley*, pp. 198–206, 228–36. On the role of private charity, see pp. 236–38.

24. Creamer and Coulter, *Labor and Shut-down of Amoskeag*, tables E-19, E-20.

25. Violette, *Franco-Americans*, chap. 15.

26. "Life Isn't All Hardware," *Worcester* [Massachusetts] *Sunday Telegram, Parade Magazine*, 9 July 1967.

27. Benoît, *Ame franco-américaine*, pp. 115–29. Father Vermette, "Par l'école," pp. 95–110, presents a spirited defense of the right of Franco-Americans to maintain their own educational system.

28. Mother Martin, *Ursuline Method*, pp. 20–22, 24–25, 57, 309, 310, 313–14.

29. *Programme d'études*, p. 3.

30. Ibid., p. 3.

31. Ibid., pp. 4–5. Carillon refers to the famous victory (1758) of Louis-Joseph, Marquis de Montcalm (1712–59), French field marshal in Canada, over British general James Abercrombie at a strategic point between Lake George and Lake Champlain. See "Bicentennaire Ticonderoga-Carillon (1758–1958)," *BSHFA* (1958), 11–46. On the flag, believed by some to be a relic of the battle, see pp. 42–43; and, especially, Hormidas Magnan, *Cinquantenaire de notre hymne national, "O Canada, terre de nos aïeux": Les origines de nos drapeaux et chants nationaux, armoiries, emblêmes, devises* (Quebec City, 1929), pp. 38–45, 39 (sketch). The fort, called Ticonderoga by the British, was the scene of a military action in 1777; see *BSHFA* (1955), 88.

32. *La Lecture par la méthode phonique, Première partie* (Montreal: Frères des Ecoles Chrétiennes, 1918). Frequently reprinted.

33. *La Lecture par la méthode phonique, Deuxième partie* (Montreal: Frères des Ecoles Chrétiennes, 1918), p. 64.

34. *Lecture, Première partie*, pp. 12, 16, 19, 23, 33, 43, 53, 56, 61.

35. *Lecture, Deuxième partie*, p. 30.

36. *Programme d'études*, pp. 1, 2.

37. *Lectures courantes, Deuxième Livre*, nouvelle édition (Montreal: Frères des Ecoles Chrétiennes, 1916).

38. *Lectures courantes*, pp. 132–33. On the Old French fabliau, see Joseph Bédier, *Les Fabliaux: Etudes de littérature populaire et d'histoire littéraire du moyen âge*,

6th ed., Bibliothèque de l'Ecole des Hautes Etudes, 4th section, Sciences Historiques et Philologiques, no. 98 (Paris: Champion, 1964), pp. 463–64.

39. Geneviève Laloux-Jain, *Les Manuels d'histoire du Canada au Québec et en
Ontario (de 1867 à 1914)*, Histoire et sociologie de la culture, no. 6 (Quebec
City: Presses de l'Université Laval, 1974). See, for example, *Histoire du Canada, Cours moyen*, 4th ed. (Montreal: Frères des Ecoles Chrétiennes, 1916),
pp. 75–76. See also *Programme de français et d'histoire nationale en usage dans
les écoles paroissiales des Etats-Unis*, part 2, p. 1. According to the librarian at the
mother house of the Sisters of the Assumption in Nicolet, Quebec, this mimeographed pamphlet was prepared by Sister Marie-Ange and used in teacher
training from 1928 to 1940 and later.

40. *Programme de français et d'histoire nationale*, part 2, p. 4.

41. Donald B. Smith, *Le "Sauvage" pendant la période héroïque de la Nouvelle-France
(1534–1663) d'après les historiens canadiens-français des XIXᵉ et XXᵉ siècles* (Ville
LaSalle, Quebec: Editions Hurtubise HMH, 1979); Sylvie Vincent and
Bernard Arcand, *L'Image de l'Amérindien dans les manuels scolaires du Québec, ou
comment les Québécois ne sont pas des sauvages* (Ville LaSalle, Quebec: Editions
Hurtubise HMH, 1979).

42. Wessel, *Ethnic Survey*, p. 12.

43. Names and photographs of early faculty are found scattered throughout "Souvenir des noces d'argent." For a list of Assumptionist Fathers attached to the
school throughout its history, see the program of the seventy-fifth anniversary celebration, 15 March 1980, *Collège de l'Assomption, 1904–1979* (1980),
[pp. 7–8]. The publication also contains a brief history of the institution.
Father Georges Bissonnette, one of the college's most distinguished alumni
(among other achievements, he served as chaplain of Americans in the USSR
from 1953 to 1955, and as president of Assumption from 1968 to 1971), has
written a lively and perceptive account of the school from its founding to the
present day. Soon to be published, the book is entitled *The Legend of a College
(Assumption)*. "Souvenir des noces d'argent," pp. 64–72, also contains a list of
all students who enrolled at Assumption from 1904 to 1928.

44. For 1921–25 enrollment, see "Souvenir des noces d'argent," p. 18; for 1926,
1934, and post–World War II, see Father Polyeucte Guissard, *Un Siècle d'histoire assomptionniste* (Worcester, Mass.: Imprimerie Caron, 1950), pp. 128, 132.

45. "Souvenir des noces d'argent," pp. 63–64, provides the names of fifty-eight
alumni who became priests.

46. Ibid., p. 18.

47. Gatineau, *Histoire des Franco-Américains*.

48. Marie-Louise Bonier, *Débuts de la colonie franco-américaine de Woonsocket, Rhode
Island* (1920; rpt., Montreal and Manchester, N.H.: Editions du 45ᵉ Parallèle
Nord, 1981), pp. 328–42; Sorrell, "Sentinelle Affair," pp. 107, 119.

49. Rumilly, *Histoire des Franco-Américains*, p. 298.

50. Ibid., pp. 323, 328–30, 339–41, 367–61, 382, 386, 388, 390–91, 395,
401, 403, 412, 413, 434, 449; *Canado-Américain* 6, no. 4 (1980), 18.

51. Sister Therriault, *Littérature française*, pp. 71–72; *Guide officiel franco-
américain 1938*, pp. 333–35.

52. *BSHFA* (1964), 56, 83.

53. *Vie Franco-Américaine* (1946), 259–61.

54. *InformACTION* 2, no. 2 (1983), 4.

55. Dion-Lévesque, *Silhouettes*, p. 335.

56. Information contained in a mimeographed list of clubs and officers kindly provided by Florence Rose Laliberté of Lewiston, Maine, 15 December 1983.
Also program of National Snowshoe Congress held at Lewiston, January
28–30, 1983.

57. Sister Therriault, *Littérature française,* pp. 202, 204, 206, 240–43, 279–86. Louis Dantin, *Le Coffret de Crusoé* (Montreal: Albert Lévesque, 1932); Rosaire Dion-Lévesque, *Les Oasis* (Rome: Desclée, 1930). Boucher's "Ode à Québec" appeared in various collections; for 1933 and 1952 versions, see *ALFANA* 7: 173–204, 205–24. For other poetry by Boucher, see Chassé, *Anthologie,* pp. 162–71, and *ALFANA* 7: 161–72, 225–69. The total (217) is in Adolphe Robert, "L'apport franco-américain à la littérature des Etats-Unis," *BSHFA* (1954), 64.

58. Santerre, "Roman franco-américain," pp. 163–77, 178–98, 199–216. See also Armand B. Chartier, "Pour une problématique de l'histoire littéraire franco-américaine," *CIF* 1, 81–100. Chartier provides a penetrating overview of Franco-American literature in French and English. See also his "Franco-American Literature: The New England Experience," in *Ethnic Perspectives in American Literature: Selected Essays on Their European Contribution,* ed. Robert J. Di Pietro and Edward Ifkovic (New York: Modern Language Association of America, 1983), pp. 15–42.

59. Alberte Gastonguay-Sasseville, *La Jeune Franco-Américaine* (Lewiston, Maine, 1933); reprinted in 1980 by the NMDC.

60. See chap. 2, n. 27.

61. See chap. 2, n. 9.

62. Paul Dufault, *Sanatorium* (Montreal, 1938); reprinted in 1982 by the NMDC. See Santerre, "Roman franco-américain," pp. 275–99.

63. Louis Dantin, *Les Enfances de Fanny* (Montreal: Chantecler, 1951). See Santerre, "Roman franco-américain," pp. 300–331.

64. Gérard Bessette, Lucien Geslin, and Charles Parent, *Histoire de la littérature canadienne-française par les textes* (Centre Educatif et Culturel, 1968), pp. 143, 145, 146, 167.

65. Sister Therriault, *Littérature française,* pp. 258–66; Bessette, Geslin, and Parent, *Histoire,* p. 92.

66. Chassé, "Poètes franco-américains," pp. 15–45, 102–8, 109–37. Selections in idem, *Anthologie,* pp. 17–21, 33–42, 44–52; also *ALFANA* 2: 220–48 (Duval-Thibault); 3: 196–256 (Roy); 4: 2–52 (Girouard). Duval-Thibault is also the author of a novel, *Les Deux Testaments* (Fall River, Mass.: Imprimerie de l'Indépendant, 1888); reprinted in 1979 by the NMDC; also *ALFANA* 2: 95–199. See Santerre, "Roman franco-américain," pp. 70–92.

67. Chassé, "Poètes franco-américains," pp. 189–253, 254–93, 305–43, 344–91; selections in idem, *Anthologie,* pp. 54–62, 64–72, 74–79, 81–88; also *ALFANA* 3: 152–92 (Daoust); 6: 211–327 (Sainte-Marie); 7: 67–141 (Nolin).

68. Chartier, "Pour une problématique," pp. 82–83. Selections in Chassé, *Anthologie,* pp. 101–21, and *ALFANA* 9: 54–127.

69. Henri d'Arles, *Laudes* (Paris: Paul Lefebvre, 1925). See Armand B. Chartier, "The Franco-American Literature of New England: A Brief Overview," in *Ethnic Literatures since 1776: The Many Voices of America* (Lubbock, Tex.: Texas Tech University Press, 1978), 1, 207–8; idem, "Pour une problématique," p. 83. Selections in Chassé, *Anthologie,* pp. 90–99, and *ALFANA* 5: 373–76.

70. Rosaire Dion-Lévesque, *Vita* (Montreal: Bernard Valiquette, 1939); idem, *Quête* (Quebec City: Garneau, 1963); idem, *Walt Whitman* (Montreal: Elzévirs, 1933). See Chartier, "Franco-American Literature of New England," pp. 208–11; idem, "Pour une problématique," pp. 83–84; and, especially, Michel Lapierre, "Rosaire Dion-Lévesque (1900–1974) et la littérature franco-américaine," M.A. thesis, Université de Montréal, Département d'Etudes Françaises, 1983. Selections in Chassé, *Anthologie,* pp. 124–49, and *ALFANA*

9: 132–274. Dion-Lévesque is also the author of *Silhouettes* (see chap. 2, n. 146). On dramatic productions in Holyoke, Massachusetts, at this time, see Ernest B. Guillet, *Un Théâtre francophone dans un milieu franco-américain* (Manchester, N.H.: NMDC, 1981).

71. Robert, "Apport franco-américain," p. 64.

72. Jacques Ducharme, *The Delusson Family: A Novel* (New York: Funk & Wagnalls, 1939); Albéric A. Archambault, *Mill Village: A Novel* (Boston: Bruce Humphries, 1943).

73. Rocheleau-Rouleau, *Laurentian Heritage.* On this remarkable woman, deaf from the age of nine and, after 1940, a resident of Montreal, see Dion-Lévesque, *Silhouettes,* pp. 782–87; and "Corinne Rocheleau-Rouleau (1881–1963)," *BSHFA* (1963), 93–94.

74. Robert Fontaine, *The Happy Time* (New York: Simon and Schuster, 1945). See Dion-Lévesque, *Silhouettes,* pp. 312–14. The Taylor adaptation was published in New York City by Random House in 1950.

75. Maximilienne Tétrault, *Le Rôle de la presse dans l'évolution du peuple franco-américain de la Nouvelle-Angleterre* (Marseilles: Imprimerie Ferran, 1935). See also Antoine Clément, "Apothéose de la presse franco-américaine," in *Quarante Ans,* pp. 585–90; idem, "L'oeuvre de la presse franco-américaine dans notre survivance," in ibid., pp. 591–96; Bernard Therrien, "Pourquoi faut-il lire le journal franco-américain catholique?" also in ibid., pp. 730–731; Ernest B. Guillet, *Essai de journalisme* (Bedford, N.H.: NMDC, 1981).

76. Sister Therriault, *Littérature française,* pp. 117–28; Rumilly, *Histoire des Franco-Américains,* p. 515; *BSHFA* (1957), 282–85; Elphège Roy, *Les Causes du déclin de la presse franco-américaine* (Manchester, N.H., 1965). See, however, Roger Lacerte, "Une thèse artificielle . . . celle de M. Elphège Roy: Une réfutation," *Travailleur,* 14 June 1969 and 21 June 1969.

77. Perreault, "Survol," p. 18. Mention is also made of *Le Courrier,* Lawrence, Massachusetts, founded in 1899, with the notation: "Existe toujours [presumably as an occasional publication] en 1983." For biographies and selections from the works of leading Franco-American historians, see Armand B. Chartier, *Littérature historique populaire franco-américaine* (Bedford, N.H.: NMDC, 1981).

78. Dion-Lévesque, *Silhouettes,* pp. 382–85; *Canado-Américain* 6, no. 2 (1980), 26.

79. Dion-Lévesque, *Silhouettes,* pp. 680–82; *BSHFA* (1967), 164–65 (obituary); *L'Union* 84, no. 6 (1984), 15 (photographs). See also Gary Samson, "Ulric Bourgeois, photographe franco-américain, 1874–1963," *Magazine OVO* (Montreal), 12, no. 46 (1982), 6–13.

80. Dion-Lévesque, *Silhouettes,* pp. 280–84; obituary in the *New York Times,* 10 November 1981.

81. Dion-Lévesque, *Silhouettes,* pp. 284–87. Durocher's autobiography is entitled *Nice Guys Finish Last* (New York: Simon and Schuster, 1975). See also Leo Trachtenberg, "Leo Durocher and the Yankees," *Yankees Magazine,* 7 July 1983, pp. 18–19; and Peter Golenbock, *Bums: An Oral History of the Brooklyn Dodgers* (New York: G. P. Putnam, 1984).

82. Dion-Lévesque, *Silhouettes,* pp. 312–14; obituaries in the *Boston Globe* and the *New York Times,* 6 August 1978.

83. Rumilly, *Histoire des Franco-Américains,* pp. 531–32; obituaries: Associated Press news release, *Centre Daily Times* (State College, Pa.), 13 October 1979; *New York Times,* 16 October 1979; *Canado-Américain* 5, no. 4 (1979), 6. See also *L'Union* 81, no. 6 (1981), 10. On Gagnon's role, see Bernard C. Nalty, *The United States Marine Corps on Iwo Jima: The Battle and the Flag Raising*

(Washington, D.C.: Historical Division, Headquarters, U.S. Marine Corps, 1970), pp. 13–14. There were actually two flag-raising ceremonies, the second having occasioned the famous photograph. However, both scenes were captured on film. See also the Public Broadcasting System's documentary "Return to Iwo Jima" shown on 27 May (Memorial Day) 1985.

84. Dion-Lévesque, *Silhouettes*, pp. 345–48; Rumilly, *Histoire des Franco-Américains*, p. 524; "Small Arms," in *Funk & Wagnalls Standard Reference Encyclopedia*, 1959 ed.; Edward C. Ezell, "An Exclusive Interview with John C. Garand," *Rifle Magazine* (September–October 1970), 14–19, 60. Also, mimeographed information courtesy of Larry Lowenthal, park historian, Springfield Armory National Historic Site, Springfield, Massachusetts. Obituary in the *New York Times,* 17 February 1974.

85. Dion-Lévesque, *Silhouettes,* pp. 872–75. Rudy Vallée's autobiography, *Let the Chips Fall . . .* (1975), was revised and reissued in paperback under the title *Rudy Vallée Kisses and Tells* (Canoga Park, Calif.: Major Books, 1976).

86. Luc Lacourcière, "Oral Tradition: New England and French Canada," in *French in New England, Acadia, and Quebec,* pp. 93–113; Julien Olivier, *D'la Boucane: Une Introduction au folklore franco-américain de la Nouvelle-Angleterre* (Cambridge, Mass.: NADC, 1979); Dupont, "Culture populaire," pp. 47–60; Lane, "Franco-American Folk Traditions."

87. Dion-Lévesque, *Silhouettes,* pp. 476–80; Armand Capistran, "Adélard Lambert (1867–1946): Folkloriste, bibliophile," *BSHFA* (1954), 70–75; Lane, "Franco-American Folk Traditions," pp. 140–45, 219, n. 1. Marius Barbeau, *Roundelays/Dansons à la ronde,* National Museum of Canada Bulletin, no. 151 (Ottawa: National Museum of Canada, 1958), p. 96, attributes most of the dances in this volume to Lambert.

88. Lane, "Franco-American Folk Traditions," pp. 15–16, 145–48, 514–32, 540–43, 549–61, *passim.*

89. Eusèbe Viau and J.-Ernest Philie, *Chants populaires des Franco-Américains,* 13th ed., 12 vols. (Woonsocket, R.I.: Union Saint-Jean-Baptiste d'Amérique, 1960). See also Eusèbe Viau, *Vieux Cantiques et hymnes religieuses* (Woonsocket, R.I.: Union Saint-Jean-Baptiste d'Amérique, 1931). See Lane, "Franco-American Folk Traditions," pp. 383–84.

90. Father Charles-Emile Gadbois, *La Bonne Chanson: Les 100 plus belles chansons* (La Prairie, Quebec: Editions Culturelles, 1937). See Lane, "Franco-American Folk Traditions," p. 383.

91. Lane, pp. 156–166, 440–446.

92. The shows at Montreal were called "Veillées du Bon Vieux Temps."

93. Lane, "Franco-American Folk Traditions," pp. 166–73, 178, n. 68.

Chapter 4. Pages from a Family History

1. This chapter is based in part on genealogical research carried out over several years in various archives and public record offices. It is a pleasure to acknowledge here the initial encouragement and guidance provided to me in this field by Father Clarence J. d'Entremont, by a distant cousin, Pierre Brault of L'Acadie, Quebec, and by a former student of mine at Penn State, Albert H. Ledoux. The best manual for beginners is Julien Olivier, *Souches et racines: Une introduction à la généalogie pour les jeunes Franco-Américains* (Bedford, N.H.: NMDC, 1981). See also Michel Langlois, *Cherchons nos ancêtres* (Quebec City: Québec Science Editeur, 1980); and *Guide des sources généalogiques au Canada* (Ottawa: Ministère des Approvisionnements et Service Canada, 1983).

2. "Colonization of Canada" and "Recruitment of Colonists" are based in part on

Trudel, *Initiation à la Nouvelle-France*. The English translation of this work is entitled *Introduction to New France* (Toronto and Montreal: Holt, Rinehart, and Winston of Canada, 1968).

3. Geneviève Massignon, *Les Parlers français d'Acadie: Enquête linguistique* (Paris: Klincksieck, 1962), 1:41–75; Andrew H. Clark, *Acadia: The Geography of Early Nova Scotia to 1760* (Madison: University of Wisconsin Press, 1968).

4. Trudel, *Introduction to New France*, p. 133.

5. Silvio Dumas, *Les Filles du roi en Nouvelle-France: Etude historique avec répertoire biographique*, Cahiers d'histoire, no. 24 (Quebec City: Société Historique de Québec, 1972).

6. Raymond Douville and Jacques-Donat Casanova, *La Vie quotidienne en Nouvelle-France: Le Canada, de Champlain à Montcalm* (Paris: Hachette, 1964), p. 37.

7. Georges Duby and Robert Mandrou, *Histoire de la civilisation française*, nouvelle édition (Paris: Librairie Armand Colin, 1962), 1: 247–48; 2: 15, 44, 100. The English translation of this work is entitled *A History of French Civilization* (New York: Random House, 1964).

8. Boris Porchnev, *Les Soulèvements populaires en France de 1623 à 1648*, Ecole Pratique des Hautes Etudes, 6th Section, Centre de Recherches Historiques, Oeuvres Etrangères, no. 4 (Paris: S.E.V.P.E.N., 1963).

9. Fernand Braudel, *The Structures of Everyday Life: The Limits of the Possible*, vol. 1 of *Civilization and Capitalism: 15th–18th Century*, trans. Siân Reynolds (New York: Harper & Row, 1981), pp. 54–56. In the original French this work is entitled *Les Structures du quotidien: Le possible et l'impossible* (Paris: Librairie Armand Colin, 1979).

10. Douville and Casanova, *Vie quotidienne*, pp. 18–24.

11. Marc Venard, *Bourgeois et paysans au XVIIe siècle: Recherche sur le rôle des bourgeois parisiens dans la vie agricole au sud de Paris au XVIIe siècle*, Ecole Pratique des Hautes Etudes, 6th Section, Centre de Recherches Historiques, Hommes et la terre, no. 3 (Paris: S.E.V.P.E.N., 1957).

12. Massignon, *Parlers français*, 1: 36–38; Claude Massé, "A propos du Bulletin no. 31 (juillet-septembre 1972)," *Bulletin de l'Association pour l'histoire de Belle-Ile-en-Mer* 10, no. 38 (1973), 5–6. Dr. Massé, a surgeon and professor at the Université de Bordeaux II, has reservations about this identification (also expressed in a letter to the author dated 10 October 1983). See, however, Bona Arsenault, *Histoire et généalogie des Acadiens* (Montreal: Leméac, 1978), 2: 466–67.

13. At Loudun in 1634 Father Urbain Grandier was burned at the stake for witchcraft, giving rise to much controversy. See Robert Mandrou, *Magistrats et sorciers en France au XVIIe siècle: Une analyse de psychologie historique* (Paris: Editions du Seuil, 1980), pp. 210–19, 264–82. (The witch trials in Salem, Massachusetts, occurred in 1692.)

14. Geneviève Massignon, "La Seigneurie de Charles de Menou d'Aulnay, Gouverneur de l'Acadie, 1635–1650," *Revue d'Histoire de l'Amérique Française* 16 (1963), 469–501.

15. Paul Lebel, *Les Noms de personnes*, Que sais-je?, no. 235 (Paris: Presses Universitaires de France, 1949), p. 58.

16. Auguste H. Longnon, *Les Noms de lieu de la France: Leur origine, leur signification, leurs transformations* (Paris: Champion, 1920–29), p. 256, nos. 1054, 1056.

17. This name is first attested in 1469 as Berault, then Brault (never, as in the Michelin map no. 69, Braux). Letter to the author, 21 September 1979, from F. Villard, director of the Archives de la Vienne.

18. Marcel Delafosse, "La Rochelle et le Canada au XVIIe siècle," *Revue d'Histoire de l'Amérique Française* 4 (1951), 469–511; idem, "La Rochelle et le Canada," in *Mémoire d'une Amérique: La Rochelle 1980* (La Rochelle: Imprimerie Rochelaise, 1980), pp. 23–25.

19. G. Debien, "Engagés pour le Canada au XVIIe siècle vus de La Rochelle," *Revue d'Histoire de l'Amérique Française* 6 (1952), 177–220.

20. Jean Boudriot, "A propos du tableau de J. Vernet Le Port de La Rochelle," in *Mémoire d'une Amérique*, pp. 32–35; *Une Année d'acquisitions remarquables 1982* (La Rochelle: Bibliothèque Municipale de La Rochelle, 1983), items 14 and 15 ("The Expulsion of the Huguenots from La Rochelle" and "The Flight of the Huguenots from La Rochelle," November 1666; engravings by Jan Luyken, 1649–1712).

21. *Musée du Nouveau Monde, Hôtel Fleuriau, La Rochelle, 14 Mai 1982* (La Rochelle: Imprimerie Rochelaise, 1982).

22. Jean Merrien, *La Vie quotidienne des marins au temps du Roi-Soleil* (Paris: Hachette, 1964). This reference is the source for much of what follows in this section. See also Gilles Proulx, *Entre France et Nouvelle-France* (La Prairie, Quebec: Editions Marcel Broquet, 1984).

23. Eric Reith, "Les navires rochelais de la fin du XVIIe siècle à travers les 'Desseins des différentes manières de vaisseaux que l'on voit dans les havres, ports et rivières depuis Nantes jusqu'à Bayonne qui servent au commerce des sujets de Sa Majesté 1679,'" in *Mémoire d'une Amérique*, pp. 18–43. The pinnace in question is said to be used by merchants in trade with "les Isles de l'Amérique et Canada." A replica of the Grande Hermine, Jacques Cartier's flagship in 1535–36, is anchored at the mouth of the Lairet River in Cartier-Brébeuf National Park, Quebec City. Guided tours are conducted by Parks Canada.

24. Samuel Eliot Morison, *Samuel de Champlain: Father of New France* (Boston: Little, Brown and Co., 1972), p. 233; see also Proulx, *France et Nouvelle France*, pp. 55–91.

25. Clark, *Acadia*, p. 100. Cf. Massignon, *Parlers français*, 1: 20, who gives the population as 300 to 400. On the sentimental view of early Acadia ("Mythique Acadie"), see Hautecoeur, *L'Acadie du discours*, pp. 68–76.

26. Clark, *Acadia*, pp. 107–8.

27. Ibid., pp. 111–12, 121, and n. 15.

28. The document is reproduced in Massignon, *Parlers français*, 2: 946–947.

29. His spouse is listed as a widow in the census taken that year. Photographic copy in the Centre d'Etudes Acadiennes, Moncton, New Brunswick.

30. Photographic copy of the 1714 census and microfilm of the register of Saint-Jean-Baptiste parish, Port Royal, 1702–55, in the Centre d'Etudes Acadiennes.

31. Clark, *Acadia*, pp. 139, 141, 148–51.

32. Photographic copy of the 1701 census in the Centre d'Etudes Acadiennes; for entry in the parish register, see above, n. 30.

33. Clark, *Acadia*, pp. 148–51, 214–17 (map, p. 209).

34. John Winslow, *Journal of Colonel John Winslow of the Provincial Troops, while Engaged in Removing the Acadian French Inhabitants from Grand Pré, and Neighbouring Settlements, in the Autumn of the Year 1755*, Collections of the Nova Scotia Historical Society, no. 4 (Halifax, Nova Scotia: William MacNabb, 1885), pp. 114–23. Original in the library of the Massachusetts Historical Society, Boston.

35. A listing of families in the Village des Brault is found on a loose sheet preserved with the original of Winslow's Journal (see n. 34). Heads of families are given as follows: Amand Brault; Joseph Brault; Joseph Brault, fils; Paul Brault; Pierre Brault; Pierre Brault, fils; Olivier Daigle; Olivier Daigle, fils; Simon Daigle,

fils; Etienne Deroy; Etienne Deroy, fils; Alexis Hébert, fils; Joseph Hébert; Manuel Hébert; Pierre Hébert; Simon Hébert, fils; Simon Pitre; Charles Richard, fils; Germain Richard; and Pierre Richard, fils. The entries for this village in Winslow (p. 116) are garbled and incomplete (the name Brault appears as Brune).

36. Clark, *Acadia*, pp. 238–42.
37. Ibid., p. 186.
38. Ibid., pp. 186–95. On Father Jean-Louis Le Loutre, a guerrilla leader against the English in Acadia, see pp. 193–94, 221, 222, 334.
39. Ibid., pp. 271–74; Bona Arsenault, *Louisbourg, 1713–1758* (Quebec City: Conseil de la Vie Française en Amérique, 1971).
40. George A. Rawlyk, *Nova Scotia's Massachusetts: A Study of Massachusetts–Nova Scotia Relations, 1630 to 1784* (Montreal and London: McGill–Queen's University Press, 1973), p. 193; Clark, *Acadia*, p. 362.
41. The Seven Years' War, the European phase of this conflict, broke out in 1756.
42. What follows is based on Winslow, *Journal;* Bona Arsenault, *L'Acadie des Ancêtres* (Quebec City: Conseil de la Vie Française en Amérique, 1955); and Rawlyk, *Nova Scotia's Massachusetts.* Much controversy swirls around this subject, of course; see N. E. S. Griffiths, *The Acadian Deportation: Deliberate Perfidy or Cruel Necessity?* Issues in Canadian History (Toronto: Copp Clark, 1969). On the significance of this event in the development of Acadian ideology, see Hautecoeur, *L'Acadie du discours*, pp. 77–80.
43. Clark, *Acadia*, p. 350.
44. Arsenault, *Acadie*, p. 282; Rawlyk, *Nova Scotia's Massachusetts*, p. 211.
45. See, however, n. 35 above.
46. Winslow, *Journal*, p. 166.
47. Manning Hawthorne and Henry Wadsworth Longfellow Dana, *The Origin and Development of Longfellow's "Evangeline"* (Portland, Maine: Anthoensen Press, 1949).
48. Ibid., p. 41, n. 74.
49. Ernest Martin, *L'Evangéline de Longfellow et la suite merveilleuse d'un poème* (Paris: Hachette, 1936); Hawthorne and Dana, *Longfellow's "Evangeline,"* p. 41.
50. Arsenault, *Acadie*, p. 303. LeBlanc, "Migrations acadiennes," p. 153, provides different figures for 1763:

Massachusetts	1,043
Maryland	810
Connecticut	666
Pennsylvania	383
South Carolina	280
Georgia	185
New York	249
Total	3,616

51. Arsenault, *Acadie*, pp. 308–11; Waddell, "Louisiane," p. 197.
52. This section is based on R. G. Lowe, "Massachusetts and the Acadians," *William and Mary Quarterly*, 3d series, 25, no. 2 (1968), 212–29; and Pierre Belliveau, *French Neutrals in Massachusetts: The Story of Acadians Rounded Up by Soldiers from Massachusetts and Their Captivity in the Bay Province, 1755–1766* (Boston: Kirk S. Giffen, 1972). See also Ronald Boucher: "Acadian Research in New England Archives and Libraries: A Student Viewpoint—The Acadians in Massachusetts," in *French in New England, Acadia, and Quebec*, pp. 67–73.

53. Massachusetts Archives (Boston), vols. 23 and 24. On this unpublished material, see Boucher, "Acadian Research."
54. Belliveau, *French Neutrals*, p. 253, citing John Adams; Rawlyk, *Nova Scotia's Massachusetts*, p. 213.
55. Lowe, "Massachusetts," p. 216; Belliveau, *French Neutrals*, p. 91.
56. Belliveau, *French Neutrals*, p. 113.
57. Massachusetts Archives, vol. 23, no. 338.
58. Ibid., vol. 23, no. 609.
59. On this family, see Arsenault, *Acadie*, p. 160.
60. Massachusetts Archives, vol. 23, nos. 607–8.
61. Ibid., vol. 23, no. 213; vol. 24, nos. 211, 383.
62. Ibid., vol. 24, nos. 388, 390, 487.
63. Ibid., vol. 24, no. 509.
64. On Louis Robichaud and his descendants, see Belliveau, *French Neutrals*, pp. 192–99; Father Clarence J. d'Entremont, "The Acadians in New England," in *French in New England, Acadia, and Quebec*, pp. 26–27; and Albert H. Ledoux, "An Acadian Minuteman," *Fleur de Lys* 1, no. 2 (1979), 40–42.
65. Arsenault, *Acadie*, pp. 306–7; Pierre Brault, *L'Acadie et son église* (Saint-Jean-sur-Richelieu, Quebec: Editions Mille Roches, 1977), p. 23; idem, *Histoire de L'Acadie du Haut-Richelieu* (Saint-Jean-sur-Richelieu, Quebec: Editions Mille Roches, 1982), pp. 38–39.
66. Jean-Claude Vernex, "Espace et appartenance: L'exemple des Acadiens au Nouveau-Brunswick," in *Continent perdu*, pp. 163–80.
67. Arsenault, *Acadie*, pp. 332–47.
68. Father S.-A. Moreau, *Histoire de L'Acadie, Province de Québec* (Montreal, 1908), pp. 46, 161. For descendants, see Albert H. Ledoux, *Les Mariages acadiens du Québec: L'Acadie (St-Jean) et la vallée du Richelieu* (State College, Pa.: Albert H. Ledoux, 1978), pp. 40, 58, 59; the latter page has the author's line of direct descent.
69. Father Moreau, *Histoire de L'Acadie*; Brault, *Histoire de L'Acadie*.
70. E. R. Adair and E. S. Wardlesworth, "The Parish and Church of L'Acadie," *Canadian Historical Association Report* (1933), 59–73; Brault, *L'Acadie et son église*.
71. Father Moreau, *Histoire de L'Acadie*, p. 161; copy of L'Acadie parish registry in the Prothonotary's Office, Superior Court, District of Iberville, St. John, Quebec. For Amand's second marriage, see Benoît Pontbriand, *Mariages de L'Acadie (1785) et Saint-Luc (1801), Comté Saint-Jean*, Publication no. 65 (Quebec City: Benoît Pontbriand, 1970), p. 28.
72. The bibliography on French-Canadian attitudes toward and involvement in the American Revolution is extensive. The essential points are covered in Rumilly, *Histoire des Franco-Américains*, pp. 10–11, 12, 13; and Wade, *French Canadians*, vol. 1, chap. 2. See also Corinne Rocheleau-Rouleau, "Une incroyable et véridique histoire: L'affaire Cazeau, 1776–1893," *BSHFA* (1946–47), 3–31; Jean-Jacques Lefebvre, "Les Canadiens [-Français] et la Révolution américaine," *BSHFA* (1946–47), 50–76 (bibliography, pp. 67–71); P. A. Lajoie, "Vlan!" *BSHFA* (1956), 156–58; Richard Ouellet and Jean-Pierre Therrien, eds., *L'Invasion par les Bastonnois: Journal de M. Sanguinet*, Civilisation du Québec, no. 14 (Quebec City: Ministère des Affaires Culturelles, 1975).
73. Arsenault, *Histoire et généalogie des Acadiens*, 3: 1129; Ledoux, *Mariages acadiens*, p. 59; and copy of L'Acadie parish registry, St. John, Quebec.
74. Copy of L'Acadie parish registry, St. John, Quebec.

75. Father Moreau, *Histoire de L'Acadie,* p. 135; Lessard and Vilandré, *Maison traditionnelle,* p. 145 (photograph); Brault, *Histoire de L'Acadie,* pp. 236–37 (photograph).
76. Gauthier-Larouche, *Evolution,* p. 234.
77. I am indebted to Pierre Brault of L'Acadie, Quebec, for a copy of Julien Brault's baptismal record preserved in the parish registry at L'Acadie; for the marriage, see Benoît Pontbriand, *Mariages du Comté de Napierville,* Publication no. 95 (Quebec City: Benoît Pontbriand, 1973), p. 75.
78. Copy of St. Cyprien (Napierville) parish registry, St. John, Quebec; see also Canadian census reports for 1851 and 1861, Napierville, St. Cyprien.
79. United States manuscript census schedule of population, Enfield, Connecticut, 1870.
80. The concern became Bigelow-Hartford in 1914, then, in 1929, Bigelow-Sanford Carpet Company, the largest such business in the United States. See John S. Ewing and Nancy P. Norton, *Broadlooms and Businessmen: A History of the Bigelow-Sanford Carpet Company,* Harvard Studies in Business History, no. 17 (Cambridge, Mass.: Harvard University Press, 1955). The Thompsonville plant shut down in 1971.
81. Town of Enfield, Connecticut, Manuscript Record of Births, Marriages, and Deaths, 1852–66; Saint Patrick's (Thompsonville) parish registry. Arthur Baribault, *Histoire et statistiques des Canadiens-français du Connecticut, 1885–1898* (Worcester, Mass.: Imprimerie de L'Opinion Publique, 1899), p. 355, lists one physician, Dr. H. J. Varneau, and the following individuals as "Canado-Américains bien connus" in Thompsonville: Jos. Manceau, A. Lemay, Louis Robillard, J. Plamondon, J. Lagrange, and J. Hamel.
82. Léon Kemner, "Les Franco-Américains du Connecticut," *Revue Franco-Américaine* (1908), 209–211, citing a report by Dr. C. J. Leclaire. Thompsonville's Franco-American population in that year is listed as 1,100 (p. 210).
83. Saint Patrick's (Thompsonville) parish registry; United States manuscript census schedule of population, Enfield, Connecticut, 1880. Julien and his family are listed in the Canadian census report for 1871 (Napierville).
84. Copy of Saint-Bernard-de-Lacolle parish registry, St. John, Quebec; see also Father Irénée Jetté et al., *Mariages du Comté de Saint-Jean (1828–1950),* Publication no. 97 (Quebec City: Benoît Pontbriand, 1974), p. 86.
85. Saint Patrick's (Thompsonville) parish registry; copy of Saint-Bernard-de-Lacolle parish registry, St. John, Quebec.
86. Charles Rostaing, *Les Noms de lieux,* Que sais-je? no. 176 (Paris: Presses Universitaires de France, 1948), p. 6; Jean Poirier, "Le toponyme Lacolle et son dérivé anglais Cole," *Revue de Géographie de Montréal* 25 (1971), 163–67.
87. Harris, *Seigneurial System,* back endpaper (government of Montreal, seigneurie no. 49).
88. Father Jules Romme, *Saint-Bernard-de-Lacolle: Centenaire de l'église paroissiale* (Saint-Jean-sur-Richelieu, 1965), [p. 6].
89. Mario Fillion, *Le Blockhaus de Lacolle: Histoire et architecture,* Retrouvailles, no. 11 (Quebec City: Ministère des Affaires Culturelles, 1983), p. 3.
90. Father Romme, *Saint-Bernard-de-Lacolle,* [p. 18]; idem, *Lacolle* (1973), pp. 3–5. The present building was constructed in 1928 (pp. 5–6).
91. Information provided by Albert H. Ledoux; cf. Father Moreau, *Histoire de L'Acadie,* p. 30; Brault, *Histoire de L'Acadie,* p. 30.
92. Pontbriand, *Mariages du Comté de Napierville,* p. 365.
93. St. Valentin (Stottsville) parish registry: (Pierre) Alexis; Méville Marcel (Aimé's tombstone is in the cemetery of Notre-Dame-du-Mont-Carmel parish, Lacolle).

94. Ministère des Affaires Culturelles, Macro-Inventaire, Code 4222-55-01-P. The *Cahier de terrain, Rapport synthèse,* and *Analyse du paysage architectural* on Lacolle were prepared by Louise Desautels and Marcel Gauthier in 1980, 1981, and 1982, respectively. Rue St. Bernard (Van Vliet) is described in the Analyse, pp. 6–8.

95. Information derived from personnel records of the Amoskeag Manufacturing Company maintained in the library of the Manchester Historic Association,, Manchester, New Hampshire.

96. Réal G. Boivin and Robert G. Boivin, *Répertoire des mariages, Ste-Marie, Manchester, New Hampshire, 1880–1973* (Manchester, N.H.: Réal G. Boivin and Robert G. Boivin, 1974), p. 28.

97. Saint Mary (Manchester, New Hampshire) parish registry; Office of the City Clerk, Manchester, New Hampshire; copy of Notre-Dame-du-Mont-Carmel (Lacolle, Quebec) parish registry, St. John, Quebec.

98. Boivin and Boivin, *Répertoire des mariages,* p. 28.

99. Copy of Notre-Dame-du-Mont-Carmel parish registry, St. John, Quebec.

100. Route recommended by the Automobilist Legal Association.

101. Father Romme, *Lacolle,* p. 15.

102. James F. Looby, "Ex-Factory Hand Here May Become Saint," *Hartford* [Connecticut] *Daily Courant,* 12 December 1937; Lachance, *Frère André.* On Franco-American devotion to Brother André, see Anctil, "Aspects of Class Ideology," pp. 254–60. Anctil, pp. 260–63, also discusses the Franco-American stigmatic Marie-Rose Ferron (1902–36) of Woonsocket, Rhode Island.

103. On various pilgrimage sites and traditions in Quebec, see Pierre Boglioni and Benoît Lacroix, eds., *Les Pèlerinages au Québec,* Travaux du Laboratoire d'Histoire Religieuse de l'Université Laval, no. 4 (Quebec City: Presses de l'Université Laval, 1981).

104. Ernst Halberstadt was born in Budingen, Germany, in 1910. Records of the commissions by the Works Progress Administration (WPA) are maintained by the National Archives and Records Service in Washington, D.C. See Karal A. Marling, *Wall-to-Wall America: A Cultural History of Post-Office Murals in the Great Depression* (Minneapolis: University of Minnesota Press, 1982). Material concerning Halberstadt's mural is found in the Civil Archives Division, file nos. 132 (proposal form), 133 (box 45), 134 (box 149), and 136 (box 200).

105. *Jubilé paroissial, Saint-Georges, 1893–1943* (Chicopee Falls, Mass., 1943). On early pressure by Franco-Americans in Chicopee Falls to found a church separate from Assumption parish in Chicopee, see Father Hamon, *Canadiens-français,* pp. 299–301.

106. A list of alumni from 1932 to 1947 is provided in *Association des anciens élèves de l'Ecole Saint-Georges, Chicopee Falls, Massachusetts: Première réunion, 12, 15, 16 novembre 1947* (1947).

107. *Courrier-Sud* (Nicolet, Quebec), 5 September 1972. The community was founded at St. Grégoire, Quebec, in 1853; the transfer of the mother house to Nicolet occurred in 1872; see *Courrier-Sud;* especially, Sister Marie-Immaculée, "Monseigneur Joseph-Calixte Marquis et les Soeurs de l'Assomption de la Sainte Vierge," in *La Société Canadienne de l'Histoire de l'Eglise Catholique: Rapport, 1943–1944* (Hull, Quebec: Imprimerie Leclerc, 1944), pp. 89–111. I am indebted to my former teacher at Saint George's School, Sister Jeanne Beliveau, for this information.

108. *Meeting Tomorrow's Challenge Today: The Chicopee Falls Urban Renewal Plan (Mass. R-111) Chicopee, Massachusetts* (1969).

109. "Souvenir des noces d'argent," pp. 50–54.
110. Ibid., pp. 54–58.
111. "Tarawa: A Study in Courage," in Hanson W. Baldwin, *Battles Lost and Won: Great Campaigns of World War II* (New York: Harper & Row, 1966), pp. 236–55 (quote by Spruance, pp. 254–55).
112. Obituary by Rolland Fleury in *BSHFA* (1966), 42–45.
113. Obituary in the *Springfield* [Massachusetts] *Union,* 31 May 1953; *BSHFA* (1955), 133.
114. Possibly an anglicization of Asselin.
115. Father Guillaume J. Morin, *La Paroisse de l'Immaculée Conception de Fitchburg, Massachusetts: Un cinquantenaire, 1886–1936* (Fitchburg, Mass.: Imprimerie de La Liberté, 1936), p. 121.
116. Ibid., p. 129.
117. Vénérande Douville-Veillet, *Souvenirs du Rapide-Nord, 1: Au temps de ma jeunesse,* Collection "Notre Passé," no. 6 (Trois-Rivières: Editions du Bien Public, 1973), p. 8 (photograph).
118. Monsignor Albert Tessier, *Petite Histoire de notre petit poisson des chenaux,* Collection "Notre Passé," no. 13 (Trois-Rivières: Editions du Bien Public, 1975).
119. Raymond Douville, *Les Premiers Seigneurs et colons de Sainte-Anne de la Pérade (1667–1681)* (Trois-Rivières: Editions du Bien Public, 1946).
120. André Vachon, *Madeleine de Verchères,* Collection "Notre Passé," no. 21 (Trois-Rivières: Editions du Bien Public, 1978).
121. Douville-Veillet, *Souvenirs d'une institutrice;* idem, *Souvenirs du Rapide-Nord, 1: Au temps de ma jeunesse;* idem, *Souvenirs du Rapide-Nord, 2: Les occupations familiales,* Collection "Notre Passé," no. 7 (Trois-Rivières: Editions du Bien Public, 1973).
122. Cathy's grandfather George Simonich is the author of an untitled, unpublished, 208-page memoir, written about 1945, that contains many shrewd observations about ethnic (including Franco-American) politics in Chicopee, Massachusetts. Born in Drasici, Yugoslavia, in 1873, he emigrated to the United States in 1889, settled in Chicopee in 1904, and served one term as alderman, from 1934 to 1935.
123. *Album-souvenir: L'Acadie 1782–1982* (1982); Pierre Brault, *Les Fêtes de L'Acadie du Haut-Richelieu, 1782–1982* (Saint-Jean-sur-Richelieu, Quebec: Editions Mille Roches, 1983).

Chapter 5. The Franco-Americans Today

1. Léon F. Bouvier, "La stratification sociale du groupe ethnique canadien-français aux Etats-Unis," *Recherches Sociographiques* 5 (1964), 371–79, tables 2, 3, 5; English trans. by Suzanne A. Hatfield in *FAO* 4: 117–22.
2. Bouvier, *FAO* 4: 118.
3. Madeleine Giguère, "The Franco-Americans: Occupational Profiles," in *Quebec and Acadian Diaspora in North America,* pp. 65–76, table 3.
4. Marcel Bellemare, "Social Networks in an Inner-City Neighborhood: Woonsocket, Rhode Island," Ph.D. diss., Catholic University of America, 1974, pp. 84 (referring to table 3) and 87 (table 7).
5. Madeleine Giguère, "Social and Economic Profile of French and English Mother Tongue Persons: Maine 1970," *FAO* 4: 148. "In 1970 in New England, the occupational patterns of those of French mother tongue were only marginally different from those of English mother tongue. The hypothesis that ethnicity is related to occupations must be reformulated. A promising hypothesis is that those Franco-Americans who are French-dominant are more

likely to retain their blue-collar occupations than those who are English-dominant" (p. 74).

6. Ashley W. Doane, Jr., *Occupational and Educational Patterns for New Hampshire's Franco-Americans* (Manchester, N.H.: Civil Liberties Union, 1979), pp. 24–37 (education), 37–60 (employment).

7. Peter Woolfson, *Franco-Americans in Vermont: A Civil Rights Perspective* (Washington, D.C.: Government Printing Office, 1983), chap. 4.

8. Cf. Doane, *Occupational and Educational Patterns*, pp. 64–65. "In the search for explanation, however, it would be entirely inappropriate to emphasize either cultural factors or the dissimilarities between Franco-American culture and the dominant culture. . . . Indeed, influences seemingly rooted in Franco-American culture, such as low aspiration levels or a low valuation of education, are more likely products of existing social and economic relationships. If explanations are to be sought, then, more fertile ground lies in those institutional mechanisms which perpetuate inequality. In a system where inequality is rooted in the social structure, division along class and ethnic lines becomes inevitable."

9. Ibid., p. 7. "Use of mother tongue as a means of identification is limited, however, by the steadily increasing number of Franco-Americans for whom the French language is no longer a factor. . . . the French mother tongue group may only comprise one-half of the total Franco-American population."

10. Walker, *Politics and Ethnocentrism*, chaps. 5–6; idem, "La politique présidentielle des Franco-Américains: Quelques observations sommaires," in *Les Conférences de l'Institut Franco-Américain de Bowdoin College*, ed. Gerard J. Brault (Brunswick, Maine, 1961), pp. 64–72. On Franco-American politics in general, see Josaphat-T. Benoît, "Attitudes des Franco-Américain en politique," in *Conferences de l'Institut Franco-Americain*, pp. 7–19; Louis-Israël Martel, "Franco-Americans and American Political Life," in *The 20th-Century Franco-American*, pp. 24–26; Paul M. Paré, "Franco-Americans in Politics: An Absence Worth Noticing," *InformACTION* 1, no. 3 (1982), 2.

11. Former United States senator Edmund S. Muskie, speaking at Lewiston, Maine, June 25, 1970.

12. Maurice R. Gravel, born in Springfield, Massachusetts, served one term as United States senator from Alaska, 1968–75.

13. Rumilly, *Histoire des Franco-Américains*, pp. 85–86, 174, 322; Walker, *Politics and Ethnocentrism*, p. 24.

14. For a perceptive analysis of Bérubé's poor showing, see Paré, "Franco-Americans in Politics," p. 2.

15. For the association's charter, see FAROG *Forum* 7, no. 8 (1980), 16.

16. Walter J. Landry, "Linguistic Liberation—Now is the Time," FAROG *Forum* 8, no. 1 (1980), 1, 18; see also 8, no. 4 (1980), 10; 9, nos. 7–8 (1982), 4; 10, no. 3 (1982), 11. I am grateful to Landry for providing me with a copy of the report (and related material) he made as chairman of the U.S. Language Policy Conference held at Chicago, Illinois, in January 1983. (The report was entered in the *Congressional Record* by the Honorable Paul Simon on 3 March 1983.) I am also indebted to Armand B. Chartier for giving me a copy of "A Franco-American Position Paper Developed by the Association of Franco-Americans" (ten typewritten pages). Chartier, former president of the AFA and one of the foremost authorities on Franco-American and Quebecois literature, is a member of the Department of Languages at the University of Rhode Island.

17. Marcus L. Hansen, "The Third Generation in America," *Commentary* 14 (1952), 492–500; Vander Zanden, *American Minority Relations*, pp. 290–92.

18. On the concept, see Vander Zanden, *American Minority Relations*, pp. 290–92; Madeleine Giguère, "Commentary," in *Les Franco-Américains: La promesse du*

passé, les réalités du présent. Colloque 1976 (Cambridge: Mass.: NADC, 1976), pp. 73–75.

19. Giguère, "Commentary," p. 74.
20. *L'Union,* July 1972, p. 7; 81, no. 4 (1981), 1; and especially, 85, no. 1 (1985), 11. For other symbols of Franco-American organizations, see the advertisements in the back pages of *BSHFA* from 1955 through 1959.
21. *L'Unité* 7, no. 6 (1983), 1; *InformACTION* 2, no. 2 (1983), 1. The flag was designed by Attorney Robert L. Couturier of Lewiston, Maine; *Inform-ACTION* 3, no. 1 (1984), 8. The placing of one device (a fleur-de-lis) upon another (a star) of the same color may strike some as inelegant; it also violates one of the fundamental rules of heraldry. For another criticism (i.e., alleged insensitivity to Acadian symbolism), see J. P. Gallant, "New Franco-American Flag Said to Exclude One Million U.S. Francos," *FAROG Forum* 12, no. 5 (1985), 1, 19. The existence, since 1972, of a flag representing the Francophones of Louisiana (i.e., the twenty-two parishes known as Acadiana) complicates matters further. For background information about the flags of Acadia (1884), Quebec (1948), and seven other Francophone groups in Canada and the United States including the Franco-Americans, see the program of the *VIIIᵉ Rencontre francophone de Québec, du 21 au 25 juin 1985, Université Laval* (Quebec City: Imprimerie Sociale Limitée, 1985). This meeting was sponsored by the Secrétariat Permanent des Peuples Francophones in Quebec City.
22. Chartier, "Franco-American Literature of New England," pp. 195–204; Richard S. Sorrell, "L'histoire en tant que roman, le roman en tant qu'histoire: Le roman ethnique franco-américain de langue anglaise," *CIF* 1, 72–76; cf. Chartier, "Pour une problématique," pp. 87–88.
23. Dion-Lévesque, *Silhouettes,* pp. 432–36. The bibliography on Kerouac is extensive; see Richard S. Sorrell, "Jack Kerouac and Grace Metalious as Franco-Americans: A Well-Kept Secret?" *Canado-Américain* 7, no. 1 (1981), 15–16.
24. On the memory of Kerouac in Lowell, Massachusetts, see Lane, "Franco-American Folk Traditions," pp. 358–65. The most detailed study of Kerouac's use of French is an unpublished paper read by Edward Harvey (Kenyon College, Gambier, Ohio) at the Kentucky Foreign Language Conference, April 22–24, 1965.
25. On Kerouac's mysticism, see Anctil, "Aspects of Class Ideology," pp. 266–67.
26. William Plummer, "Jack Kerouac: The Beat Goes On," *New York Times Magazine,* 30 December 1979; William E. Schmidt, "Beat Generation Elders Meet to Praise Kerouac," *New York Times,* 30 July 1982. *Moody Street Irregulars: A Jack Kerouac Newsletter,* a clearinghouse for information about the author, has been appearing since 1977. The editor is Joy Walsh, P.O. Box 157, Clarence Center, New York 14032. *Visions of Kerouac* by Martin Duberman was performed off-off-Broadway at the Lion Theater in 1976.
27. The club is sponsored by the Secrétariat Permanent des Peuples Francophones, Quebec City.
28. Emily Toth, *Inside Peyton Place: The Life of Grace Metalious* (Garden City, N.Y.: Doubleday, 1981).
29. Grace Metalious, *Peyton Place* (New York: Julian Messner, 1956). In May 1985, NBC broadcast "Peyton Place: The Next Generation."
30. Grace Metalious, *The Tight White Collar* (New York: Julian Messner, 1960); idem, *No Adam in Eden* (New York: Trident Press, 1963). See Emily Toth, "Fatherless and Dispossessed: Grace Metalious as a French-Canadian Writer," *Journal of Popular Culture* 15, no. 3 (1981), 28–38.
31. Robert Cormier, *Now and at the Hour* (New York: Coward-McCann, 1960); idem, *A Little Raw on Monday Mornings* (New York: Sheed and Ward, 1963); idem, *Take Me Where the Good Times Are* (New York: Macmillan, 1965); idem,

8 plus 1 (New York: Pantheon, 1980). See Sorrell, "Histoire en tant que roman," pp. 70–72.

32. Gérard Robichaud, *Papa Martel: A Novel in Ten Parts* (Garden City, N.Y.: Doubleday, 1961); idem, *The Apple of His Eye* (Garden City, N.Y.: Doubleday, 1965). See Chartier, "Franco-American Literature of New England," pp. 204–7; idem, "Pour une problématique," p. 88; Sorrell, "Histoire en tant que roman," pp. 66–68.

33. David Plante, *The Family* (New York: Farrar, Straus, and Giroux, 1978); idem, *The Country* (New York: Atheneum, 1981); idem, *The Woods* (New York: Atheneum, 1984); also published as *The Francoeur Novels: The Family, The Woods, The Country* (New York: Dutton/Obelisk, 1984); idem, *The Foreigner* (New York: Atheneum, 1984); idem, *Difficult Women: A Memoir of Three* (New York: Atheneum, 1983).

34. Robert B. Perreault, *L'Héritage* (Durham, N.H.: NMDC, 1983); idem, *One Piece in the Great American Mosaic;* idem, *Joseph Laferrière: Ecrivain lowellois* (Bedford, N.H.: NMDC, 1982). See also idem, "Les Franco-Américains," *Magazine OVO* (Montreal), 12, no. 46 (1982), 14–17 (photographs; others, pp. 18–45); and above, chap. 2, n. 92.

35. Biographies and selections in Chassé, *Anthologie,* pp. 245–58, 266–71; for selections, see also François Roche, *Les Francos de la Nouvelle-Angleterre: Anthologie franco-américaine (XIXᵉ et XXᵉ siècles)* (Paris: Belles Lettres [for LARC Centre d'Action Culturelle, Le Creusot], 1981), pp. 35–40, 189–93. Dubé's poetry appeared in his *Un Mot de chez nous* (Fall River, Mass.: NADC, 1976); *La Broderie inachevée* (Cambridge, Mass.: NADC, 1976); and *Le Nuage de ma pensée* (Bedford, N.H.: NMDC, 1981).

36. Grégoire Chabot, *Un Jacques Cartier errant: Pièce en un acte* (Fall River, Mass.: NADC, 1977). For an earlier performance, see *Les Franco-Américains: La promesse du passé, les réalités du présent. Colloque 1976,* pp. 172–73 (also other skits by Chabot and Paul M. Paré, pp. 148–70). *Criquette: Huit pièces pour jeunes gens,* by Julien Olivier and Normand C. Dubé (Cambridge, Mass.: NADC, 1980), is a collection of eight short plays designed to acquaint students with Franco-American customs, daily living, and folklore.

37. Elizabeth Aubé, "Les écrivains au travail," *L'Unité* 6, no. 8 (1982), 7; idem, "Premier rassemblement des artistes franco-américains," *L'Unité* 6, no. 9 (1982), 6; *FAROG Forum* 10, no. 2 (1982), 8; Gérard Robichaud, "Report from the 'Rassemblement,'" *FAROG Forum* 10, no. 3 (1982), 12; Paul Grégoire, "Participants Review Rassemblement '84," *FAROG Forum* 12, no. 1 (1984), 1, 4; Julien Olivier, "Le rassemblement des artistes," *FAROG Forum* 12, no. 1 (1984), 1, 5; Lorraine L. Chalifoux, "My First Rassemblement," *FAROG Forum* 12, no. 1 (1984), 8. The fourth gathering, organized by Eloise A. Brière, was held at Albany, New York, July 5–7, 1985. See announcement in *FAROG Forum* 12, no. 5 (1985), 4.

38. Beaupré, *Enclume et couteau.*

39. Julien Olivier, *Pas de gêne: L'histoire d'Omer Marcoux, violoneux et sculpteur* (Bedford, N.H.: NMDC, 1981).

40. *Canado-Américain,* 7, no. 2 (1981), 14. See also Olivier, *D'la Boucane,* pp. 35–53.

41. Olivier, *D'la Boucane,* pp. 36, 141; and especially, Roger Paradis, *Gilbert O. Roy: Peintre populaire de la vallée Saint-Jean* (Cambridge, Mass.: NADC, 1979).

42. *FAROG Forum* 8, no. 3 (1980), 9. Lilianne Labbé's long-playing record, "Un Canadien errant: French Music in the North American Tradition" (Philo Forerunner Series 41069) was produced by Philo Records, The Barn, North Ferrisburg, Vermont 05473, in 1980. Her accompanist on the guitar and piano was Don Hinkley.

43. See, for example, *L'Union* 78, no. 3 (1978), 10 (campaign by the Comité de Vie Franco-Américaine).
44. Jacques Casanova and Armour Landry, *America's French Heritage* (Quebec City: Documentation Française and the Quebec Official Publisher, 1976); Claire Quintal, *Sur les Traces de l'héritage français en Nouvelle-Angleterre: Boston* (Fall River, Mass.: NADC, 1977), includes teacher's guide; Benoît Brouillette, *La Pénétration du continent américain par les Canadiens français, 1763–1846: Traitants, explorateurs, missionnaires,* 2d ed. (Montreal: Fides, 1979). One notable exception is Sister Eugena Poulin and Claire Quintal, *The French Experience in North America: An Activities Packet* (Rochambeau Education Committee and Rhode Island Heritage Commission, 1981). This mimeographed volume devotes considerable space to the Franco-Americans. It is available from the Union Saint-Jean-Baptiste d'Amérique, Woonsocket, Rhode Island.
45. Solomon, *Ancestors and Immigrants,* pp. 161–63; Peter Woolfson and André Sénécal, *The French in Vermont: Some Current Views,* Occasional Paper, no. 6 (Burlington, Vt.: Center for Research on Vermont, University of Vermont, 1983), pp. 24, n. 12; 35.
46. Bernard C. Rosen, "Race, Ethnicity, and the Achievement Syndrome," *American Sociological Review* 24 (1959), 47–60, tables 2, 3, 4; reprinted in *FAO* 4: 84–101; summary in Vander Zanden, *American Minority Relations,* pp. 187–89.
47. Patricia Wood Adrian, "Ethnic and Social Class Differences in Role Strain and Mechanisms Adjustment," Ph.D. diss., Catholic University of America, 1970.
48. Peter Woolfson, "Publish or Parish: A Study of Differences in Acculturation of Franco-American Schoolchildren," *Man in the Northeast,* no. 8 (1974), 65–75; reprinted in *FAO* 4: 6–18. See also idem, "Le Franco-Américain campagnard dans l'état du Vermont," *CIF* 2, 81–98; idem, *Franco-Americans in Vermont;* and idem (with Sénécal), *French in Vermont,* pp. 1–26.
49. Vinay, "Français en Amérique du Nord," p. 422.
50. Haden, "French Dialect Geography in North America," pp. 423–24, 426.
51. Jean-Paul Vinay, "Bout de la langue ou fond de la gorge?" *French Review* 23 (1950), 489–98; J.-D. Gendron, *Tendances phonétiques du français parlé au Canada* (Paris: Klincksieck, and Quebec City: Presses de l'Université Laval, 1966), p. 135; Juneau, *Contribution à l'histoire de la prononciation française au Québec,* pp. 159–77; Jean Clermont and Henriette Jonas Cedergren, "Les R de ma mère sont perdus dans l'air," in *Le Français parlé: Etudes sociolinguistiques,* ed. Pierrette Thibault, Current Inquiry into Language and Linguistics, no. 30 (Edmonton, Alberta: Linguistics Research, Inc., 1978), pp. 13–28.
52. Orkin, *Speaking Canadian French,* pp. 16–17, 105–8; Edith Bédard, *La Qualité de la langue: Survol des préoccupations récentes* (Quebec City: Gouvernement du Québec, 1979).
53. The best introduction to New England French is Robert A. Fischer, "La langue franco-américaine," *CIF* 1, 37–60 (bibliography, pp. 56–60). More recent studies include Henry Kelley, "Phonological Variation in a New England Speech Community," Ph.D. diss., Cornell University, 1980; Irène Mailhot-Bernard, "Facteurs sociaux et leur rapport avec le choix de vocabulaire chez les Franco-Américains de Lewiston, Maine," *CIF* 2, 99–122; Louise Péloquin-Faré, *L'Identité culturelle: Les Franco-Américains de la Nouvelle-Angleterre* (Paris: Centre de Recherche et d'Etude pour la Diffusion du Français, 1983); idem, "Les attitudes des Franco-Américains envers la langue française," *French Review* 57 (1984), 657–68.
54. Nancy Lee Schweda, "Goal-Oriented Interaction in the French-Speaking St. John River Valley of Northern Maine: A Sociolinguistic and Ethnomethodological Study of the Use of Verbal Strategies by Professional Community

Members Living in a Bilingual Society with a French-English Speech Continuum," Ph.D. diss., Georgetown University, 1979, chap. 6.

55. Haugen, *Bilingualism in the Americas,* chap. 4. Locke, *Pronunciation,* p. 23, n. 1. Maurice Cagnon, "New England Franco-American Terms Used in Spoken English," *Romance Notes* 11 (1969), 1–7.

56. Gerard J. Brault, "Kinesics and the Classroom: Some Typical French Gestures," *French Review* 36 (1963), 382, n. 23.

57. Sister Maris Stella, "Pronunciation of New England French."

58. Gerard J. Brault, "Some Misconceptions about Teaching American Ethnic Children Their Mother Tongue," *Modern Language Journal* 48 (1964), 67–71.

59. Robert Muckley, "After Childhood, What Then? An Overview of Ethnic Language Retention (Elret) Programs in the United States," *Revista Interamericana Review* 2 (1972), 53–67.

60. See, for example, Andy Rooney, "You Have to Know the Lingo," *Philadelphia Inquirer,* 18 November 1979; idem, "Language of the U.S. Is English," *Philadelphia Inquirer,* 8 March 1981; S. I. Hayakawa, "English by Law," *New York Times,* 1 October 1981; "In Plain English," *New York Times* (editorial), 10 October 1981.

61. Calvin J. Veltman, *The Retention of Minority Languages in the United States* (Washington, D.C.: Department of Education, National Center for Education Statistics, 1980), p. 79. This publication includes the proceedings of a seminar on Veltman's study held at the National Center for Education Statistics on May 13, 1980 (summary of reactions, pp. viii–ix).

62. Ibid., p. viii.

63. Calvin J. Veltman, "Le sort de la francophonie aux Etats-Unis," *Cahiers Québécois de Démographie* 9, no. 1 (1980), 48–54, tables 1–3, graphs 1–2.

64. Vander Zanden, *American Minority Relations,* pp. 282–84.

65. According to T. J. Samuel, *The Migration of Canadian-Born between Canada and the United States of America 1955 to 1968* (Ottawa: Department of Manpower and Immigration, 1970), the average annual rate of emigration of Canadian-born to the United States during this period was about 29,000; however an estimated 10,000 per year returned to Canada, reducing the annual rate of net migration to about 19,000 (pp. 4–5). Connecticut, Maine, Massachusetts, New Hampshire, and Rhode Island continued to attract many Canadian-born but, except for Connecticut, at a lower rate than before World War II (p. 26). There has also been a decline in the percentage of French Canadians in this migration, from 33.6 percent in 1900 to 24.0 percent in 1950 (p. 26).

66. *Pour Résoudre la Crise de l'enseignement du français dans nos écoles paroissiales: Actes du IXe Congrès des Franco-Américains tenu à Providence, Rhode Island, les 11 et 12 novembre 1966* (Comité de Vie Franco-Américaine, 1967). The principal address was by Dr. Robert A. Beaudoin, "Quelques détails et observations sur ce qui se passe au New Hampshire depuis ie Congrès d'octobre 1965," pp. 13–21.

67. Nathan Glazer and Daniel P. Moynihan, eds., *Ethnicity: Theory and Experience* (Cambridge, Mass.: Harvard University Press, 1975); Howard F. Stein and Robert F. Hill, *The Ethnic Imperative: Examining the New White Ethnic Movement* (University Park, Pa.: Pennsylvania State University Press, 1977).

68. Alex Haley, *Roots* (Garden City, N.Y.: Doubleday, 1976).

69. Gerard J. Brault, "The Special NDEA Institute at Bowdoin College for French Teachers of Canadian Descent," *PMLA* 77 (1962), 2, n. 10; Gerard J. Brault et al., *Cours de langue française destiné aux jeunes Franco-Américains ("Bowdoin Materials")* (Manchester, N.H.: Association des Professeurs Franco-Américains, 1965), p. i.

70. Brault, "Special NDEA Institute," pp. 1–5. For two early overviews of the group's efforts to maintain its mother tongue, see Hervé B. Lemaire, "Franco-American Efforts on Behalf of the French Language in New England," in *Language Loyalty in the United States*, ed. Joshua A. Fishman, Janua Linguarum, Series Maior, no. 21 (The Hague: Mouton, 1966), pp. 253–79; and Donald G. Dugas, "Franco-American Language Maintenance Efforts in New England: Realities and Issues," in *Identité culturelle et Francophonie dans les Amériques*, Travaux du Centre International de Recherche sur le Bilinguisme (Quebec City: Presses de l'Université Laval, 1976), 1: 44–57.

71. Brault, "Teaching American Ethnic Children Their Mother Tongue."

72. Brault et al., *Cours de langue française*.

73. "NMDC Books Now Available from University of New Hampshire," *Inform-ACTION* 1, no. 4 (1982), 1; "Fermeture du NMDC," p. 6.

74. An excellent overview is provided by Phyllis L. Jacobson, "The Social Context of Franco-American Schooling in New England," *French Review* 57 (1984), 641–56. For specific programs, see also Kathy Holmes, "Nous autres à Berkshire," *FAROG Forum* 8, no. 5 (1981), 6; Elizabeth A. Gosselin, "Bonjour Bébittes!" 9, no. 4 (1981), 7; Paula B. Johnson, "La fin d'un commencement," *FAROG Forum* 9, no. 7/8 (1982), 8. With ESEA support, Normand C. Dubé wrote a series of textbooks for the St. John Valley Bilingual Education Program. The case for bilingual education is succinctly made by Paul M. Paré, "Les Franco-Américains et le recensement 1980: La législation sur le bilinguisme et le biculturalisme," *FAROG Forum* 8, no. 3 (1980), 7, 11; no. 4, p. 12. See also Cynthia Parsons, "Bilingualism—Are You For It or Against It?" *FAROG Forum* 8, no. 1 (1980), 15 (reprint of an article in the *Christian Science Monitor*, 9 June 1980).

75. Schweda, "Goal-Oriented Interaction," pp. 175–78.

76. Frank Anshen, "Tongues and Myths," *New York Times*, 19 October 1980; Fred M. Hechinger, "A Humane Look at Bilingual Schooling," *New York Times*, 31 May 1983.

77. Georges-Henri Dagneau, "L'histoire doucement tragique des Franco-Américains," *FAROG Forum* 8, no. 1 (1980), 2; "Bien des mots ont changé (Les Franco-Américains de la Nouvelle-Angleterre)," *FAROG Forum* 8, no. 1 (1980), 18.

78. An excellent teacher's manual was also produced with NEH funds: Stanley L. Freeman, Jr., and Raymond J. Pelletier, *Initiating Franco-American Studies: A Handbook for Teachers* (Orono, Maine: University of Maine, 1981).

79. *BSHFA* (1968), 85–86.

80. Richard R. Santerre, "Historique de la célébration de la fête Saint-Jean-Baptiste à Lowell, Massachusetts, 1868 à 1968," in *Centenaire de la Fête Saint-Jean-Baptiste* (Lowell, Mass.: Imprimerie L'Etoile, 1968), pp. 1–36.

81. "La Saint-Jean," *L'Union* 82, no. 4 (1982), 11.

82. *L'Union* 77, no. 2 (1977), 3, 12; no. 3, p. 5; no. 4, p. 4. Franco-American ethnic fairs are listed by ActFANE in periodic press releases; for 1985, see *L'Union* 85, no. 2 (1985), 14; and *FAROG Forum* 12, no. 8 (1985), 10.

83. U.S. Department of Housing and Urban Development, *The Urban Fair: How Cities Celebrate Themselves* (Washington, D.C.: Government Printing Office, 1981). Cf. Marie Chicoine, Louise de Grosbois, and Francine Poirier, *Lâchés lousses: Les fêtes populaires au Québec, en Acadie et en Louisiane* (Montmagny, Quebec: VLB Editeur, 1982). Neither source mentions Franco-American fairs. A list of festivals in Quebec is available from the Société des Festivals Populaires du Québec, 1415, rue Jarry est, Montreal, Quebec.

84. Roger Lacerte, "Le Festival Franco-Américain 1978: Un demi-succès," *FAROG Forum* 6, no. 2 (1978), 1–2; Yvon Labbé, "Yvongélisations," 8, no. 1 (1980),

23 (see also "Thumbs Down," back page); Liz Cash, "D'ici au mois prochain, salut," no. 2, p. 7 (the last three items concern Old Town, Maine's fair); 9, no. 1 (1981), back page ("Thumbs Up"); 10, no. 1 (1982), 12 (full-page sketch), 13; 10, no. 3 (1982), 14 (letter to the editor from Clifton Beamis about Old Town's fair).

85. Georges-E. Lapalme, "Le Ministère des Affaires Culturelles de la Province de Québec," in *Les Conférences de l'Institut Franco-Américain de Bowdoin College, deuxième série,* ed. Gerard J. Brault (Brunswick, Maine, 1962), pp. 28–52; W. Donald Moisan, "The Present State of Relations between Franco-Americans and French Canada," in *The 20th-Century Franco-American,* pp. 43–46; Robert Couturier, "The Franco-Americans and French Canada (Quebec)," in ibid., pp. 47–50; Armand B. Chartier, "Franco-Americans and Quebec: Linkages and Potential in the Northeast," in *Problems and Opportunities in U.S.-Quebec Relations,* ed. Alfred O. Hess, Jr., and Marcel Daneau (Boulder, Colo.: Westview Press, 1984), pp. 151–68.

86. See, for example, "Ministre québécois en Nouvelle-Angleterre," *L'Unité* 6, no. 3 (1982), 1. On the Secrétariat Permanent des Peuples Francophones, established by the Quebec government in 1981 to facilitate contacts between Francophone groups in North America, see *L'Union* 83, no. 3 (1983), 5. The bureau's telephone number in Quebec City is (418) 692-5177.

87. The Quebec Government Bureau was first established in Boston in 1969. It is now the Quebec Government Delegation in New England. See "Quebec in New England," *FAROG Forum* 9, no. 3 (1981), 5.

88. The genesis of this agency is described in a press release published in *Canado-Américain* 6, no. 2 (1980), 24–25; see also Paul M. Paré, "Premier rapport annuel du Secrétariat de l'ActFANE, juillet '81 à septembre '82," *InformACTION* 1, no. 4 (1982), 2, 5–7. In 1984 ActFANE held nine regional seminars for Franco-American leaders. See *InformACTION* 4, no. 1 (1985), 2. ActFANE has its office at 52 Concord Street (Association Canado-Américaine building), Manchester, New Hampshire. The telephone number is (603) 622-2883.

89. "Visite du vice-premier ministre du Québec, M. Jacques-Yvan Morin," *Canado-Américain* 8, no. 1 (1982), 31.

90. "New England Pact for Quebec Power," *New York Times,* 22 March 1983.

91. "New England Utilities to Buy Canada Power," *New York Times,* 20 June 1984; "Quebec in New England," p. 5.

92. Pierre Tourangeau, "Un ancien consul US ne prisait guère l'aide venant du Québec," *Soleil* (Quebec City), 26 March 1984.

93. Chinlund, "Renaissance of French Pride," p. 40. According to *Journal de Lowell* 8, no. 2 (1982), 7, the Comité pour l'Avancement du Français en Amérique (CAFA) is an organization fostering the Quebec independence movement. Officers are listed as Dr. Georges-André Lussier of Woonsocket, Rhode Island, president; Roger Lacerte of Manchester, New Hampshire, secretary-treasurer; Denis Baillargeon of Putnam, Connecticut; and Father Richard Brunelle, of Worcester, Massachusetts.

94. Edward B. Ham, "The Library of the Union Saint-Jean-Baptiste d'Amérique," *Franco-American Review* 1 (1937), 271–75; see also *L'Union* 77, no. 4 (1977), 2, 8; 82, no. 1 (1982), 5.

95. *L'Union* 75, no. 1 (1975), 1; 82, no. 5 (1982), 11.

96. "Project FAITH Will Help Retarded," *L'Union* 77, no. 1 (1977), 1.

97. "New Slate Takes Over at ACA," *FAROG Forum* 8, no. 1 (1980), 11.

98. *Canado-Américain* 6, no. 3 (1980), 3, 16–17.

99. Edward B. Ham, "The Library of the Association Canado-Américaine," *MLN* 52 (1937), 542–44; *Canado-Américain* 8, no. 2 (1982), 8.

100. Monsignor Adrien Verrette, "Inventaire des Archives franco-américaines," *BSHFA* (1951), 29–31; idem, "Rapport de la Commission des Archives," *BSHFA* (1956), 225; idem, "L'Institut Franco-Américain," *BSHFA* (1957), 160–63; idem, *BSHFA* (1962), 10 ("la bibliothèque nationale des Franco-Américains").

101. See, for example, *La Femme francophone aux Etats-Unis,* Actes du 16ᵉ Congrès biennal de la Fédération Féminine Franco-Américaine de la Nouvelle-Angleterre tenu au Collège Rivier, Nashua, New Hampshire, les 27, 28, et 29 avril 1984 (Manchester, N.H.: Imprimerie Lafayette, 1984).

102. Information derived from mimeographed documents entitled *Guide du nouveau Richelieu* and *Annuaire Richelieu—District 9 et Floride et Louisiane— 1983* received from Richelieu International Associate General Director Jean-Marie Beaulieu, 18 February 1983. The organization's policy toward women members was confirmed in a telephone conversation with General Director G. Mathias Page, 11 July 1985.

103. *Les Franco-Américains: La promesse du passé, les réalités du présent.* Publication of these proceedings was made possible by grants from the NMDC and the French government.

104. *CIF* 1–5. On Claire Quintal, see Chassé, *Anthologie,* p. 206; Roche, *Francos,* pp. 12, 13, 41, 211; *L'Union* 80, no. 4 (1980), 8; and the *Bulletin de la Fédération Féminine Franco-Américaine* 21 (1981), 14.

105. "Souscription en faveur de l'Institut Français," *L'Union* 82, no. 6 (1982), 14.

106. FAROG has also published a useful eighty-seven-page illustrated pamphlet entitled *A Franco-American Resources Inventory of New England* (FARINE) (1979). The project was funded by grants from the government of Quebec, the Boston University Bilingual Resources and Training Center, and the NMDC.

107. On the program called FACET (Franco-American Children's Education Team) to teach children at the Governor Baxter School for the Deaf in Portland, Maine, see *FAROG Forum* 8, no. 5 (1981), 3; "Student Testifies in Favor of St. John Baptist Day," 10, no. 5 (1983), 2 (testimony of a hearing-impaired student in Augusta); also Renelle Côté, "Merci à tous," pp. 2, 15; "On vous présente Renelle Côté," no. 7/8, p. 24.

108. *FAROG Forum* 10, no. 1 (1982), 11 (full-page sketch); no. 4, p. 6; "Une boîte à chansons," no. 5, pp. 9–10; 12, no. 7 (1985), 3; no. 8, pp. 1, 12–13, 23.

109. For a list of French-language radio broadcasts in New England, prepared by ActFANE, see *L'Union* 84, no. 4 (1984), 15.

110. *Le Journal de Lowell,* founded in 1974, appears monthly; see profile in *L'Unité* 6, no. 3 (1982), 4. *L'Unité,* established in 1976 as the official organ of L'Unité Franco-Américaine of Lewiston, Maine, also appeared monthly until April 1984. Whether it will resume publication is unclear.

111. La Librairie Populaire is located at 18 Orange Street, Manchester, New Hampshire. The telephone number is (603) 669-3788.

112. Richard L. Fortin, "La Société Généalogique Américaine-Canadienne déménage à l'Association Canado-Américaine," *Canado-Américain* 7, no. 4 (1981), 16–17; "Nouvelle société généalogique," 6, no. 4 (1980), 9; *FAROG Forum* 12, no. 6 (1985), 6. For names and addresses of local and national Franco-American genealogical societies, see *FAROG Forum* 12, no. 8 (1985), 18. See also Father d'Entremont, "Survivance acadienne en Nouvelle-Angleterre," pp. 18–23. The ACGS publishes *The Genealogist* twice yearly.

113. *Je me souviens* is the quarterly publication of the AFGS. On genealogy, see chap. 4, n. 1.

114. Jean Blouin and Jean-Pierre Myette, "Les Francos: Agonie ou renaissance?" *L'Actualité* (Montreal), 7, no. 1 (1983), 33–35; Charles Hillinger, "Maine's Quiet Minority Makes No Waves," *Washington Post,* 16 February 1985.

115. For excellent recommendations about enhancing prospects for Franco-American cultural survival, see Chartier, "Franco-Americans and Quebec," pp. 162–67. I am also indebted to Dean R. Louder, Department of Geography, Laval University, for giving me a copy of his 101-page unpublished report dated December 1984 entitled "La Franco-Américanie, 1968–1984," prepared for Quebec's Ministry of International Relations. Louder interviewed several Franco-American leaders and provides much inside information about present-day Franco-American organizations.

Appendix

1. *20 Ans au service de la culture ça se fête* (Quebec City: Ministère des Affaires Culturelles, 1981); *Les Biens culturels du Québec classés ou reconnus au 1ᵉʳ janvier 1981* (Quebec City: Ministère des Affaires Culturelles, 1981), dossier 50; *Ministère des Affaires Culturelles: Rapport annuel, 1982–1983* (Quebec City: Ministère des Affaires Culturelles, 1983); *Des Actions culturelles pour aujourd'hui: Programme d'action du Ministère des Affaires Culturelles* (Quebec City: Ministère des Affaires Culturelles, 1983).
2. Ministry of Finance, Quebec, to author, 16 April 1984.
3. *Le Macro-Inventaire: Guide explicatif* (Quebec City: Ministère des Affaires Culturelles, 1983). See also the illustrated brochure, *Le Macro-Inventaire: Banque de données sur les biens culturels du Québec* (Quebec City: Ministère des Affaires Culturelles, 1981).
4. Information based on the brochure entitled *La Grande Ferme: Centre d'initiation au patrimoine* (Quebec City: Ministère des Affaires Culturelles, n.d.); mimeographed syllabi; and an on-site visit, 12 April 1984. I am grateful to instructors Marc Fleury and Pierre Gaudin for their hospitality on this occasion.
5. Jean-Claude Dupont, "Le Centre d'Etudes sur la langue, les arts et les traditions populaires des francophones en Amérique du Nord (CELAT), Université Laval (Québec)," in *Quatre Siècles d'identité canadienne* (Montreal: Bellarmin, 1982), pp. 83–96.
6. Information provided by Carole Saulnier, archivist, Archives de Folklore. On small-format holy pictures, see Pierre Lessard, *Les Petites Images dévotes: Leur utilisation traditionnelle au Québec* (Quebec City: Presses de l'Université Laval, 1981).
7. Lise Gauvin and Laurent Mailhot, *Guide culturel du Québec* (Montreal: Boréal Express, 1982), p. 259.
8. Father Anselme Chiasson, "Le Centre d'Etudes Acadiennes de l'Université de Moncton," in *The French in New England, Acadia, and Quebec*, pp. 43–48; *Inventaire général des sources documentaires sur les Acadiens* (Moncton: Editions d'Acadie, 1975), 1: 13–14.

BIBLIOGRAPHY

The best bibliography dealing with Franco-American studies and including critical notes is Pierre Anctil, *A Franco-American Bibliography: New England* (Bedford, N.H.: NMDC, 1979). See also Richard S. Sorrell, "Research Notes: Franco-Americans in New England," *FAO* 4:193–98. The fifteen volumes of *La Vie Franco-Américaine* recorded the many facets of Franco-American life from 1937 to 1952; this labor of love by Monsignor Adrien Verrette was continued by him in the *BSHFA* from 1955 (includes information relative to the years 1953–55) through 1973.

In addition to the surveys by Benoît, Ducharme, Rumilly, and Perreault mentioned in the preface, one may also consult with profit the entry by Elliott R. Barkan, "French Canadians," in *Harvard Encyclopedia of American Ethnic Groups,* ed. Stephan Thernstrom (Cambridge, Mass.: Belknap Press of Harvard University Press, 1980), pp. 388–401.

Useful oral history may be found in Tamara K. Hareven and Randolph Langenbach, *Amoskeag: Life and Work in an American Factory-City* (New York: Pantheon Books, 1968); *Jim: L'histoire de Jim Caron, jeune homme, racontée par lui-même (à 101 ans) telle qu'interprétée par Julien Olivier* (Bedford, N.H.: NMDC, 1977); Dyke Hendrickson, *Quiet Presence: Dramatic, First-Person Accounts—The True Stories of Franco-Americans in New England* (Portland, Maine: Guy Gannett Publishing Co., 1980); Julien Olivier, *Pas de gêne: L'histoire d'Omer Marcoux, violoneux et sculpteur* (Bedford, N.H.: NMDC, 1981); idem, *Prendre le large: Big Jim Cote, pêcheur* (Bedford, N.H.: NMDC, 1981); and C. Stewart Doty, *The First Franco-Americans: New England Life Histories from the Federal Writers' Project, 1938–1939* (Orono, Maine: University of Maine at Orono Press, 1985).

On Canadian studies in the United States, see Richard A. Preston, *The Squat Pyramid: Canadian Studies in the United States, Problems and Prospects,* Duke University Center for International Studies, Occasional Papers Series, no. 9 (Durham, N.C.: Canadian Studies Center, 1980), and *Canadian Studies Activity in the United States: A Profile* (Washington, D.C.: Association for Canadian Studies in the United States, 1983).

The following bibliography lists all publications mentioned in the notes, except for brief, unsigned, newspaper items.

Adair, E. R., and E. S. Wardlesworth. "The Parish and Church of L'Acadie." *Canadian Historical Association Report* (1933), 59–73.
Adrian, Patricia Wood. "Ethnic and Social Class Differences in Role Strain and Mechanisms Adjustment." Ph.D. diss., Catholic University of America, 1970.

L'Aide-mémoire: Répertoire pour la mise en valeur du patrimoine québécois, Version préliminaire. Quebec City: Télé-université, 1979.

Albert, Renaud S., ed. *A Franco-American Overview.* Vol. 1. Cambridge, Mass.: NADC, 1979.

Album-souvenir: L'Acadie 1782–1982. N.p.: n.p., 1982.

Allen, James P. "Catholics in Maine: A Social Geography." Ph.D. diss., Syracuse University, 1970.

Almanach franco-américain et catholique. N.p.: n.p., 1911.

Anctil, Pierre. "Aspects of Class Ideology in a New England Ethnic Minority: The Franco-Americans of Woonsocket, Rhode Island (1865–1929)." Ph.D. diss., New School for Social Research, 1980.

———. "L'attachement à la terre et l'émigration dans certains romans du terroir québécois." *CIF* 2, 61–80.

———. "Un point tournant de l'histoire du Québec: L'épisode des 'Chinese of the Eastern States' de 1881." *Canado-Américain* 7, no. 2 (1981), 17–19.

———. "Vie et Survie: A Portrait of the Franco-American Press." *Société Historique Franco-Américaine,* Cahier no. 1 (1983), 37–41.

Anderson, Elin L. *We Americans: A Study of Cleavage in an American City.* 1937. Reprint. New York: Russell & Russell, 1964.

Une Année d'acquisitions remarquables 1982. La Rochelle: Bibliothèque Municipale de La Rochelle, 1983.

Anshen, Frank. "Tongues and Myths." *New York Times,* 19 October 1980.

Archambault, Albéric A. *Mill Village: A Novel.* Boston: Bruce Humphries, 1943.

Arsenault, Bona. *L'Acadie des Ancêtres.* Quebec City: Conseil de la Vie Française en Amérique, 1955.

———. *Histoire et généalogie des Acadiens.* 6 vols. Montreal: Leméac, 1978.

———. *Louisbourg, 1713–1758.* Quebec City: Conseil de la Vie Française en Amérique, 1971.

Arsenault, Georges. *Courir la Chandeleur.* Moncton, New Brunswick: Editions d'Acadie, 1982.

Arseneault, Jeanne. "La survie du costume traditionnel français en Acadie." In *La Vie quotidienne au Québec,* ed. René Bouchard, pp. 249–52. Montreal: Presses de l'Université du Québec, 1983.

Association des anciens élèves de l'Ecole Saint-Georges, Chicopee Falls, Massachusetts: Première réunion, 12, 15, 16 novembre 1947. N.p.: n.p., 1947.

Aubé, Elizabeth. "Les écrivains au travail." *L'Unité* 6, no. 8 (1982), 7.

———. "Premier rassemblement des artistes franco-américains." *L'Unité* 6, no. 9 (1982), 6.

Audet, Louis-Philippe, and Armand Gauthier. *Le Système scolaire du Québec: Organisation et fonctionnement.* Montreal: Beauchemin, 1967.

"Autour des conférences Podea-Wade." *BSHFA* (1950), 68–71.

Ayotte, Alfred, and Victor Tremblay. *L'Aventure Louis Hémon.* Montreal: Fides, 1974.

Baldwin, Hanson W. *Battles Lost and Won: Great Campaigns of World War II.* New York: Harper & Row, 1966.

Barbeau, Marius. *Ceinture fléchée.* 1945. Reprint. Montreal: Editions l'Etincelle, 1973.

———. *Jongleur Songs of Old Quebec.* New Brunswick, N.J.: Rutgers University Press, 1962.

———. *Roundelays/Dansons à la ronde.* National Museum of Canada Bulletin, no. 151. Ottawa: National Museum of Canada, 1958.

Baribault, Arthur. *Histoire et statistiques des Canadiens-français du Connecticut, 1885–1898.* Worcester, Mass.: Imprimerie de L'Opinion Publique, 1899.

Beamis, Clifton. Letter to the editor. *FAROG Forum* 10, no. 3 (1982), 14.

Beaudoin, Robert A. "Le nom 'Franco-Américain.'" *BSHFA* (1967), 151–54.

———. "Quelques détails et observations sur ce qui se passe au New Hampshire depuis le Congrès d'octobre 1965." In *Pour Résoudre la Crise de l'enseignement du français dans nos écoles paroissiales: Actes du IXe Congrès des Franco-Américains tenu à Providence, Rhode Island, les 11 et 12 novembre 1966,* pp. 13–21. Comité de Vie Franco-Américaine, 1967.

Beaugrand, Honoré. *Jeanne la fileuse: Episode de l'émigration franco-canadienne aux Etats-Unis.* Fall River, Mass., 1878. Reprinted with an introduction by Roger Le Moine. Montreal: Fides, 1980. Also reprinted under the title *Jeanne la fileuse.* Bedford, N.H.: NMDC, 1980.

Beaulieu, Mireille. *Les Meilleures Récettes du Québec.* Montreal: La Presse, 1974.

Beaulieu, Oda, ed. "Actes du Symposium tenu à l'occasion de l'ouverture des Archives Wilfrid Beaulieu–*Le Travailleur* sous les auspices conjoints de la Société Historique Franco-Américaine et de la Bibliothèque Publique de Boston." *Société Historique Franco-Américaine,* Cahier no. 1 (1983).

Beaupré, Normand R. *L'Enclume et le couteau: The Life and Work of Adelard Coté, Folk Artist.* Manchester, N.H.: NMDC, 1982.

Bédard, Edith. *La Qualité de la langue: Survol des préoccupations récentes.* Quebec City: Gouvernement du Québec, 1979.

Bédier, Joseph. *Les Fabliaux: Etudes de littérature populaire et d'histoire littéraire du moyen âge.* 6th ed. Bibliothèque de l'Ecole des Hautes Etudes, 4th section, Sciences Historiques et Philologiques, no. 98. Paris: Champion, 1964.

Bélanger, Albert A., ed. *Guide officiel des Franco-Américains 1938.* Providence, R.I.: Guide Franco-Américain, Inc., 1938.

Belisle, Alexandre. *Histoire de la presse franco-américaine.* Worcester, Mass.: L'Opinion Publique, 1911.

Bellemare, Marcel. "Social Networks in an Inner-City Neighborhood: Woonsocket, Rhode Island." Ph.D. diss., Catholic University of America, 1974.

Belliveau, Pierre. *French Neutrals in Massachusetts: The Story of Acadians Rounded Up by Soldiers from Massachusetts and Their Captivity in the Bay Province, 1755–1766.* Boston: Kirk S. Giffen, 1972.

Benoît, Josaphat-T. *L'Ame franco-américaine.* Montreal: Editions Albert Lévesque, 1935.

———. "Attitudes des Franco-Américains en politique." In *Les Conférences de l'Institut Franco-Américain de Bowdoin College,* ed. Gerard J. Brault, pp. 64–72. Brunswick, Maine, 1961.

———. "Les Franco-Américains en politique." In *Guide officiel franco-américain,* pp. 157–64. Woonsocket, R.I.: Sansouci, 1946.

Bernard, Jean-Paul. *Les Rouges: Libéralisme, nationalisme et anticléricalisme au milieu du XIXe siècle.* Montreal: Presses de l'Université du Québec, 1971.

Bessette, Gérard, Lucien Geslin, and Charles Parent. *Histoire de la littérature canadienne-française par les textes.* Centre Educatif et Culturel, 1968.

"Bicentenaire Ticonderoga-Carillon (1758–1958)." *BSHFA* (1958), 11–46.

"Bien des mots ont changé (Les Franco-Américains de la Nouvelle-Angleterre)." *FAROG Forum* 8, no. 1 (1980), 18.

Les Biens culturels du Québec classés ou reconnus au 1er janvier 1981. Dossier 50. Quebec City: Ministère des Affaires Culturelles, 1981.

Blouin, Jean, and Jean-Pierre Myette. "Les Francos: Agonie ou renaissance?" *L'Actualité* (Montreal), 7, no. 1 (1983), 33–35.

B.M.L. "Portée et signification historique du personnage de 'Jeanne' dans le roman d'Honoré Beaugrand, 'Jeanne la fileuse.'" *L'Unité* 6, no. 7 (1982), 5, 8, 9.

Boglioni, Pierre, and Benoît Lacroix, eds. *Les Pèlerinages au Québec.* Travaux du

Laboratoire d'Histoire Religieuse de l'Université Laval, no. 4. Quebec City: Presses de l'Université Laval, 1981.

Boivin, Réal G, and Robert G. Boivin. *Répertoire des mariages, Ste-Marie, Manchester, New Hampshire, 1880–1973.* Manchester, N.H.: Réal G. Boivin and Robert G. Boivin, 1974.

Bolduc, Claire. "Les Franco-Américains eux-mêmes, veulent-ils d'une renaissance culturelle?" In *Les Franco-Américains: La promesse du passé, les réalités du présent. Colloque 1976,* pp. 99–106. Cambridge, Mass.: NADC, 1976.

Bonier, Marie-Louise. *Débuts de la colonie franco-américaine de Woonsocket, Rhode Island.* 1920. Reprint. Montreal, and Manchester, N.H.: Editions du 45ᵉ Parallèle Nord, 1981.

Bouchard, René, ed. *Culture populaire et littératures au Québec.* Stanford French and Italian Studies, no. 19. Saratoga, Calif.: Anma Libri and Co., 1980.

———, ed. *La Vie quotidienne au Québec.* Montreal: Presses de l'Université du Québec, 1983.

Boucher, Ronald. "Acadian Research in New England Archives and Libraries: A Student Viewpoint—The Acadians in Massachusetts." In *The French in New England, Acadia, and Quebec,* pp. 67–73. Orono, Maine: New England–Atlantic Provinces–Quebec Center, 1973.

Boudreau, Marielle, and Melvin Gallant. *La Cuisine traditionnelle en Acadie.* Moncton, New Brunswick: Editions d'Acadie, 1975.

Boudriot, Jean. "A propos du tableau de J. Vernet Le Port de La Rochelle." In *Mémoire d'une Amérique: La Rochelle 1980,* pp. 32–35. La Rochelle: Imprimerie Rochelaise, 1980.

Bourget, Benoît. "Gens du pays . . . c'est à mon tour!" *FAROG Forum* 10, no. 7/8 (1983), 22.

Bourret, Françoise, and Lucie Lavigne. *Le Fléché.* Montreal: Editions de l'Homme, 1973.

Bouvier, Léon F. "La stratification sociale du groupe ethnique canadien-français aux Etats-Unis." *Recherches Sociographiques* 5 (1964), 371–79. English trans. by Suzanne A. Hatfield in *FAO* 4: 117–22.

Braudel, Fernand. *The Structures of Everyday Life: The Limits of the Possible.* Vol. 1 of *Civilization and Capitalism: 15th–18th Century.* Trans. Siân Reynolds. New York: Harper & Row, 1981.

Brault, Gerard J. "Etat présent des études sur les centres franco-américains de la Nouvelle-Angleterre." *CIF* 1, 9–25.

———. "Le français en Nouvelle-Angleterre." In *Le Français hors de France,* ed. Albert Valdman, pp. 75–91. Paris: Champion, 1979.

———. "Kinesics and the Classroom: Some Typical French Gestures." *French Review* 36 (1963), 374–82.

———. "New England French Culture." *French Review* 45 (1972), 831–37.

———. "Photographs of French-Canadian Children Working in New England Textile Mills by Lewis W. Hine, 1908–1916." *French-Canadian and Acadian Genealogical Review* 8, nos. 3–4 (1980), 131–40.

———. "Some Misconceptions about Teaching American Ethnic Children Their Mother Tongue." *Modern Language Journal* 48 (1964), 67–71.

———. "The Special NDEA Institute at Bowdoin College for French Teachers of Canadian Descent." *PMLA* 77 (1962), 1–5.

———, ed. *Les Conférences de l'Institut Franco-Américain de Bowdoin College.* Brunswick, Maine, 1961.

———, ed. *Les Conférences de l'Institut Franco-Américain de Bowdoin College, deuxième série.* Brunswick, Maine, 1962.

Brault, Gerard J., Alexander Hull, Norman D. Deschenes, Solange Duboff, and Emmanuel Jacquart. *Cours de langue française destiné aux jeunes Franco-Américains ("Bowdoin Materials")*. Manchester, N.H.: Association des Professeurs Franco-Américains, 1965.

Brault, Pierre. *L'Acadie et son église*. Saint-Jean-sur-Richelieu, Quebec: Editions Mille Roches, 1977.

———. *Les Fêtes de L'Acadie du Haut-Richelieu, 1782–1982*. Saint-Jean-sur-Richelieu, Quebec: Editions Mille Roches, 1983.

———. *Histoire de L'Acadie du Haut-Richelieu*. Saint-Jean-sur-Richelieu, Quebec: Editions Mille Roches, 1982.

Brent, Edmund. "Canadian French: A Synthesis." Ph.D. diss., Cornell University, 1971.

Breton, Raymond, and Pierre Savard, eds. *The Quebec and Acadian Diaspora in North America*. Toronto: Multicultural History Society of Ontario, 1982.

Breton, Roland J.-L., and Dean R. Louder. "La géographie linguistique de l'Acadiana, 1970." In *Du Continent perdu à l'archipel retrouvé: Le Québec et l'Amérique française,* Ed. Dean R. Louder and Eric Waddell, pp. 213–34.Quebec City: Presses de l'Université Laval, 1983.

Brouillette, Benoît. *La Pénétration du continent américain par les Canadiens français, 1763–1846: Traitants, explorateurs, missionnaires*. 2d ed. Montreal: Fides, 1979.

Cagnon, Maurice. "The Dialectal Origins of the French-Canadian Lexicon." Ph.D. diss., University of Pennsylvania, 1967.

———. "New England Franco-American Terms Used in Spoken English." *Romance Notes* 11 (1969), 1–7.

Capistran, Armand. "Adélard Lambert (1867–1946): Folkloriste, bibliophile." *BSHFA* (1954), 70–75.

Carpentier, Paul. *La Croix de chemin: Au-delà du signe*. Ottawa: National Museum of Canada, 1981.

Carufel, Hélène de. *Le Lin*. Montreal: Leméac, 1980.

Casanova, Jacques, and Armour Landry. *America's French Heritage*. Quebec City: Documentation Française and the Quebec Official Publisher, 1976.

Cash, Liz. "D'ici au mois prochain, salut." *FAROG Forum* 8, no. 2 (1980), 7.

Centenaire de la Fête Saint-Jean-Baptiste. Lowell, Mass.: Imprimerie L'Etoile, 1968.

Chabot, Grégoire. *Un Jacques Cartier errant: Pièce en un acte*. Fall River, Mass.: NADC, 1977.

———. "Un Noël chabotant." *FAROG Forum* 8, no. 4 (1980), 3.

Chalifoux, Lorraine L. "My First Rassemblement." *FAROG Forum* 12, no. 1 (1984), 8.

Chaput, Donald. "Some Repatriement Dilemmas." *Canadian Historical Review* 49 (1968), 400–412.

Chaput, Sister Hélène. *Mère Marie-du-Rosaire*. Histoire de la Congrégation des Soeurs des SS. NN. de Jésus et de Marie. St. Boniface, Manitoba: Éditions du Blé, 1982.

Charbonneau, Hélène. *L'Albani: Sa carrière artistique et triomphale*. Montreal: Imprimerie Jacques-Cartier, 1938.

Charlebois, Joseph. *La Bêche (The Spade) ou les assimilateurs en action: Album de dessins gais*. Montreal: J. A. Lefebvre, 1911.

Chartier, Armand B. "The Franco-American Literature of New England: A Brief Overview." In *Ethnic Literatures since 1776: The Many Voices of America,* 1 : 207–8. Lubbock, Tex.: Texas Tech University Press, 1978.

———. "Franco-American Literature: The New England Experience." In *Ethnic Perspectives in American Literature: Selected Essays on Their European Contribution,* ed. Robert J. Di Pietro and Edward Ifkovic, pp. 15–42. New York: Modern Language Association of America, 1983.

————. "Franco-Americans and Quebec: Linkages and Potential in the Northeast." In *Problems and Opportunities in U.S.-Quebec Relations,* ed. Alfred O. Hess, Jr., and Marcel Daneau, pp. 151–68. Boulder, Colo.: Westview Press, 1984.

————. *Littérature historique populaire franco-américaine.* Bedford, N.H.: NMDC, 1981.

————. "Pour une problématique de l'histoire littéraire franco-américaine." *CIF* 1, 81–100.

————. "Wilfrid Beaulieu: L'homme et l'oeuvre." *CIF* 4, 50–80.

Chassé, Paul P. *Anthologie de la poésie franco-américaine.* Rhode Island Bicentennial Commission, 1976.

————. *Church.* Franco-American Ethnic Heritage Studies Program. Title IX (ESEA) grant. Worcester, Mass.: Assumption College, 1976.

————. "Les Poètes franco-américains de la Nouvelle-Angleterre, 1875–1925." Ph.D. diss., Laval University, 1968.

————. *La Presse chez les Franco-Américains.* Cambridge, Mass.: NADC, 1979.

Chevalier, Sister Florence M. "The Role of French National Societies in the Sociocultural Evolution of the Franco-Americans of New England from 1860 to the Present: An Analytical Macro-Sociological Case Study in Ethnic Integration Based on Current Social System Models." Ph.D. diss., Catholic University of America, 1972.

Chiasson, Father Anselme. "Le Centre d'Etudes Acadiennes de l'Université de Moncton." In *The French in New England, Acadia, and Quebec,* pp. 43–48. Orono, Maine: New England–Atlantic Provinces–Quebec Center, 1973.

————. "Traditions and Oral Literature in Acadia." In *The Acadians of the Maritimes: Thematic Studies,* ed. Jean Daigle, pp. 477–512. Moncton, New Brunswick: Centre d'Etudes Acadiennes, 1982.

Chicoine, Marie, Louise de Grosbois, and Francine Poirier. *Lâchés lousses: Les fêtes populaires au Québec, en Acadie et en Louisiane.* Montmagny, Quebec: VLB Editeur, 1982.

Chinlund, Chris. "A Renaissance of French Pride." *Boston Globe,* 6 February 1983.

Clark, Andrew H. *Acadia: The Geography of Early Nova Scotia to 1760.* Madison: University of Wisconsin Press, 1968.

Clément, Antoine. "Apothéose de la presse franco-américaine." In *Les Quarante Ans de la Société Historique Franco-Américaine,* pp. 585–90. Boston: Société Historique Franco-Américaine, 1940.

————. "L'oeuvre de la presse franco-américaine dans notre survivance." In *Les Quarante Ans de la Société Historique Franco-Américaine,* pp. 591–96. Boston: Société Historique Franco-Américaine, 1940.

Clermont, Jean, and Henriette Jonas Cedergren. "Les R de ma mère sont perdus dans l'air." In *Le Français parlé: Etudes sociologiques,* ed. Pierrette Thibault, pp. 13–28. Current Inquiry into Language and Linguistics, no. 30. Edmonton, Alberta: Linguistics Research, Inc., 1978.

Coelho, Anthony. "A Row of Nationalities: Life in a Working-Class Community: The Irish, English, and French Canadians of Fall River, Massachusetts, 1850–1890." Ph.D. diss., Brown University, 1980.

Cole, Donald B. *Immigrant City: Lawrence, Massachusetts, 1845–1921.* Chapel Hill: University of North Carolina Press, 1963.

Collège de l'Assomption, 1904–1979. N.p.: n.p., 1980.

Collet, Paulette. *L'Hiver dans le roman canadien-français.* Quebec City: Presses de l'Université Laval, 1965.

Cormier, Robert. *8 plus 1.* New York: Pantheon, 1980.

————. *A Little Raw on Monday Mornings.* New York: Sheed and Ward, 1963.

————. *Now and at the Hour.* New York: Coward-McCann, 1960.

————. *Take Me Where the Good Times Are*. New York: Macmillan, 1965.

Côté, Renelle. "Merci à tous." *FAROG Forum* 10, no. 5 (1983), 2, 15.

Couturier, Robert. "The Franco-Americans and French Canada (Quebec)." In *The 20th-Century Franco-American,* pp. 47–50. Comité de Vie Franco-Américaine, 1976.

Creamer, Daniel, and Charles W. Coulter. *Labor and the Shut-down of the Amoskeag Textile Mills.* 1939. Reprint. New York: Arno and New York Times, 1971.

Croteau, Michèle Paradis. "Le temps de boucherie chez nos ancêtres à St-Edouard de Maskinongé." *Culture et Tradition* 7 (1983), 87–105.

Cusson, Théodore J., Sr. "On va tuer un cochon! Killing a Pig—in Three Acts." *Canado-Américain* 7 (1981), 16–18.

Dagneau, Georges-Henri. "L'histoire doucement tragique des Franco-Américains." *FAROG Forum* 8, no. 1 (1980), 2.

Daigle, Jean, ed. *The Acadians of the Maritimes: Thematic Studies.* Moncton, New Brunswick: Centre d'Etudes Acadiennes, 1982.

Daignault, Elphège-J. *Le Vrai Mouvement sentinelliste en Nouvelle-Angleterre, 1923 – 1929, et l'affaire du Rhode Island.* Montreal: Editions du Zodiaque, 1935.

Daignault, Pierre. *En Place pour un set.* Montreal: Editions de l'Homme, 1964.

Danses et costumes régionaux du Québec. 2 vols. Montreal: Fédération des Loisirs-Danse du Québec, 1977.

Dantin, Louis. *Le Coffret de Crusoé.* Montreal: Albert Lévesque, 1932.

————. *Les Enfances de Fanny.* Montreal: Chantecler, 1951.

D'Arles, Henri. *Laudes.* Paris: Paul Lefebvre, 1925.

Dawson, Nora. *La Vie traditionnelle à Saint-Pierre (Ile d'Orléans).* Quebec City: Presses de l'Université Laval, 1960.

Debien, G. "Engagés pour le Canada au XVIIe siècle vus de La Rochelle." *Revue d'Histoire de l'Amérique Française* 6 (1952), 177–220.

Deffontaines, Pierre. *Le Rang, type de peuplement rural du Canada français.* Quebec City: Presses de l'Université Laval, 1953.

Delafosse, Marcel. "La Rochelle et le Canada." In *Mémoire d'une Amérique: La Rochelle 1980,* pp. 23–25. La Rochelle: Imprimerie Rochelaise, 1980.

————. "La Rochelle et le Canada au XVIIe siècle." *Revue d'Histoire de l'Amérique Française* 4 (1951), 469–511.

D'Entremont, Father Clarence J. "The Acadians in New England." In *The French in New England, Acadia, and Quebec,* pp. 23–42. Orono, Maine: New England–Atlantic Provinces–Quebec Center, 1973.

————. "The Franco-Americans and Louisiana." In *The 20th-Century Franco-American,* pp. 51–65. Comité de Vie Franco-Américaine, 1976.

————. "La survivance acadienne en Nouvelle-Angleterre." *CIF* 5, 8–25.

Des Actions culturelles pour aujourd'hui: Programme d'action du Ministère des Affaires Culturelles. Quebec City: Ministère des Affaires Culturelles, 1983.

Deschamps, Nicole, Raymonde Héroux, and Normand Villeneuve. *Le Mythe de Maria Chapdelaine.* Montreal: Presses de l'Université de Montréal, 1980.

Dion-Lévesque, Rosaire. *Les Oasis.* Rome: Desclée, 1930.

————. *Quête.* Quebec City: Garneau, 1963.

————. *Silhouettes franco-américaines.* Manchester, N.H.: Association Canado-Américaine, 1957.

————. *Vita.* Montreal: Bernard Valiquette, 1939.

————. *Walt Whitman.* Montreal: Elzévirs, 1933.

Di Pietro, Robert J., and Edward Ifkovic, eds. *Ethnic Perspectives in American Literature: Selected Essays on Their European Contribution.* New York: Modern Language Association of America, 1983.

Doane, Ashley W., Jr. *Occupational and Educational Patterns for New Hampshire's Franco-Americans.* Manchester, N.H.: Civil Liberties Union, 1979.

Dorion, Jacques. *Les Ecoles de rang au Québec.* Montreal: Editions de l'Homme, 1979.

Douville, Raymond. *Les Premiers Seigneurs et colons de Sainte-Anne de la Pérade (1667–1681).* Trois-Rivières: Editions du Bien Public, 1946.

Douville, Raymond, and Jacques-Donat Casanova. *La Vie quotidienne en Nouvelle-France: Le Canada, de Champlain à Montcalm.* Paris: Hachette, 1964.

Douville-Veillet, Vénérande. *Souvenirs d'une institutrice de petite école de rang.* Collection "Notre Passé," no. 2. Trois-Rivières: Editions du Bien Public, 1973.

———. *Souvenirs du Rapide-Nord, 1: Au temps de ma jeunesse.* Collection "Notre Passé," no. 6. Trois-Rivières: Editions du Bien Public, 1973.

———. *Souvenirs du Rapide-Nord, 2: Les occupations familiales.* Collection "Notre Passé," no. 7. Trois-Rivières: Editions du Bien Public, 1973.

Doyon-Ferland, Madeleine. "Le costume traditionnel féminin: Documents beaucerons recueillis et présentés." *Archives de Folklore* 1 (1946), 112–20.

———. "Le costume traditionnel féminin (deuxième série): Documents de Charlevoix recueillis et présentés." *Archives de Folklore* 2 (1947), 183–89.

———. *Jeux, rythmes et divertissements traditionnels.* Montreal: Leméac, 1980.

Dubé, Normand C. *La Broderie inachevée.* Cambridge, Mass.: NADC, 1976.

———. "Commentary." *CIF* 1, 61–63.

———. *Un Mot de chez nous.* Fall River, Mass.: NADC, 1976.

———. *Le Nuage de ma pensée.* Bedford, N.H.: NMDC, 1981.

Du Berger, Jean. *Introduction aux études en arts et traditions populaires, première partie: Eléments de bibliographie et choix de textes historiques.* Quebec City: Archives de Folklore, 1973.

Duby, Georges, and Robert Mandrou. *Histoire de la civilisation française.* Nouvelle édition. 2 vols. Paris: Librairie Armand Colin, 1962. English trans., *A History of French Civilization.* New York: Random House, 1964.

Ducharme, Jacques. *The Delusson Family: A Novel.* New York: Funk & Wagnalls, 1939.

———. *The Shadows of the Trees: The Story of French-Canadians in New England.* New York: Harper & Brothers, 1943.

Dufault, Paul. "Notes sur la médecine franco-américaine." *BSHFA* (1943), 98–109.

———. *Sanatorium.* Montreal, 1938. Reprint. Manchester, N.H.: NMDC, 1982.

Dugas, Donald G. "Franco-American Language Maintenance Efforts in New England: Realities and Issues." In *Identité culturelle et Francophonie dans les Amériques,* 1:44–57. Travaux du Centre International de Recherche sur le Bilinguisme. Quebec City: Presses de l'Université Laval, 1976.

Dulong, Gaston. *Bibliographie linguistique du Canada français.* Bibliothèque française et romane. Série E: Langue et littérature françaises au Canada, no. 1. Quebec City: Presses de l'Université Laval, and Paris: Klincksieck, 1966.

———. "Histoire du français en Amérique du Nord." In *Current Trends in Linguistics,* ed. Thomas A. Sebeok, 10:407–21. The Hague and Paris: Mouton, 1973.

Dulong, Gaston, and Gaston Bergeron. *Le Parler populaire du Québec et de ses régions voisines: Atlas linguistique de l'Est du Canada.* 10 vols. Quebec City: Ministère des Communications, 1980.

Dumas, Silvio. *Les Filles du roi en Nouvelle-France: Etude historique avec répertoire biographique.* Cahiers d'histoire, no. 24. Quebec City: Société Historique de Québec, 1972.

Dupont, Jean-Claude. *L'Artisan forgeron.* Quebec City: Presses de l'Université Laval, 1979.

————. "Le Centre d'Etudes sur la langue, les arts et les traditions populaires des francophones en Amérique du Nord (CELAT), Université Laval (Québec)." In *Quatre Siècles d'identité canadienne,* pp. 83–96. Montreal: Bellarmin, 1982.

————. "Culture populaire de l'émigrant québécois, 1850–1920." *CIF* 2, 47–60.

————. *Le Fromage de l'île d'Orléans.* Montreal: Leméac, 1977.

————. *Héritage d'Acadie.* Montreal: Leméac, 1977.

————. *Histoire populaire de l'Acadie.* Montreal: Leméac, 1979.

————. *Le Légendaire de la Beauce.* Montreal: Leméac, 1978.

————. *Le Pain d'habitant.* Montreal: Leméac, 1974.

————. *Le Sucre du pays.* Montreal: Leméac, 1975.

Dupont, Jean-Claude, and Jacques Mathieu. *Les Métiers de cuir.* Quebec City: Presses de l'Université Laval, 1981.

Durocher, Leo. *Nice Guys Finish Last.* New York: Simon and Schuster, 1975.

Duval-Thibault, Anna. *Les Deux Testaments.* Fall River, Mass.: Imprimerie de l'Indépendant, 1888. Reprint. Bedford, N.H.: NMDC, 1979.

Early, Frances H. "French-Canadian Beginnings in an American Community: Lowell, Massachusetts, 1868–1886." Ph.D. diss., Concordia University, 1980.

————. "The Rise and Fall of Félix Albert: Some Reflections on the Aspirations of Habitant Immigrants to Lowell, Massachusetts, in the Late Nineteenth Century." In *The Quebec and Acadian Diaspora in North America,* eds. Raymond Breton and Pierre Savard, pp. 25–38. Toronto: Multicultural History Society of Ontario, 1982.

————. "The Settling-In Process: The Beginnings of Little Canada in Lowell, Massachusetts, in the Late Nineteenth Century." *CIF* 3, 23–43.

Eno, Arthur L. *Les Avocats franco-américains de Lowell, Massachusetts, 1886–1936.* Lowell, Mass.: Eno Printing Company, 1936.

Ewing, John S., and Nancy P. Norton. *Broadlooms and Businessmen: A History of the Bigelow-Sanford Carpet Company.* Harvard Studies in Business History, no. 17. Cambridge, Mass.: Harvard University Press, 1955.

Ezell, Edward C. "An Exclusive Interview with John C. Garand." *Rifle Magazine,* September–October 1970, 14–19, 60.

Falardeau, Jean C. "Les Canadiens français et leur idéologie." In *Canadian Dualism: Studies of French-English Relations,* ed. Mason Wade, pp. 23–31. Toronto: University of Toronto Press, and Quebec City: Presses de l'Université Laval, 1960.

————, ed. *Essais sur le Québec contemporain.* Quebec City: Presses de l'Université Laval, 1953.

La Femme francophone aux Etats-Unis. Actes du 16ᵉ Congrès biennal de la Fédération Féminine Franco-Américaine de la Nouvelle-Angleterre tenu au Collège Rivier, Nashua, New Hampshire, les 27, 28, et 29 avril 1984. Manchester, N.H.: Imprimerie Lafayette, 1984.

Fillion, Mario. *Le Blockhaus de Lacolle: Histoire et architecture.* Retrouvailles, no. 11. Quebec City: Ministère des Affaires Culturelles, 1983.

Fischer, Robert A. "La langue franco-américaine." *CIF* 1, 37–60.

Fishman, Joshua A., ed. *Language Loyalty in the United States.* Janua Linguarum. Series Maior, no. 21. The Hague: Mouton, 1966.

Fontaine, Robert. *The Happy Time.* New York: Simon and Schuster, 1945. A new edition was adapted by Samuel A. Taylor. New York: Random House, 1950.

Forget, Danielle. "Quel est le français standard au Québec?" In *Le Français parlé: Études sociologiques,* ed. Pierrette Thibault, pp. 153–61. Current Inquiry into Language and Linguistics, no. 30. Edmonton, Alberta: Linguistics Research, Inc., 1978.

Forget, Ulysse. "Les Franco-Américains et le 'Melting Pot.'" *BSHFA* (1946–47), 32–49.

Fortin, Richard L. "La Société Généalogique Américaine-Canadienne déménage à l'Association Canado-Américaine." *Canado-Américain* 7, no. 4 (1981), 16–17.

Fournier, Hélène. "Examen comparatif des quadrilles charentais et québécois." *Culture et Tradition* 6 (1982), 52–72.

Les Franco-Américains: La promesse du passé, les réalités du présent. Colloque 1976. Cambridge, Mass.: NADC, 1976.

Les Franco-Américains peints par eux-mêmes. Montreal: Albert Lévesque (for the Association Canado-Américaine), 1936.

A Franco-American Resources Inventory of New England (FARINE). N.p.: n.p., 1979.

Freeman, Stanley L., Jr., and Raymond J. Pelletier. *Initiating Franco-American Studies: A Handbook for Teachers.* Orono, Maine: University of Maine, 1981.

The French in New England, Acadia and Quebec. Orono, Maine: New England–Atlantic Provinces–Quebec Center, 1973.

Frenière, Maxime O. "Une catastrophe à Holyoke, 1875." *BSHFA* (1961), 103–9.

———. "Les maires franco-américains des villes des Etats-Unis, 1684–1942." *BSHFA* (1942), 109–13. Additions and corrections, *BSHFA* (1943), 110.

Funk & Wagnalls Standard Reference Encyclopedia. 25 vols. Gen. ed. Joseph Laffan Morse. New York: Standard Reference Works Publishing Co., 1959.

Gadbois, Father Charles-Emile. *La Bonne Chanson: Les 100 plus belles chansons.* La Prairie, Quebec: Editions Culturelles, 1937.

Galarneau, Claude. *Les Collèges classiques au Canada français (1620–1970).* Montreal: Fides, 1978.

Galarneau, Laurent. *Histoire de la garde Lafayette, ou compagnie A, du premier régiment d'infanterie de la garde nationale de l'état du New Hampshire.* Manchester, N.H.: L'Avenir National, 1937.

Gallant, J. P. "New Franco-American Flag Said to Exclude One Million U.S. Francos." *FAROG Forum* 12, no. 5 (1985), 1, 19.

Garigue, Philippe. *La Vie familiale des Canadiens français.* Montreal: Presses de l'Université de Montréal, and Paris: Presses Universitaires de France, 1962.

Gastonguay-Sasseville, Alberte. *La Jeune Franco-Américaine.* Lewiston, Maine, 1933. Reprint. Bedford, N.H.: NMDC, 1980.

Gatineau, Félix. *Histoire des Franco-Américains de Southbridge, Massachusetts.* Framingham, Mass.: Lakeview Press, 1919.

———. *Historique des conventions générales des Canadiens-français aux Etats-Unis, 1865–1901.* Woonsocket, R.I.: Union Saint-Jean-Baptiste d'Amérique, 1927.

Gauthier-Larouche, Georges. *Evolution de la maison rurale traditionnelle dans la région de Québec (Etude ethnographique).* Quebec City: Presses de l'Université Laval, 1974.

Gauvin, Lise, and Laurent Mailhot. *Guide culturel du Québec.* Montreal: Boréal Express, 1982.

Gendron, J.-D. *Tendances phonétiques du français parlé au Canada.* Paris: Klincksieck, and Quebec City: Presses de l'Université Laval, 1966.

Giguère, Madeleine. "Commentary." In *Les Franco-Américains: La promesse du passé, les réalités du présent. Colloque 1976,* pp. 73–75. Cambridge, Mass.: NADC, 1976.

———. "The Franco-Americans: Occupational Profiles." In *The Quebec and Acadian Diaspora in North America,* ed. Raymond Breton and Pierre Savard, pp. 65–76. Toronto: Multicultural History Society of Ontario, 1982.

———. "Social and Economic Profile of French and English Mother Tongue Persons: Maine 1970." In *FAO* 4:145–64.

———, ed. *A Franco-American Overview.* Vol. 3, *New England (Part 1).* Cambridge, Mass.: NADC, 1981.

————, ed. *A Franco-American Overview*. Vol. 4, *New England (Part 2)*. Cambridge, Mass.: NADC, 1981.

Glazer, Nathan, and Daniel P. Moynihan, eds. *Ethnicity: Theory and Experience*. Cambridge, Mass.: Harvard University Press, 1975.

Glossaire du parler français au Canada. Quebec City: L'Action Sociale, 1930.

Godbout, Father Archange. "Nos hérédités provinciales françaises." *Archives de Folklore* 1 (1946), 26–40.

Goësbriand, The Most Reverend Louis Joseph de. Letter to the editor of *Le Protecteur Canadien*. In Father Edouard Hamon, *Les Canadiens-français de la Nouvelle-Angleterre*, pp. 171–76. Quebec City: Hardy, 1891.

Golden, Daniel. "Franco-Americans in Search of Roots." *Boston Globe*, 30 May 1983.

Golenbock, Peter. *Bums: An Oral History of the Brooklyn Dodgers*. New York: G. P. Putnam, 1984.

Gosselin, Elizabeth A. "Bonjour Bébittes!" *FAROG Forum* 9, no. 4 (1981), 7.

La Grande Ferme: Centre d'initiation au patrimoine. Quebec City: Ministère des Affaires Culturelles, n.d.

Grégoire, Paul. "Participants Review Rassemblement '84." *FAROG Forum* 12, no. 1 (1984), 1, 4.

Griffiths, N. E. S. *The Acadian Deportation: Deliberate Perfidy or Cruel Necessity?* Issues in Canadian History. Toronto: Copp Clark, 1969.

Guide des sources généalogiques au Canada. Ottawa: Ministère des Approvisionnements et Service Canada, 1983.

Guide officiel des Franco-Américains 1931. Auburn, R.I.: Albert A. Bélanger, 1931.

Guide officiel franco-américain. Woonsocket, R.I.: Sansouci, 1946.

Guignard, Michael J. "Ethnic Survival in a New England Mill Town: The Franco-Americans of Biddeford, Maine." Ph.D. diss., Syracuse University, 1976.

————. *La Foi, la Langue, la Culture: The Franco-Americans of Biddeford, Maine*. N.p.: n.p., 1982.

————. "Maine's Corporation Sole Controversy." *Maine Historical Society Newsletter* 12 (1973), 111–26.

Guilbault, Nicole. *Henri Julien et la tradition orale*. Montreal: Boréal Express, 1980.

Guillet, Ernest B. *Essai de journalisme*. Bedford, N.H.: NMDC, 1981.

————. "French Ethnic Literature and Culture in an American City: Holyoke, Massachusetts." Ph.D. diss., University of Massachusetts, 1978.

————. *Un Théâtre francophone dans un milieu franco-américain*. Manchester, N.H.: NMDC, 1981.

Guissard, Father Polyeucte. *Un Siècle d'histoire assomptionniste*. Worcester, Mass.: Imprimerie Caron, 1950.

Haden, Ernest F. "French Dialect Geography in North America." In *Current Trends in Linguistics*, ed. Thomas A. Sebeok, 10:422–39. The Hague and Paris: Mouton, 1973.

Haebler, Peter. "Habitants in Holyoke: The Development of the French-Canadian Community in a Massachusetts City, 1865–1910." Ph.D. diss., University of New Hampshire, 1976.

Haley, Alex. *Roots*. Garden City, N.Y.: Doubleday, 1976.

Ham, Edward B. "French National Societies in New England." *New England Quarterly* 12 (1939), 315–32.

————. "Journalism and the French Survival in New England." *New England Quarterly* 11 (1938), 89–107.

————. "The Library of the Association Canado-Américaine." *MLN* 52 (1937), 542–44.

————. "The Library of the Union Saint-Jean-Baptiste d'Amérique." *Franco-American Review* 1 (1937), 271–75.

Hamon, Father Edouard. *Les Canadiens-français de la Nouvelle-Angleterre.* Quebec City: Hardy, 1891.

Hansen, Marcus L. "The Third Generation in America." *Commentary* 14 (1952), 492–500.

Hareven, Tamara K. *Family Time and Industrial Time: The Relationship between the Family and Work in a New England Industrial Community.* New York: Cambridge University Press, 1982.

———. "The Laborers of Manchester, New Hampshire, 1912–1922: The Role of Family and Ethnicity in Adjustment to Industrial Life." *Labor History* 16 (1975), 249–65.

Harney, Robert F. "Franco-Americans and Ethnic Studies: Notes on a Mill Town." In *The Quebec and Acadian Diaspora in North America,* ed. Raymond Breton and Pierre Savard, pp. 77–88. Toronto: Multicultural History Society of Ontario, 1982.

Harris, Richard C. *The Seigneurial System in Early Canada: A Geographical Study.* Madison: University of Wisconsin Press, 1968.

Harth, Morris, and Theodore M. Bernstein, eds. *Family Almanac '72.* New York: New York Times, 1971.

Haugen, Einar. *Bilingualism in the Americas: A Bibliography and Research Guide.* Publication of the American Dialect Society, no. 26. University, Ala.: University of Alabama Press, 1956.

———. "Bilingualism, Language Contact, and Immigrant Languages in the United States: A Research Report, 1956–1970." In *Current Trends in Linguistics,* ed. Thomas A. Sebeok, 10:513–20. The Hague and Paris: Mouton, 1973.

Hautecoeur, Jean-Paul. *L'Acadie du discours: Pour une sociologie de la culture acadienne.* Quebec City: Presses de l'Université Laval, 1975.

Hawthorne, Manning, and Henry Wadsworth Longfellow Dana. *The Origin and Development of Longfellow's "Evangeline".* Portland, Maine: Anthoensen Press, 1949.

Hayakawa, S. I. "English by Law." *New York Times,* 1 October 1981.

Hechinger, Fred M. "A Humane Look at Bilingual Schooling." *New York Times,* 31 May 1983.

Hémon, Louis. *Maria Chapdelaine.* Ed. Nicole Deschamps and Ghislaine Legendre. Montreal: Boréal Express, 1983.

Hess, Alfred O., Jr., and Marcel Daneau, eds. *Problems and Opportunities in U.S.-Quebec Relations.* Boulder, Colo.: Westview Press, 1984.

Hillinger, Charles. "Maine's Quiet Minority Makes No Waves." *Washington Post,* 16 February 1985.

Histoire du Canada, Cours moyen. 4th ed. Montreal: Frères des Ecoles Chrétiennes, 1916.

Holmes, Kathy. "Nous autres à Berkshire." *FAROG Forum* 8, no. 5 (1981), 6.

VIIIᵉ Rencontre francophone de Québec, du 21 au 25 juin 1985, Université Laval. Quebec City: Imprimerie Sociale Limitée, 1985.

Hume, Bonnie. "Education and Parents' Rights." *Religious Education* 60 (1965), 460–66, 472.

Identité culturelle et Francophonie dans les Amériques. Vol. 1. Travaux du Centre International de Recherche sur le Bilinguisme. Quebec City: Presses de l'Université Laval, 1976.

"In Plain English." *New York Times,* 10 October 1981.

Inventaire général des sources documentaires sur les Acadiens. Vol. 1. Moncton, New Brunswick: Editions d'Acadie, 1975.

Jacobson, Phyllis L. "The Social Context of Franco-American Schooling in New England." *French Review* 57 (1984), 641–56.

Jetté, Father Irénée, et al. *Mariages du Comté de Saint-Jean (1828-1950)*. Publication no. 97. Quebec City: Benoît Pontbriand, 1974.

Johnson, Paula B. "La fin d'un commencement." *FAROG Forum* 9, no. 7/8 (1982), 8.

Jolicoeur, Catherine. *Les Plus Belles Légendes acadiennes*. Montreal and Paris: Stanké, 1981.

Jubilé d'or paroissial (1872–1922). Paroisse du Précieux Sang, Holyoke, Massachusetts. Holyoke, Mass., 1922.

Jubilé paroissial, Saint-Georges, 1893–1943. Chicopee Falls, Mass., 1943.

Juneau, Marcel. *Contribution à l'histoire de la prononciation française au Québec: Etude des graphies des documents d'archives*. Langue et littérature françaises au Québec, no. 8. Quebec City: Presses de l'Université Laval, 1972.

———. *Problèmes de lexicologie québécoise: Prolégomènes à un Trésor de la langue française au Québec*. Quebec City: Presses de l'Université Laval, 1977.

Kelley, Henry. "Phonological Variation in a New England Speech Community." Ph.D. diss., Cornell University, 1980.

Kemner, Léon. "Les Franco-Américains du Connecticut." *Revue Franco-Américaine* (1908), 209–211.

Kenngott, George F. *The Record of a City: A Social Survey of Lowell, Massachusetts*. New York: Macmillan, 1912.

Kirkland, Edward C. *Brunswick's Golden Age*. Lewiston, Maine: Loring, 1941.

Knowlton, Evelyn H. *Pepperell's Progress: History of a Cotton Textile Company, 1844–1945*. Cambridge, Mass.: Harvard University Press, 1948.

Labbé, Yvon. "Yvongélisations." *FAROG Forum* 8, no. 1 (1980), 23.

Labelle, Ronald. "L'eau de Pâques: Coutume religieuse populaire." *Culture et Tradition* 2 (1977), 1–11.

Lacerte, Roger. "Comptines et chansons grivoises de chez nous." *FAROG Forum* 8, no. 6 (1981), 1, 12.

———. "Du neuf sur nos comptines." *FAROG Forum* 7, no. 8 (1980), 17.

———. "Le Festival Franco-Américain 1978: Un demi-succès." *FAROG Forum* 6, no. 2 (1978), 1–2.

———. "Une thèse artificielle . . . celle de M. Elphège Roy: Une réfutation." *Travailleur*, 14 June 1969 and 21 June 1969.

Lachance, Micheline. *Le Frère André*. Montreal: Editions de l'Homme, 1979.

Lacourcière, Luc. "Comptines canadiennes." *Archives de Folklore* 3 (1948), 109–57.

———. "Le conte populaire français en Amérique du Nord." Quebec City: Archives de Folklore, 1959. Mimeo.

———. "Oral Tradition: New England and French Canada." In *The French in New England, Acadia, and Quebec*, pp. 93–113. Orono, Maine: New England–Atlantic Provinces–Quebec Center, 1973.

Lacroix, Father Benoît. "L'Oratoire Saint-Joseph (1904–1979): Fait religieux populaire." In Micheline Lachance, *Le Frère André*, Appendix 3. Montreal: Editions de l'Homme, 1979.

Laflamme, J. K. L., David E. Lavigne, and J. Arthur Favreau. "French Catholics in the United States." *Catholic Encyclopedia*, 1909 ed. Reprinted in *FAO* 3:23–35.

Laforte, Conrad. *Catalogue de la chanson folklorique française*. 6 vols. Quebec City: Presses de l'Université Laval, 1977–83.

Lahaie, Rose, and Irène Bilodeau. "Le costume traditionnel d'hiver de la région de Charlevoix de la fin du XIXᵉ siècle au début du XXᵉ." *Culture et Tradition* 4 (1979), 11–18.

Lajoie, P. A. "Vlan!" *BSHFA* (1956), 156–58.

Laliberté, Monique. "Le poisson d'avril." *Culture et Tradition* 5 (1980), 79–89.

Laloux-Jain, Geneviève. *Les Manuels d'histoire du Canada au Québec et en Ontario (de 1867 à 1914)*. Histoire et sociologie de la culture, no. 6. Quebec City: Presses de l'Université Laval, 1974.

Lamontagne, Sophie-Laurence. *L'Hiver dans la culture québécoise (XVIIe–XIXe siècles)*. Quebec City: Institut Québécois de Recherche sur la Culture, 1983.

Landry, Father Thomas-M. "Le centenaire franco-américain de 1949." *BSHFA* (1950), 34–38.

Landry, Walter J. "Linguistic Liberation—Now is the Time." *FAROG Forum* 8, no. 1 (1980), 1, 18.

Lane, Brigitte Marie. "Franco-American Folk Traditions and Popular Culture in a Former Milltown: Aspects of Ethnic Urban Folklore and the Dynamics of Folklore Change in Lowell, Massachusetts." Ph.D. diss., Harvard University, 1983.

Langlois, Michel. *Cherchons nos ancêtres*. Quebec City: Québec Science Editeur, 1980.

Lapalme, Georges-E. "Le Ministère des Affaires Culturelles de la Province de Québec." In *Les Conférences de l'Institut Franco-Américain de Bowdoin College, deuxième série*, ed. Gerard J. Brault, pp. 28–52. Brunswick, Maine, 1962.

Lapierre, Eugène. "Calixa Lavallée." *BSHFA* (1970), 15–23.

———. *Calixa Lavallée: Musicien national du Canada*. 1936. Revised edition. Montreal: Fides, 1966.

Lapierre, Michel. "Rosaire Dion-Lévesque (1900–1974) et la littérature franco-américaine." M.A. thesis, Université de Montréal, Département d'Etudes Françaises, 1983.

Lavoie, Yolande. *L'Emigration des Québécois aux Etats-Unis de 1840 à 1930*. Quebec City: Editeur officiel du Québec, 1979.

Lebel, Paul. *Les Noms de personnes*. Que sais-je?, no. 235. Paris: Presses Universitaires de France, 1949.

LeBlanc, Robert G. "Colonisation et rapatriement au Lac Saint-Jean (1895–1905)." *Revue d'Histoire de l'Amérique Française* 38 (1985), 379–408.

———. "Les migrations acadiennes." In *Du Continent perdu à l'archipel retrouvé: Le Québec et l'Amérique française*, eds. Dean R. Louder and Eric Waddell, pp. 137–62. Quebec City: Presses de l'Université Laval, 1983.

———. "Regional Competition for Franco-American Repatriates, 1870–1930." *Quebec Studies* 1 (1983), 110–29.

La Lecture par la méthode phonique: Deuxième partie. Montreal: Frères des Ecoles Chrétiennes, 1918.

La Lecture par la méthode phonique: Première partie. Montreal: Frères des Ecoles Chrétiennes, 1918.

Lectures courantes: Deuxième Livre. Nouvelle édition. Montreal: Frères des Ecoles Chrétiennes, 1916.

Ledoux, Albert H. "An Acadian Minuteman." *Fleur de Lys* 1, no. 2 (1979), 40–42.

———. "Franco-American Veterans of the Civil War (Massachusetts Residents)." *Fleur de Lys* 2, no. 3 (1980), 3–24; no. 4, 6–38.

———. *Les Mariages acadiens du Québec: L'Acadie (St-Jean) et la vallée du Richelieu*. State College, Pa.: Albert H. Ledoux, 1978.

Lefebvre, Jean-Jacques. "Les Canadiens [-Français] et la Révolution américaine." *BSHFA* (1946–47), 50–76.

Léger, Lauraine. "L'émigrant acadien et sa culture populaire." *CIF* 5, 86–100.

Lemaire, Hervé B. "Franco-American Efforts on Behalf of the French Language in New England." In *Language Loyalty in the United States*, ed. Joshua A. Fishman, pp. 253–79. Janua Linguarum. Series Maior, no. 21. The Hague: Mouton, 1966.

Lessard, Camille. *Canuck*. Lewiston, Maine: Messager, 1936. Reprint. Bedford, N.H.: NMDC, 1980.

Lessard, Michel, and Huguette Marquis. *Encyclopédie de la maison québécoise*. Montreal: Editions de l'Homme, 1972.

Lessard, Michel, and Gilles Vilandré. *La Maison traditionnelle au Québec*. Montreal: Editions de l'Homme, 1974.

Lessard, Pierre. *Les Petites Images dévotes: Leur utilisation traditionnelle au Québec*. Quebec City: Presses de l'Université Laval, 1981.

"Life Isn't All Hardware." *Worcester* [Massachusetts] *Sunday Telegram. Parade Magazine*, 9 July 1967.

Lindsay, Betty A. Lausier. *Nothing Went to Waste . . . in Grandmother's Kitchen*. Bedford, N.H.: NMDC, 1981.

Locke, William N. "The French Colony at Brunswick, Maine: A Historical Sketch." *Archives de Folklore* 1 (1946), 97–111.

———. *Pronunciation of the French Spoken at Brunswick, Maine*. Publication of the American Dialect Society, no. 12. Greensboro, N.C.: American Dialect Society, 1949.

Longnon, Auguste H. *Les Noms de lieu de la France: Leur origine, leur signification, leurs transformations*. Paris: Champion, 1920–29.

Looby, James F. "Ex-Factory Hand Here May Become Saint." *Hartford* [Connecticut] *Daily Courant*, 12 December 1937.

Lortie, Jeanne d'Arc. *La Poésie nationaliste au Canada français (1606–1867)*. Quebec City: Presses de l'Université Laval, 1975.

Louder, Dean R., and Eric Waddell, eds. *Du Continent perdu à l'archipel retrouvé: Le Québec et l'Amérique française*. Quebec City: Presses de l'Université Laval, 1983.

Lowe, R. G. "Massachusetts and the Acadians." *William and Mary Quarterly*, 3d series, 25, no. 2 (1968), 212–29.

Lumpkin, Katherine Du Pre. *Shutdowns in the Connecticut Valley: A Study of Worker Displacement in the Small Industrial Community*. Smith College Studies in History, no. 29. Northampton, Mass.: Department of History, Smith College, 1934.

Mackensen, Lutz. *Der singende Knochen: Ein Beitrag zur vergleichenden Märchenforschung*. Folklore Fellows Communications, no. 49. Helsinki: Suomlainen tiedeakatemia, 1923.

Le Macro-Inventaire: Banque de données sur les biens culturels du Québec. Quebec City: Ministère des Affaires Culturelles, 1981.

Le Macro-Inventaire: Guide explicatif. Quebec City: Ministère des Affaires Culturelles, 1983.

Magnan, Hormidas. *Cinquantenaire de notre hymne national, "O Canada, terre de nos aïeux": Les origines de nos drapeaux et chants nationaux, armoiries, emblêmes, devises*. Quebec City, 1929.

Mailhot-Bernard, Irène. "Facteurs sociaux et leur rapport avec le choix de vocabulaire chez les Franco-Américains de Lewiston, Maine." *CIF* 2, 99–122.

Mandrou, Robert. *Magistrats et sorciers en France au XVIIᵉ siècle: Une analyse de psychologie historique*. Paris: Editions du Seuil, 1980.

Marie-Immaculée, Sister. "Monseigneur Joseph-Calixte Marquis et les Soeurs de l'Assomption de la Sainte Vierge." In *La Société Canadienne de l'Histoire de l'Eglise Catholique: Rapport, 1943–1944*, pp. 89–111. Hull, Quebec: Imprimerie Leclerc, 1944.

Marie-Ursule, Sister. *Civilisation traditionnelle des Lavalois*. Quebec City: Presses de l'Université Laval, 1951.

Maris Stella, Sister. "A Note on the Pronunciation of New England French." *French Review* 32 (1959), 363–66.

Marling, Karal A. *Wall-to-Wall America: A Cultural History of Post-Office Murals in the Great Depression*. Minneapolis: University of Minnesota Press, 1982.

Martel, Louis-Israël. "Franco-Americans and American Political Life." In *The*

20th-Century Franco-American, pp. 24–26. Comité de Vie Franco-Américaine, 1976.

———. Letter to the editor. *FAROG Forum* 8, nos. 7–8 (1981), 20.

Martin, Ernest. *L'Evangéline de Longfellow et la suite merveilleuse d'un poème*. Paris: Hachette, 1936.

Martin, Mother Marie de Saint Jean. *Ursuline Method of Education*. Rahway, N.J.: Quinn and Boden, 1946.

Massachusetts Bureau of Statistics of Labor. *Twelfth Annual Report, 1881*.

Massé, Claude. "A propos du Bulletin no. 31 (juillet–septembre 1972)." *Bulletin de l'Association pour l'histoire de Belle-Ile-en-Mer* 10, no. 38 (1973), 5–6.

Massicotte, Edmond J. *Nos Canadiens d'autrefois: 12 grandes compositions*. Montreal: Granger Frères, 1923.

Massignon, Geneviève. *Les Parlers français d'Acadie: Enquête linguistique*. 2 vols. Paris: Klincksieck, 1962.

———. "La Seigneurie de Charles de Menou d'Aulnay, Gouverneur de l'Acadie, 1635–1650." *Revue d'Histoire de l'Amérique Française* 16 (1963), 469–501.

Meeting Tomorrow's Challenge Today: The Chicopee Falls Urban Renewal Plan (Mass. R-111) Chicopee, Massachusetts. N.p.: n.p., 1969.

Mémoire d'une Amérique: La Rochelle 1980. La Rochelle: Imprimerie Rochelaise, 1980.

Merrien, Jean. *La Vie quotidienne des marins au temps du Roi-Soleil*. Paris: Hachette, 1964.

Metalious, Grace. *No Adam in Eden*. New York: Trident Press, 1963.

———. *Peyton Place*. New York: Julian Messner, 1956.

———. *The Tight White Collar*. New York: Julian Messner, 1960.

Miner, Horace. *St. Denis: A French-Canadian Parish*. 1939. Reprint. Chicago: University of Chicago Press, 1963.

Ministère des Affaires Culturelles: Rapport annuel, 1982–1983. Quebec City: Ministère des Affaires Culturelles, 1983.

Moisan, E. Donald. "The Present State of Relations between Franco-Americans and French Canada." In *The 20th-Century Franco-American*, pp. 43–56. Comité de Vie Franco-Américaine, 1976.

Monseur, Eugène. "L'os qui chante." *Bulletin de Folklore* 1 (1891–92), 39–51, 89–149; 2 (1893–95), 219–41, 245–51.

Monteiro, George. "Histoire de Montferrand: L'Athlète Canadien and Joe Mufraw." *Journal of American Folklore* 73 (1960), 24–34.

Montpetit, Raymond. *Le Temps des Fêtes au Québec*. Montreal: Editions de l'Homme, 1978.

Moreau, Father S.-A. *Histoire de L'Acadie, Province de Québec*. Montreal, 1908.

Morin, Father Guillaume J. *La Paroisse de l'Immaculée Conception de Fitchburg, Massachusetts: Un cinquantenaire, 1886–1936*. Fitchburg, Mass.: Imprimerie de La Liberté, 1936.

Morison, Samuel Eliot. *Samuel de Champlain: Father of New France*. Boston: Little, Brown and Co., 1972.

Moussette, Marcel. *Le Chauffage domestique au Canada des origines à l'industrialisation*. Quebec City: Presses de l'Université Laval, 1983.

Muckley, Robert. "After Childhood, What Then? An Overview of Ethnic Language Retention (Elret) Programs in the United States." *Revista Interamericana Review* 2 (1972), 53–67.

Musée du Nouveau Monde, Hôtel Fleuriau, La Rochelle, 14 Mai 1982. La Rochelle: Imprimerie Rochelaise, 1982.

Nadeau, Gabriel. "La blessure du Major Maillet." *BSHFA* (1953), 32–40.

———. "L'oeuvre historique d'Edmond Mallet." *BSHFA* (1941), 49–60.

————. "Le théâtre chez les Franco-Américains." *BSHFA* (1955), 69–74.

Nalty, Bernard C. *The United States Marine Corps on Iwo Jima: The Battle and the Flag Raising.* Washington, D.C.: Historical Division, Headquarters, U.S. Marine Corps, 1970.

Nevers, Edmond de. *L'Ame américaine: Les origines, la vie historique.* 2 vols. Paris: Jouve and Boyer, 1900.

Notre Vie franco-américaine. Manchester, N.H.: L'Avenir National (for the Comité d'Orientation Franco-Américaine), 1949.

O'Brien, Kenneth B., Jr. "Education, Americanization at the Supreme Court: The 1920s." *American Quarterly* 13 (1961), 161–71.

Official Catholic Directory. New York: Kenedy, 1972.

Olivier, Julien. *D'la Boucane: Une Introduction au folklore franco-américain de la Nouvelle-Angleterre.* Cambridge, Mass.: NADC, 1979.

————. *Pas de gêne: L'histoire d'Omer Marcoux, violoneux et sculpteur.* Bedford, N.H.: NMDC, 1981.

————. "Le rassemblement des artistes." *FAROG Forum* 12, no. 1 (1984), 1, 5.

————. *Souches et racines: Une introduction à la généalogie pour les jeunes Franco-Américains.* Bedford, N.H.: NMDC, 1981.

Olivier, Julien, and Normand C. Dubé. *Criquette: Huit pièces pour jeunes gens.* Cambridge, Mass.: NADC, 1980.

100th Anniversary: St. Joseph's Church, Cohoes, New York. N.p.: n.p., 1984.

Orkin, Mark M. *Speaking Canadian French.* Revised edition. Toronto: General Publishing Co., 1971.

Ouellet, Fernand. *Le Bas-Canada, 1791–1840: Changements structuraux et crise.* Ottawa: Editions de l'Université d'Ottawa, 1976.

Ouellet, Richard, and Jean-Pierre Therrien, eds. *L'Invasion par les Bastonnois: Journal de M. Sanguinet.* Civilisation du Québec, no. 14. Quebec City: Ministère des Affaires Culturelles, 1975.

Paradis, Roger. *Gilbert O. Roy: Peintre populaire de la vallée Saint-Jean.* Cambridge, Mass.: NADC, 1979.

Paré, Paul M. "Les Franco-Américains et le recensement 1980: La législation sur le bilinguisme et le biculturalisme." *FAROG Forum* 8, no. 3 (1980), 7, 11; no. 4, p. 12.

————. "Franco-Americans and Credit Unions." *InformACTION* 3, no. 1 (1984), 4–5, 7.

————. "Franco-Americans in Politics: An Absence Worth Noticing." *InformACTION* 1, no. 3 (1982), 2.

————. "Premier rapport annuel du Secrétariat de l'ActFANE, juillet '81 à septembre '82." *InformACTION* 1, no. 4 (1982), 2, 5–7.

————. "Les vingt premières années du *Messager* de Lewiston, Maine." *CIF* 4, 81–96.

Paroisse Saint-Pierre et Saint-Paul: Centenaire, album souvenir. Lewiston, Maine, 1971.

Parsons, Cynthia. "Bilingualism—Are You For It or Against It?" *FAROG Forum* 8, no. 1 (1980), 15. Reprinted from the *Christian Science Monitor,* 9 June 1980.

Péloquin-Faré, Louise. "Les attitudes des Franco-Américains envers la langue française." *French Review* 57 (1984), 657–68.

————. *L'Identité culturelle: Les Franco-Américains de la Nouvelle-Angleterre.* Paris: Centre de Recherche et d'Etude pour la Diffusion du Français, 1983.

Perreault, Robert B. *Elphège-J. Daignault et le mouvement sentinelliste à Manchester, New Hampshire.* Bedford, N.H.: NMDC, 1981.

————. "Les Franco-Américains." *Magazine OVO* (Montreal), 12, no. 46 (1982), 14–17.

————. *L'Héritage.* Durham, N.H.: NMDC, 1983.

————. *Joseph Laferrière: Ecrivain lowellois.* Bedford, N.H.: NMDC, 1982.

————. *One Piece in the Great American Mosaic: The Franco-Americans of New England.* Manchester, N.H.: Association Canado-Américaine, 1976. Special issue of *Canado-Américain* 2, no. 2, 1976.

————. *La Presse franco-américaine et la politique: L'oeuvre de Charles-Roger Daoust.* Bedford, N.H.: NMDC, 1981.

————. "Survol de la presse franco-américaine," *CIF* 4, 9–34.

Petrin, Ronald A. "Culture, Community, and Politics: French Canadians in Massachusetts, 1885–1915." *CIF* 3, 66–77.

Plante, David. *The Country.* New York: Atheneum, 1981.

————. *Difficult Women: A Memoir of Three.* New York: Atheneum, 1983.

————. *The Family.* New York: Farrar, Straus, and Giroux, 1978.

————. *The Foreigner.* New York: Atheneum, 1984.

————. *The Francoeur Novels: The Family, The Woods, The Country.* New York: Dutton/Obelisk, 1984.

————. *The Woods.* New York: Atheneum, 1984.

Plourde, Father Antonin. "Cent ans de vie paroissiale, SS. Pierre et Paul de Lewiston." In *Paroisse Saint-Pierre et Saint-Paul: Centenaire, album souvenir,* pp. 1–53. Lewiston, Maine, 1971.

Plummer, William. "Jack Kerouac: The Beat Goes On." *New York Times Magazine,* 30 December 1979.

Poirier, Claude. "Chronique du Trésor de la langue française au Québec." *Québec Français,* March 1982, pp. 20–22.

————. "Le lexique québécois: Son évolution, ses composantes." In *Culture populaire et littératures au Québec,* ed. René Bouchard, pp. 43–80. Stanford French and Italian Studies, no. 19. Saratoga, Calif.: Anma Libri and Co., 1980.

Poirier, Jean. "Le toponyme Lacolle est son dérivé anglais Cole." *Revue de Géographie de Montréal* 25 (1971), 163–67.

Pontbriand, Benoît. *Mariages de L'Acadie (1785) et Saint-Luc (1801), Comté Saint-Jean.* Publication no. 65. Quebec City: Benoît Pontbriand, 1970.

————. *Mariages du Comté de Napierville.* Publication no. 95. Quebec City: Benoît Pontbriand, 1973.

Porchnev, Boris. *Les Soulèvements populaires en France de 1623 à 1648.* Ecole Pratique des Hautes Etudes. 6th Section. Centre de Recherches Historiques. Oeuvres Etrangères, no. 4. Paris: S.E.V.P.E.N., 1963.

Portes, Jacques. "Le réveil des Franco-Américains." *Le Monde,* 29 November 1981. English trans. in the *Manchester Guardian,* 3 January 1982; reprinted in the *Boston Globe,* 21 February 1982.

Port-Joli, Emma. *Mirbah.* Holyoke, Mass.: La Justice Publishing Co., 1910–12. Reprint. Bedford, N.H.: NMDC, 1979. Also reprinted in *ALFANA* 4 : 56–312.

Poulin, Sister Eugena, and Claire Quintal. *The French Experience in North America: An Activities Packet.* Rochambeau Education Committee and Rhode Island Heritage Commission, 1981.

Pour Résoudre la Crise de l'enseignement du français dans nos écoles paroissiales: Actes du IXᵉ Congrès des Franco-Américains tenu à Providence, Rhode Island, les 11 et 12 novembre 1966. Comité de Vie Franco-Américaine, 1967.

Programme de français et d'histoire nationale en usage dans les écoles paroissiales des Etats-Unis. N.p.: n.p., n.d.

Programme d'études et Directoire à l'usage des SS. de l'Assomption de la S.V. pour les écoles bilingues. Nicolet, Quebec, 1912.

Programme d'études pour les pensionnats des Soeurs de l'Assomption. Nicolet, Quebec, 1905.

Programme-souvenir du huitième congrès de la Brigade des volontaires franco-américains des Etats-Unis. Lowell: J. E. Lambert, 1915.

Proulx, Gilles. *Entre France et Nouvelle-France.* La Prairie, Quebec: Editions Marcel Broquet, 1984.

Provost, Robert. "Les Canadiens français à la Guerre de Sécession." *BSHFA* (1956), 143–55.

Putnam, Donald F., and Robert G. Putnam. *Canada: A Regional Analysis.* Toronto: Dent, 1970.

Les Quarante Ans de la Société Historique Franco-Américaine, 1899–1939. Boston: Société Historique Franco-Américaine, 1940.

Quatre Siècles d'identité canadienne. Montreal: Bellarmin, 1982.

Quintal, Claire. *Sur les traces de l'héritage français en Nouvelle-Angleterre: Boston.* Fall River, Mass.: NADC, 1977.

———, ed. "L'Emigrant acadien vers les Etats-Unis, 1842–1950." *CIF* 5.

———, ed. "L'Emigrant québécois vers les Etats-Unis, 1850–1920." *CIF* 2.

———, ed. "Le Journalisme de langue française aux Etats-Unis." *CIF* 4.

———, ed. "The Little Canadas of New England." *CIF* 3.

———, ed. "Situation de la recherche sur la Franco-Américanie." *CIF* 1.

Rawlyk, George A. *Nova Scotia's Massachusetts: A Study of Massachusetts–Nova Scotia Relations, 1630 to 1784.* Montreal and London: McGill–Queen's University Press, 1973.

Reith, Eric. "Les navires rochelais de la fin du XVIIe siècle à travers les 'Desseins des différentes manières de vaisseaux que l'on voit dans les havres, ports et rivières depuis Nantes jusqu'à Bayonne qui servent au commerce des sujets de Sa Majesté 1679.'" In *Mémoire d'une Amérique: La Rochelle 1980,* pp. 18–43. La Rochelle: Imprimerie Rochelaise, 1980.

Robert, Adolphe. "L'apport franco-américain à la littérature des Etats-Unis." *BSHFA* (1954), 64–69.

———. "L'inviolabilité de la paroisse nationale." *Vie Franco-Américaine* (1948), 115–24.

Robert, Adolphe, and Father Thomas-M. Landry. "Les catholiques américains de langue française en Nouvelle-Angleterre." In *Notre Vie franco-américaine,* pp. 18–21. Manchester, N.H.: L'Avenir National (for the Comité d'Orientation Franco-Américaine), 1949.

Robert, Hermanita, and Roseline Moore, eds. *La Bonne Croûte, livre de récettes.* Chicopee-Holyoke, Mass.: Festival Franco-Américain, Inc., 1983.

Robichaud, Gérard. *The Apple of His Eye.* Garden City, N.Y.: Doubleday, 1965.

———. *Papa Martel: A Novel in Ten Parts.* Garden City, N.Y.: Doubleday, 1961.

———. "Report from the 'Rassemblement.'" *FAROG Forum* 10, no. 3 (1982), 12.

Robinson, Sinclair, and Donald Smith. *Practical Handbook of Quebec and Acadian French.* Toronto: Anansi, 1984.

Roby, Yves. "L'évolution économique du Québec et l'émigrant (1850–1929)." *CIF* 2, 8–20.

———. "Un Québec émigré aux Etats-Unis." In *Les Rapports culturels entre le Québec et les Etats-Unis,* ed. Claude Savary, pp. 105–129. Quebec City: Institut Québécois de Recherche sur la Culture, 1984.

Roche, François. *Les Francos de la Nouvelle-Angleterre: Anthologie franco-américaine (XIXe et XXe siècles).* Paris: Belles Lettres (for LARC Centre d'Action Culturelle, Le Creusot), 1981.

Rocheleau-Rouleau, Corinne. "Une incroyable et véridique histoire: L'affaire Cazeau, 1776–1893." *BSHFA* (1946–47), 3–31.

———. *Laurentian Heritage.* Toronto: Longmans, Green and Co., 1948.

———. "Silhouettes et cadres franco-américains, 1880–1900." *BSHFA* (1942), 58–78.

Rodrigue, Denise. *Le Cycle de Pâques au Québec et dans l'Ouest de la France.* Quebec City: Presses de l'Université Laval, 1983.

Romme, Father Jules. *Lacolle.* N.p.: n.p., 1973.

————. *Saint-Bernard-de-Lacolle: Centenaire de l'église paroissiale.* Saint-Jean-sur-Richelieu, 1965.

Rooney, Andy. "Language of the U.S. Is English." *Philadelphia Inquirer,* 8 March 1981.

————. "You Have to Know the Lingo." *Philadelphia Inquirer,* 18 November 1979.

Rosen, Bernard C. "Race, Ethnicity, and the Achievement Syndrome." *American Sociological Review* 24 (1959), 47–60. Reprinted in *FAO* 4:84–101.

Rostaing, Charles. *Les Noms de lieux.* Que sais-je?, no. 176. Paris: Presses Universitaires de France, 1948.

Roy, Elphège. *Les Causes du déclin de la presse franco-américaine.* Manchester, N.H., 1965.

Rumilly, Robert. *Histoire des Franco-Américains.* Montreal: Robert Rumilly (under the auspices of the Union Saint-Jean-Baptiste d'Amérique), 1958.

Sabourin, Conrad, and Rolande Lamarche. *Le Français québécois (Bibliographie analytique).* Montreal: Office de la langue française, 1979.

Samson, Gary. "Ulric Bourgeois, photographe franco-américain, 1874–1963." *Magazine OVO* (Montreal), 12, no. 46 (1982), 6–13.

Samuel, T. J. *The Migration of Canadian-Born between Canada and the United States of America 1955 to 1968.* Ottawa: Department of Manpower and Immigration, 1970.

Santerre, Albert. "The Champagne Family: Strauss of New England." *FAROG Forum* 6, no. 8 (1979), 15.

Santerre, Richard R. *Anthologie de la littérature franco-américaine de la Nouvelle-Angleterre.* 9 vols. Bedford, N.H.: NMDC, 1980–81.

————. "Bibliographie des imprimés franco-américains parus à Lowell, Massachusetts, de 1837 à 1968." *BSHFA* (1968), 153–211.

————. *The Franco-Americans of Lowell, Massachusetts.* Lowell, Mass.: Franco-American Day Committee, 1972.

————. "Historique de la célébration de la fête Saint-Jean-Baptiste à Lowell, Massachusetts, 1868 à 1968." In *Centenaire de la Fête Saint-Jean-Baptiste,* pp. 1–36. Lowell, Mass.: Imprimerie L'Etoile, 1968.

————. "Le Roman franco-américain en Nouvelle-Angleterre, 1878–1943." Ph.D. diss., Boston College, 1974.

Schmidt, William E. "Beat Generation Elders Meet to Praise Kerouac." *New York Times,* 30 July 1982.

Schweda, Nancy Lee. "Goal-Oriented Interaction in the French-Speaking St. John River Valley of Northern Maine: A Sociolinguistic and Ethnomethodological Study of the Use of Verbal Strategies by Professional Community Members Living in a Bilingual Society with a French-English Speech Continuum." Ph.D. diss., Georgetown University, 1979.

Sebeok, Thomas A., ed. *Current Trends in Linguistics.* Vol. 10. The Hague and Paris: Mouton, 1973.

Séguin, Robert-Lionel. *La Vie libertine en Nouvelle-France au XVIIe siècle.* Montreal: Leméac, 1972.

Servais-Maquoi, Mireille. *Le Roman de la terre au Québec.* Quebec City: Presses de l'Université Laval, 1974.

Shlakman, Vera. *Economic History of a Factory Town: A Study of Chicopee, Massachusetts.* Smith College Studies in History, vol. 20, nos. 1–4. Northampton, Mass.: Department of History, Smith College, 1935.

Silvia, Philip T., Jr., "The Spindle City: Labor, Politics, and Religion in Fall River, Massachusetts, 1870–1905." Ph.D. diss., Fordham University, 1973.

Simard, Jean, ed. *Un Patrimoine méprisé: La religion populaire des Québécois.* Ville LaSalle, Quebec: Hurtubise HMH, 1979.

Smith, Donald B. *Le "Sauvage" pendant la période héroïque de la Nouvelle-France (1534–1663) d'après les historiens canadiens-français des XIXᵉ et XXᵉ siècles.* Ville LaSalle, Quebec: Editions Hurtubise HMH, 1979.

Solomon, Barbara M. *Ancestors and Immigrants: A Changing New England Tradition.* Cambridge, Mass.: Harvard University Press, 1956.

Sorrell, Richard S. "L'histoire en tant que roman, le roman en tant qu'histoire: Le roman ethnique franco-américain de langue anglaise." *CIF* 1, 64–80.

———. "Jack Kerouac and Grace Metalious as Franco-Americans: A Well-Kept Secret?" *Canado-Américain* 7, no. 1 (1981), 15–16.

———. "The Sentinelle Affair (1924–1929) and Militant 'Survivance': The Franco-American Experience in Woonsocket, Rhode Island." Ph.D. diss., State University of New York at Buffalo, 1975.

———. "The Sentinelle Affair (1924–1929): Religion and Militant Survivance in Woonsocket, Rhode Island." *Rhode Island History* 36 (1977), 67–80.

———. "La *Sentinelle* et la *Tribune:* Le rôle joué par ces journaux de Woonsocket dans l'affaire de la *Sentinelle.*" *CIF* 4, 35–49.

———. "Sports and Franco-Americans in Woonsocket, 1870–1930." *Rhode Island History* 31 (1972), 116–26.

"Souvenir des noces d'argent, 1904–1929." *L'Assomption,* April–May 1929 (special issue).

Springfield's Ethnic Heritage: The French and French-Canadian Community. Springfield, Mass.: U.S.A. Bicentennial Committee of Springfield, 1976.

Stein, Howard F., and Robert F. Hill. *The Ethnic Imperative: Examining the New White Ethnic Movement.* University Park, Pa.: Pennsylvania State University Press, 1977.

Tessier, Monsignor Albert. *Petite Histoire de notre petit poisson des chenaux.* Collection "Notre Passé," no. 13. Trois-Rivières: Editions du Bien Public, 1975.

Tétrault, Maximilienne. *Le Rôle de la presse dans l'évolution du peuple franco-américain de la Nouvelle-Angleterre.* Marseilles: Imprimerie Ferran, 1935.

Theriault, George F. "The Franco-Americans in a New England Community: An Experiment in Survival." Ph.D. diss., Harvard University, 1951.

———. "The Franco-Americans of New England." In *Canadian Dualism: Studies of French-English Relations,* ed. Mason Wade, pp. 392–411. Toronto: University of Toronto Press, and Quebec City: Presses de l'Université Laval, 1960.

Therriault, Sister Mary-Carmel. *La Littérature française de Nouvelle-Angleterre.* Montreal: Fides, 1946.

Therrien, Bernard. "Pourquoi faut-il lire le journal franco-américain catholique?" In *Les Quarante Ans de la Société Historique Franco-Americaine,* pp. 730–31. Boston: Société Historique Franco-Américaine, 1940.

Thibault, Pierrette, ed. *Le Français parlé: Etudes sociologiques.* Current Inquiry into Language and Linguistics, no. 30. Edmonton, Alberta: Linguistics Research, Inc., 1978.

Thompson, Stith. *The Folktale.* Berkeley: University of California Press, 1977.

———. *Motif-Index of Folk Literature: A Classification of Narrative Elements in Folktales, Ballads, Myths, Fables, Mediaeval Romances, Exempla, Fabliaux, Jest-Books, and Local Legends.* 6 vols. Revised and enlarged edition. Bloomington: Indiana University Press, 1955–58.

Toth, Emily. "Fatherless and Dispossessed: Grace Metalious as a French-Canadian Writer." *Journal of Popular Culture* 15, no. 3 (1981), 28–38.

———. *Inside Peyton Place: The Life of Grace Metalious.* Garden City, N.Y.: Doubleday, 1981.

Tourangeau, Pierre. "Un ancien consul US ne prisait guère l'aide venant du Québec." *Soleil* (Quebec City), 26 March 1984.

Trachtenberg, Leo. "Leo Durocher and the Yankees." *Yankees Magazine,* 7 July 1983, pp. 18–19.

Tremblay, M. "Orientations de la pensée sociale." In *Essais sur le Québec contemporain,* ed. Jean C. Falardeau, chap. 9. Quebec City: Presses de l'Université Laval, 1953.

Tremblay, Rémi. *Un Revenant.* Bedford, N.H.: NMDC, 1980.

———. *Un Revenant: Épisode de la Guerre de Sécession aux Etats-Unis.* Montreal: Typographie de la Patrie, 1884.

Trudel, Marcel. *Initiation à la Nouvelle-France: Histoire et institutions.* Montreal: Editions HRW, 1971. English trans., *Introduction to New France.* Toronto and Montreal: Holt, Rinehart, and Winston of Canada, 1968.

The 20th-Century Franco-American. Comité de Vie Franco-Américaine, 1976.

Tyrchniewicz, Peggy. *Ethnic Folk Costumes in Canada.* Winnipeg: Hyperion Press, 1979.

U.S. Department of Commerce. Bureau of the Census. *Census of Population: General Social and Economic Characteristics.* Washington, D.C.: Government Printing Office, 1972.

———. *1980 Census of Population: Ancestry of the Population by State.* Supplement Report, PC 80-Sl-10. Washington, D.C.: Government Printing Office, 1983.

U.S. Department of Housing and Urban Development. *The Urban Fair: How Cities Celebrate Themselves.* Washington, D.C.: Government Printing Office, 1981.

Vachon, André. *Madeleine de Verchères.* Collection "Notre Passé," no. 21. Trois-Rivières: Editions du Bien Public, 1978.

Valdman, Albert, ed. *Le Français hors de France.* Paris: Champion, 1979.

Vallée, Rudy. *Rudy Vallée Kisses and Tells.* Canoga Park, Calif.: Major Books, 1976.

Vander Zanden, James W. *American Minority Relations.* 4th ed. New York: Knopf, 1983.

Veltman, Calvin, J. *The Retention of Minority Languages in the United States.* Washington, D.C.: Department of Education, National Center for Education Statistics, 1980.

———. "Le sort de la francophonie aux Etats-Unis." *Cahiers Québécois de Démographie* 9, no. 1 (1980), 45–57.

Venard, Marc. *Bourgeois et paysans au XVIIᵉ siècle: Recherche sur le rôle des bourgeois parisiens dans la vie agricole au sud de Paris au XVIIᵉ siècle.* Ecole Pratique des Hautes Etudes. 6th Section. Centre de Recherches Historiques. Hommes et la terre, no. 3. Paris: S.E.V.P.E.N., 1957.

Vermette, Father Joseph S. "Par l'école." In *Les Franco-Américains peints par eux-mêmes,* pp. 195–210. Montreal: Albert Lévesque (for the Association Canado-Américaine), 1936.

Vernex, Jean-Claude. "Espace et appartenance: L'exemple des Acadiens au Nouveau-Brunswick." In *Du Continent perdu à l'archipel retrouvé: Le Québec et l'Amérique française,* pp. 163–80. Quebec City: Presses de l'Université Laval, 1983.

Verrette, Monsignor Adrien. "Les Acadiens aux Etats-Unis, 1755–1955." *BSHFA* (1955), 75–85.

———. "L'Institut Franco-Américain." *BSHFA* (1957), 160–63.

———. "Inventaire des Archives franco-américaines." *BSHFA* (1951), 29–31.

———. "La paroisse franco-américaine." *Vie Franco-Américaine* (1948), 125–40.

———. *Paroisse Sainte-Marie, Manchester, New Hampshire: Cinquantenaire, 1880–1930.* Manchester, N.H.: Imprimerie Lafayette, 1931.

———. "Rapport de la Commission des Archives." *BSHFA* (1956), 225.

Vers Une Nouvelle Cuisine québécoise. 2d ed. Institut de tourisme et d'hôtellerie du Québec. Quebec City: Editions Elysée, 1979.

Viatte, Auguste. *Histoire de la Congrégation de Jésus-Marie, 1818–1950.* Quebec City: Charrier and Dugal, 1952.

Viau, Eusèbe. *Vieux Cantiques et hymnes religieuses.* Woonsocket, R.I.: Union Saint-Jean-Baptiste d'Amérique, 1931.

Viau, Eusèbe, and J.-Ernest Philie. *Chants populaires des Franco-Américains.* 12 vols. 13th ed. Woonsocket, R.I.: Union Saint-Jean-Baptiste d'Amérique, 1960.

Vicero, Ralph D. "Immigration of French Canadians to New England, 1840–1900: A Geographical Analysis." Ph.D. diss., University of Wisconsin, 1968.

Vinay, Jean-Paul. "Bout de la langue ou fond de la gorge?" *French Review* 23 (1950), 489–98.

———. "Le français en Amérique du Nord: Problèmes et réalisations." In *Current Trends in Linguistics,* ed. Thomas A. Sebeok, 10:323–406. The Hague and Paris: Mouton, 1973.

Vincent, Sylvie, and Bernard Arcand. *L'Image de l'Amérindien dans les manuels scolaires du Québec, ou comment les Québécois ne sont pas des sauvages.* Ville LaSalle, Quebec: Editions Hurtubise HMH, 1979.

20 Ans au service de la culture ça se fête. Quebec City: Ministère des Affaires Culturelles, 1981.

Violette, Maurice. *The Franco-Americans: A Franco-American's Chronicle of Historical and Cultural Environment: Augusta Revisited.* New York: Vantage Press, 1976.

Voisine, Nive. "Les valeurs religieuses de l'émigrant québécois (1850–1920)." *CIF* 2, 21–37.

Waddell, Eric. "La Louisiane: Un poste outre-frontière de l'Amérique française ou un autre pays et une autre culture?" In *Du Continent perdu à l'archipel retrouvé: Le Québec et l'Amérique française,* ed. Dean R. Louder and Eric Waddell, pp. 195–211. Quebec City: Presses de l'Université Laval, 1983.

Wade, Mason. *The French Canadians, 1760–1967.* Laurentian Library, no. 33. 1968. Reprint. Toronto: Macmillan of Canada, 1975.

———. "The French Parish and *Survivance* in Nineteenth-Century New England." *Catholic Historical Review* 36 (1950), 163–89. Reprinted in *FAO* 3:235–53.

———, ed. *Canadian Dualism: Studies of French-English Relations.* Toronto: University of Toronto Press, and Quebec City: Presses de l'Université Laval, 1960.

Walker, David B. *Politics and Ethnocentrism: The Case of the Franco-Americans.* Brunswick, Maine: Bowdoin College, Bureau for Research in Municipal Government, 1961.

———. "La politique présidentielle des Franco-Américains: Quelques observations sommaires." In *Les Conférences de l'Institut Franco-Américain de Bowdoin College,* ed. Gerard J. Brault, pp. 64–72. Brunswick, Maine, 1961.

Walkowitz, Daniel J. *Worker City, Company Town: Iron and Cotton Worker Protest in Troy and Cohoes, New York.* Urbana: University of Illinois Press, 1978.

Wallot, Jean-Pierre. "Religion and French-Canadian Mores in the Early Nineteenth Century." *Canadian Historical Review* 52 (1971), 51–94.

Warner, W. Lloyd, and Paul S. Lunt. *The Social Life of a Modern Community.* New Haven: Yale University Press, 1941.

Warner, W. Lloyd, and Leo Srole. *The Social Systems of American Ethnic Groups.* New Haven: Yale University Press, 1945.

Weider, Ben. *Les Hommes forts du Québec.* Montreal: Editions du Jour, 1973.

Wessel, Bessie Bloom. *An Ethnic Survey of Woonsocket, Rhode Island.* Chicago: University of Chicago Press, 1931.

Wink, Robin W. "The Creation of a Myth: 'Canadian' Enlistments in the Northern Armies during the American Civil War." *Canadian Historical Review* 39 (1958), 24–40.

Winslow, John. *Journal of Colonel John Winslow of the Provincial Troops, while Engaged in Removing the Acadian French Inhabitants from Grand Pré, and Neighbouring Settlements, in the Autumn of the Year 1755.* Collections of the Nova Scotia Historical Society, no. 4. Halifax, Nova Scotia: William MacNab, 1885.

Woolfson, Peter. "Le Franco-Américain campagnard dans l'état du Vermont." *CIF* 2, 81–98.

———. *Franco-Americans in Vermont: A Civil Rights Perspective.* Washington, D.C.: Government Printing Office, 1983.

———. "Publish or Parish: A Study of Differences in Acculturation of Franco-American Schoolchildren." *Man in the Northeast,* no. 8 (1974), 65–75. Reprinted in *FAO* 4:6–18.

Woolfson, Peter, and André Sénécal. *The French in Vermont: Some Current Views.* Occasional Paper, no. 6. Burlington, Vt.: Center for Research on Vermont, University of Vermont, 1983.

INDEX

Acadia: dikes, 119, 153; deputies, 120; marshland farming, 119; population in 1755, 121–22; "villages," 118–19; mentioned, 109. *See also* Flags

Acadiana (parishes in La.), 2, 233n21

Acadian colonists, provincial origins of, 110

Acadian French language, 167. *See also* Canadian French (the language)

Acadian Genealogical Historical Association, 183

Acadians in Acadia: deportation in 1755, 121–24, 153; and unqualified oath, 121. *See also* Brault family (Acadians)

Acadians in Canada. *See* Centre d'Etudes Acadiennes; Société L'Assomption

Acadians in exile: at Boston in 1755 and 1760, 124, 129; in Massachusetts, 124–30; removed to Quebec in 1766, 130. *See also* Brault family (Acadians)

Acadians in Quebec. *See* Brault family (Acadians)

Acadians in U.S. *See* Acadian Genealogical Historical Association; Cajuns of Louisiana; Census of 1980, U.S.; Franco-Americans of New England; Parishes; Société L'Assomption; Symbols

Acculturation, 86

Achievement orientation, 166

ActFANE. *See* Action for Franco-Americans in New England

Action for Franco-Americans in New England, 178, 180, 238n88

Adolescence, 34

Advent, 17, 95

"Ah! Qui me passera le bois?" (folk song), 45

Aix-la-Chapelle, Treaty of, 120, 121

"A la claire fontaine" (folk song), 44

Alaska. *See* Gravel, Maurice R.

Albani. *See* Lajeunesse, Emma

Albany, N.Y., 136, 138

Albert, Félix (met immigrants at Lowell, Mass., railroad station), 59

Alcoholism, 67

Aldenville (Chicopee), Mass., 138

ALEC. *See* Atlas linguistique de l'Est du Canada

Alienation, 102

Alliance Française, 79

All Saints' Day, 29, 94

All Souls' Day, 29, 95

"Alouette!" (folk song), 45

Amaron, Rev. Calvin E. (author and proselytizer), 68

American and Canadian French Cultural Exchange Commission, 176

American Association of Teachers of French, 175

American-Canadian Genealogical Society, 180, 183

American Federation of Labor, 63

American-French Genealogical Society, 183

American Indians in French-Canadian textbooks, 97

American International College. *See* Collège Franco-Américain

Americanism and New England Protestant groups, 68

Americanization, 87, 100

American Legion, Americanization campaign, 87

American Revolution, 132, 134, 165. *See also* Loyalists

American Revolution Bicentennial, 172, 179

American Snowshoe Union, 100

Amoskeag Manufacturing Co.: former employees interviewed, 62; 1922 strike, 90; wages in 1923 and 1934, 91; mentioned, 137, 154

"Amour c'est comme la salade, L'." *See* Champagne, Octave

265

Lussier, Georges-André. *See* Comité pour l'Avancement du Français en Amérique
Lynn, Mass., St. John the Baptist Church, 220n17

Macro-Inventaire. *See* Quebec Ministry of Cultural Affairs
Magnan, Father Aristide D.M. (poet), 103
Maiden without Hands (folk motif), 39
Maine Council for the Humanities and Public Policy, 175, 181
Maine Public Broadcasting Network, 175
Maison de l'Acadie. *See* La Chaussée (Vienne), France
Mallet, Edmond: in Union Army, 53; collection of Franco-Americana, 179
Maltais, Beatrice (teacher), 175
Manchester, N. H.: Franco-Americans in 1930s, 90–91; Manchester Historic Association, 230n95; and 1922 strike, 90; St. John the Baptist Church, 149; St. Mary's Church, 137, 218n156; St. Mary's Cooperative Association, 80; mentioned, 137–38, 150, 152, 153. *See also* Amoskeag Manufacturing Co.; Association Canado-Américaine; American-Canadian Genealogical Society; Librairie Populaire, La; Metalious, Grace
Manseau, Abraham (early resident of Enfield, Conn.), 133
Manseau, Joseph (early resident of Thompsonville, Conn.), 133, 229n81
Manseau, Leonard (victim of explosion at Enfield, Conn.), 83
Manseau, Otha (early resident of Enfield, Conn.), 133
Manseau, Roger (Douville family in-law), 152
Maple leaf, 160
Maple-sugaring time, 25–26, 154
Marchandes de Bonheur founded in 1929, 100
Marcoux, Omer (fiddler and wood-carver), 164
Marguilliers (church board members), 9, 19, 132
Marin, Samuel P. (recruited French-Canadian laborers), 55
Marion, Raymond J. (professor at Assumption College), 146
Marist Fathers, 69
Marlboro, Mass., early girls' boarding school, 75
Martel, Edgar J. (president of Union Saint-Jean-Baptiste d'Amérique), 179
Martel, Louis J. (founder of *Le Messager*), 81
Massachusetts Bay Colony and Acadian exiles, 124–25, 129–30
Massachusetts Bureau of Statistics of Labor and Franco-Americans in 1881, 67–68

Massachusetts Historical Society, 122
Massé, Claude (genealogist), 225n12
Massicotte, Edmond J. (French-Canadian artist), 7
Master Thief (folk motif), 39
May Day, 27–28
Mayors, 67, 147, 158, 218n146. *See also* Talbot, Edmund P.
Media, 183
Mental health, 166
Messager, Le (early newspaper), 81–82
Metalious, Grace (DeRepentigny [novelist]), 161–62
Mexican Border Campaign, 79
Meyer v. Nebraska (U.S. Supreme Court decision in 1923), 87
Michaud, Bp. John Stephen (diocese of Burlington), 7
Middle Atlantic Conference for Canadian Studies, 182
Middle class, 57, 64, 183–84. *See also* Social classes
"Milltown" (video film), 175
Mock funeral, 36
Modern Language Association of America, 182
Molin, Father Laurent, and 1671 census of Acadia, 117
Monast, Louis (congressman), 158
Monckton, Robert, and deportation of Acadians, 121
Moncton, New Brunswick. *See* Société L'Assomption
Monferrand, Jos (legendary strongman), 46
Monsieur Beausoleil. *See* "Franco-File, The"
Mon Soldat program, 148
Montcalm, Louis-Joseph, Marquis de, 220n31
Montreal, 136, 137, 140–41, 151, 175
Montreal School (French-Canadian literary group), 102
Moody Street Irregulars: A Jack Kerouac Newsletter, 233n26
Mooers Forks, N.Y., 148
Moosup, Conn., 141
Morin, Jacques-Yvan (Quebec cabinet minister), 178
Mortagne-au-Perche, France and the colonization of New France, 112
Mother's Day, 95
Mother tongue: and the term Franco-American, 232n9; loyalty, 159, 184; maintenance, 90, 169, 170–71, 174, 184, 237n70
Mount Saint Charles Academy, 88–89
Murray, James, and Acadian exiles, 130
Museums, Franco-American, 180–81
Music, 85, 199. *See also* Blé d'Inde Contraband; Bands; Folk musicians; Orchestras

Parti Québécois, 173, 177
Patriote Canadien, Le (early newspaper), 80
Patriotes: movement defined, 16; mentioned, 12, 44, 48, 51, 76, 80, 132. *See also* Chénier, Jean Olivier; Duvernay, Ludger
Patriot's Day, 95
Pawtucket, R.I. *See* American-French Genealogical Society
Peck, Frederick, bill in Rhode Island legislature opposed, 87
Pedagogical and research materials, 173–74
Peddlers, 11, 39, 45
Pépin, Joseph (early resident of Enfield, Conn.), 133
Pepin family (Canadians), Guillaume, 148
Pepin family (Franco-Americans): Amédée Edouard, 148 (his wife, Eveline [Lambert], 148, 149, 152; their children, Alice Rosina, 148, 149, 152; Carl Edward, 148; Esther Marie, 149, 152); Arthur Lambert, son of Amédée Edouard, 149, 150, 152 (his wife, Beatrice [Douville], 149, 150, 152); Edward Lawrence, son of Arthur Lambert, 149, 152 (his wife, Catherine [Rouillard], 152; their children, Carol, 152; Catherine Ann, 152; Edward Mark, 152; Joan [Mrs. Robert King], 152); for Jeanne Lambert, daughter of Arthur Lambert, *see* Brault, Gerard J. *See also* Lambert, François P.; Lambert, Rosina (Ashline)
Peppermint leaves. *See* "P'tites Paparmanes, Les"
Perrault, Charles (French author), 39
Perreault, Robert B. (author), 163
Petit Poucet. *See* Hansel and Gretel; Tom Thumb
Philie, J.-Ernest (song publisher), 107
Physicians, 218n146. *See also* Beauchamp family; Beaudoin, Robert A.; Chénier, Jean-Olivier; Laroche, Armand; Leclaire, Charles J.; Literature; Nadeau, Gabriel; Paré, Onésime; Varneau, H. J.
Pierre (Assumption College mascot), 146
Pike, Robert (author), 165
Pinette, Raoul, and Bates College colloquium, 181
Pitre, Simon (Acadian at Grand Pré in 1755), 122
Plainfield, Conn., 141, 145
Plamondon, J. (early resident of Thompsonville, Conn.), 229n81
Plante, David (novelist), 163
Poitiers, France, 112, 113
Politics, 66–67, 158–59, 176–77. *See also* Chicopee, Mass.; Elected officials; Mayors; Quincy, Josiah
Pontifical Zouaves. *See* Zouaves

Population centers: central and southeastern New England, 3; northern Maine, 2–3; western Vermont and upper New York State, 3
Port Royal, Acadia, 116–18
Pothier, Aram J. (governor of Rhode Island), 67, 158
Prefigurative society, 74
Presentation of Mary, feast of the, 94
Primeau, Bp. Ernest J. (diocese of Manchester), 160
Prince, Father W. A. (pastor of St. Louis Church), 88
Producteurs de sucre d'érable du Québec, 207n81
Protecteur Canadien, Le (early newspaper), 80
Protestant groups in New England, proselytizing efforts, 68
Proulx, Aux. Bp. Amédée W. (diocese of Portland), 160
Proulx, Joseph (recruited French-Canadian laborers), 55
"P'tites Paparmanes, Les" (folktale), 40–42, 43–44
Public television programs, 183

Quadrilles, 34, 107
Quebec: geography and climate, 52; exports to U.S., 178; independence movement, 178; and New England tourists, 178; mentioned, 179, 183. *See also* Comité pour l'Avancement du Français en Amérique; Flags; Quiet Revolution
Quebec, government of, subsidies to Franco-Americans, 177–78, 182
Quebec (nineteenth-century): agriculture, 52; population, 52
Quebec City: founded in 1608, 6; falls to British in 1759, 6, 120, 125; Place Royale, 198; mentioned, 147, 150, 175, 178, 233n21
Quebec Government Delegation in New England, 238n87
Quebec Ministry of Cultural Affairs: La Grande Ferme, 198–99; Macro-Inventaire des biens culturels du Québec, 198; Service du Patrimoine, 198; mentioned, 177
Quebec Ministry of Finance, 240n2
Quebec Ministry of Intergovernmental Relations. *See* Quebec Ministry of International Relations
Quebec Ministry of International Relations, 177, 240n115
Quebecois (the language). *See* Canadian French (the language)
Quebecois (the people) and Franco-Americans of New England, 160

Quiet Revolution: defined, 168; mentioned, 160, 173, 182, 184
Quincy, Josiah (secretary of National Democratic Party), 80–81
Quintal, Claire: director of Franco-American Heritage Studies Program, 175; of French Institute, 181

Radio programs, 183
Raiche, Félix (early resident of Enfield, Conn.), 133
Raiffeisen, Friedrich Wilhelm, and credit union movement, 80
Rang defined, 8
Rassemblement des Artistes Franco-Américains, 164
Ratisbonne, Louis (French author), 97
Rawson and Acadian exiles in Braintree, Mass., 127
Reagan, Ronald, administration of, 174
Recipes, 205 n45
"Reflets et Lumière" (public television series), 175
Rehabilitations, 70
Reims, France, xii
Religion, 68–70, 159, 160, 166, 172, 184
Religious disputes: with Irish parishioners, 62, 71; with Irish-dominated hierarchy, 70–73, 87–88, 159
Religious of Jesus and Mary. See Fall River, Mass., Notre Dame de Lourdes Church
Rémillard family (Canadians): François Hyacinthe, 135 (his first wife, Marie Amable [Bourgeois], 135; his second wife, Charlotte [Lamoureux], 135); Gédéon, 135–36, 139–40 (his first wife, Virginie [Thibodeau], 136; their children, Aimé, 136; Albert, 136, 140 [his first wife, Clorinde (Landry), 140; their son, Louis, 140]; Alexandre, 136; Alexis, 136; Blanche [Mrs. Victor Julien], 136; Jeannette [Mrs. Alfred Hébert], 136; Méville Marcel, 136; Zénaïde [Mrs. Eugène Hébert], 136; for other daughter Aline, see Brault, Philias J.; for other son Joseph, see Rémillard family [Franco-Americans])
Rémillard family (Franco-Americans): children of Gédéon, Aline (see Brault, Philias J.); Joseph, 136, 138 (his wife, Bernadette, 138)
Repatriation, 81, 82
Repentir (play performed at Springfield, Mass.), 79
Republican Party, 66, 67, 158
Research. See Pedagogical and research material
Resignation, 166
Rhéaume, Miss (teacher), 73

Rhode Island College, 175
Rhode Island Folklore Project, 107
Rhys, Jean, and David Plante, 163
Richard, Germain (Acadian at Grand Pré in 1755), 122
Richelieu, Armand-Jean du Plessis, Cardinal: and siege of La Rochelle, 114; mentioned, 111
Richelieu Clubs, 180
Richford, Vt., ESEA program, 174
Rivier College, 181
Rivière aux Canards, Acadia, 118, 119, 153
Roadside crosses, 47, 154
Robert, Adolphe, and library of Association Canado-Américaine, 180
Robichaud, Gérard (novelist), 162–63
Robichaud, Louis (Acadian in Massachusetts [eighteenth century]), 228 n64
Robillard, Louis (early resident of Thompsonville, Conn.), 229 n81
Robinson, Rowland (author), 165
Rocheleau-Rouleau, Corinne (author), 103
Rodier, Louis (early resident of Enfield, Conn.), 133
Rosenthal, Joe (photographer), 106
Rotary International, 180
Rouleau, Wilfrid (teacher), 73
Round dances, 32–33, 154
Roux, Luc (Brault family in-law), 134, 138
Roy, Alphonse (congressman), 158
Roy, Gilbert O. (folk painter), 164
Roy, Joseph-Hormidas (poet), 102–3
Roy Lumber Co., J. G., 150
Rutland, Vt., Immaculate Heart of Mary Church, parochial school, 74, 75

Sacred Heart League. See Parish societies
St. Albans, Vt.: Société Jacques Cartier, 76; early newspaper, 80
St. Anne de Beaupré, Quebec, 141, 199
St. Anne's Church. See Woonsocket, R.I.
St. Anne's Sodality. See Parish societies
St. Anselm's College, 160
St. Bernadette Soubirous, feast of, 95
St. Bernard Church. See Lacolle, Quebec
St. Blaise, feast of, 95
St. Casimir, Quebec, 151
St. Catherine's Day, 29
St. Cecilia, feast of, 95
St. Charles Church. See Grand Pré, Quebec
St. Cyprien Church. See Napierville, Quebec
Saint-David-de-Lévis, Quebec, 150
Sainte-Anne-de-la-Pérade, Quebec: ice-fishing, 151; local historical society, 151; mentioned, 141, 150. See also Verchères, Madeleine de
Sainte-Brigitte-de-Laval, Quebec, 207 n99
Sainte-Marie, Philippe (poet), 103

Spruance, Raymond A., and Tarawa, 146
Sputnik and NDEA, 172
Square dances, 34, 107
Stages of life. *See* French Canadians at turn of century
Star, 160, 161
State cultural commissions, 176
State University of New York at Albany, 182
Stevens Arms, J., 138, 142
Stottsville, Quebec, St. Valentin Church, 136
Stoudtbeck-Kluckhohn Value Orientation Model, 167
Supreme Court, U.S. *See Lau v. Nichols; Meyer v. Nebraska*
Surnames, anglicization of, 70
Surprenant, Lorenzo (character in Hémon), 8, 55
Survivance: defined, 2; Evangeline as Acadian symbol of, 123; and Franco-American ideology, 65, 66, 87; in nineteenth-century Quebec, 7, 65; prospects for, 240n115. *See also* Curés
Survivance Française, founded in 1942, 100
Symbols: Acadian, 233n21; Franco-American organizations, 233n20. *See also* Flags; Fleur-de-lis; Maple leaf; Star; Survivance
Syndique (parish corporation), 71

Talbot, Edmund P. (mayor of Fall River, Mass., in 1922), 67
Talon, Jean (French intendant in New France), 109
Tanguay, Eva ("I Don't Care Girl"), 84–85
Tarawa (battle in World War II), 146
Taylor, Samuel L. (adapter of Fontaine's play), 103
Télesphore (Assumption College mascot), 146
Teleuron (public officer at La Rochelle, France), 113
Television programs, 175
Tenney, A. G. (editor of *Brunswick Telegraph*), 61
Tessier, Catherine (Crète [wife of Paul-Edouard Tessier]), 151
Tessier, Georgette (Douville family cousin), 151
Tessier, Paul-Edouard (Douville family cousin), 151
Textile mills in New England: accidents, 83; early history, 54; Franco-American employees in 1900, 61; and the Great Depression, 90; wages in 1873, 57; working conditions in 1890, 57, 59. *See also* Amoskeag Manufacturing Co.; Granite Mill
Textile mills in New York State, at Cohoes in 1880, 61

Thanksgiving, 95
Thayer, Capt., and Acadian exiles in Braintree, Mass., 127, 129
Theater, early amateur groups, 78
Thibodeau, Pierre Gustave (Rémillard family relative), 40
Thibodeau, Victorine (née Dozois [Rémillard family relative]), 40
Third generation, 159
Thirty Years' War, 111
Thivierge, Hélène (Paquet [teacher]), 73
Thivierge, Narcisse (pharmacist), 73
Thompson, Orrin (owner of carpet mill in Thompsonville, Conn.), 133
Thompsonville, Conn.: Franco-American population in 1908, 229n82; St. Patrick's Church, 133, 134; mentioned, 135, 153
Ti-Jean and Dragon Slayer (folk motif), 40
Tinian (battle in World War II), 146
Tizoune and Manda. *See* Troupes
TLFQ. *See Trésor de la langue française au Québec*
Tomcod, 151
Tom Thumb and Le Petit Poucet, 40–41
Traditional trades, 45–47
Travailleur, Le: newspaper founded in 1874, 81; founded anew in 1931, 88
Tremblay, Rémi (author), 53
Trésor de la langue française au Québec (computerized dictionary of Canadian French), 199, 210n151
Trois-Rivières, Quebec, 141, 148, 150
Troupes, 78, 216n119
Two Sisters. *See* "P'tites Paparmanes, Les"

Union Saint-Jean-Baptiste d'Amérique: founded in 1900, 77; and Sentinelle Affair, 88; library, 179; logo and official seal, 160; newsletter, 179, 183; Project FAITH, 179; mentioned, 88, 180, 181, 235n44
Union Saint-Joseph (women's group founded in 1902), 78
University of Lowell, 181
University of Maine, Lewiston-Auburn Center, 180–81
University of Maine at Augusta, 182
University of Maine at Fort Kent, 182
University of Maine at Orono, 175, 182. *See also* Franco-American Resource Opportunity Group
University of Maine at Presque Isle, 182
University of Massachusetts, 181, 182
University of Moncton, 199
University of New Hampshire, 174, 175
University of Rhode Island, 232n16
University of Southern Maine, 191
University of Vermont, 174
Ursulines. *See* Waterville, Maine
Utrecht, Treaty of, 19

DATE DUE

DEMCO 38-297